CLASSICAL IMITATION

AND INTERPRETATION

IN CHAUCER'S *TROILUS*

CLASSICAL IMITATION

AND INTERPRETATION

IN CHAUCER'S

Troilus

JOHN V. FLEMING

University of Nebraska Press | Lincoln & London

The paper in this book meets the minimum
requirements of American National Standard
for Information Sciences—Permanence of
Paper for Printed Library Materials, ANSI
Z39.48–1984.

Library of Congress
Cataloging-in-Publication Data
Fleming, John V.
Classical imitation and interpretation in
Chaucer's Troilus / John V. Fleming.
p.   cm.
Includes bibliographical references.
ISBN 0-8032-1977-6 (alk. paper)
1. Chaucer, Geoffrey, d. 1400. Troilus and
Criseyde.   2. Chaucer, Geoffrey, d. 1400—
Knowledge—Literature.   3. Troilus (Greek
mythology) in literature.   4. English poetry
—Classical influences.   5. Imitation (in
literature)   6. Trojan War in literature.
7. Classicism—England.   I. Title.
PR1896.F86   1990
821'.1—dc20   90–12011
                                        CIP

For Rich Fleming, '87,

who never took the course

CONTENTS

ABBREVIATIONS

AA	*Ars amatoria*
BEC	*Bibliothèque de l'Ecole des Chartes*
BICS	*Bulletin of the Institute of Classical Studies*
ChR	*Chaucer Review*
CJ	*Classical Journal*
CP	*Consolatio Philosophiae*
CL	*Comparative Literature*
ELN	*English Language Notes*
ES	*Englische Studien*
Fil.	*Filostrato*
HF	*House of Fame*
HSCP	*Harvard Studies in Classical Philology*
JEGP	*Journal of English and Germanic Philology*
JTS	*Journal of Theological Studies*
MED	*Middle English Dictionary*
Met.	*Metamorphoses*
MLN	*Modern Language Notes*
MLQ	*Modern Language Quarterly*
MLR	*Modern Language Review*
N&Q	*Notes and Queries*
NED	*New English Dictionary on Historical Principles*
NLH	*New Literary History*
NM	*Neuphilologische Mitteilungen*
PMLA	*Publications of the Modern Language Association*
PQ	*Philological Quarterly*
RA	*Remedia amoris*
RR	*Roman de la Rose*

SAC   *Studies in the Age of Chaucer*
SIFC   *Studi Italiani di Filologia Classica*
TAPA   *Transactions of the American Philological Association*
TC   *Troilus and Criseyde*
TLL   *Thesaurus Linguae Latinae*
YES   *Yearbook of English Studies*

A Note on Translations

Unless otherwise specifically identified, the translators of the modern English versions of ancient and medieval works cited in this book include the following. Specific publication details may be found in the bibliography. Other translations are by the author.

Boccaccio, *Filostrato:* Nathaniel Griffin and Arthur Myrick
Boethius, *Consolatio Philosophiae:* Richard Green
Cicero, *Tusculanes:* J. E. King
Dante Alighieri, *Divina Commedia:* Charles Singleton
Horace: E. C. Wickham
Ovid, *Amores, Heroides:* Grant Showerman
Ovid, *Ars amatoria, Remedia amoris:* J. H. Mozley
Ovid, *Metamorphoses:* Mary Innes
Roman de la Rose: Charles Dahlberg
Statius, *Thebaid:* J. H. Mozley
Virgil, *Aeneid:* W. F. Jackson Knight

PREFACE

Habent sua fata libelli. Everyone knows *that,* but only authors know that it may well be a fate worse than death, such as, for instance, the ennui of their readers. *Troilus and Criseyde* can hardly be regarded as a neglected poem, and the author, or perhaps perpetrator, of another study of it owes it to the generous reader to explain something of what he is up to and what he is not up to. What he is not up to is fairly easy to describe. Although a good deal of my book is given over to discussions of the theme of interpretation, it has not been my intention to offer a comprehensive new interpretation of the poem myself. As a matter of fact, I doubt that there is a comprehensive new interpretation—as opposed to a repartition or redistribution of various interpretations already in the public domain—still undiscovered in the text. Of them there are no doubt a nearly infinite number, and each of them another vibrant testimony to the attractive powers of the poem.

On the whole my researches have confirmed my acceptance of the brief and general account of the poem as Christian tragedy first offered by my great teacher D. W. Robertson and since augmented, elaborated, and modified by one set of scholars, and controverted, denied, or dismissed by another set. Discussion and debate have moved on at a rapid pace in the last three decades, and although I invoke the specific terms of Robertson's work in this book on occasion to exploit its incidental brilliances, I more generally view that work primarily as part of what might be thought of as a set of ideas inescapably and usually controversially present or implicit in recent discussions of the poem.

In this regard I find it useful to examine in some detail the critical history of a few textual dilemmas on which interpretive controversy has focused in an attempt to clarify some theoretical issues concerning the nature of poetic ambiguity, the nature of classical imitation, and the parameters of medieval Christian humanism, among others subjects. There are often enough ironies

in literary criticism no less than in literature itself, and I am particularly interested in the fact that the critique of Robertson's historical criticism, invariably
and explicitly pursued as a rejection of historical or interpretive reduction or
oversimplification, has invariably if often implicitly involved the imposition
of what I consider radical and wholly unacceptable *theoretical* limitations on
Chaucer's intelligence, his learning, the range and sensitivity of his reading of
poetry, the pluralism of his thought, his moral seriousness, the intellectual and
linguistic complexity of his poems, and even the extent of the verbal lexicon
at his command.

But I should find no justification for offering yet another book about the
Troilus did I not think that my own agenda, however clear its intellectual ante-
cedents, was fundamentally new: new in its principal concerns, in its central
arguments, and perhaps above all in its examination of primary evidence. I
first became seriously engaged with the *Troilus* during the course of protracted
and continuing investigations into the *Roman de la Rose* of Jean de Meun,
a writer whose enormous and varied influence upon Chaucer still awaits a
deep and detailed exposition. The intellectual style of Jean's appropriation
of texts by Ovid, Virgil, and Seneca—the details of which are presently irrelevant—and the intellectual style of Chaucer's own appropriation of certain
Magdunian texts—some of which will be explored in this book—led me to
appreciate, after some years of thought and considerable reading in the field
of classical philology, a set of complex but elegant patterns of textual relationships operative among the major Latin poets of antiquity and among the
great poet-classicists of the European Middle Ages such as the authors of the
twelfth-century *romans d'antiquité*, Chrétien, Jean de Meun, Dante, Boccaccio, Petrarch, and Chaucer. To treat these phenomena in a synoptic fashion
that at once honored their cultural pervasiveness and respected the individu-
ality and inventiveness of their variety would be highly desirable; but such
an undertaking is, unfortunately, not within my capacities. I must limit my
investigations to a single author and a single poem, Geoffrey Chaucer's *Troilus
and Criseyde*. I believe that the kind of analysis I undertake with regard to this
poem has very considerable potential value for a wide spectrum of medieval
texts, but for the moment I limit myself to local, not global ambitions.

Having silently moved on to the subject of what I *am* up to, or think I am up
to, I should make explicit an assumption that underlies my study, and which I
came to embrace only gradually and against the judgment of my earlier opinion and that of many others. It is that Chaucer was, for his day, a considerable

and sophisticated "classicist." I do not mean simply what we have known since the time of Edgar Shannon's still useful book *Chaucer and the Roman Poets* (1929) and before—to wit, that Chaucer's works are full of "classical story" and specific reminiscences of classical poetry. I mean that by the time he wrote the *Troilus* he had firsthand knowledge of the major works of the major Latin poets and that, furthermore, he had thought deeply about the *poetic* techniques he found there. The demonstrable presence in Chaucer's poetry of trace elements of errant Latin philology, both in terms of the construction of individual phrases of text and in terms of occasional narrative inaccuracy, certainly shows that like most other medieval poets, Chaucer frequently indulged in rather superficial "classical" ornamentation drawn from the rhetorical stockbooks of his day, from intermediate vernacular adaptations and paraphrases, and from earlier vernacular imitations and redactions of classical texts. It is this fact, perhaps, that has masked the evidence of his much more profound engagement with primary Latin materials. A close study of his practice would probably allow us to make a useful discrimination of Chaucerian "classicisms," one shallow, one deep.

Though there are elements of both in the *Troilus*, the prevailing mode of the poem is what I shall call "deep classicism." In this poem Chaucer made an attempt without parallel in the rest of his poetry, and with relatively few parallels in medieval poetry generally, to imagine and to reconstruct a spiritually foreign ancient culture. Here I need to stress that Chaucer's originality was a matter of degree rather than a matter of kind. The Homeric poetic subjects were for the Latin Middle Ages *historical* subjects transmitted in texts that often claimed the genre of history. In the very center of the medieval phase of the Trojan legend is the *Historia destructionis Troiae* of Guido delle Colonne, a genuine research scholar of sorts, and every medieval poet who wrote in his shadow wrote to some extent as a historian. There is a considerable element of genuine historical imagination in Benoît, as in other authors of the *romans d'antiquité*, and in the "pagan" romances of Boccaccio, especially the *Filostrato* and the *Teseida*. One subject of particular interest in the *Troilus*—what might be called religious archaeology—is especially prominent in these texts.

In Chaucer's *Troilus* antique authority—authority that imposes itself both as to historical content and as to the manner of poetical treatment—is embodied in the cleverly invented Lollius, a genuine antique poet, who both authorizes and demands a close attention to antique historical detail. There is accordingly in the *Troilus* a notable thickening of the sense of historical fiction, a phenomenon that has been observed and acutely described from a number of different points of view by scholars ancient and modern, including James W. Broatch (*JEGP*, 1898), Daniel C. Boughner (*ELH*, 1939), and Morton Bloomfield (*JEGP*, 1952).

To invoke the work of earlier scholars is to evoke another signal difficulty of our text. As the greatest writer of the English Middle Ages, and often enough the only one taught in college curricula, Chaucer has by now attracted a vast nation of commentators and interpreters. The "bibliographical problem" attendant to his study, while still not quite so daunting as that facing the student of, say, Shakespeare, is nonetheless *mighty* daunting; and it certainly is a challenge to someone like myself who has in the past preached to graduate students the pious professional necessity of surveying in comprehensive fashion the available secondary opinion before presuming to offer a new opinion of one's own. An attempt to make even a quite incomplete review of scholarship on *Troilus and Criseyde* recently resulted in a book as long as this one, and it easily could have been twice as long. I cannot and do not cite in this book all the materials relating to the poem that I have reviewed. My aim is to encourage the consideration of several new perspectives on Chaucer, and to this end my first concern with regard to secondary studies has been to invoke a body of scholarship largely new to the published conversation of Chaucerians.

There is so much that has been written about the *Troilus* that the laws of probability alone would determine that a good deal that has been written is exciting, illuminating, and challenging; what the laws of probability cannot explain, at least to me, is what I take to be the disproportionately large number of brilliant medievalists who have written on *Troilus* during the past decade alone. There is no way that I can catalog the plenitude of what they have taught me. I do of course make the attempt to acknowledge quite specific debts (and grievances) through footnote citation. Since I continue to think that literature is important and that it must necessarily elicit from those who have made it their life's work what Robert Frost called a "passionate preference," I continue to think that it merits the investment of argument and debate. There is a certain amount of that in my book, though it is strictly limited by a propaedeutic agenda and rigorously controlled by a "no first strike" policy.

I hope that it might nonetheless be useful to potential readers, browsing through this introduction in the university bookstore and as yet financially uncommitted, to try to situate my own study within the context of recent work on the *Troilus*. My motive here is not to offer a series of unsolicited book reviews, but to try to identify a context for my undertaking within the recent history of Chaucer criticism. I must limit myself to studies relating quite specifically to Chaucer and the classical Latin tradition and to some, not even all, of the monographs on *Troilus* of the last decade. It appears that few classicists have ever written about Chaucer directly, but one of the few to do so impressed me considerably. In 1963 Katherine Lever published a brief article or long note called "The Christian Classicist's Dilemma" (*CJ* 58 [1963]:356–61). The piece was in some ways a surprising one to find in a scholarly journal, for in it Lever drew a parallel between Geoffrey Chaucer and herself as Christians with a Christian point of view and as readers deeply drawn to Latin poetry. In identifying the cultural "dilemma" of a literary scholar interested both in old books and in Christian truth, Lever's essay very nearly identified the energy source behind Chaucer's enterprise in the *Troilus*, then sank to the bottom of the great bibliographical sea with hardly a ripple. John Norton-Smith's *Geoffrey Chaucer* (1974), a book deserving wider currency, pursues certain formalist aims that necessarily involve a serious-minded and often detailed consideration of Latin authors and texts. Though I share few of Norton-Smith's ideas about Chaucer's artistic vision, I learned a good deal from his book. I found John Fyler's *Chaucer and Ovid* (1979), another challenging work with a perspective very different from my own, highly engaging; among its many merits the one that is for me most prominent is its author's working assumption that Chaucer could, and did, respond to sophisticated Latin poetry with poetic sophistication. A brilliant essay by Eugene Vance (*NLH* 10 [1979], reprinted in revised form in *Mervelous Signals*, 1986) encouraged my serious thinking about Chaucer's poem in its possible relation to medieval linguistic theory.

A. J. Minnis's *Chaucer and Pagan Antiquity* (1982) deals extensively with a wide variety of relevant but often neglected primary materials in an attempt to provide an intellectual and cultural context in which to appreciate Chaucer's considerable historical researches into antique subjects and his poetic uses of the past. It is unquestionably the most important work yet published on its subject, and I have inevitably learned much from it. At the same time I find it fundamentally unsatisfactory in its general characterization of Chaucer's historical attitudes and in some of its specific poetic interpretations. Although my own essay would be an inappropriate context in which to conduct a protracted debate with Minnis concerning the general character of the historical attitudes of Jean de Meun, the "classicizing friars," and the fourteenth-century Italian poets, I do offer criticisms of some parts of Minnis's argument that relate to specific interpretations of Chaucerian text.

Chauncey Wood's *The Elements of Chaucer's Troilus* (1984) expands the work of D. W. Robertson and offers an interpretation of the poem with which I am in basic agreement. What I find particularly new and valuable in this book is the careful consideration of the moral tone of Boccaccio's *Filostrato* and the sophisticated appreciation of Chaucer's use of the strategies of Jean de Meun. Although it appeared too late for me to use it in this book, the fine study of David Anderson, *Before the Knight's Tale* (Philadelphia: Pennsylvania University Press, 1988), shares a number of the central concerns of my own enterprise.

So far as my own specific enterprise is concerned the most interesting recent book on *Troilus* is probably Winthrop Wetherbee's *Chaucer and the Poets* (1984), a study that argues Chaucer's self-conscious and inventive vernacular classicism after the manner of Dante Alighieri. Wetherbee's demonstration of the complexity of several literary relationships often ignored or underestimated is a major contribution to our understanding of Chaucer's poetic methods.

"Underestimation" is my characterization of Howard Schless's *Chaucer and Dante* (1984), a book that necessarily engages the attention of any reader interested in Chaucer's relationship to the classical poetic tradition. One man's scholarly rigor is another man's timidity; and from my perspective the narrowly positivistic criteria adopted by Schless for the demonstration of textual relationship forbid more than they enable a more just appreciation of Chaucer's very substantial imaginative debt to Dante. On the other hand I must be, like all Chaucerians, deeply grateful for a piece of work whose usefulness goes far beyond commitment to any particular interpretive point of view. So far as relations between Chaucer and Dante are concerned, I have found myself more taken with the kind of approach exemplified by Wetherbee and R. A. Shoaf.

I have had an uneasy relationship with Alice R. Kaminsky's *Chaucer's "Troilus and Criseyde" and the Critics* (1980), so far as its interpretive conclusions are concerned. But the book is, among other things, an impressively ambitious critical bibliography which I—no doubt in common with many others—have used with great profit and convenience.

Just before I began to write my book, Barry Windeatt's edition of *Troilus & Crideyde* (1984) appeared. I join the general chorus of applause at its appearance and appreciate its importance. It is quite clearly the product of an an enormous labor, and it will have indispensable reference value for many years to come. I have myself consulted it at every turn, but I nonetheless persevere in using Root's text as a practical and accessible book. The edition of the poem prepared by Stephen A. Barney in the third edition of *The Riverside Chaucer* (1987) appeared only after my manuscript was essentially complete, and beyond testing the editor's opinion on two or three disputed points of interpretation I have not been able to make use of it.

This book has been written in the altogether too narrow contemplative margins surrounding a life too much occupied with active administrative responsibilities. I am aware of its imperfections, but aware also that it never could have been written at all without the help of many friends. I am most grateful to Dean Aaron Lemonick for a semester's leave to pursue the project, and to the Master and Fellows of Jesus College, Oxford, who offered an alumnus hospitality that allowed me to hide out for a few months in the Bodleian. The Princeton community has as always provided me with every scholarly encouragement: splendid library resources, demanding students, and above all such generous colleagues as Madelein Brainerd, Peter Brown, Giles Constable, Kevin Cureton, Michael Curschmann, Roberta Davidson, Robert Hollander, Frank Ordiway, and Seth Lerer, to name but some of those faculty collaborators and graduate students whose conversation has helped shape my recent work. To one student in particular—Gwen Crane, my sharp-eyed research assistant—I owe special thanks. I am also grateful to the press readers of my manuscript, known or unknown, approving or appalled, who have shared with me their reactions to the book's ideas. I must mention in particular Paul A. Olson, whose learned, judicious, and voluminous commentary led me to reconsider and I hope improve many pages in the book.

Chaucer, like other great authors, is different in every age. He also varies, of course, according to place. It is from my students that I have learned most about this wonderful poem as about so many things. For years I dutifully tried to teach *Troilus* as a *love* poem, but they gradually taught me what I should have learned from Thomas Usk, namely that Chaucer is "the noble *philosophical* poet in English." I did not presume to write about Chaucer's *Troilus* until after I had for twenty years studied it with what now has to be well over a thousand wonderfully rewarding, bright, eager, and often highly skeptical undergraduate students at Princeton University. Much changed during those years, especially the objects of student skepticism. I well remember that on the very first day I first "taught" the book, as one of the preceptors in Robertson's locally famous English 307, I had grave difficulty in getting students even to consider the possibility presented by the lecturer that there was something morally questionable about its major characters. The difficulty now, I often find, is getting them to entertain, at least for purposes of argument, the possible dignity and seriousness of what seem to them wholly preposterous images of "love" and "truth."

Today's undergraduates—whether liberated women, political idealists, careerists, calculating preprofessionals, seekers after truth, or all of the above —are often bemused by the romantic *Troilus* of my own undergraduate years. There seem to be two major problems. In the first place most students seem to think that politically prominent people have social obligations that override the claims of personal gratification; and they are willing to extend to this ancient fiction the censoriousness which they bring to the judgment of public figures of our own day who privilege personal gain over the public weal. Thus they find weaknesses in the hero that the calumniation of the heroine is insufficient to excuse. Second, they all know more about sex than Troilus does, so that they tend to be quite skeptical concerning what they take to be the poem's culpable exaggeration both of the technical difficulties involved and the philosophical rewards accrued.

I cannot wholly approve this point of view. My book finds Chaucer to be no more a modern cynic than a modern romantic. He is something quite different from either, a medieval classicist. Yet my debt to my students remains decisive. After these years I still from time to time realize with a start the nearly miraculous fact that someone is paying me to talk about *Troilus and Criseyde* with wonderful young fresh folks, he or she. In dedicating this book to one of their number, I offer my sincere if inadequate gratitude for the remarkable privilege.

ONE | QUAINT LIGHT IN TROY

I t would appear that no poem has ever been more finally ambiguous—
or more welcomely so to its audience—than *Troilus and Criseyde*. My
reading of major critics finds them just about evenly divided between
those who assign Troilus to some kind of a heaven at the end of the poem
and those who assign him to some kind of a hell. This is a remarkable fact
since experts assure us that there is a substantial and unresolvable difference
between heaven and hell, a difference at least as marked as that between a
hawk and a handsaw, even if, as Chaucer himself once reminds us, we have
little by the way of experimental evidence to go on. Furthermore, the ambiguity of the poem's ending is only the beginning of the poem's ambiguity,
which critics have found—usually praising it as one of Chaucer's major artistic achievements—in nearly every aspect of its treatment of historical theme,
its delineation of major character, and, above all, its exploration of the theme
of love. It is hardly surprising that one of the best books on the poem in the
last generation is subtitled "A Study of Ambiguities in *Troilus and Criseyde*."

Under these circumstances it is, to say the least, appropriate that it was
Chaucer, and this poem of Chaucer's, that introduced the very vocabulary of
ambiguity into the English language. I refer to the remarkable words *amphibologies* (TC 4.1406) and *ambages* (5.897), both of which refer to the tricky
language of pagan oracles, and specifically, to the oracular pronouncements to
and from Calchas. Diomede, trying to bed Criseyde a little more quickly, tells
her that Troy will certainly be destroyed "but if Calkas lede us with ambages"
—adding, lest she not know the word, "that is to seyn, with double wordes
slye / Swich as men clepe a word with two visages."

An *ambage,* then, is a sly ambiguity, that is, one intentionally present in the
utterance. In its context within Chaucer's poem, the ambage calls into question
the veracity and intentions of the pagan gods and their oracular mediators;

but we may also apply the concept to our understanding of Chaucer's own intentional poetic language, since much of the controversy surrounding the interpretation of his poem is a controversy concerning ambiguous language, its presence or absence, its meaning or meanings. For example, we may wish to consider the exegetical history of Troilus' soliloquy upon revisiting Criseyde's empty house in book 5:

> Than seide he thus, "O paleys desolat,
> O hous of houses whilom best ihight
> O paleys empty and disconsolat,
> O thow lanterne of which queynt is the light,
> O paleys, whilom day, that now art nyght,
> Wel oughtestow to falle, and I to dye,
> Syn she is went that wont was us to gye!

> "O paleis, whilom crowne of houses alle,
> Enlumyned with sonne of alle blisse,
> O ryng, fro which the ruby is out falle,
> O cause of wo, that cause hast ben of lisse,
> Yit, syn I may no bet, fayn wolde I kisse
> Thi colde dores, dorste I for this route;
> And farewel, shryne of which the seynt is oute!"
>   (5.540–53)

This passage has been much discussed. Indeed, it was the central text taken up in the 1984 Biennial Lecture to the New Chaucer Society, a fact that offers sufficient warrant of its continuing interest to Chaucerians and sufficient justification of my use of it for propadeutic purposes. In this instance the history of a scholarly *crux* can provide us with something of an anthology of critical attitudes relevant to the chief question that occupies my attention in this chapter: the question of linguistic ambiguity in its relationship to the classical poetic tradition.

Time spent in critical review of that history is not time wasted, even though the task must of necessity be controversial. For controversial the passage, and its exegesis, has certainly become.[1] It was D. W. Robertson, in his famous or

---

1. There is a partial history of the controversy in Alice Kaminsky, *Chaucer's "Troilus and Criseyde" and the Critics* (Athens: Ohio University Press, 1980), 110–13.

infamous essay on "Chaucerian Tragedy" that subsequently became the basis of his discussion of the *Troilus* in *A Preface to Chaucer*, who first suggested the presence of an ambage in the lines under consideratation. "The ironic pun on 'queynt' is a bitter comment on what it is that Troilus actually misses, and the change from day to night is, ironically again, the fulfillment of his wish in Book III."[2] Robertson was in no wise tentative about the presence of a pun which, he implied, is rather obvious on the text's surface; and he paused not at all to argue the validity of his suggestion. He did not even say what the pun or supposed pun is, though discusssion elsewhere in his work makes it clear enought what he meant. Robertson quite seriously proposes that the word *queynt* has an artistically conscious double meaning. One meaning is the past participle "quenched"; the other is a vulgar noun meaning a woman's vagina. Thus he implied that what "Troilus actually missed" is sexual intercourse— denoted by a coarse or at any rate clinical ribaldry. This was, to say nothing more, a revolutionary "reading" of a passage frequently mentioned in terms of its elevated rhetorical style and elevated sentiment, and it is hardly surprising that it was soon attacked.

C. L. Wrenn, one of the greatest English philologists of this century, published a long review of *A Preface to Chaucer* in 1963. The review, though generally favorable, offered numerous criticisms both of Robertson's methods and of his specific interpretations. Concerning the putative pudendum Wrenn wrote this: "We may notice in this book how sometimes the author's zeal for moral theology leads him to read more into the language of Chaucer than is there. Thus, for instance, the obscene pun (as one would now call it) which he sees in the word *queynt* in the exquisite lament of Troilus on revisiting Criseyde's palace after her final departure, will seem not to exist to most students who have a feeling for Middle English and know its syntax."[3]

Now either there is or there is not an intentional pun on the word *queynt* in this passage, and when one distinguished scholar says that there is and another, reviewing his claim, says that there is not, it may be instructive to examine the grounds of discord. Wrenn's objection is that Robertson is guilty of misreading or overreading stemming from intellectual prejudice: his "zeal

2. D. W. Robertson, *A Preface to Chaucer* (Princeton: Princeton University Press, 1962), 500.
3. C. L. Wrenn, in *JEGP* 62 (1963): 800.

for moral theology leads him to read more into the language of Chaucer than is there"; and it is posed in scholarly terms, as an objection based in philology.

It appears to me, however, that the objection is not one of scholarly substance only. It includes a definite dimension of temperamental inclination. Wrenn does not note, for example, that the syntax of the line "O thow lanterne of which queynt is the light" is just as peculiar if the word *queynt* is a past participle as it is if it is a noun, nor that it rhymes with a line ("O hous of houses whilom best ihight") equally abnormal in its syntax, nor that there is hardly a stanza in the entire *Troilus* that does not witness a surrender of "normal" Middle English syntax to the requirements of meter and rhyme.

Denying the pun removes no syntactical difficulty, for in fact the appeal to those "who have a feeling for Middle English and know its syntax" is not in this instance an appeal to scholarly expertise but an appeal to a certain predetermined assumption about the poem. The passage in question is "exquisite" and, by implication, no exquisite passage can contain the substantive *queynt*. Wrenn's specific criticism here is part of a more general indictment of moral simplism and tunnel vision in *A Preface to Chaucer*, a "theological" predisposition to deny the complexity of poetry. The critical irony is instructive: Robertson is here arguing for complexity and Wrenn for simplicity. Robertson claims that *queynt* is a complex word that infuses the entire passage with complex meaning. Wrenn denied the verbal complexity and, with it, the poetic complexity.

Wrenn denied the pun but not the *possibility* of the pun—that more radical attack awaited, as we shall see, a more august moment. He seems to have accepted the view now published in the *Chaucer Glossary* that *queynt* means, among other things, the "genitals (female)." The question was, and is, whether, as Robertson claimed, the word *queynt* was an ambage in Calchas' sense: a sly ambiguity, that is, one artistically and intentionally contrived by an author. Authorial intention is never a matter easily adjudicated, but we find help in the very history of the word *ambage* as a technical term. What might be called its poetic history will occupy our attention soon enough. I speak now of the technical connotations of Latin *ambag(i)o*.

The word occurs less frequently in medieval philosophical texts than does the commoner *ambiguitas,* but one can adduce a sufficient number of important examples to demonstrate its currency in the vocabulary of dialectical and logical analysis. Peter Abelard, for example, uses it in a commonplace context of some poetic interest in an analysis that reminds us that "Homer" can mean either a poet or a poem.[4] By Jean de Meun's time the classic school-text on ambiguous terms had long since become Aristotle's *Sophistical Refutations*, to which Jean makes a specific reference. In Chaucer's day a large and complex literature, much of it from the pens of such English logicians as his friend Strode, had grown up around the question of insoluble sentences. There were also, however, important texts from Christian antiquity. Although Aristotle's logic was for many centuries lost to Western thinkers, much of its tradition had been transmitted through the rhetorical works of Cicero and "christianized" by Augustine. A work of particular significance in this regard—though one too often neglected by students of the liberal arts in the later Middle Ages —is the *De dialectica*.

Its relevance to the present discussion derives from several circumstances. In the first place, it is explicitly an essay on the uses of language in the liberal arts—an essay in philosophical as opposed to theological hermeneutics, if you like. Although many of its central ideas are taken up again and amplified in Augustine's theoretical writings on scriptural interpretation—and especially in the *De doctrina christiana*—the *De dialectica* is resolutely "secular" in character. Its relationship to Christian exegesis is the relationship of the *De vera religione* to the anti-Pelagian polemics. Its textual grounding is not in the Christian Scriptures but in the Latin philosophical and poetic traditions as represented by Cicero and Virgil. Indeed the work is contemporary, or nearly so, with Augustine's study of the *Aeneid* at Cassiciacum. Finally, we may note its intimate connection with the central concern of the Cassiciacum enterprise: the defense, against the powerful schools of academic skepticism, of reason's capacity to know truth. Augustine says in so many words that "the business of dialectic is to discern the truth."[5]

This statement is the explicit introduction to Augustine's discussion of ambiguity. Ambiguity claims a place in the study of the arts precisely because "ambiguity hinders the hearer from discerning the truth in words." We note that ambiguity is here described as a hindrance or barrier to truth. There is no suggestion that unresolved ambiguity is desirable or admirable or artistically satisfying. The task of the reader (hearer) is to move through ambiguity, using the techniques of dialectic, to truth. Truth is the goal. This is a principle to be

4. P. Abelard, *Dialectica*, ed. L. M. De Rijk (Assen: n.p., 1966), 169.
5. Augustine, *De dialectica* 8; ed. J. Pinborg and trans. B. Darrell Jackson (Dortrecht: North Holland, 1975), 103.

kept in the forefront of the mind as we evaluate Troilus' own analysis of ambiguity, or as we try to account for Chaucer's consciously artistic ambiguous language.

Troilus laments to Criseyde's empty house "O thow lanterne of which queynt is the light." What does the house say to Troilus? What do his ambiguous words say to us? Augustine confronts the linguistic skeptics at their most radical formulation. The Stoic logicians maintained that all words are ambiguous, and to this statement Augustine gives a tentative and limited assent. But if all words be ambiguous, what hope is there for the dialectical resolution of ambiguity, that is, the explanation of words by other words? On this question the sweet voice of sophistical skepticism is the voice of Hortensius. "It is beside the point when Hortensius in Cicero misrepresents [the dialecticians] in this way: 'They say that they listen for ambiguous words in order to explain them clearly; and yet they say that every word is ambiguous. How will they explain ambiguities by ambiguities? This is like bringing an unlighted lamp into the darkness.'"[6] *Extinctum lumen/queynt light.*

The limited truth that Augustine allows to the statement that "all words are ambiguous" is simply this: all words in *isolation* are ambiguous. The isolated articulation "beta" will mean the letter *B* to a Greek and a vegetable to a Roman. "For when it is said that all words are ambiguous, it is said of isolated words. But ambiguities are explained through discussion and certainly no one carries on a discussion by means of isolated words. Thus no one explains ambiguous words by ambiguous words; and although every word is ambiguous, no one will explain the ambiguity of the words except by means of words, but words already combined which will not be ambiguous."[7]

Augustine actually uses the word *ambag(i)o* when discussing the ambiguous disjunction of written and spoken words. The written ambiguity *leporem* is not present in the spoken word "leporem" when the quantity of the penultimate syllable indicates whether it be a form of *lepos* or *lepus*. This principle is in general relevant to English as well, especially to Chaucer's English, where many ambiguous words or rhetorically ironical expressions demand an adjudication of a speaking voice not required by silent reading.

6. Ibid., 107/109. On the general relationship between the *De dialectica* and traditional themes in antique linguistics, see Karl Barwick, *Probleme der stoischen Sprachlehre und Rhetorik* (Berlin: Akademie Verlag, 1957), 8–28.
7. *De dialectica*, 109.

In general terms the Augustinian technique for the resolution of ambiguous words is examination within context, and this technique we must apply to the line "O thow lanterne of which queynt is the light." Just about the time Wrenn's views appeared in print, John F. Adams was publishing his elegant essay "Irony in Troilus' Apostrophe to the Vacant House of Criseyde."[8] He took as his starting point the correctness of Robertson's identification of a pun on *queynt* and searched out cognate implications elsewhere in the two stanzas of Troilus' speech, concluding that "it can be demonstrated with some certainty that a specific pun and pattern of wordplay was intended and that these contribute to an ironic view of Troilus, thus qualifying the approval which is to be given to the love affair and perhaps to courtly love in general."[9] Robinson had regarded as striking the fact that Chaucer calls Criseyde's house (*casa* in Boccaccio's Italian) a "palace," and Adams suggests that he has done so to introduce the idea of an astrological mansion, and with it the specific parallel (abundantly developed elsewhere in the poem) between Troilus' adoration of Venus and his love for Criseyde. He also introduces into the discussion compelling evidence supporting a sexual interpretation of the "light" imagery in general—first in the form of the famous "Venus Tray," with its fourteenth-century painting of lovers, Troilus among them, kneeling before a nude Venus and bathed in golden beams of light emanating from her crotch; and second, in the form of metaphorical commonplaces in Middle English religious literature, commonplaces biblical in origin, linking the ideas of illumination and chastity. Finally, Adams suggests, somewhat more tentatively, that the "ryng, fro which the ruby is out falle" is "a standard sexual figure. The lost ruby itself probably represents sexual passion."[10]

The matter was next raised by Ida Gordon in her crisp study of *Troilus* in 1970, and again raised in part to scold Robertson for being simple in pointing out complexity never before noticed. "When D. W. Robertson drew attention to the (possible) pun on 'queynt' . . . he was putting an unfortunately simple view of what is far from being a simple piece of writing."[11] Gordon's commitment to her theory that the language of *Troilus* rests in unresolved ambiguity

8. John F. Adams, "Irony in Troilus' Apostrophe to the Vacant House of Criseyde," *MLQ* 24 (1963): 61–65.

9. Ibid., 61.

10. Ibid., 65.

11. Ida L. Gordon, *The Double Sorrow of Troilus: A Study of Ambiguities in Troilus and Criseyde* (Oxford: Clarendon, 1970), 133.

explains the fact that, despite her acceptance of Adams's argument, she still finds a pun merely "possible." Her own analysis in fact makes the pun nearly impossible to deny, for it extends a confirming context of sexual double entendre to the following stanza. Adams's somewhat vague suggestion about the ruby and the ring (line 549) makes no mention of the parallel text that Gordon cites, with consummate appropriateness, from book 2. Pandarus is soliciting Criseyde, for the first time openly, on Troilus' behalf:

> "And right good thrifte, I pray to god, have ye,
> That han swich oon ykaught withoute net;
> And be ye wis, as ye be fair to see,
> Wel in the rynge than is the ruby set.
> There were nevere two so wel ymet,
> Whan ye ben his al hool, as he is youre;
> Ther myghty God yit graunte us see that houre."
>
> "Nay, therof spak I nought, a, ha!" quod she;
> "As helpe me god, ye shenden every deel."
> "A! mercy, dere nece," anon quod he,
> "What so I spak, I mente nat but wel . . ."
>   (2.582–92)

Once again, as it happens, an American colleague was simultaneously and independently publishing an analysis of these very lines: Thomas Ross, in the *Chaucer Review* for 1970.[12] Ross claims that Pandarus is offering a filthy suggestion, that Criseyde clearly understands its sexual innuendo, and that Pandarus then deceitfully or playfully tries to withdraw behind the innocent side of verbal ambiguities. Specifically, *hool* is a particularly coarse term for the vagina, *rynge* a slightly less coarse one, and the ruby which is to be set in the ring is a ribald indirection for Troilus' penis. There is a remarkable ratification of the probability of Ross's identifications in the fact that he does not link the passage in book 2 with its reprise in book 5, and in the fact that his own discovery is entirely independent not only of Gordon but of Adams. And neither Adams nor Ross nor Gordon invokes the classical text that could well explain the apparently bizarre appearance of genital rings in a medieval poem, namely the fifteenth elegy in the second book of Ovid's *Amores*, a poem in which "Ovid" thus addresses the ring which he sends as a gift to his beloved:

12. Thomas Ross, "*Troilus and Criseyde*, ii, 582–587: A Note," *ChR* 5 (1970): 137–39.

Anule, formosae digitum vincture puellae . . .
tam bene convenias, quam mecum convenit illi,
et digitum iusto commodus orbe teras. (1.5–6)

(O ring, that art to circle the finger of my fair lady . . . mayst thou fit her
as well as she fits me, and press her finger with aptly adjusted circle.)

It is not unlikely that this lewd text is to be associated with certain "signet-ring graffiti" found at Pompeii and elsewhere which probably preserve varying forms of an actual inscription engraved in gift rings or accompanying them:

gemma velim fieri hora non amplius una,
ut tibi signanti oscula pressa darem.[13]

(That I could be this gem only for an hour, that I might give you
impressed kisses in the act of sealing.)

The possibility that generations of Chaucer's readers never saw the double en-tendre that Criseyde herself clearly sees ("Nay, therof spak I nought, a, ha!") forcefully suggests that, given our moral and linguistic distance from the four-teenth century, our misreadings are quite as likely to be underreadings as overreadings.

Ross made a number of other contributions to an analysis of the passage, and I shall return to them in due course. I must now continue, however, with a history of the attempt to discredit Robertson's alleged pun, an attempt that grew more rhetorically heated as it became more philologically exotic. The next adversary to enter the lists was the formidable Morton Bloomfield of Harvard who in 1972 published a learned article entitled "Troilus' Paraclausi-thyron and Its Setting."[14] His ostensible purpose is to place Troilus' address to Criseyde's house within the literary genre, theme, or topos of the "paraclausi-thyron"—the lover's lament before the door of the beloved from which he has been barred. This undertaking supplies the occasion for lively and engaging

---

13. See W. D. Lebek, "Ein lateinisches Epigramm aus Pompei (vellem essem gemma eqs.) und Ovids Gedicht vom Siegelring (Am. 2.15)," *Zeitschrift für Papyrologie und Epi-graphik* 23 (1976): 21–40. Note Pandarus' "graunte us see that houre." Chaucer was certainly aware, presumably from literary texts, of the inscribed signet rings of the ancients. See lines 3.1352–55.

14. Morton W. Bloomfield, "Troilus' Paraclausithyron and Its Setting," *NM* 73 (1972): 15–24.

polemics against "some critics," either identical with Robertson and Adams or represented by them, who are the practitioners of "this type of Manichaean criticism." They hold an "un-Christian Christian attitude" that condemns Troilus "for deifying his beloved and for taking pleasure in such a wicked activity as sexual intercourse outside of marriage" and which maintains that all Troilus "was interested in . . . was Criseyde's sexual charms and apparatus." Bloomfield rejects the view that "the relentless puritanical Chaucer, who hated the flesh, loved nothing but the Trinity itself and ignored God's creation and handiwork."[15] I shall leave it to others to determine whether "some critics" or indeed any critic imaginable ever actually held the views refuted. As a general rule, refuters of Robertson have had more luck with those of his ideas which they themselves have invented than with those in which his own thought has played some role. Bloomfield himself reckons that his article pretty well disposes of Adams's suggestion that the word "palace" is to be connected with the idea of an astrological mansion. He seems also to deny a pun on *queynt*. "Aside from the confusion of imagery which would equate the inner light rather than the door itself with the pudendum, the proposed interpretation is an example of the unnuanced view of Troilus which is characteristic of this type of Manichaean criticism."[16] Bloomfield is one of the great scholars of our generation, and his erudite essay certainly has something to teach us all—beginning with the word "paraclausithyron" perhaps. Yet I find that like Wrenn's appeal to Middle English and its syntax, his appeal to the literary history of the paraclausithyron as an implicit test for the presence or absence of ambiguous language is actually an appeal to a preconceived and essentially romantic interpretation of the poem, not to objectively verifiable philological fact. Of course that interpretation may be right, wrong, or a nuanced bit of both; but the invocation of the paraclausithyron tells us precisely nothing about the alleged pun on *queynt* in line 543, especially, I must add, when there is no paraclausithyron in the poem.

For my first and stolid objection is this: whatever else Troilus' speech may be, it is not a paraclausithyron. According to its historian the paraclausithyron is "the song of the shut-out lover."[17] Troilus is not a shut-out lover; he is a ludicrously impatient lover whose girl friend is out of town for a few days.

---

15. Ibid., 24.
16. Ibid.
17. F. O. Copley, *Exclusus Amator* (Madison: University of Wisconsin Press, 1954), 1.

A paraclausithyron is a lament directed to a door or a doorkeeper. Troilus' lament is directed not to a door but to a palace, alias a house, alias a lantern, alias a ring, alias a cause of woe. The lover of the paraclausithyron may wander desperately through the streets seeking his beloved. Troilus does not search for Criseyde, since he knows where she is and thinks that he knows when she will return. If we require a generic name for the literary type represented by Troilus' speech, we shall surely call it, with Richard Schrader, the topos of the "Deserted Chamber." [18] Now to be sure, Troilus' lament is related to the "paraclausithyron tradition," but rather in the way a zebra is related to the "horse tradition" or a moose is related to the "mouse tradition"—in a way, that is, that invites us to appreciate significant differences as well as features commonly shared. According to Bloomfield, Troilus' speech is "obviously" a paraclausithyron and equally "obviously" of the subtype tragic paraclausithyron; but there is, I fear, nothing obvious about this matter. One might even find that to ignore radical differential in the name of critical sensitivity or "nuance" is an unpromising procedure at the theoretical level. Even if it *were* a paraclausithyron, what difference would it make for the interpretive question contested by Robertson and Bloomfield? I myself conclude that Troilus' speech before Criseyde's house certainly reflects a prominent classical theme with which the paraclausithyron enriched the Latin elegy—a satirical condemnation of the sexual passion of literary lovers—but that is so general a topic in antique philosophy and literature as to be a genuine commonplace.[19] It is scarcely an afternoon's work to read every surviving example of Latin paraclausithyron. Such a pleasant afternoon has convinced me that Troilus' lament to an empty house is modeled on no extant classical door-song, though, as I shall attempt to demonstrate, it "obviously" does reflect the influence of a famous medieval burlesque of certain themes of Latin elegy. None of Robertson's censors has so much as suggested that Troilus' elaborate declamation to a vacant house is less than wholly solemn at either the rhetorical or the intellectual level, but it seems to me that the genuine literary tradition of the passage—a tradition made up of witty medieval poets trained by witty classical poets—is far from humorless.

18. Richard Schrader, "The Deserted Chamber: An Unnoticed Topos in the 'Father's Lament' of Beowulf," *Journal of the Rocky Mountain Medieval and Renaissance Association* 5 (1984): 1–5.
19. See the stimulating essay of Claudio Soria, "El Paraclausithyron como presupuesto cultural de la elegia latina," *Revista de Estudios Clásicos* 8 (1963): 55–94, esp. 66–68.

For ecumenical purposes I should mention the brief article by William Frost called "A Chaucerian Crux" published in 1977.[20] The author's purposes are not polemical, and he essays an evenhanded review of arguments on both sides of the question before moving to his own somewhat ambiguous conclusion which is, as best I understand it, that since a dirty pun by Mercutio in *Romeo and Juliet* is probably irrelevant to Tennyson's *In Memoriam*, so also a pun on *queynt* is probably irrelevant (or worse) to *Troilus*. The style of this elegant essay does not call for footnote documentation, so that its reader cannot know whose ideas Frost has or has not reviewed, aside from those of Adams; he appears to have neglected, for instance, his most powerful ally, Morton Bloomfield. He does in passing cite the collateral text from the Wife of Bath's prologue (331–35) which seems to me to demonstrate absolutely a semantic field inescapable in Troilus' soliloquy.

The next author I have read on this subject, Winthrop Wetherbee, finds a "probably punning significance" in the word *queynt* in Troilus' speech, a probability he is willing to entertain because of his appreciation of the smutty associations of the ruby and the ring in the next stanza. At the same time, he clearly thinks that Adams has gone too far, and he finds that Frost and Bloomfield offer "sensible criticisms" of his reading.[21] This peripheral speculation occupies a mere moment in Wetherbee's rich book, however; and even as it was rolling off the presses some hundreds of professional Chaucerians gathered in York at the international congress of the New Chaucer Society were listening to Larry D. Benson deliver the distinguished Biennial Lecture of the New Chaucer Society, "The 'Queynte' Punnings of Chaucer's Critics."[22] Benson's treatment of his subject, as witty as it was revolutionary, raises the discussion to a new abyss. According to him no disturbing pun on *queynt* is possible in the *Troilus*—or in most of the Chaucerian passages in which critics have pretended to discover it—because the word *queynt* never meant the female organ in the first place. It was instead, in the passages in the "Miller's Tale" and the Wife of Bath's prologue so well known to Chaucerians, an absolute form of the adjective meaning "curious, elegant, pleasing." As such, it did of course refer

20. William Frost, "A Chaucerian Crux," *Yale Review* 66 (1977): 551–61.
21. Winthrop Wetherbee, *Chaucer and the Poets: An Essay on Troilus and Criseyde* (Ithaca: Cornell University Press, 1984), 217 and note.
22. Benson's lecture, "'Queynte' Punnings," is published in the New Chaucer Society's supplementary volume, *Proceedings* no. 1 (1984): *Reconstructing Chaucer*, ed. Paul Strohm and Thomas J. Heffernan (Knoxville, Tenn., 1985), 23–47.

to that curious, elegant, and pleasing part of the female anatomy that hende Nicholas grabbed and that Alison of Bath dispensed freely to her husbands, but only by way of a euphemism made intelligible by quite specific context. He caught her by the elegant; she allowed as how he was getting plenty of curious of an evening. Elsewhere, and especially in the "most beautiful example of paraclausithyron in our language," no pun was even possible. Before the powers of Benson's oratory, a word retreated from the English lexicon, shamed not by its obscenity but by its nonentity. Presumably, various literary critics—Robertson, Ross, and Bolton in particular—were expected to skulk off silently into the shadows with it as the dirty-minded inventors and champions of a philological fiction. Benson quoted Dennis with approval: "A man who would make so vile a pun would not scruple to pick a pocket." One especially curious, elegant, and pleasing feature of Benson's argument was that, as he made clear, he was not its inventor. That distinction belonged to the younger Francis Junius, friend of Milton, who had recorded his speculation in his *Etymologicon* published in the century after his death, in 1743. Thus Benson's own argument could fairly be described as quaint as well as crafty.

I hope that in what follows the focus of my criticism of Benson's truly delightful argument will be clear; I object not to the antiquity of Junius' retooled philological hypothesis but to its inadequacy. I, too, am a college professor, and I know that the reinvention of the wheel is the noble duty of each generation of scholars. But to reinvent the flat tire suggests a culpable want of imagination. The feisty tone of Benson's anti-Robertsonianism is refreshing and invigorating, but it does invite some friendly feistiness in response. For example, even if I were disposed to accept Benson's philological argument without cavil—and of course I am not so prepared—I should point out that the severe reprimand it authorizes has been misdirected. The castigation surely should fall on lexicographers, not on literary critics. According to Benson most "indecent puns" adduced in scholarly print have been illusory. "In most cases the critic would have been better advised to have stopped by the library to consult the dictionaries."[23] I can absolve that "most" as the hyperbole of the orator, but I must point out that the "dictionaries" would hardly have deterred a critic tempted to posit a pun based on a supposition that the word *queynt* was a noun meaning the female organ. The glossaries in all important editions of Chaucer from Skeat to Norman Blake, as well as the *Oxford English Dictionary*,

23. Ibid., 25.

Robertson, whose claim to see a pun in *TC* 5.543, becomes the special object
of Benson's proemial *sarcasmos,* never said that the pun was "obscene." His
word was "ironic." Of course, he did assume that the word *queynt* meant the
female sexual organ. And so, in my opinion, it did.

Any scholar offended by the fashions of the moment, which often value mere
verbal ingenuity above faithful toil among primary documents, may share Benson's regret that "in the critical climate of our time a vial of pun is worth a
bucket of philology"; but even a philological bucket cannot hold water if it has
a hole in its bottom. The philological heart of Benson's argument is simplicity
itself. "Junius's suggestion that *queynt* is the English equivalent of *bel chose,*
'elegant, pleasing thing,' must be correct."[25] I conclude on the contrary that it
must be wrong. Let me attempt to explain why. I begin with the French phrase
bele chose, which, as Benson notes, appeared as *bely chose* in the manuscript
Junius was reading. Now there is no doubt that the French word *chose* could
be used as a euphemism for the sexual organ, but the language is not unique
in that regard. Obviously the English word *thing* could have exactly the same
meaning, as it does in the Wife of Bath's prologue (WBP) 121 in "oure bothe
thynges smale." Yet the Wife of Bath never says "my queynt thing"; instead
she twice says "my bele chose." Before speculating about this phrase I should
point out that she does not say "my cointe chose" either, and indeed I think
that Benson is mistaken in suggesting that English *queynt* is a fair "equivalent"
of French *bele.* I note that the English *Romaunt* has the adjective *queynt* nine
times and the adverb *queyntly* twice. In no instance is the French original *bel-.*
It is usually *coint-.* At the same time there are about fifty appearances of the
adjective *bel(e)* in Guillaume de Lorris alone. Though the constraints of verse
translations usually smoke out the most latitudinarian possibilities in a word,
French *bel(e)* is nowhere rendered *queynt* in the *Romaunt.* The expected Middle
English equivalent of *bel(e)* would be *faire,* as we get in "faire dame" (WBP 296),
which obviously reflects the French commonplace *beldame.* If we search out
Chaucer's uncontroversial uses of the adjective *queynt*—as in "As clerkes ben
ful subtile and ful queynt" or "My fader nought, for all his queynt pley," we
shall nowhere find an example where the word *queynt* easily means the same
thing as the French *bel(e).* There is considerable doubt in my mind that the
qualities suggested by the word—elaboration, cunning, artifice, learning, or
deviousness—would encourage the creation of an adjective absolute meaning

25. Ibid., 36.

the female organ. In any event, the English adjective *queynt* is not a synonym for the French adjective *bel(e)*, and the hypothesis of their synonymity proposed by Junius in the early seventeenth century and delightfully revived by Benson in 1984, remains as implausible as ever.

Then why does the Wife of Bath—pardon her French—say *bele chose*? If the question seems simple enough, the answer to it is necessarily complex, for the Wife of Bath, as we see from her prologue and her tale alike, loves both to use and to confuse texts from the classical literary tradition. The two words with which she rhymes *chose, glose* and *rose,* suggest the most likely source of inquiry, the *Roman de la Rose*, the only other poem known to me in world literature in which we shall find the verb "to gloss" elaborately applied to sexual organs. Benson himself allows the possibility, which he characterizes as "slight," that the *Roman* is the source of the "euphemism" *queynt* "and some of the Wife of Bath's other expressions (such as *bele chose*)."[26] This seems a promising suggestion, and one that deserves to be pursued further, since, as a matter of fact, the *Roman* has long been recogized as a principal source of Chaucer's inspiration in his creation of the Wife of Bath, and about a third of the lines in her prologue have clearly generative parallels in the text of Jean de Meun, particularly though not exclusively in the speeches of La Vieille and Amis. The pervasive pattern of imitation is of considerable generic significance: Chaucer remakes after Jean de Meun the erotic pedagogy that Jean himself remade after the *Ars amatoria* of Ovid. Quite unsurprisingly, the *Roman* provides a parallel use of *chose* in a context that makes it certain that it is Chaucer's "source." Amis, speaking of jealous husbands, says this:

Autel fetes de Jalousie,
que nostres sires la maudie!
la doulereuse, la sauvage,
qui tourjorz d'autri joie enrage,
qui est si cruieuse et si glote
que tel chose veut avoir tote,
s'el en lessoit a chascun prendre,
qu'el ne la troveroit ja mendre.
Mout est fols qui tel chose esperne;
c'est la chandele en la lanterne:

26. Ibid., 41. Benson's consideration of the French vocabulary of the *Roman* is confined to a solitary and in my view misleading footnote (p. 41, n. 44).

qui mil en i alumeroit,
ja meins de feu n'i troveroit.
                    (RR 7371–82)

(Do the same with Jealousy—may our lord curse her—the suffering, wild
woman whom the joy of others always enrages. She is so cruel and greedy
that if she left something for everyone to take a share, she would want to
have the whole of it so that she would never find her portion smaller.
Whoever would monopolize such a thing is a fool. It is the candle in the
lantern: whoever brought light with it to a thousand would never find its
flame smaller.)

I shall return to the concluding lines of this passage; for the moment it is sufficient to note that they specify the repeated phrase *tel chose* (7376, 7379) in
such a way that it is clear that it means not merely sex, sexual intercourse, or
sexual favors, but the female sexual organ itself. Since the extended passage in
the *Roman* is clearly enough the direct inspiration for the extended passage in
the Wife's prologue, we can safely suppose that the Wife's *bele chose* is related
to Amis's *tel chose*. But the Wife does not say *tel chose;* she says *bele chose,* and
to understand why must involve the speculative examination of another sort
of Magdunian context: to wit, a *con*-text. Before adducing it, however, I want
to make two quick and related points that bear on the positivist assumptions
behind Benson's linguistic argument.

    In my view it would be fundamentally mistaken to think that the Wife of
Bath's prologue is written in "normal" Middle English, if we mean by that the
language once spoken by a native English-speaker, let alone that spoken by
a late fourteenth-century monoglot milliner of Bath. Her speech, thick with
Latinisms and Gallicisms swallowed nearly whole from the Vulgate, Jerome's
Adversus Jovinianum, the *Roman de la Rose,* and half a dozen other learned
texts, bears about the same relationship to "normal" conversational English of
Chaucer's day as does the language of the *Faerie Queene* to the normal conversational English of Queen Elizabeth. If Spenser writ no language, Alison of
Bath spake no language, and if we seek to know what "octogamye" (WBP 33)
means, we shall learn not from parallel examples of the usage documented by
the *MED* but by reading the ascetic polemics of Jerome.

    The related point is that, *pace* Benson, the Wife of Bath—in common with
many other characters in the *Canterbury Tales*—frequently plays on words.

Often enough Chaucer's wordplay is bilingual, dependent upon more or less learned command of the relationships between words or phrases in different languages. Benson himself allows such a bilingual pun: the word *ars-metrik* in the "Summoner's Tale." One could adduce many others. At the end of the Wife's prologue, for example, the Friar laughs at her "long preamble of a tale" and the Summoner counters with an insult dependent upon slovenly punning on English *preamble,* French *perambulacioun,* and Latin *ambulare.* Such word-play implies at least the authorial hope for a highly literate audience (and in the fourteenth-century English court that means an audience with a supple appreciation of French and Latin) but it never commits the success of the narrative to that hope. The arithmetical problem of the "Summoner's Tale" is funny or gross, depending upon a reader's sensibilities, quite without reference to the pun.

With particular regard to the *Troilus*—a poem that owes practically nothing to any anterior text written in the English language—we may safely adopt the a priori assumption that linguistic curiosities are likely to be related to texts written in antique Latin or in its medieval Romance vernaculars. There is a certain sense in which the question of the "English" word *queynt* is irrelevant; we are not concerned with an *English* word but with a *Chaucerian* word. Furthermore, if we seek to understand wordplay in a poet like Chaucer, positivist "philology" is but one, and by no means always the most helpful, tool at the critic's disposal. James Joyce's *Ulysses* is laced with philologically "impossible" puns which quite clearly insist on existing in spite of the fact that "philology" would tell us they are not supposed to. I am not convinced that Geoffrey Chaucer had a less interesting mind than did James Joyce.

With this in mind we may return to the Wife's *bele chose* and to the *con*-text —a nonce word I repeat in order to suggest that puns create meanings as well as play off against them—that in my opinion helps to explain it. There is in the long speech of La Vieille, in the context of a passage demonstrably implicated both in the Wife's prologue and in her tale, the following paraphrase of Horace:

> [E qui vodroit Horace croire . . .]
> Jadis avant Helen furent
> batailles que li con esmurent,
> don cil a grant douleur perirent
> qui por eus les batailles firent

(mes les morz n'en sunt pas seües,
quant en escrit ne sunt leües).
                    (*RR* 13893–98)

([Whoever would believe Horace knows that] formerly, before the time of
Helen, there were battles spurred by *con,* in which those who fought for it
perished with great suffering; but the dead are not known when we do not
read about them in written records.)

Here the word *con* is as unavoidable as is its specifically Horatian ancestry.
I presume that Geoffrey Chaucer and Alison of Bath knew the original Latin
quite as well as did Jean de Meun and La Vieille. It is

Nam fuit ante Helenam cunnus taeterrima belli
causa, sed ignotis perierunt mortibus illi
quos uenerem incertam rapientis more ferarum
uiribus editior caedebat ut in grege taurus.
                    (Horace, *Satires,* 1.3.107–10)

(Even before the time of Helen, the cunt was a shameful cause of war; but
in those days died inglorious deaths those whom, snatching the pleasures
of lawless love after the manner of beasts, some superior in physical
strength struck down like the bull in a herd.)

That is the text that Jean de Meun's Old Woman remembers from Horace,
and that Geoffrey Chaucer's Old Woman remembers after Jean de Meun. We
may note that the noun *cunnus* is the subject of a sentence of which the predi-
cate complement is *belli causa.* Latin *cunnus* became French *con,* and *causa*
became *chose.* It was left to the ingenious imagination of the Wife of Bath
merely to belie *belli* in order to remake Horace's phrase as *bele chose.* We here
see the Wife of Bath casually refuting Benson's fundamental and fundamentally flawed iron law of the pun ("one cannot pun on a meaning that does
not exist"). It should not surprise us that she prefers the medieval style of
etymology to the modern; she is, after all, a medieval woman.

Her learned *gauloiserie* might help explain the curious reading in Junius'
manuscript, *bely chose,* though it would be dangerous to depend too much on
the sophistication of scriveners. Jean could have quite realistically had higher
hopes for his clerical and academic readers, most of whom thought in Latin,
so to speak. Or he may have had no ambition greater than self-amusement,

an ambition after all fully authorized by Ovid and other poets of his choice. My point is that a particular bizarre "philological" phenomenon may on occasion have more to do with the creative processes of the poet's imagination than with the historical development of the Romance languages. On occasion fiction is stranger than truth. We have already seen that *bele chose* is not an equivalent for *queynt [thing]*. We now see that it is not merely a French euphemism either, but a learned if trivial poetical joke, tossed off without fanfare or exalted expectation, but not without significance either.

There are in the *Roman de la Rose* several other examples of play, at once bawdy and philosophically serious, on the vernacular words for the genitals; but though Chaucer clearly found Jean de Meun a writer of great moral weight, I doubt that he found him "exquisite." Yet quite possibly a related pun exists even in the most "exquisite" poem produced by the vernacular Middle Ages, Dante's *Commedia*.[27] Chaucer is apparently conspicuous among fourteenth-century realist poets for not using genital puns if indeed he does not do so. The phenomenon is, however, so far removed from modern expectations of exalted poetry as to make its very suggestion "dazzlingly bad taste."

27. In *Inferno* 18 Dante encounters as the type of a pimp Venedico Caccianemico, a man who procured his own sister for his princely friend, the Marquis d'Este—just as, incidentally, Troilus and Pandarus each offer to do for each other at one point. Venedico's brief speech is terminated by a demon-torturer who says "Via, / ruffian! qui non son femmine da conio" (18.65–66). The principal ambiguity in *conio* involves the ideas of "coining" and of "conning," as Isidoro del Longo, *Dante ne' tempi di Danti* (Bologna: N. Zanichelli, 1888), 199–269, demonstrates at length; but one cannot dismiss the obscene implications suggested by Giovanni Alessio in the *Dizionario etimologico italiano* (s.v. *conio*, 1); see further Pico Luri di Vassano, "Modi di dire proverbiali e motti popolari italiani," *Il Propugnatore* 12:2 (1879), 207. Here we have the possibility of sexual as well as verbal ambiguity, since *conio* (derived from L. *cuneus*, "wedge") has a phallic connotation that can be collated with the *con*-notation in *conno* (from L. *cunnus*). The possibility of an obscene pun in these lines has, of course, been denied by some readers, largely on "exquisite" grounds; see Wayne Conner in *Italica* 32 (1955), 95ff. Incidentally, I suggest that the Dantesque passage has been twice echoed by Chaucer in the *Troilus*. In the scene in which the pander Pandarus begins his mission of procuring his own niece for his princely friend, she says to him in lighthearted jest, "Uncle, youre maistresse is nat here" (2.98). Likewise Hector, expressing what is unfortunately a minority opinion in the city of Troy, says of the proposal to exchange Criseyde for Antenor, "We usen here no wommen for to selle" (4.182). In the former, Chaucer captures something of Dante's sense of sexual deprivation; in the latter Dante's collocation of fraud (through Antenor) and mercantile exchange.

I find that Benson's zeal for purging Chaucer's lexicon of the substantive *queynt* leads him into special pleading as he sets out to dismantle the lexicography of four centuries. He dismisses the testimony of Florio's Italian-English dictionary of 1598, because, he says, Florio must be citing Chaucer rather than common usage. "Had the word been common, Junius, writing about the same time, would probably not have restricted his attention to its uses in Chaucer and would almost certainly have cited its contemporary forms."[28] Curiously, Junius' silence has here become more powerful than Florio's clear speech.

There is no reason to believe, as Benson apparently does, that Florio did not know what a word meant simply because he uses Chaucer to document its usage. I presume, rather, that Chaucer was the only written source he had. To be fair, Benson is here addressing the highly dubious notion—the source of which is to me unknown—that the genital meaning of *queynt* was *common* usage. Florio's testimony is of interest, however, precisely for the reason that it tells us what he thought the word meant *in Chaucer*. I find wholly unconvincing Benson's unexamined assertion that Junius would, under any circumstances, "almost certainly" have cited a current English ribaldry from the *spoken* language. He, too, is largely restricted to "literary" words, and he is generally silent when the texts are silent. He has no article on *cunt,* for example, though I presume that most Englishwomen had one in the early seventeenth century or, for that matter, even in the severer days of the Protectorate.

Benson's discovery of the word *quaint* in the *Sir Tristram* is of interest, and, as he justly remarks, it is unlikely to be obscene in its context. I should add that it is even less likely to be a euphemistic adjective absolute and less likely still to be the place where Chaucer learned the word. It has in context a nearly medical specificity, as it relates directly to the question of who has or has not had sexual intercourse with Isolde. There may also be, though I doubt it, something of the special French sense of the *con* as visibly exposed by a woman when she lifts her skirts to warm her rump or to urinate (*convoi,* or *convoistisson*), a bawdy pun made much of by Béroalde de Verville and possibly visually present in the iconography of the *Roman de la Rose* in the portraits of Convoitise and Villenie.[29]

---

28. Benson, " 'Queynte' Punnings," 39.
29. See Béroalde de Verville, *Le Moyen de Parvenir,* ed. H. Moreau and A. Tournon (Aix-en-Provence: Publications de l'Université, 1984), 2:22, 122. A visual analogue is common in illustrations of the *Roman.*

As for the relationship between the English synonyms (as I regard them) *queynt* and *cunte* I can offer no more illumination than our great lexicographers, who must perforce be content to leave *queynt* among the very large number of English words whose origins are "obscure." That the form *queynt* cannot have developed by normal etymological mutation from the Germanic root *kunta* I of course recognize; no less do I recognize that our lexicon is full of etymological "abnormalities." I speculate, along with Eric Partridge, Norman Davis, and others, that *queynt* as a "literary" version of *cunt*—and it has been found only in *Sir Tristram* and Chaucer, so far as I know—does indeed represent a kind of Gallicization of the Germanic root. This operation may have been euphemistic or intentionally facetious, as when modern English speakers humorously dignify the word "garbage" by pronouncing it to rhyme with American "garage." Certainly the appearance of *cunte* in the *Proverbs of Hendyng* as recorded in the *MED*—where the Germanic form plays on the word cunni[n]g—seems to assume that *cunt* is to *cunning* as *queynt* is to *cointise*.

This is, I repeat, speculation, and I claim no privilege for it. At the same time it seems to me a good deal more probable than Benson's hypothesis that *queynt* is an absolute adjective meaning the pudendum. For that hypothesis he says that he has "not much evidence." As winningly modest as this disclaimer is, it is still not modest enough; for, in fact, he has no evidence at all. Outside of the closed circle of poetic texts which are the subject of the inquiry and cannot really be invoked to prove themselves—four undisputed appearances in Chaucer and one in *Sir Tristram*—the dictionaries offer no parallel English readings. Under these circumstances we are left precisely in the situation of the Oxford and Ann Arbor lexicographers, of Skeat and Davis, in the situation, indeed, of any principled reader trying to make sense of a difficult word.

The genital meaning of the word *queynt* is not to be banished by appeals to syntax, to literary genre, or to etymology—which are for Wrenn, Bloomfield, and Benson, respectively, the ostensible grounds of its indictment—but this is of course not the same as to say that there is a pun or rather an ambage in the word in *Troilus* 5.545, or in any other specific passage. We have had to overcome a formidable amount of scholarly prejudice to defend simply the *possibility* of such verbal complexity, and indeed the possibility may be all that is demonstrable. If we wish to go further, we shall be thrown back upon our contextual understanding of the passage. Such is the Augustinian technique for the solution of ambiguities. Fortunately, the poem does not leave us without some guidance, for Troilus does not merely utter an ambiguous monosyllable into a vacuum. We are given a context—literary, psychological, and narrative —and it is to that context that we must now turn our attention.

To be fair to Larry Benson I note that he, too, insists upon the examination of context, though he appears to mean by that word something much narrower than I. He means, I take it, little more than a word's lexical neighborhood in a text. "Is there then a pun of dazzlingly bad taste in the line 'O thow lanterne of which queynt is the light'?" he asks. "No. The only way one can make such a pun is to use it in a context that will evoke the obscenity. There is no such context in Troilus's apostrophe."[30]

If that is a demonstration of contextual absence, I permit myself to wonder what a demonstration of contextual presence might look like. Such context is apparently present in the "Miller's Tale." When the Miller tells us that hende Nicholas "caughte her by the queynt," I take it that we know what he means, according to Benson, not because the word *queynt* actually denotes any specific quaint thing but because the context—that is, the sexual nature of Nicholas's apparent interest in Alison and his act of "catching" her—signals what the Miller must mean, and that is what Benson calls "the obscene word." Yet there is in the philological principles that guide him nothing to justify our under-standing that Nicholas caught her by the obscene word. Why does not this context suggest instead that he caught her by the waist, or the thigh, or the breast, or the earlobe, or an intimate item of apparel, or any one of a number of other equally sexually suggestive and considerably more credibly catchable quaintities?

Surely lexical context is only one of *many* contexts leading the reader to a silent act of interpretation? In the phrase "lanterne of which queynt is the light," lexical context—that is, specifically, the nouns *lanterne* and *light*—gives the reader the obvious indication that the word *queynt* means "quenched." No one, least of all Robertson, ever denied so elementary a truth, and if the only kind of context that a reader of Chaucer had to deal with were lexical con-text, that would be the end of the matter. However, things are not so easy, for Chaucer was not writing simple exercises for a book designed to teach Mid-dle English as a second language but a complex poem deeply informed by a learned poetic tradition.

In point of fact, a certain amount of the extralexical defining context of Chaucer's quaint light has already been adduced. The image of a woman's pri-

30. Benson, "'Queynte' Punnings," 46.

vate parts as a source of light is bizarre and indeed grotesque, and to posit its reality in the line "O thow lanterne of which queynt is the light" on the solitary basis of the identification of theoretical homophones would in my opinion be absurd. Such an objection was implicit in my passing reference to William Empson earlier.

We have already seen, however, that a literal and visual parallel of the grotesquerie exists in the so-called Venus Tray.[31] In this painting, Troilus, clearly and identifiably captioned, is among a group of the world's most conspicuous lovers who kneel in adoration of Venus, bathed in the beams of light emanating from her crotch. At least that is what I claim is in the picture. Interestingly enough the equivalent of the "philologists" among the art historians would be fully capable of denying that it is possible to draw a picture of something that does not exist. I find the evidence of the "Venus Tray" telling, but it is of course a somewhat remote visual analogue with no known specific connections in English art or in the documented commerce of Chaucer's intellectual relations. To be useful, it needs the support of more definite literary analogues. These are to be found, I suggest, in the Ovidian texts that provide the specific tradition of Chaucer's treatment of the theme of the disconsolate lover.

Among the several issues at stake in this discussion is the fundamental question of whether there is or is not a definite and frankly sexual element in Troilus' grief. The adjudication of that question cannot decide the presence or absence of a pun on *queynt,* but it can at least help confirm or deny the plausibility of adducing a sexual vocabulary in the passage. What Troilus does or does not say in this scene, that is, may be illuminated by what literary tradition would expect him to say. To this end it is necessary to invoke one absolutely cardinal literary relationship that has gone unremarked in all the elaborate exegesis to which the passage has been subjected, and that is its relationship to the antierotic precepts of Ovid.

Though both Boccaccio and Chaucer appear to have taken some care to avoid the name of Ovid and thus to avoid anachronism within their imagined pre-Roman setting, the old poet is surely powerfully there in spirit and in text. Pandaro, who thinks that a good way for Troilo to get over Criseida would be to take up with some other woman, says that he has often heard it said that

31. The painting has been frequently published. One standard and easily accessible source is Roger S. Loomis, *Arthurian Legends in Medieval Art* (New York: Columbia University Press, 1938), plate 135.

"il nuovo amor sempre caccia l'antico" (*Fil.* 4.49). Chaucer, who is generally more ambitious in his aspirations to a pseudoantique local color, allows his Pandarus to supplant the hearsay evidence of the *Filostrato* with definite textual authority, the authority of "Zanzis, that was ful wys" and who wrote (not said) that "the newe love out chaceth ofte the olde" (*TC* 4.415). As everybody knows (and, I would add, as everybody knew), that advice actually comes from Ovid's *Remedia amoris;* nor should we expect in a medieval context and on the subject of falling out of love any other text or any other teacher.

It is only in the fifth book that Troilus' erotic grief reaches its highest and maddest pitch—as he curses the gods, caresses a pillow, stipulates the maudlin terms of his funeral, and so forth—and only then that he most needs love's remedies. It seems to me quite certain that in the episodes of the fifth book of the *Filostrato* (the festivities at Sarpedon's and the secret visitation to Criseida's empty house) Boccaccio was schematically playing off against the themes of Ovid's *Remedia.*

Although Chaucer's remaking of these episodes, and especially of the latter, departs substantially from the Boccaccian model, he has taken pains to acknowledge and to endorse the Ovidian text that he found there. Pandarus acts out in the fifth book the role of the consoling friend recommended as so helpful by Ovid (*RA* 587–88), and his specific advice—that they divert themselves at Sarpedon's house party for a week—echoes the counsel of Ovid to avoid solitude and to enjoy the company of the crowd (*RA* 579–91) But it is the advice that Troilus *fails* to heed that perhaps most clearly signals Ovid's complicating presence in the passage. The crowd does not distract Troilus, who spends much of his time daydreaming about his beloved (*RA* 583–84; *Fil.* 4.45; *TC* 5.453–55). And two of Ovid's most concrete and hence most memorable suggestions are schematically violated. Ovid (*RA* 718) counsels the lover in search of his sanity to burn all the old letters from his mistress: *Constantes animos scripta relecta movent* (Letters read over again move even constant minds). Troilo reads them a hundred times at Sarpedon's house (*Fil.* 5.45) and Troilus, a speed-reader, reads them a hundred times "atwixen noon and prime" (*TC* 5.472).

Immediately following the advice concerning letters in the *Remedia amoris* comes an urgent warning against frequenting the sites of former erotic pleasure, the sexual nature of which is quite explicitly denoted by the unflinching word *concubitus,* which is Latin for doing the obscene thing. Ovid dramatizes the plight of the hapless lover who looks upon the old familiar places only to be tortured by their memories of lust assuaged:

> Hic fuit, hic cubuit; thalamo dormivimus illo:
> Hic mihi lasciva gaudia nocte dedit. (*RA* 727–28)

> (Here was she, here she lay; in that chamber did we sleep; here did she give me wanton joys at night.)

And once again Troilus' behavior is determined—in an ironic fashion perhaps better described as parody than as echo—by the Ovidian text. The secret visitation to Criseyde's house is, after all, simply the set piece in Troilus' elaborately imitative trip down Memory Lane (5.519–616) to the various "places of the town / In which he whilom hadde al his plesaunce." If we honor the Ovidian tradition, we must conclude that (if nothing more) Troilus is acting out a disastrous amatory pattern, a course of action explicitly defined by the greatest authority on such matters as the course to be avoided at all costs. The text of the *Remedia amoris* is, at this point in the *Troilus*, a stress-bearing element, not a decorative or whimsical addition. Anyone familiar with its teachings and aware of their authority in the medieval schools might thus be more likely to imagine that Troilus' lament before Criseyde's empty house is more pathological than that it is "exquisite."[32] Yet it requires neither such a predisposition nor a pun on the word *queynt* to suggest what it is that "Troilus actually missed," since Ovid tells us quite clearly it is *concubitus*.

Obscenity in Latin poetry was largely a function of genre.[33] The same thing can be said by and large of the aristocratic poetry of medieval Europe. Satire authorizes subjects, styles, themes, and lexicon that would elsewhere be inappropriate. This explains why the grave moralist Horace, practitioner of a "poetry of ethics," could use the word *cunnus* and why the vernacular satirist Jean de Meun would follow him with impunity. Chaucer is not about to play with the word *queynt* in the "Book of the Duchess." He does so almost as a matter of instinct in the "Miller's Tale."

What of the oration of Troilus, prince of Troy, to a piece of unoccupied real

32. Elisabeth Pellegrin, "Les 'Remedia Amoris' d'Ovide, texte scolaire médiévale," *BEC* 115 (1957): 172–79.
33. See the excellent essay of H. Bardon, "Rome et l'impudeur," *Latomus* 24 (1965): 495–518.

estate? The critical tradition has protected this particular passage of Chaucerian text with various questionable acts of literary appreciation that give it
a spurious generic privilege. It is "exquisite"; it is "the most beautiful example
of paraclausithyron in our language." What if, instead, its genuine literary
filiations are with classical satire and antierotic doxography? Might we not
then licitly find here some aspects of a satirical episode wildly implausible in
its want of psychological and narrative verisimilitude, risibly maudlin in its
sentimentality, and embarrassingly overblown in its rhetoric?

Latin or "Ur-Ovid" certainly can point us in the right direction, but Chaucer's
poem, an elaborate exercise in the transformation of the classical to the vernacular, is likewise richly informed by anterior vernacular Ovidianism, particularly that of the *Roman de la Rose* and of Boccaccio. There is a vernacular
Ovidian text in the *Canterbury Tales* which, to my mind, ought to lay our
narrowest question to rest:

> For certeyn, olde dotard, by your leve,
> Ye shul have queynt right ynogh at eve.
> He is to greet a nygard that wold werne
> A man to light a candle at his lanterne;
> He shul have never the lasse light, pardee.
>   (WBP 331–35)

Though it seems to me impossible that the word *queynt* is here an adjective
absolute, I am not concerned to argue the point. I *am* concerned to point out
that in this entirely unambiguous text the female sexual organ is equated with
a candle in a lantern. Discussion of the line "O thow lanterne of which queynt
is the light" has been blunted by the failure of certain critics to realize that the
word "light" is here a concrete rather than an abstract noun. It means "candle."
The passage in *Troilus* thus shares with the passage in the Wife' prologue the
crucial words *queynt* and *lanterne* and the synonyms light and candle. The
specific literary source of the idea is also perfectly clear. It is the passage from
the *Roman de la Rose* cited earlier:

> Mout est fols qui tel chose esperne;
> c'est la chandele en la lanterne:
> qui mil en i alumeroit,
> ja meins de feu n'i troveroit.
>   (7379–82)

(Whoever would monopolize such a thing is a fool. It is the candle in the lantern: whoever brought light with it to a thousand would never find its flame smaller.)

Here the speaker is Friend (one of the literary ancestors of Pandarus) speaking to the Lover about Jealousy, one of the guardians of the rose. Jealousy wants to keep the rose to herself, and Friend counsels the Lover in those deceitful practices best suited to circumvent the difficulty. Since the rosebud is for Jean de Meun an emblem of Chaucerian *queynt,* and since Jealousy represents among other things the sexual possessiveness of husbands, the generic relationship is plain enough.

So are the specific lexical filiations. *Queynte, tel chose, bele chose, con, la chandele en la lanterne* are all the same things. Furthermore, they all have a common source in a bland Ovidian euphemism—*illa pars*—in a text wholly predictable if not inevitable, the *Ars amatoria.*[34] The image of a source of illumination that "is" queynt, were it dependent upon an isolated and possibly accidental homophone alone, would not be enough to encourage our acceptance. But when I see it in the uncompromising medium of painted wood, and when I find it unmistakably present in an Ovidian passage in Jean de Meun which Geoffrey Chaucer reworks in a fashion that makes it even more explicit, I have to admit that the image is not merely a theoretical if grotesque philological possibility but an actual artistic reality within the sphere of the poet's experience.

The discovery of a link with the *Roman de la Rose* is a crucial step in reconstructing the itinerary of Chaucer's poetical imagination with regard to "quaint light," but we note that it is a complex contextual pattern, and not isolated words or images, that points the way. In the *Roman de la Rose* what might be called sexual light has a bawdy potential, and the Wife of Bath transforms the potentiality into an actuality. Another Chaucerian text, based in these same lines of Jean de Meun's, shows that this need not always happen. The idea that the candle's light is in no wise decreased by the fires borrowed from it is so commonplace in texts between Cicero and Chaucer that those editors who

---

34. "Conteritur ferrum, silices tenuantur ab usu: / Sufficit et damni pars caret illa metu. / Quis vetet adposito lumen de lumine sumi?" (*AA* 3.91–93). (Iron is worn away, and flints are diminished by use; that part endures, and has no fear of loss. Who would forbid to take light from a candle set before you?) In its context in the third book, "Ovid's advice to the girls," the lines are part of an exhortation to female promiscuity; that context informs their use first by Jean de Meun and then by Chaucer.

have called it "proverbial" have not been without justification. For a naive or innocent use of the image I would point to the description of the good Fair White in the "Book of the Duchess":

> She was lyk to torche bryght
> That every man may take of lyght
> Ynogh, and hyt hath never the lesse.
> (963–65)

The good Fair White is as nearly a morally unambiguous character as we shall find in Chaucer's poetry. The locus of such moral ambiguity as there is in the "Book of the Duchess" will be found in the dialectic between the narrator and the Black Knight. White herself is not without complexity, but it is the complexity of hagiography, in which the more customary moral adjudication of literary character becomes instead the search for any traces of the real woman beneath the stylized portraits of perfection in the Song of Songs and the handbooks of the rhetoricians. All the central facts of the "Book of the Duchess"—its historical circumstances, the probable historical identification of the Black Knight, the certain identification of Fair White—lead me to think it inconceivable that Chaucer here intends, or that his passage here allows, a smutty implication. I am tempted to describe the moral context here as unambiguously black-and-blanche, a context wholly incapable of the off-color. Yet the two allegedly smutty images from the *Troilus*—the undiminished light and the ornament without its stone—are prominently here:

> She was lyk to torche bryght
> That every man may take of lyght
> Ynogh, and hyt hath never the lesse.
> (963–65)

The ornament here is a crown, not a ring, but the metaphoric sense is still clearly related:

> Me thoughte the felawsshyppe as naked
> Withouten hir, that sawgh I oones,
> As a corowne withoute stones.
> (978–80)

I would argue that the image of "undiminished light" involves an ambage (as distinguished from a mere lexical ambiguity) neither in the "Book of the

Duchess" nor in the prologue to the Wife of Bath's tale. In the one case the image is contextually free from sexual suggestion; in the second it is radically implicated in it. It would be a fallacious reading that imputed sexual implication to the one or denied it to the other. Only the passage in the *Troilus* presents a true poetic ambiguity, that is to say, an image capable of a coherent understanding from two quite different perspectives.

In analyzing the covert darknesses of the "paleys desolat," John Adams writes that "Troilus is betrayed by areas of suggestion in his language which are not under his control."[35] I like his verb "betray." We do not have here a "Freudian slip," a momentary and involuntary flash of unconscious motive, but a systematic and protracted linguistic "betrayal" of conscious motivation in which the radically intentional nature of language overcomes even the most powerfully willed of deceptions, self-deception.

The philosopher J. Engels, bringing to bear on Augustine's theory of signification his profound knowledge of the vocabulary of antique semantics, has suggested an enriching subtlety highly relevant to the linguistic "betrayal" of Chaucerian ambages.[36] Augustine distinguishes two classes of signs: *signa naturalia* and *signa data,* and he assigns words to the latter category. The phrase *signa data* has been translated as "conventional signs" by nearly all students of Augustinian linguistics, thus making his verbal *signa* cognate with Boethian *nomina* as translated from the *Peri Hermeneias* of Aristotle. "Nomen ergo est vox significativa secundum placitum" (A name [noun] is a word which signifies according to convention). Concerning Augustine's belief in the conventional nature of *signa data* there can be no doubt, but Engels suggests that the translation of the phrase as "conventional signs" is inexact. Rather, he argues, *data* means intentionally given or given with the will to express, with a distinct emphasis on intentional and volitional expression. I find that Troilus' language, here and elsewhere in the poem, "deconstructs" certain structures of self-deception and penetrates certain barriers of imperfect moral awareness.

The "ambiguous" potential of Chaucerian language is a function both of lexicon and of literary style, arising both from the denotative range of such words as "light" and "palace" and from implications of poetic tone and context. The latter feature strikes me as particularly important throughout the *Troilus,*

35. Adams, "Vacant House," 62.
36. J. Engels, "La Doctrine du signe chez saint Augustin," *Studia Patristica* 6 (1962): 366–73.

where text so often wars with context, and where words are so seldom cousin
to the deed. Neither the *Filostrato* nor the *Consolation of Philosophy*, the two
texts to which Chaucer is most explicitly indebted in the *Troilus*, could offer
him a model of that precise mode of ambiguous poetic texture; and he turned
to his great predecessor in Boethian love fiction, Jean de Meun. The *Roman
de la Rose* provided both the poet and his audience with a context in which
only a powerfully volitional act of critical blindness will fail to see the glow of
Chaucer's quaint light.

Robertson has already drawn attention to the fact that Troilus' erotic desire
of the third book, the lover's wish for an endless night, finds its ironic and
unsatisfying reality in Criseyde's absence: "O paleys, whilom day, that now
art nyght." The ironic play of light and dark, day and night, is extensively
developed in stanzas 74 through 79 (5.512–53), as in the fine couplet

> And unto tyme that it gan to nyghte,
> They spaken of Criseyde the bright.
>   (5.515–16)

Yet it has not been noticed, I think, that the whole episode of the lover's visit
to the empty house has been ironically structured about the values of day and
night in an Ovidian moment of the *Roman de la Rose*. A single stanza of the
Filostrato (5.50) is expanded to two in the *Troilus* (5.74 and 75) in a fashion that both increases the weight of the episode and further attenuates its
already considerable sentimentality. Troilus wakes Pandarus with the plan to
visit Criseyde's house as the dawn lightens, "On morwe, as soone as day bygan
to clere" (5.519). As annotators have been aware, this last phrase, "as soone as
day bygan to clere" is textually and contextually related to a line in the *Roman
de la Rose*:

> Gart que tu soies repairiez
> *ainz que li jorz soit esclariez*
>   (2527–28)

(Take care that you have left before the light of day.)

The context in the *Roman de la Rose*, as well as another notable borrowing
in stanza 79, shows that Chaucer is using Guillaume de Lorris with conscious
design. The code of Ovidian love that Guillaume's Cupid delivers to Amant is
characterized by various self-serving extravagances, many borrowed directly
from Ovid and others merely imitated after him, intended to help a lover dem-

onstrate to his woman the extraordinary quality of his passion. One ploy is to go secretly by night to the woman's house, where "you will perch like a crane all alone, outside in the wind and rain." The practical objective here is that the woman may wake up and hear the lover's rehearsed moans and groans and thus be moved to pity. The lover must, however, be sure to leave by break of day so as not to be seen. Chaucer has reworked the Italian Ovidianism of Boccaccio in the idiom of the French Ovidianism of the *Roman de la Rose*, but he has underscored the dramatic reversal of Troilus' amatory fortunes by having him go to his beloved's (empty) house at daybreak, rather than leave it then. This is not paraclausithyron, exquisite or otherwise, but it is engaging vernacular burlesque of some of the themes of Ovidian elegy.

Two other details link Chaucer's passage with the *Roman de la Rose* and with the Ovid who sits laughing behind its pages. Troilus, upon perceiving the emptiness of the house, blanches "with chaunged dedlich pale face" (5.536). Once again, what is prescriptive for lovers in the *Roman* has become descriptive for the individual lover Troilus. Chaucer has returned the lines that link pallor with the visit to the beloved's house,

> Il covient que tu t'esseïmes,
> car bien saches qu'amors ne lesse
> sor fin amant color ne gresse
> (2534–36)

(It is normal that you should waste away, for love, you understand, leaves no color or fat on true lovers)

to their Latin source in Ovid:

> Palleat omnis amans: hic est color aptus amanti.
> (*AA* 1.729)

(Let every lover be pale; this is the lover's hue.)

The whiting of Troilus is not limited to this single episode, since he does it on an average of once every twenty minutes during daylight hours (1.441), and some readers may think it too general a symptom of medieval love-sickness to argue its specific textual connections here.[37] Even so, the possibility seems

---

37. In the Latin elegiac tradition, "to blanch" is virtually identical with "to suffer from the disease of love." See Saara Lilja, *The Roman Elegists' Attitude to Women* (Helsinki, 1965), 108.

confirmed by the extraordinary suggestion of stanza 79 that Troilus *kiss the door* of Criseyde's house.

> Yit, syn I may no bet, fayn wolde I kisse
> Thi colde dores, dorste I for this route.
>   (5.551–52)

This is a certain echo of the preposterous advice of the god of Love:

> Si te dirai que tu doiz faire
> par amor dou haut seintuaire
> de quoi tu ne puez avoir aise:
> au revenir la porte baise . . .
>   (2521–24)

(Now I will tell you what you should do for the love of that high sanctuary whose comfort you cannot possess: on your return, kiss the door . . .)

Bloomfield justly notes that door kissing is a feature of the classical para-clausithyron, but Chaucer's identifiable source here—Guillaume's parodic extrapolation on an elegiac theme already treated by Ovid with irreverent facetiousness—leads me to suspect a deep and somewhat undifferentiated obscene potential, probably complicated by a near blasphemy.

Chaucer could never have intended that the sumptuous text he created would be unraveled, thread by thread, in laborious argument. The utility, as also the beauty, of a textile is in its finished unity, not in the individual materials of its construction. But if we are to gauge the tensile strength of a fabric, we must first know of what it has been constructed and how it has been put together. What may be a work of elaborate analysis in a laboratory is something the weaver himself takes in at a glance.

My conclusion is that he knew the *Roman de la Rose* very well indeed, and that he fully appreciated both Guillaume's Ovidianism and Jean's satirical critique of it. He knew that the *haut seintuaire* (2522), later called the *saintuaire precieus* (2711), whatever implications it would have for Guillaume, would have a sexual meaning for Jean. At the end of his poem both the pilgrim-lover's gear and the shrine to which he brings them are given specifically genital meanings that no reader is likely to miss. That Geoffrey Chaucer did not miss them is clear from some of the more memorable lines in the *Canterbury Tales*, such as "This Somonour bar to hym a stif burdoun" (General Prologue, 673) or "I wolde I hadde thy coillons in my hand / Instead of relikes or of seintuarie" ("Pardoner's Tale," 962).

Paragraph 79 concludes with this line: "And farewel, shryne of which the seynt is oute!" We may recall the line "O thow lanterne of which queynt is the light": *queynt* rhymes with *seynt,* and one means, the other is, "out." Aside from the repeated reference to God the Creator, in whom many pagans shared the belief of Christians, there are not many religious syncretisms in the *Troilus*— passages in which the specific vocabulary of Christian cult is inappropriately imposed upon the world and speech of ancient pagans—but this is one. What is the "seynt" of a "shryne"? The answer is that it is the body, or part thereof —a "relic"—of a holy person, or a sacred image of a holy person, or an image reliquary containing a relic. This is what is no longer at the "shrine." In this context the word *seynt* cannot mean a living person or a spiritual abstraction: it means a body or a member of a body or an image of a body. Another Middle English word—*corseynt*—makes the idea of the body clearer.

If we seek to know how and why the living daughter of an ancient augur can be a "seynt," Jean de Meun once again can offer guidance. Chaucer is playing with the idea of idolatry, a theme he would find in the *Roman de la Rose*, but also in the *Canzoniere* of Petrarch and several other texts used in the *Troilus* including, conspicuously, the *Filostrato* itself. This theme is so essential to the *Troilus*, and developed by Chaucer with such imaginative brilliance, that I elect to devote another chapter of this book to its examination. Here it is perhaps sufficient to say that, in my opinion, it is the textual invocation of the theme of idolatry that transforms Troilus' lament before Criseyde's empty house from a maudlin or satiric imitation of Ovidian elegy to an episode with intellectual bite and philosophical importance.

What of the alleged wordplay on *queynt?* Is it possible to lend credence to the actuality of a pun so shocking and grotesque, a pun of "dazzlingly bad taste"? Certainly it is not easy to do so, but the alternative to reluctant belief would appear to me to be a preposterous credulity. For if we deny the pun we must then explain away as coincidences and mere random fortuities the lengthy catalog of contextual congruences examined earlier. The bizarre iconography of the "Venus Tray" is a mere coincidence. The Wife of Bath's image of a woman's cunt as a lantern is also coincidental. The repetition of the image of the shrine from the *Roman de la Rose* is accidental. Likewise accidental are the structural congruences of Chaucer's text with the *Remedia amoris* of Ovid, and the parallel presence of Ovid in Jean de Meun and in Boccaccio. Any similarity between the phrases *bele chose* and *belli causa* is merely fortuitous and nothing more.

The clues are, to be sure, of differing kinds and differing weights, reflecting the often playful and even whimsical imagination of the working poet. There are, however, quite a large number of them. To dismiss their implications we must not merely credulously accept as coincidental each individual piece of the adduced evidence; we must, as a final act of faith, embrace the belief that a very large number of coincidences coincidentally coincide in a single verse paragraph of Chaucer's *Troilus*. To be sure, there are things harder to believe. One of them, at least so far as I am concerned, is that the word *queynt* is an adjective absolute. But there are also things that are easier; it is easier to believe that we have discovered a modest "congruence of objectivities," to use an art historian's useful phrase. Faced with the alternative of accepting what is preposterous and what is merely unexpected and surprising, I must choose the latter.

Thus I do believe that Chaucer has constructed a pun, an ambage, a "sly" ambiguity in the line "O thow lanterne of which queynt is the light." That is my conclusion concerning that particular line, but it is not my point in writing this chapter. The point of the chapter is to raise certain issues of a theoretical nature concerning the poetry of the *Troilus*. Among the questions that commanded my initial inquiries, two were conspicuous; one was quite broad and the other quite narrow. The broad question was this: what might have been Chaucer's own understanding of the phenomenon of ambiguous language? The much narrower was this: what was so powerfully offensive in Robertson's perception of a pun on the word *queynt* as to incite a philological panic in Harvard Yard? The issue on which the two questions converge is the issue of interpretation.

The pun that I claim is in Chaucer's text is not uninteresting, but its interest is strictly limited. In and of itself, it would not merit the extended attention I have given it in this chapter. It should be obvious that my interest in the passage I allege to contain the pun—like that of several others who have discussed the passage before me—is to raise some questions about the fundamental nature of Chaucer's poem. The silent issue at debate is not in fact linguistic at all, but what might follow if a certain linguistic possibility were allowed. The silent issue on the minds of many who have denied the pun has been this: *if* there is a pun on *queynt,* then Robertson's general interpretation of the poem becomes more plausible and certain other interpretations less plausible. The alarm may have been premature all along, incidentally, since the alternatives may not be that stark. I mentioned in passing that Wetherbee, whose interpretation of the *Troilus* is far from "Robertsonian," accepts the pun as probable.

We are invited to make explicit some of the theoretical issues involved, and to see how their resolution may help us to understand the *kind* of poem Chaucer has written. On the question of the use of evidence, I take it that Benson's central premise is that a certain interpretive predisposition has led "Robertsonians" to invoke textual evidence that simply cannot exist.[38] That there is such a thing as critical wishful thinking I should be foolish to deny. I wish I could claim exemption from this general failing that too often leads a scholar to see in or around a text what he or she expects to see there. But predisposition is as likely to determine what the critic does *not* see as what the critic does see. In this instance what most interests *me* is the fashion in which silent commitment to a strictly limited set of interpretive possibilities may have led certain anti-Robertsonians to deny even the *possible existence* of textual phenomena that I find to exist in the poem.

There is a kind of critical Berkleianism that rules over literary study: *esse est percipi.* If the tree falls in the forest unseen and unheard, there is no tree. In literary study this philosophical predisposition is pragmatically invoked by anti-interpreters in terms already made familiar by the anti-interpreters among the art historians: such and such cannot be true because it is so complex, convoluted, learned, or whatever that no audience could have conceivably gotten it. Since there is a good deal of wildly irresponsible "allegorical" interpretation about, enough to suggest that for some critics poems and paintings alike have the status of inkblots in a Rorschach test, this has become a powerful argument.

But such an approach addresses only one interpretive disease, and by no means necessarily the most dangerous. I shall repeat that at least my own study of poetic and visual allegory in the Gothic and Baroque periods persuades me that modern misinterpretation is as likely to be underinterpretation as overinterpretation. The Berkleian argument shields the underinterpreter and the anti-interpreter because it would limit the genius of great artists to the capacities or predispositions of their readers and viewers. Yet does any reader of the *Divine Comedy* or observer of the Ghent altarpiece actually believe that he or she has "gotten" everything there is in those works, or that scholars who make

38. For a similar point of view, see Kaminsky, *"Troilus" and the Critics*, 112.

a specialty of such things have not gotten more than they, or that it is perfectly reasonable to suppose, given the deducible aesthetic principles governing the works involved, that there are things in them that no one has ever gotten and that, perhaps, no one ever will?

Some of the objections that have been voiced against what I shall call "Robertson's pun," objections often more remarkable for their rhetoric of indignation than for their intellectual conviction, are perhaps best explained in terms of interpretive Berkleianism. What Robertson did, in my view, was to "get" something for the first time, at least for the first time within the quite brief history of modern Chaucer criticism. Since what he had gotten was apparently inconsistent with an established and decorously limited understanding of the poem, it became necessary either to allow the poem's interpretive limits to expand or else to maintain that he had not actually gotten anything at all. If what he claimed to have perceived could be shown to be forbidden by those who have a feeling for Middle English and know its syntax, or by the generic power of the "tragic paraclausithyron," or by the nonentity of the noun *queynt,* he could not have perceived it. And if he never perceived it, it never was: *esse est percipi.*

Thus even the limited question of "Robertson's pun" seems to me to introduce major issues of literary interpretation and critical theory. As for the larger question—that of Chaucer's likely attitude toward the phenomenon of ambiguous language itself, as artistic tool and as artistic technique—it will command my protracted attention in future chapters. Before I proceed with such investigation, however, it is only fair to state certain claims, or assumptions, about the *Troilus* that may help to explain what might at first appear to some as eccentric emphasis on Chaucer's continental and antique Latin models.

The extraordinary originality of the *Troilus,* viewed from the perspective of the anterior history of the English romance, encourages me in the following rash and heady generalization: there is not a line of Chaucer's poem that would be different if no other poet than Chaucer had ever written in English. The novelty of his pioneering work within his own vernacular was greater than that of Dante, considerably greater than that of Jean de Meun, and vastly greater than that of his principal textual source, Boccaccio. *Troilus* is an essentially classical poem accidentally English in its language; and if we seek to enroll it in an "English tradition," the only tradition we shall find is that of the Anglo-Norman *roman d'antiquité,* a group of pseudoarchaic poems written in a

French rapidly becoming genuinely archaic by Chaucer's day—the "romances" (meaning the "French books") of Aeneas, of Troy, and of Thebes.

Above all, Chaucer looks to the Latin epic tradition, and he looks to it not only in matters of mythic conception and of style but also in matters of poetic technique. One remarkable feature of Roman literature, and in particular of Roman poetry, is its comfortably derivative and traditional character. While it has required the penetrating expositions of such modern classicists as Georg Knauer, Andrée Thill, and Gordon Williams to characterize the nature of Latin poetic "imitation" in all its depth, subtlety, complexity, and paradoxical stimulation of originality, two central facts about Roman poetry are obvious to anyone who has read very much of it. The first is that as a body of literature it is radically dependent upon Greek poetry for its genres, subjects, themes, techniques, and dramatis personae.

The second is that the major Roman poets constantly imitate their Latin literary ancestors and contemporaries as well. The mere appreciation of the first point, incidentally, depends in no wise upon the reader's knowledge of the Greek language, since the fact itself is trumpeted in the actual Latin texts of Virgil, Horace, Ovid, and many others, and since it is enshrined in the "critical tradition"—that is, in the textbooks of primary education and in the most widely circulated poetic commentaries—from the time in classical antiquity when cultivated Latins read Greek literature to the time in the Renaissance when they once again did so. Hence the mere existence of "Greek originals" behind much Latin poetry was as much a certainty for Geoffrey Chaucer as for Georg Knauer.

In a very general sense the relationship between Greek and Roman literature is relevant to Chaucer's enterprise in the *Troilus*, since the Roman remaking of a classical tradition into what was for the Romans after all the vulgar tongue provided a precedent for Chaucer's remaking of the Roman tradition in English. The fact or fiction behind two of his explicitly cited sources, the *Ephemerides belli trojani* of Dictys the Cretan and the *De excidio Troiae* of "Dares the Phrygian," is that the Latin texts are translations of Greek originals, just as Chaucer's *Troilus*, a similar fiction, is an English translation of the Latin original of "Lollius." Because neither Chaucer nor his intended audience read Greek, however, the actual relationships between the two ancient literatures are irrelevant to this study.

Much more important for Chaucer were the literary postures that the Roman poets whom he knew took toward one another, from which he deduced that whatever else a successful pseudo-Latin poem might be, it would be one that imitated other Latin poems. Hence the "Lollius" whom he translates is a great imitator of Virgil, Horace, Ovid, Statius, and Lucan, not to mention Chaucer's own vernacular predecessors in the *roman d'antiquité,* the authors of the *Roman de la Rose,* and Dante Alighieri. We see the results of Chaucer's meditation upon the Latin poetic tradition in a wide variety of artistic techniques that are perhaps more easily observed than defined. Since it is the classicists who have best written on the subject, it is perhaps safest to use their vocabulary. We may perhaps speak of "allusive art." This was the term used by the Italian classicist Giorgio Pasquali, from whom it was borrowed by various influential *dantisti,* who in turn introduced it to medieval studies generally.[39] Another scholar has sought to explore the distinctive terms used by Roman authors themselves— *interpretatio, imitatio,* and *aemulatio.*[40]

D. A. Russell, in a wonderfully illuminating essay, has gone so far as to summarize the phenomenon of "creative" poetic imitation in terms of five rules: (1) "The object must be worth imitating." (2) "The spirit rather than the letter must be reproduced." (3) "The imitation must be tacitly acknowledged, on the understanding that the informed reader will recognize and approve the borrowing." (4) "The borrowing must be 'made one's own,' by individual treatment and assimilation to its new place and purpose." (5) "The imitator must think of himself as competing with his model, even if he knows he cannot win."[41] These "rules" are as fully serviceable for describing Chaucer's relationship with the classical poetic tradition as they are for describing the relationships within Latin poetry themselves. That is, Chaucer writes in the *Troilus* as an "allusive artist" whose attitude to anterior poetic tradition is in varying degrees that of interpreter, imitator, and emulator; and in his interpretation, imitation, and emulation he operates in general according to a pattern already clearly established in ancient poetry.

This means that we must take the anterior Latin tradition seriously, but I shall claim that we must be no less attentive to the crucial fact that separates

39. G. Pasquali, "Arte allusiva," in *Stravaganze quarte e supreme* (Venice: Pozza, 1951), 11–20.

40. A. Reiff, *Interpretatio, imitatio, aemulatio: Begriff und Vorstellung literarischer Abhängigkeit bei den Römern* (Würzburg: Triltsch, 1959).

41. D. A. Russell, "De imitatione," in *Creative Imitation and Latin Literature,* ed. David West and Tony Woodman (Cambridge: Cambridge University Press, 1979), 16.

Chaucer from that tradition. That fact is not that he is a "modern" writing in English—I believe that he accepted as valid the implicit claims of several vernacular writers, especially Dante but also Boccaccio, to have written classical poems—but the fact that he is a Christian. Chaucer, again following Dante but with his own increment of striking originality, makes the dialogue of the Christian classicist and the pagan poets part of the dialectic of his poem.

To return for the last time in this chapter to the by now tiresome word *queynt,* I find that among critics who have taken offense at the suggestion of the pun none has written more vehemently, or more righteously, than Derek Brewer. "Why should this peculiarly pointless crudity be attributed to Chaucer?" he asks. "What would the passage gain, compared with the vastness of the loss, if it were accepted?"[42] The terms in which the questions are posed reveal the peculiar difficulties of a text caught up in a conflict of critical sensibilities. Brewer apparently believes that to allow the reality of a pun on *queynt* would measurably diminish the moral stature of the man Geoffrey Chaucer. Disagreement with a view so sincerely held and so forcefully expressed might appear to be closer to moral turpitude or character assassination than to a difference of philological opinion.

Obviously, it would hardly seem a promising critical maneuver to impute a peculiarly pointless crudity to Chaucer, or to any other poet for that matter, but if we for a moment entertain the hypothetical possibility that the fact that an individual critic does not see a point is not identical with a demonstration that there is no point to be seen, we may perhaps appreciate one humble example of Chaucer's practical classicism at work. It would be neither crude nor pointless for Chaucer to point toward the theme of sexual idolatry through the intertextual invocation of Jean de Meun and Horace. What Chaucer might have lost by constructing such an ambiguity, the approbation of readers of Victorian sensibility, does not strike me as a vast loss. To be fair, his gain would not have been vast either, though it would have been measurable and advantageous. He would have gained ingress to the stylistic sophistication of the Latin love elegy, in which peculiarly pointed crudities repeatedly poke through a punning surface of elegance and exquisiteness.[43] He would also have gained a desirable element of surprise over his readers.

42. Derek S. Brewer, *Chaucer*, 3d ed. (London: Longmans, 1973), 203.
43. Ovid, for example, is a great punster with a well-developed subspeciality in puns concerning sexual organs. See J. M. Frecaut, *L'Esprit et l'humour chez Ovide* (Grenoble: Presses universitaires, 1972), 30–31 for texts and bibliography.

One of the "philological" objections lodged against the possibility of word-play on *queynt* in the passage is an alleged inelegance or syntactical inconsistency. In one reading *queynt* is an adjectival past participle modifying "light," in the other a noun. Yet if we look to classical literature we find that conscious ambiguation based in alternative syntactical possibility is a quite common artistic device and that it is evidently regarded as an elegance. Characteristically it defines the more complex and ambitious nature of the amphibolia as compared with the simple homonomia of the unitary pun. The scholars who have written about the nature of ambiguous language in Latin poetry have thus differentiated between "lexical" ambiguity on the one hand and "phrasal" or "syntactical" ambiguity on the other. To these categories D. N. Levin, in an excellent essay, has added a third, which he calls "psychological ambiguity," ambiguity that "depends for its effect on the reader's first making an understandable error of interpretation, then correcting it as his knowledge is increased through further perusal of the passage."[44]

In this instance the error from which the reader recovers with a certain psychological shock is not the belief that the word *queynt* means "extinguished" but that it means *only* that. We discover that the text suggests, in a highly allusive and indirect way, that Troilus has adored, with quasi-religious affection, "queynt." Such crudity as there may be in either the idea or its expression certainly finds a sanction in the precedent of approved Christian authors.

It is demonstrable that Chaucer's construction of these stanzas is implicated in his reading of the *Roman de la Rose*, far and away the best-known poem in the vernacular canon of Chaucer's literary education, and a poem in which the central character "worships" at the rosebud "shrine" of a woman's sexual organs. When around the year 1400 this grotesque poetic image was attacked as a pointless crudity, one of Chaucer's classically educated contemporaries, Pierre Col, wrote thus: "When Master Jean de Meun calls a woman's secret parts 'sanctuary' and 'relic,' he does so to demonstrate the great foolishness that there is in the Foolish Lover; for a foolish lover thinks of no other thing but this bud; and it is his god, and he worships it as his god."[45]

44. D. N. Levin, "Propertius, Catullus, and Three Kinds of Ambiguous Expression," *Proceedings of the American Philological Association* 100 (1969), 222.
45. "Et quant maistre Jehan de Meung appelle les secres membres de fame 'saintuaires' et 'reliques,' il le fist pour monstrer la grant folie qui est en Fol Amoureux: car ung fol amoureux ne pense a autre chose que a ce bouton; et est son dieu, e l'aoure come

I see here a probable echo of Phil. 3.19, and of Paul's memorable crudity concerning those "whose god is their belly." Certainly the poetic apotheosis of the vagina strikes me as neither more nor less remarkable than the metaphorical deification of the great bowel. That a special dimension of *poetic* language was involved was of course obvious to Pierre Col as well. That is why he appropriately cited the *Ars poetica* of Horace on the license accorded to poets and painters.[46] The citation may be even apter than he realized, for it is the interjection of Horace's startled pupil, shaken by the opening lines of the *Ars poetica*, in which Horace suggests the risible impropriety of a human head on a plumed horse. Surely, he counters, *anything* is allowed to the poet. The answer of the *Ars poetica* is that not quite *anything* is allowed; what is allowed is the imaginative imitation of universally accepted authors. And that is what Geoffrey Chaucer, with the manipulated collusion of his creature Lollius, pursues.

His readers must also pursue that object, after a fashion. The preparatory enterprise of this chapter has been to explore in some depth a single possible instance of artistically ambiguous language in Chaucer's poem. My intention has been less to make a positive demonstration of a specific lexical ambiguity than to suggest—so far as I know for the first time in the history of discussion of the *Troilus*—that the phenomenon of ambiguous language within the poem has important connections with the techniques of "creative imitation" in the classical manner, techniques that Geoffrey Chaucer, following in the footsteps of Jean de Meun and a few other medieval vernacular classicists, recognized and appropriated. In this regard, poetic ambiguity was for Chaucer a feature of classicizing poetic style. At the same time it was more, much more. In a sense, indeed, it was Chaucer's theme. The two strange words that I invoked at the beginning of this chapter—*amphibologies* and *ambages*—are technical terms from the vocabulary of ancient divination, the cursed rites of old pagans. Chaucer chose to write a special kind of historical epic, a poem in which the world of the past was not merely "setting" but argument, a backdrop against which he could explore, in their bold philosophical relief, contrasting modes

---

son dieu," in *Le Débat sur le Roman de la Rose*, ed. Eric Hicks (Paris: Champion, 1977), 93.

46. "Aux poetes et paintres a tousjours este licence pareille de toute feindre, comme dit Orace." Ibid., 93. The Latin is "Pictoribus atque poetis / quidlibet audendi semper fuit aequa potestas" (Poets and painters have always had an equal license in daring invention; *Ars poetica* 9–10).

of signifying, of interpreting, and of loving. In the pursuit of these themes, as in other aspects of his poetic vocation, Chaucer was a "creative imitator." We shall be better readers of Chaucer, better able to evaluate and affirm his creating art, if we follow him first along some of the meandering paths of poetic imitation.

TWO | AMBAGES; OR, THE GENEALOGY OF AMBIGUITY

How does Chaucer make of ambiguity a philosophical and religious theme? What is the relationship of that theme to concrete instances of ambiguous language? How is his interest in ambiguity served by the "creative imitation" of classical poets? Finally, how might the poet's thematic interests in truth and ambiguation overlap with the anxieties of the artist? We might begin to address these questions by noting that there is another context within the *Troilus* that could have provided an alternative path to appreciating the ambiguity of the line "O thow lanterne of which queynt is the light" and, indeed, to understanding the poetic nature of Chaucerian *ambages* generally. Early in the fourth book, in his first outburst of anguish at the prospect of losing Criseyde to the Greek camp, Troilus, in addressing his two eyes as worthless objects if they have no Criseyde to look upon, asks whether they might not weep themselves into blindness—

> wepen out youre sighte?
> Syn she is queynt, that wont was yow to lighte.
>
> (4.312–13)

It is this last line, obviously enough, that is the object of a conscious reprise in the first paragraph of the address to Criseyde's vacant house in the fifth book:

> O thow lanterne of which queynt is the light . . .
> Wel oughtestow to falle, and I to dye,
> Syn she is went that wont was us to gye!
>
> (5.543–45)

The passage in the fourth book is part of Troilus' elaborate comparison of his own situation with that of Oedipus:

45

"What shal I don? I shal, while I may dure,
On lyve in torment and in cruel peyne,
This infortune or this disaventure,
Allone as I was born, iwys, compleyne;
Ne nevere wol I seen it shyne or reyne;
But ende I wol, as Edippe, in derknesse
My sorwful lif, and dyen in distresse."
                    (4.295–301)

The reference to Oedipus presented certain scribes with difficulty and therefore with an invitation to simplism to which they responded, as Windeatt's
helpful notes make clear, by eliminating the difficult "classical allusion" altogether and supplying in its place various simple contrasts of lightness and
darkness in the manner of "shyne or reyne" in line 299. The parallel with the
treatment of *queynt* (5.543), which according to Windeatt's collations has on
occasion been replaced by *quenched,* is obvious: in both cases scribal initiative
secures a simple metaphoric pattern and disallows complicated and complicating literary context. After all it does no more damage to Chaucer's *story*
to replace line 4.300 with "Ne hevenes light and thus I in derknesse" than it
does to replace "queynt" with "quenched"; it merely excises of field of possible
poetic signification from critical scrutiny.

    No critic to my knowledge has actually followed the scribal lead in ban-
ishing Chaucer's "classical allusion" to Oedipus, though most have ignored it
until quite recently, when it has become the subject of diverse but illuminating
comment. Windeatt says that "there may be some comparison of the blinding
of Oedipus and the blindness of love." In fact Julia Ebel's brief but convincing essay shows precisely the poetic and iconographic associations exploited
by Chaucer to make that connection as powerful as it is obvious.[1] Whether
or not we agree with her that the blind Oedipus is "the poem's most significant image," we are unlikely to deny its considerable significance or to find
in it with Chauncey Wood the culmination of a persistent imagery pattern of
blindness that speaks most clearly to Troilus' spiritual state. Another critic is
struck as much by the distance between Oedipus and Troilus as by the parallels between them. Thus Wetherbee writes that Troilus' invocation of the
ancient royal victim is in context melodramatic, "startling and surprising . . .

---

1. Julia Ebel, "Troilus and Oedipus: The Genealogy of an Image," *ES* 55 (1974): 14–21.

Oedipus' darkness is the result of far more than a young man's first setback in love."[2] Though from a certain point of view "a young man's first setback in love" is as good a plot summary of Seneca's *Oedipus* as of Chaucer's *Troilus*, I share Wetherbee's disquiet and, with him, seek the illumination of broader patterns of contextual suggestion.

To follow the blind Oedipus more deeply into Chaucer's poem is, admittedly, a risky business despite Pandarus' assurance that he has "seyn a blynd man go, / Ther as he fel that koude loken wide" (1.628–29). Oedipus leads us immediately to dense literary complexity—that is, into a highly complicated and intentionally directed literary context. Chaucer's relationship with great literary works in the classical tradition, Latin and vernacular alike, is still taken by many and perhaps by most Chaucerians to be rather primitive, casual or shallow in character. That Chaucer "uses" Virgil or Dante is readily granted by all. That he had a keen reader's sophisticated and coherent understanding of their poems, that he meditated upon their intertextual relationships, and that he must have regularly consulted their works during his own process of composition is implicitly denied by many. Unless the reader has already been convinced by independent study of the extraordinary allusiveness of Chaucer's *Troilus*, my necessarily brusque and breathless introduction of a number of anterior texts may seem initially startling; yet I am convinced that it will no more do to limit Oedipus by interpretive underreading than to banish him by scribal emendation. Chaucer's subject is the "double sorwe of Troilus," a man whose very name reminds us that he is the microcosmic analogue of Great Troy. Yet Troy, too, mirrors another world—that of ancient Thebes, of which it is at once the echo and the supererogator. Donald Howard has written eloquently of the poetic function of the Theban world within the fictive Trojan world, a world "as old again as Troy is to us."[3] The temporal relationships between Thebes and Troy enjoy the licit inconsistency of myth. In Chaucer's poem Thebes is as remote as the ancient curse on Oedipus; it is as near as the threat of Diomedes, "son of Tideus."

Two Latin texts taught the clerks of the Middle Ages most of what they knew of ancient Thebes: the *Oedipus* of Seneca and the *Thebaid* of Statius. Both are highly relevant to the *Troilus*, though it is only the latter, because of its explicit,

---

2. Wetherbee, *Chaucer and the Poets*, 209–10.
3. Donald Howard, *The Three Temptations* (Princeton: Princeton University Press, 1966), 113.

clever, and repeated appearance at the surface of Chaucer's text, that has thus far received much attention from critics. By the time that Troilus comes to despair of his eyes in the fifth book, old Oedipus has already entered Chaucer's text twice, once explicitly and once implicitly, and both times through the mediation of Statius. Criseyde's summary of the plot of the *Thebaid* (2.101–5) is "how that Kyng Layus deyde, / Thorugh Edippus his sone, and al that dede." An earlier, implicit reference, is more pointedly relevant still, as Wetherbee has shown us.[4] The opening stanza of Chaucer's poem includes an arresting invocation of the Fury Tesiphone.

> To the clepe I, thow goddesse of torment,
> Thow cruel furie sorwynge evere yn peyne
>
> (1.8–9)

Three of the cardinal words in this passage—*torment, cruel,* and *pain*—are repeated in precisely that order in Troilus' comparison of himself with Oedipus at 4.295–301; Chaucer echoes his first invocaton. But as is well known that invocation itself is an echo, for it recaptures a unique moment in classical literature; namely, Oedipus' similar invocation of Tesiphone in the opening lines of the *Thebaid*.

This prominent connection between the *Thebaid* and *Troilus* was recognized already by Chaucerians in the nineteenth century, but numerous textual relationships require further exploration and, in their totality, suggest that Chaucer's interest in Statius defined an important part of his poetic agenda. One fact that has not been commented upon, probably because it bore no obvious relevance to the *Troilus*, is that Oedipus' invocation of Tesiphone is related to the theme of divine ambiguity through the word *ambages;* for Oedipus thus recalls the ironic exploit of his youth—when he saved Thebes from the ravages of the Sphinx by solving her riddle: "Sphingos iniquae / . . . ambages . . . resolvi" (I solved the riddles of the evil Sphinx; *Thebaid* 1.66–67). Statius' language in this passage is heavy with the reverberations of Seneca's *Oedipus*, a text in which the old king's claim to have the gift of solving *ambigua* is almost terrifyingly ironic. I think that this perception brings us to the threshhold of one of Chaucer's greatest and least-appreciated philosophical themes; but first it may be useful to note how Statius' presence clarifies other aspects of Chaucer's proemium.

4. Wetherbee, *Chaucer and the Poets*, 31–34.

His radical investment in Statius is, I believe, signaled by his very incipit itself: "The double sorwe of Troilus."[5] The curious phrase "double sorwe" has a parallel in Boccaccio (*doppia doglia,* 4.118.2) but context demands that we recognize that its *source* is Dante's *doppia trestizia di Giocasta* (*Purgatorio* 22.56), a phrase used by Virgil as a summary statement of the contents of the *Thebaid* and, as it were, that poem's subtitle. The double sorrow of Jocasta is usually taken, and probably correctly so, to be her two sons Polinices and Eteocles, whose strife is the principal subject of the *Thebaid* and who in the end kill each other in single combat. In passing I suggest as a possible cognate alternative that the "double sorwe" may refer specifically to the two phrases *fraternas acies* (wars between brothers) and *alterna regna* (alternating regnancies) that Statius proposes, in the first line of his poem, as his own subject: "Fraternas acies alternaque regna . . . incidit." In this case it becomes even clearer that the beginning of Chaucer's poem makes sharp and definite allusion to the beginning of the *Thebaid* even as its ending (5.1786–87) makes sharp allusion to Statius' ending (12.810–19). I am further convinced by the brilliant argument of Winthrop Wetherbee that, for Chaucer, Statius had been "baptized" by full immersion in the text of Dante's *Commedia.* To the very considerable extent that Chaucer is concerned with the continuites and discontinuities of pagan and Christian truth, Dante's intervention probably had a decisive impact on him in this as in so many subjects related to modes of meaning in the *Troilus.* To explore it in depth would be the worthy task of a book, though not one I am competent to attempt.

In returning to my more specific and more limited purpose of examining certain acts of creative imitation in his poem, I note that the phrases *doppia trestizia* and *double sorwe* may well derive from a specific passage in Statius' text. As one who met his death by violence, King Laius, father of Oedipus, is forbidden the passage of Lethe (1.295–97); and it is on the "horrid shore of Cocytus" that the *vates* Amphiaraus addresses to him dark enigmas concerning the future of Thebes:

"Certa est victoria Thebis,
ne trepida, nec regna ferox germanus habebit,
sed Furiae geminumque nefas, miserosque per ensis,

---

5. Again here is an ideographic parallel with the "Knight's Tale," for which the *incipit* of the *Thebaid* is used as an epigraph.

ei mihi! crudelis vincit pater." Haec ubi fatus,
labitur et flexa dubios ambage relinquit. (4.641–45)

("Victory is certain for Thebes, fear not; the fierce brother will not have the
kingdom, but the Furies and a double evil and through cursed swords—
ah me!—the cruel father triumphs." This spoken, he leaves him wavering
in uncertainty at his doubtful ambiguities.)

As critics have observed, this passage is in context a reprise of Statius' opening
scene in which Oedipus invokes Tesiphone.[6] It thus has a prima facie relevance to the intertextual concerns of Chaucer's proemium. What is from the
domestic or sentimental point of view of the maternal Jocasta a double "sorrow" is from the political and dynastic point of view of the paternal Laius a
double "evil" of Polinices and Eteocles. Likewise, Troilus' tragedy will be at
once private and universal. But it is perhaps the word *ambage* that should most
immediately capture our attention in this passage, for it directs us both to
Chaucer's fascination with pagan ambiguity and to the figure of Oedipus who
appears in faint palimpsest outline in the opening stanza of the *Troilus*. In the
theme of ambages Statius, Dante, and Chaucer for a moment merge in a single,
implicit "macrotext." I have alluded to the intense irony of Oedipus' supposed
gift of interpreting verbal ambiguities. It is this: the prize won by Oedipus for
his riddle solving was Jocasta, whom he took as wife without realizing that
she was also his mother, thus initiating the tragic course of events that is the
poetic history of Thebes and Troy.

Although they are synonyms, Chaucer's two English neologisms for the
tricky ambiguities of oracles, *amphibologies* and *ambages,* have markedly differing philological histories. The first one is a common technical term of rhetorical
analysis, the second an ornament of a highly specialized poetic diction. Each
is sufficiently rare in their vernacular appearances to allow us to construct a
quite precise philological genealogy for their Chaucerian issue. It seems quite
clear to me that in this instance to recover the history of Chaucer's words is to
recover the history of his reading and his thought.

As we shall see, Chaucer would have had excellent literary precedent in
using the word *amphibology,* or at least something like that word, to denote the

6. Statius, *Opere di Publio Papinio Stazio,* ed. Antonio Traglia and Giuseppe Arciò (Turin:
UTET, 1980), 297n.

ambiguous utterance of an oracle; but that usage is, in fact, merely one specific application of the word's more general meaning of "ambiguity." Latin *amphibolia* is, as its appearance suggests, a direct transliteration of a Greek word. It exists alongside the more recognizably Latin term *ambiguitas,* with which it is synonymous. The *amphibolia,* however, is the more distinctly literary term. Its appearance as a technical term in Latin grammatical and rhetorical texts is commonplace, and it became part of the stable critical vocabulary of medieval rhetoricians.[7]

A few general points about *amphibolia* and *ambigua* are useful to bear in mind. The first is that ambiguity is in antique and medieval literary theory considered a vice or an obstacle to be overcome, as we have already seen in a passage of Augustine's *De dialectica.* Antique "criticism" will in this regard seem very foreign indeed to readers nourished by Wellek and Warren.

According to ancient theoreticians, verbal ambiguity is a shortcoming that serious writers should avoid in so far as is possible.[8] In general the suggestion is that ambiguity is a mistake, that is, something the writer would avoid were he aware of it—but of course the rhetoricians were alert to the distinction between accidental and willed ambiguity.[9] Unintended ambiguity is spoken of as a vice to be extirpated from writing through vigilant revision. Willed ambiguity, on the other hand, always has an oblique purpose. A legitimate purpose of willed ambiguity is facetiousness.[10] More commonly, but also more culpably, the motive is deception or evasion. It is in this context that the

7. See H. Lausberg, *Handbuch der literarischen Rhetorik,* 2d ed. (Munich: Heuber, 1960), 1:122.

8. The potential offensiveness of this mode of thinking to the modern critical sensibility may be suggested by R. G. Austin's reaction, in his commentary on Virgil's first book, to Quintillian's discovery of an amphibolia in Virgil's description of the death of Troilus (*Aeneid* 1.477): "an interesting glimpse of arid school-pedantry." Quintillian suggests that orators should not use ambiguous language: *Institutionis oratoriae libri duodecim,* ed. M. Winterbottom (Oxford: Clarendon, 1970), 6.3.46–48.

9. E.g., Julius Victor: "Ambiguitas est, quotiens varia pronunciatione vel varia significatione quaestio nascitur. Fit autem vel in scripto vel in voluntate scripti." *Rhetores latini minores,* ed. C. Halm (Leipzig: Teubner, 1863), 383.

10. Cicero (*De oratore* 2.253, ed. A. S. Wilkins [Oxford: Clarendon, 1881], p. 323) reports a brilliant witticism of Vespa Terentius concerning the statue-basher Titus, whose absence from a certain gathering was noticed: ". . . cum in campam non venisset, requirerunt, excusavit Vespa Terentius, quod eum brachium fregisse diceret."

vocabulary of ambiguity came to be used of oracular utterances. The notorious reputation of oracles for ambigutiy, certainly based in actual religious practice, was considerably augmented by a poetic tradition that repeatedly turned to oracular materials in its delineation of the bizarre, the baroque, and the morally dubious. It is clear from the testimony of several ancient witnesses that even many people who sincerely believed in divination were aware that many diviners were fakers, and some principal classical authorities rejected the truth of divination altogether. In the Latin tradition the most notable of these by far was the augur Cicero, whose *De divinatione* must have seemed to many medieval Christians to have been written expressly to further their own radical assault on pagan religion. One famous passage in the *De divinatione* in particular forever linked the quack oracle and the *amphibolia* and made even more renowned than it already was the most notorious tricky oracle in Latin literature.

In this passage (*De divinatione* 2.56.116) Cicero quotes the Stoic Chrysippus as saying directly to Apollo that his oracles are in part true and in part false, but accidentally so, as with any blind guess. They are also in part intentionally ambiguous (*partim flexiloquis et obscuris*), so that "the interpreter requires another interpreter." He cites by way of example the most celebrated amphibology in the Latin literary tradition, the Delphic oracle given to Pyrrhus when he sought to know whether he could defeat the Romans in battle: "Aio, te Aeachida, Romanos vincere posse" (I say that you, offspring of Aechus, the Romans can defeat). The point here, as Cicero notes, is the syntactic ambiguity present in the double accusative structure. The sentence can mean either that Pyrrhus can defeat the Romans or that the Romans can defeat Pyrrhus. Pyrrhus rashly believed and acted upon the former grammatical possibility, but it was the second that was ratified by the historical event. In this passage of the *De divinatione*, and repeatedly throughout that work, Cicero hints at a moral truth that would be made much of in Christian apologetic: the fraud of the diviners requires the gullibility of the self-seeking, the ambitious, the avaricious, those greedy for empire. In this analysis, oracular ambiguity was a technique for telling people what they wanted to hear. It is a willed deception requiring the active collusion of the hearer. Of all such oracles the "victory oracle" is perhaps the cruelest in the clarity of this sad symbiosis. It exposes both the falseness of the gods and the philosophical blindness of men. Both of those themes are prominent in the text in which Chaucer explicitly uses the "victory oracle," the "Knight's Tale." The oracle transmitted through the idol of

Mars to Arcite is the single word "Victory," a promise that turns out to be, as
Alastair Minnis says, both "mean and misleading."[11]

That Chaucer knew and used the *De divinatione* I take to be certain. His
explicit citation of it in his Boethius translation may reflect an intermediate
Latin commentary; but Cicero was the natural, nearly inevitable authority to
which Christian writers with a serious interest in pagan divination naturally
turned, as may be suggested by Augustine's own prominent use of it (along
with the *De natura deorum*) in the *City of God*, a book that remained a primary
text for "classicists" of all stripes during the long centuries of the Middle Ages.
Cicero's book is also cited by Nicole Oresme, the contemporary of Chaucer's
from whom (I suggest by way of a working hypothesis) the English poet took
his definition of ambages put into the mouth of Diomede at *TC* 5.897–98.
There can be no doubt that Chaucer's *hapax amphibologies* at 4.1406 corresponds to the *amphiboliae* of the classical and medieval rhetorical vocabulary.
At the same time the form in *-ogie* may suggest an intermediate French form,
amphibologie, actual or implied, in Chaucer's mind. Chaucer would have found
exactly this in Oresme's *De divinacions*. In a passage that brings together several of the themes that concern me in this chapter, Oresme has thus cataloged
a number of the traditional frauds of the pagan oracles:

> Item, autres dient ou escripsent les choses apres le fait, et faignent que
> ainsi avoit il este prenostique devant, et en telle maniere. Ce dit Saint
> Augustin; (et) descript Virgille l'estat et les proesces du Rommain du
> temps passe, et imposoit a une sibille que ainsi l'avoit elle divine devant.
> Item, leurs paroles sont aucunefois doubles, amphiboliques, a deux vis-
> ages, comme on trouve en plusieurs hystoires, et aucunefois son obscures
> et peuent este appliquees a plusieurs effects ou personnes, come sont
> aucunes prophecies des papes et plusieurs autres. . . . Item, se leurs pro-
> nosticacions sont cleres, lors sont elles aucunefois vrais a l'avanture, et
> aucunefois fausses. Et ceste sentence n'est pas inoye ou nouvelle mais
> est chose anciennement examinee et determinee par les sages philoso-
> phes. De quoy dit Tulles, ou *Livres de Divinacions*, "O Appollo," dit il,
> "tes responses sont en partie fausses et en partie vrayes a l'aventure, en

---

11. See the excellent remarks in A. Minnis, *Chaucer and Pagan Antiquity* (Cambridge:
Boydell and Brewer, 1982), 136. At pp. 34–35 Minnis discusses the Phyrric oracle as
cited in Isidore of Seville. This oracle is so widely reported in medieval texts as to be a
genuine commonplace.

partie doubteuses et obscures, en tant que l'expositeur a mestier d'autre expositeur." [12]

Oresme's sentence "leurs paroles sont aucunefois doubles, amphiboliques, a deux visages" seems to be reflected in Chaucer's definition of ambages: "double wordes slye . . . a word with two visages." In any event, Oresme provides the first definite parallel that has ever been adduced for this difficult Chaucerian passage. It further appears that Oresme himself has anticipated his readers' possible difficulty with the adjective *amphiboliques* by glossing it with the synonyms that surround it. This suggests that he took the word to be a difficult one and perhaps (as with Chaucer) a neologism that he himself self-consciously introduced into his own vernacular. Thus the philological evidence, while by no means absolutely conclusive, suggests to me that Chaucer has Oresme's book in mind if not in view when he wrote the passage. The philological evidence, furthermore, is entirely consistent with the inferences to be drawn from the character and intellectual context of Oresme's book.

Oresme was one of the leading French intellectuals of the fourteenth century. His competence as a classicist is attested to by his well-known translations of Aristotle, but he was something of a polymath, with wide-ranging intellectual interests. In the 1360s he wrote two works on divination—the work in French from which I have quoted, called the *Livre de Divinacions* in imitation of Cicero, and a Latin *Tractatus contra judicarios astronomos*. These works were by no means merely antiquarian in character. Certain widespread aristocratic superstitions, particularly those relating to judicial astrology, gave his schol-

---

12. Oresme's *Livre*, in G. W. Coopland, *Nicole Oresme and the Astrologers: A Study of His Livre de Divinacions* (Liverpool: Liverpool University Press, 1952), 94. "Again, some diviners say or write things after they have happened and pretend they had prophesied them beforehand. We read in St. Augustine that Virgil put into the mouth of a sibyl a description of the estate and prowess of the Romans of past time, as if she had divined it beforehand. And, again, the words of the diviners are sometimes of double meaning, amphibolic, two-faced, as we see in many histories; and they can be applied to more than one event or person, as in the case of some of the prophecies about the Popes and others. . . . And if their prognostications are unambiguous, then they are sometimes right and sometimes wrong, according to chance. And this opinion is not a new one, but was anciently examined and decided by the wise philosophers. On this matter Tully in the *De Divinatione*, says, 'Apollo, thy responses are sometimes true, sometimes false, according to chance, in part doubtful and obscure, so much so that the expositor has need of another expositor'" (trans. Coopland, p. 95).

arly researches a contemporary relevance, as he himself demonstrates. His enterprise was shared by the younger generation of scholars in his immediate intellectual milieu, notably Jean Gerson and Pierre d'Ailly, and substantial evidence testifies to the extensive circulation of his books. It is thus no exaggeration to say that in Chaucer's day, at least in France, there was a lively polemical interest in the old and cursed rites of pagans. No one who reads the *Livre de Divinacions* can fail to see that far from being the neutral historian of divination Oresme is a scholarly controversialist. It is of considerable interest that, in Coopland's words, "there is no important difference of kind" between Oresme's French and Latin works on the subject. I draw attention to this fact because of the common and commonly unstated assumption that there is a necessarily major difference between Latin and vernacular erudition in the fourteenth century. The *Livre de Divinacions* is one of many French books of the period that is deeply learned, making no condescensions to its intended vernacular audience. Oresme's learned sources are precisely the ones we would expect: Cicero, Augustine, the early Christian polemicists, the epic poets, and all important earlier medieval writers on the subject.

Rich investigations since the 1950s make it increasingly obvious that Chaucer had undertaken significant researches into the matter of antiquity. Was Oresme's book among the sources he consulted? So far as the nature and error of pagan divination was concerned, he could have found no book more helpful than the *Livre de Divinacions*. It was not a book unknown to Chaucer's poetic circle. It is conceivable that it was drawn to his attention by his colleague and admirer Eustache Deschamps, who had plundered it in writing his own little "Demoustraciouns contre sortilèges."[13] In the absence of other evidence, I suggest that Oresme's positive influence on Chaucer is reflected in two lines of the fourth book of *Troilus and Criseyde;* we may perhaps add another volume to the "Chaucer Library." But whether this hypothesis be confirmed or disproved, Oresme's book remains valuable testimony to the ways in which a learned authority of the fourteenth century, a man of catholic poetic tastes and of urgently engaged secular sensibilities, anticipated in discursive argument Chaucer's own imaginative response to the religious rites of ancient pagans.

13. Deschamps, *Oeuvres complètes*, ed. Q. de Sainte-Hilaire and Gaston Raynaud (Paris: SATF, 1878–1903), 7:192–99; see further G. W. Coopland, "Eustache Deschamps and Nicolas Oresme: A Note on the Demoustraciouns contre sortilèges," *Romania* 52 (1926): 355–61.

That is, there is a contemporary social context to the fourteenth-century discussion of ancient religion which can illuminate the religious archaeology in Chaucer's poem.

Whether or not Chaucer took his own internal gloss to his neologism *ambages* from Oresme's similar gloss to his inkhorn term *amphiboliques,* it is plain enough that in his mind the two words were essentially identical in meaning. Yet why should he "explain" the one but not the other? One possibility, not absolutely farfetched, relates to the intended audience. Diomede uses the word *ambages* in a speech designed to seduce Criseyde, a woman whom he appears to pursue for sexual as opposed to intellectual companionship, and his gloss may be a condescension to her assumed female limitations. If the suggestion is not a particularly nice one, we may remember that Diomede is not a particularly nice man; and he has not yet gotten to know Criseyde well enough to hear that she uses words like "amphibologies" herself, no doubt a household word in the household of a diviner. On the other hand he does know his Latin, "more than the Crede" as the poet says of him in a different but highly relevant context.

What Chaucer saw in the text of the *Filostrato* was "se Calcas per ambage e per errori / qui non ci mena"; but I suggest that he himself would have known what the unglossed Italian word *ambage* meant only because he knew the Latin texts from which it was derived. It is accordingly in the Latin poets that we must conduct a preliminary search. The five poets to whom Chaucer implicitly stands sixth at the end of his own works are Virgil, Ovid, Homer, Lucan, and Statius.[14] Homer's presence is demanded by a kind of literary piety alone, for Chaucer knew little more of him than the name. The Latin poets on the other hand, here named in their proper chronological order and possibly also in their order of merit as Chaucer saw things, are the "olde clerkes" in whom we may read of "olde payens corsed rites." It is from them, certainly, that we shall learn of poetic ambages; and we must begin with the first and greatest of them, Virgil.

The Latin word *ambages* has three principal meanings: (1) the pathways of a

14. Chaucer is here matriculating in the academy of great modern classical poets including Jean de Meun, Dante, and Boccaccio; see David Wallace, "Chaucer and Boccaccio's Early Writings," in *Chaucer and the Italian Trecento,* ed. Piero Boitani (Cambridge: Cambridge University Press, 1983), 150–51.

labyrinth; (2) the meanderings of literary digression; and (3) dark ambiguities, especially those of oracles. Virgil uses the word six times in his poetry, and he invokes all three of these meanings; but the passage that clearly established the poetic context of the word as it relates to the world of *Troilus and Criseyde* is the account of Aeneas' seance with the Cumaean Sibyl in the sixth book of the *Aeneid*. This scene was probably the single best-known episode of baroque paganism known to the Christian Middle Ages. As Apollo takes possession of her frenzied body, the Sibyl shrieks from her cave awful and riddling glimpses of the future:

Talibus ex adyto dictis Cumaea Sibylla
horrendas canit ambages antroque remugit,
obscuris vera involvens. (6.98–100)

(Such were the words of mystery and dread which the Cumaean Sibyl spoke from her shrine; the cavern made her voice a roar as she uttered truth wrapped in obscurity.)

My investigations into the philological history of this strange word convince me that the concept of ambages in Chaucer's literary tradition are quite certainly Virgilian, and that in tracing out the genealogy of ambiguity we are tracing out what is for the English poet a carefully defined philosophical theme. The philological self-consciousness with which he introduces the word to English readers signals both its importance for his thematic purposes and his awareness of its traditional philosophical and moral contexts. His use of the word provides another small ratification of Wetherbee's thesis concerning Chaucer's ambition to enroll his poem in the classical poetic tradition. At the same time, I conclude, Chaucer was aware that the Latin poets themselves revealed differing attitudes toward the rites of divination, and that what might be taken as the reverence of Virgil had been complicated by his Silver Age followers, Lucan and Statius. Both writers followed Virgil's practice in exploiting the poetic potentialities of religious archaeology, but there is more to the matter than that. It is quite true that the ancient protocols of soothsaying provided them with excellent "topics"; but in both the *Pharsalia* and the *Thebaid* divination moves beyond historical local color to become an articulated philosophical theme.

Lucan's attitude toward Virgil is in many respects wonderfully "medieval" by anticipation, the attitude that finds its artistically richest expression in Dante's *Inferno*. On the one hand it is clear that, for Lucan, Virgil is the very model of the poet, the standard he holds before himself for emulation and for competition; and there are in the *Pharsalia* many hundreds of Virgilian quotations, echoes, and imitations. On the other hand there is also clear evidence of Lucan's confident and principled dissent from his poetic master on important philosophical matters. In Lucan we shall find a Stoic Virgilianism.

The word *ambages* does not appear in Lucan's description of the consultation at Delphi. Indeed it is nearly conspicuous by its absence, so throughly has Lucan plundered Virgil's technical vocabulary in his remaking of the mantic interview. But the oracular ambiguity itself—and here in marked distinction to the Virgilian passage—is conspicuously present. One peculiar feature of the speech of the Cumaean Sibyl is its eventually unambiguous and benign nature. Her opening words (*Aeneid* 6.83–97), characterized as *horrendae ambages,* are to be sure elliptical and perhaps overcharged; but she soon moves on to giving directions of a markedly unambiguous and controlled nature (125–55). She tells Aeneas in clear and unemotive terms the difficulty he faces in the task he must undertake, and the specific means by which he must prepare.[15] The idea that a philosophically serious hero would piously and effectively turn to divination was one that was destined eventually to cause offense to Christian readers of Virgil, but it seems first to have caused offense to some of his pagan admirers, among them Lucan, the nephew of a great Roman Stoic philosopher.

Lucan's *refacimento* of Aeneas' consultation of the Cumaean Sibyl is not merely oblique; it is pointedly subversive.[16] In the first place he transfers the Cumaean manticism briefly described by Virgil to Delphi, the site of by far the greatest and most prestigious of the ancient oracles, then expands it in a baroque prolusion of well over a hundred lines. His vision of the pythoness as a rabid, hysterical, and sinister medium, though the product of polemical imagination rather than historical observation, did much to create the popular notion of Apollonian manticism that survives to the present time. It is but a short step from Lucan to Prudentius and other Christian poets who can

15. R. G. Austin (commentary to book 1, p. 78) writes thus: "The prophetess speaks solemnly and unambiguously: the *horrendae ambages* have gone, her part as inspired seer is over, and she begins to take on the character of a guide."

16. See Jean Bayet, "La Mort de la Pythie," *Mélanges dédiés à la mémoire de Félix Grat*, I (Paris: Pecqueur-Grat, 1946), 53–76; and Bernard F. Dick, "The Role of the Oracle in Lucan's de Bello Civili," *Hermes* 93 (1965), esp. pp. 464–65.

present the prophetic ecstasy as demon-possession.[17] Appius, whom Lucan casts in the role of Aeneas, is an unattractive trimmer who consults the oracle to learn which side he should back in the civil war. Within the moral framework so insistently established in the *Pharsalia*, merely to consult the oracle in these terms is a signal act of ethical pusillanimity, since the moral imperative is as clear as the military prognosis is doubtful. In this regard Appius is an artistically primed antithesis to the heroic Cato who pointedly refuses to hear the advice of the oracle of Jupiter under precisely similar circumstances. In the most famous line he ever wrote Lucan showed that if the paths of virtue and victory must diverge, the wise man's course was unequivocal and in no way dependent upon divination: *Victrix causa deis placuit sed victa Catoni* (The victor's cause was pleasing to the gods, but the cause of the vanquished to Cato; 1.128). Under these circumstances Appius gets from the Delphic priestess exactly what he deserves, classical ambages, a comfortable and profoundly deceptive prophecy, the truth of which lies hidden in the mocking relationship of spirit and letter:

> effugis ingentis tanti discriminis expers
> bellorum, o Romane, minas: solusque quietem
> Euboci uasta lateris conualle tenebis.
>
> (5.194–96)

> (Roman, thou shalt have no part in the mighty ordeal and shalt escape the awful threats of war; and though alone shalt stay at peace in a broad hollow of the Euboean coast.)

This famous ambiguity, reported by Valerius Maximus among others, encouraged Appius to think that he could safely retire in neutrality to Euboea and wait things out. What it actually turned out to have meant was that he would die obscurely and ingloriously far from the fray.

Statius, the poet par excellence of divination, is perforce the poet par excellence of ambages.[18] Divination is much more central to his poem than it is to Lucan's, for the closest approximation Statius has for a hero is Amphia-

---

17. See Jacques Fontaine, "Demons et sibylles: La peinture des possédés dans la poésie de Prudence," *Hommages à Jean Bayet* (Brussels: Latomus, 1964), 196–213.

18. Boyd Ashby Wise, *The Influence of Statius upon Chaucer* (Baltimore: J. H. Furst, 1911), 24–25, was of the opinion that Chaucer took the word directly from the *Thebaid*, in which its most important uses are at 1.67, 1.495, 3.615, and 4.645.

raus, a professional diviner and priest of Apollo who is, at the very least, the best of a bad lot of the Seven against Thebes.[19] Chaucer has preserved in his own Calchas as much Amphiaraus as was decorous for his purposes. Though Statius lacks Lucan's committed Stoicism and with it, perhaps, Lucan's desire to subvert Virgil even as he apes him, his presentation of the mantic art is not free from philosophical disquiet. Vessey puts the matter thus: "Divination, Statius maintains, is an aspect of mankind's pitiable depravity, because it is put to evil uses. He does not question its efficacy or reality; he stresses only that it is undesirable, for it is a stimulus to crime."[20]

19. We may recall that Pandarus interrupts the reading at Criseyde's house precisely "at thise lettres rede, / How the bisshop, as the book kan telle, / Amphiorax, fil thorugh the ground to helle" (2.103–5). The theory of John Norton-Smith, *Geoffrey Chaucer* (London: Routledge, 1974), 90–91, seconded by Wetherbee, *Chaucer and the Poets*, 115, is that Chaucer is here invoking the "mid-point" of the *Thebaid*. This strikes me as unlikely given the fact that the episode appears at the *end* of the *seventh* book. My own suggestion is that Chaucer chooses this moment in the history of Amphiaraus because it allows him to invoke, simultaneously, the complementary moral contexts of Statius and Dante (*Inferno* 20.31–39). Dante rewrites Statius in a way that offers a clear Christian judgment on divination, the crime of Amphiaraus. Statius' text, on the other hand, focuses on the innocence of Amphiaraus and the guilt of Eriphyle his wife (8.120–22), who betrayed him for the brooch of Thebes. Hence unlike Wetherbee I find considerable merit in the suggestion of David Anderson, "Theban History in Chaucer's Troilus," *SAC* 4 (1982): 112–28, that Chaucer implies a comparison between Eriphyle and Criseyde, who will betray Troilus with a brooch. To my mind the question is not whether these are one and the same jewel but whether they are thematically linked. In the *Thebaid* (8.120–25) Amphiaraus anticipates with pleasure the day when Eriphyle the betrayer may, like him, sink into hell ("Si quando nefanda huc aderit coniunx"). Of Amphiaraus, Criseyde says that he "fil thorugh the ground to helle." Of herself she says, shortly before betraying Troilus, that the day she betrays Troilus will be the day that the River Simois runs backward, "And I with body and soule synke in helle" (*TC* 4.1554). I find the reprise of the Statian passage no less clear than that of the Ovidian passage in the same stanza. Chaucer may well have recognized, as many readers after him have done, the Senecan origins of Statius' principal description of the *monile Harmoniae* (*Thebaid* 2.265–68) which thematically links the jewel with the mad fury of Medea and with the treachery of Deinara to Hercules. Indeed there is textual evidence to suggest that in his poetic imagination Chaucer thought that, for Troilus, Criseyde was herself like the brooch of Thebes. Cf. Troilus' "double sorwe" in having and losing Criseyde with the "double wo" of possessing and losing the brooch ("Complaint of Mars," 255).
20. David Vessey, *Statius and the Thebaid* (Cambridge: Cambridge University Press, 1973), 156.

Thus it is that there is already in the Latin epic an implicit moral critique of the same cursed rites that Chaucer has drawn into his poem as "historical background." Indeed, the ancient poets educated their medieval followers in the means of thematizing the past. Medieval writers of course went much further. In the literary tradition most imaginatively exploited by Dante and, I assume, accepted by Chaucer, Amphiaraus became the very type of the pagan diviner as viewed from a censorious Christian point of view. Though he is not an actual religious reformer like Lucan, Statius displays a perceptible moral hesitation in his own most explicit imitation of Virgil's description of the Cumaean Sibyl. It comes in the third book in a scene in which Capaneus madly rails against Amphiaraus. What Chaucer might have taken to be Statius' philosophical agenda in this scene will demand our attention in the next chapter. What is of interest in the present context is its vocabulary:

> Quae tanta ignavia," clamat
> "Inachidae vosque o socio de sanguine Achivi?
> Unius—heu pudeat!—plebeia ad limina civis
> tot ferro accinctae gentes animisque paratae
> pendemus? Non si ipse cavo sub vertice Cirrhae,
> quisquis is est, timidis famaeque ita visus, Apollo
> mugiat insano penitus seclusus in antro,
> expectare queam, dum pallida virgo tremendas
> nuntiet ambages." (3.607–15)

(What baseness is this, you sons of Inacus and you of Achive race? Is it no disgrace that such a people, girded in steel and by disposition eager for battle stand waiting before the doorstep of an ordinary citizen? Even if Apollo himself—as rumor and the cowardly call him—were to sit in the cavern of Mount Cirrha, a madman enclosed within his cave, I could not dawdle to hear some pale maiden announce to me her frightful riddles.)

The fact that this is in its context rash impiety is not enough in itself to make the mantic consultation pious. Like Lucan, Statius "translated" Virgilian ambages from Cumae to Delphi and, again like Lucan, he associates divination with human depravity.

Thus it was that the theme of divination in the Latin epic poets was as potentially double-faced as the utterances of the oracles themselves. The Christian critique of the mantic practices of paganism, so prominent a topic in early

apologetic and polemic, had been prepared not merely by the pagan philosophers but also by their greatest poets.[21] Somewhat curiously, early Christian
writers could, without contradiction, treat the epic stories both as empty fables
and as true history. This attitude is pellucid in Augustine's *City of God*, for
example, the book that for the later Middle Ages would be the unchallenged
authority on the mores and religious customs of the ancient Romans, and to
which Nicole Oresme made explicit allusion in the passage from the *Livre de
Divinacions* cited earlier. In the sixth book of the *Aeneid* the Sibyl predicts
to Aeneas the future course of Roman empire. Augustine's response to this
scene is nearly embarrassing. He says that the Sibyl describes events that have
already transpired in the past as though they were to happen in the future: a
typical fraud of written oracles. Virgil gets no credit for an imaginative fiction,
merely the obloquy due to a lie. In other words the oracle is treated as a fiction,
but the fact of the fictive oracle as a truth.[22]

We see already in Augustine and other early Christian writers that blur-
ring of the historical facts of pagan religion with the baroque extravagances
of the poets, useful for the purposes of religious polemicism but dangerous
for the scientific study of comparative religions, that continues to complicate
the investigations of Greco-Roman cults even today. (For example, the alleged
"frenzy" of the Pythia at Delphi appears to be a poetic fiction rather than a historical reality.) Although I doubt that the great medieval poets were as naively
accepting of the historical truth of their ancient epic materials as is sometimes
maintained, they had every right to follow such writers as Augustine, and indeed the ancients themselves, in treating them as "history." And the "history"
of pagan religion as it thus came to them brought with it its own powerful
self-criticism.

It is central to the larger argument of this book that the strong element of

21. Considerable evidence is gathered by Dieter Harmening, *Superstitio: Uberlieferungs-
und theoriegeschichtliche Untersuchungen zur kirchlich-theologischen Aberglaubensliteratur
des Mittelalters* (Berlin: E. Schmidt, 1979).

22. Augustine, *De civitate Dei* 18.23. Augustine did, of course, credit the validity of
some sibylline pronouncements including, conspicuously, the famous prediction of
the birth of Christ in the fourth ecloque of Virgil. See Alfons Kurfess, "Die Sibylle in
Augustins Gottesstaat," *Theologische Quartalschrift* 107 (1936): 532–42. Hence medieval attacks on divination distinguish between the Cumaean Sibyls of the sixth *Aeneid*
and the fourth ecloque. See, e.g., Chaucer's contemporary Pierre d'Ailly, "De falsis
prophetis," in Jean Gerson, *Opera Omnia* (Paris, 1706), 1:578–79.

rigorous moral philosophy discernible in the *Troilus*, far from being an exotic importation from the world of clerical and ascetic Christianity or a historically false imposition, is consistent, indeed continuous with, the strong moral element of Latin epic. So far as the theme of pagan religion is concerned I have eschewed, except for purposes of incidental illustration, the rich body of Christian poetry from the early medieval centuries in which there is an explicit and polemical confrontation of Christian truth and pagan superstition; and I have done so because it was precisely this kind of poem that Chaucer chose *not* to write, although, even in his day, it was a possible option for him.

Jacques Fontaine, who has written most illuminatingly of the formation of a Christian Latin poetry in the early Middle Ages, had drawn attention to the taxing problems faced by writers who were by the burden of their education cultural Virgilians and by the commitment of their religion implacable anti-pagans. The cultural tensions so interestingly present in Augustine and Jerome were in fact never generally resolved in medieval Christendom and they reappear in endless variety in the "humanism" of the most narrowly ascetic and the cultural asceticism of the most enthusiastically humanistic. There is a marked difference between attempting to decapitate Goliath with his own sword—which I think roughly describes the enterprise of Prudentius—and sheltering the monuments of ancient thought and poetry in the intellectual museum of Christian humanism. Both enterprises required a certain kind of admiration of the past, but they depended upon radically differing attitudes toward the present. The attitudes of Christian humanism discernible in such major writers as Jean de Meun, Petrarch, and Chaucer, while sharing an unbroken intellectual continuity with certain currents of patristic thought, inevitably exercised themselves in radically altered historical circumstances. Putting the matter somewhat crudely, the actual cultural struggle against actual paganism had long since been won by the time Chaucer wrote *Troilus and Criseyde*. Lactantius appears to have thought of himself as a *Christian* Cicero, Petrarch of himself as a Christian *Cicero*. It is the latter attitude, actually, that shows the greater confidence in Christianity.

I cannot say when the attitude of Christian Latin poetry toward pagan myth moves decisively away from simple confrontation to the much more subtle and subdued polemic of historically sympathetic competition, though I have elsewhere used as my example of the process the influential Carolingian school-poem the *Ecloga Theoduli*. The process had of course long since happened in Chaucer's day, and long since appeared in the vernacular *romans d'antiquité*. The most brilliant practitioner of this kind of literary competition in the fourteenth century, and the man from whom Chaucer had most to learn concerning it, was undoubtedly Dante Alighieri. It is only to be expected that Dante was the Christian mediator between the ambages of Virgil and those of Boccaccio and Chaucer, so that the argument of this chapter must inevitably lead us to his poem.

In the seventeenth canto of *Paradiso* the pilgrim Dante, continuing his interview with Cacciaguida, asks for the favor of a glimpse into his own future. In this episode, as in so many in the *Commedia*, Dante manages to be at once both a committed Virgilian and a superior anti-Virgilian. The episode as a whole is clearly modeled upon Aeneas' interviews with the Cumaean Sibyl and with Anchises in the sixth book of the *Aeneid*. His ancestor Cacciaguida will play for him the role played for Aeneas by *his* ancestor Anchises. Cacciaguida responds with a matter-of-fact prediction that Dante is to be condemned and exiled from Florence:

> Né per ambage, in che la gente folle
> gia s'inviscava pria che fosse anciso
> l'Agnel di Dio che le peccata tolle,
>
>   ma per chiare parole e con preciso
> latin rispuose quello amor paterno,
> chiuso e parvente del suo proprio riso:
>
>   "La contingenza, che fuor del quaderno
> de la vostra matera non si stende,
> tutta e dipinta nel cospetto etterno . . ."
>   (*Paradiso* 17.31–39)

(In no dark sayings, such as those in which the foolish folk of old once ensnared themselves, before the Lamb of God who takes away sins was slain, but in clear words and with precise discourse that paternal love replied, hidden and revealed by his own smile. "Contingency, which does not extend beyond the volume of your material world, is all depicted in the Eternal Vision . . .")

That we have here a classical imitation is, I presume, obvious to all readers. The connections with Aeneas in the underworld, so manifest in the persistent verbal echoes of the sixth book of the *Aeneid*, have been made explicit by Dante's mention of the shade of Anchises at Cacciaguida's first appearance

(15.26). But even as Dante stresses the similarities he underscores also the differences. His request for prophetic guidance from Cacciaguida is somewhat curiously linked with a new and explicit reminiscence of Virgil and with the kind of prophetic knowledge he gained while under his guidance:

> mentre che io era a Virgilio congiunto
>   su per lo monte che l'anime cura
>   e discendendo nel mondo defunto,
> dette mi fuor di mia vita futura
>   parole gravi, avvegna ch'io mi senta
>   ben tetragono ai colpi di ventura.
>   (17.19–24)

(While I was in Virgil's company, up the mountain that heals the souls, and while descending through the dead world, heavy words were said to me about my future life, though I feel myself truly foursquare against the blows of chance.)

What he will get from Cacciaguida is, of course, the old trick of the Cumaean Sibyl: a "prediction" that is in fact past history. He is surely aware of the Augustinian objection, but he outflanks Augustine to the left, theologically speaking, by invoking an Augustinian concept, that of the obliteration of temporal contingencies in the mind of God. Cacciaguida, in *paradiso* and therefore in the presence of God, is at "that point in which all time is present time" (17.17–18). Grant to Dante his one big fiction, and his thousand subordinate fictions become facts. Cacciaguida can and does predict the future with a clarity and a plausibility that no augur or pythoness could ever command. The contrast toward which Dante moves is one between the kind of knowing he could have in Virgil's realm and the kind he can have in that realm which Virgil can never enter. It is the distinction between ambage and *preciso latin*.

The tragedy of Virgil is a tragedy of human time.[23] There is a precise moment in human history when the tyranny of ambiguity gave way to the possibility of pellucid truth: the moment of Christ's Incarnation, when the idols fell from their stone columns and the oracles of Egypt were silenced. Ambages characterize that time "in che la gente folle gia s'inviscava pria che fosse anciso l'Agnel

---

23. See Robert Hollander, *Il Virgilio dantesco: Tragedia nella "Commedia"* (Florence: Olschki, 1983), esp. 117–18.

di Dio che le peccata tolle," but even as Dante makes the historical point he disallows the plea of history as an exculpation for ancient religious error. The idolators were madmen (*gente folle*); in Paul's phrase they were "without excuse." As the pilgrim Dante grows in knowledge and spiritual confidence, he becomes more, not less strident, in his censorious judgments of pagan antiquity, conspicuously including the pagan antiquity of his master Virgil. There is another passage in the *Paradiso*, where Dante makes the connection between pagan religion and pagan love, which is usefully kept in mind as we read Chaucer:

> Solea creder lo mondo in suo periclo
>   che la bella Ciprigna il folle amore
>   raggiasse, volta nel terzo epiciclo;
> per che non pur a lei faceano onore
>   di sacrificio e di votivo grido
>   le genti antiche ne l'antico errore;
> ma Dione onoravano e Cupido
>   questa per madre sua, queto perfiglio;
>   e dicean ch'el sedette in grembo a Dido . . .
>
> (8.1-9)

(The world was wont to believe, to its peril, that the fair Cyprian, wheeling in the third epicycle, rayed down mad love; wherefore the ancient people in their ancient error not only to her did honor with sacrifice and votive cry, but they honored Dione and Cupid, the one as her mother, the other as her son, and they told that he had sat in Dido's lap . . .)

Dante takes as his example of "crazy love" that "crazy people" used to believe in nothing less than the greatest love story in the Latin poetic tradition, the love affair of Dido and Aeneas. The Virgilian moment invoked brings together the three pagan errors that Chaucer joins with Dante in placing at the center of their philosophical criticism of that antique world which in so many ways attracts and even awes them in its grandeur: namely, falseness in religion, falseness in love, and falseness in language. Against the backdrop of the *Aeneid* we can see in its philosophical finality the chasm forever fixed between the two worlds of the pagan poet and the Christian pilgrim, two ways of life, what Augustine, reading that same text, would call two cities. The one honors "false and lying gods," the other "that sooth-fast Crist." Love is for one a capricious and malign passion of invincible virulence, a poison, a cancer in the bone; for the other it is a new song, a motion of the soul that leads the mind to God. The language of the one is a labyrinth of dark and deceptive enigmas; that of the other, *preciso latin*.

For the moment recalled, of course, is what happens at the end of the first book of the *Aeneid*. Venus plots against Dido with a fantastic and cruel subterfuge that fully justifies both of the adjectives Augustine uses of the old gods, *falsus* and *fallax*. She kidnaps Aeneas' little boy Ascanius, and replaces him with her own son, Cupid, transformed by Venereal magic to the exact external appearance of the other. To the false Ascanius falls the task of presenting to Dido the ceremonial gifts offered by the Trojans in gratitude for her hospitality, but his real mission is that of a *bacillus*. These are his orders:

> tu facime illius noctem non amplius unam
> falle dolo et notos pueri puer indue uultus,
> ut, cum te gremio accipiet laetissima Dido
> regalis inter mensas laticemque Lyaeum,
> cum dabit amplexus atque oscula dulcia friget,
> occultum inspires ignem fallasque ueneno.
> (1.683–88)

(You must just for one night assume his shape as a disguise, and wear his familiar features; after all, he is a boy like you. Then during the royal entertainment, when the wine is flowing, and Dido in her great happiness clasps you to her, embracing you and planting on you her sweet kisses, you shall breathe into her invisible fire, and poison her, without her knowing.)

It is a passage in which loving and lying are inextricable, but so far as the poetic history of Troy is concerned there is a good deal more to it than that. Dido accepts the gifts and the giver alike. The ceremonial world of adult society commissions schoolgirls to present bouquets to their majesties and their mezzosopranos in part to exploit the freshness, the sincerity, above all the innocence of childhood. The gift is augmented by the guilelessness of the giver. No wonder that Dido takes the dear boy onto her lap; he is so—cute![24] The scene is thus directed by a semiotics of utter falseness.

24. See W. T. Slater, "Pueri, turba minuta," *BICS* 2 (1974): 133–40.

Virgil then does something very remarkable. The poet who had identified himself in the first person in the first line of his poem now relinquishes its narration to a powerful competitor; for the second and third books of the *Aeneid*, by any reckoning among the very best of the poem, are sung not by Virgil but by Aeneas. For this long and important moment Virgil himself adopts the role we shall see in Dante, who calls himself a mere scribe, and in Chaucer, who insists that he reports another man's words. Before we see Aeneas as hero we shall see him as lover. But before he is a lover, indeed we may wish to say in preparation to becoming a lover, we see him as a historical poet of extraordinary power and unique eyewitness authority, a man who could rival Homer in technique and Dares and Dictys in his truth-claims. I think that it is not wrong to imagine that the false Ascanius nestles in Dido's lap through the duration of his story, a story that centers on the false gift fatally introduced to Troy through the guile of an enemy impersonating a friend. In Virgil the operation of the love-infection is instantaneous, and from the moment the lad comes into Dido's lap she is *infelix,* one poisoned, infected to the bone, a woman on fire. Yet as Virgil's use of the word *iamdudum* in the memorable opening sentence of the fourth book shows, there is an incremental quality to the pathology. It is not forcing the text to see that the recitation of the destruction of Troy and Dido's "falling in love" are coterminous no less than thematically cognate events. That is Virgil's way.

Given Virgil's deeply pessimistic attitude toward eroticism, we can easily enough imagine a medieval Christian poet invoking this text in a rather simple censoriousness toward sexual passion. In fact Dante's representation of Virgil in this matter is something of a misrepresentation. He uses the passage for *historical* purposes. That is what people used to believe about love, he says, somewhat disingenuously failing to add that Virgil also believed that it was all a bad business. The pagan world "used to believe that Venus rayed down mad love from the third epicycle." Boccaccio *dantista* took Dante's historical generalization and showed it operating in the psychology of an individual pagan, the Trojan prince Troilo who, in celebration of the most satisfying sensual experience of his life, sings out in praise of Venus, "O luce eterna, il cui lieto splendore / fa bello il terzo ciel . . ." (O eternal light, whose cheerful radiance makes the third heaven beautiful; *Fil.* 3.74.1–2). This beautiful song, its beauty enhanced in Chaucer's adaptation, then reappears—now in the pagan voice of the narrator Lollius—in the famous proemium to the third book of the *Troilus.* By wishful critical thinking it is often said to be "Boethian"; but in my view it is pure literary paganism.[25] Dante's mediation is here crucial. This is what people *used* to believe to their peril, what by implication it is no longer appropriate to believe. The pagan Troilo believed it, and the pagan Troilus

---

25. It would not be relevant to pursue this very complex matter here, but I owe a brief amplification of a judgment that will seem heretical to some. Troilo's love song (*Fil.* 3.74–89) has been remade by Chaucer in two parts. The first occupies the proemium to book 3 (1–49), and the second—a postcoital aria, as in Boccaccio—occupies four stanzas beginning at 3.1744. In the latter Chaucer introduces extensive quotations from *CP* 2m8. This initiative is highly significant, but I say nothing more concerning it here except that it has, in my opinion, misled critics into seeing Boethius in Chaucer's proemium as well and, indeed, in Troilo's song in the *Filostrato* which, according to Windeatt is "itself derived from Boethius." I do not believe that this is correct. There are no compelling verbal parallels, as Morton Bloomfield has pointed out, and nothing elsewhere in Boccaccio's text prepares for the introduction of Boethius into this startling context. On the other hand, the idea advanced by Bloomfield (*Classical Philology* 47 [1952], 162–65) that the passage is based on Boccaccio's direct reading of the *De rerum natura* of Lucretius is no less unconvincing; and it has been rejected by classicists and Italianists alike. (See in particular the editorial comments of K. Buechner in his edition of Lucretius, *De rerum natura* [Wiesbaden: Steiner, 1966], xix; and V. Branca in *Tutte le opere di Giovanni Boccaccio* [Verona: A. Mondadori, 1964], 2:855.) This seems to leave the field clear for my own rash speculation. There is an obvious text from a favorite author of both Boccaccio and Chaucer that has been insufficiently appreciated in previous discussion of the Chaucerian passage: the hymn to Venus at the beginning of the fourth book of Ovid's *Fasti*. The verbal parallels, though once again rather vague, are numerous; and there are some distinctively Ovidian ideas. Branca identifies as the most "Boethian" part of Boccaccio's text the stanza (3.79) beginning "Tu legge, o dea, poni all' universo, / per la quale esso in esser si mantiene," a passage represented in Chaucer's text (3.36) by the line "Ye folk a lawe han set in universe." Boccaccio's lines seem to me a reasonable representation of *Fasti* 4.93–94: "Juraque dat caelo, terrae, natalibus undis, perque suos initus continet omne genus," a line that itself probably derives from the most famous celebrations of divine order in Latin poetry, that of *Georgics* 4.221–22. The commonplace sequence of heaven, earth, and sea, which has been taken as a Boethian element (*CP* 2.8.14–15) is explicitly present at *Fil.* 3.75.1 and *TC* 3.8, but we note that the Christian poets have added "hell" as an arena where Venus' laws can be seen to hold sway—the only possibly Boethian idea I find in the proemium. Boccaccio's lines stress the dangers of crossing Venus' "little boy" (*figliuolo*), a distinctively Ovidian touch. Chaucer replaces Cupid with Venus, facilitating the narrator's self-identification as Venus' "clerk" (3.41). The one time that Chaucer uses the actual phrase "Venus' clerk" (*HF* 3.397), it is of course applied to Ovid. I thus tentatively conclude that in the proemium, Chaucer, following Boccaccio, adopts a pagan/Ovidian voice, not a Christian/Boethian one.

believed it. But the Christian poets who wrote out the phrases "le genti anti-
che ne l'antico errore" and "payens corsed olde rites" most emphatically did
not believe it. In generalizing about the religious and erotic systems operating
in the text he had translated Chaucer, now the undisguided, wholly conventional Christian commentator, gives a broad historical footnote to the primary
sources that provided the historical materials for research into ancient error
in love and religion: "the forme of olde clerkes speech in poetrie." Dante puts
the general condemnation of the pagan gods into the mouth of Virgil himself
(*Inferno* 1.72) and illustrates with a specific Virgilian reading the trickiness
of their operations. Both poets posit a contrast, and an unbridgeable gap,
between two kinds of loving and two kinds of language.

When taxed by Cupid in *The Legend of Good Women* (prologue, 471–72) for
having dared to translate the *Roman de la Rose*—a "heresy" against Cupid's law
—and to write *Troilus and Criseyde*, the persona of the poet defends himself
by saying that "God woot, yt was myn entente / To forthren trouthe in love
and yt cheryce." I take the phrase "forthren trouthe in love" to be intentionally
ambiguous. It means "to spread the truth about love" on the one hand, and
on the other "to encourage honorable behavior on the part of lovers" on the
other. Somewhere among the meanings is a scriptural allusion to Paul's phrase
"to tell the truth in love"—that is, to offer moral criticism in a spirit of charity.
It is one of many Chaucerian passages that stress the doubtful relationships
between language and truth on the one hand, and language and love on the
other.

Those relationships are, I believe, central to Chaucer's artistic conception
in the *Troilus*. They manifest themselves in numerous gestures that draw self-
conscious attention to the difficulties faced by an artist who must use ambiguous words in the paradoxical pursuit of truth through fiction. Chaucer's
concern with the twin problems of the lying of art and the art of lying is
both moody and imaginative, and it might well merit an independent and detailed study. But the present chapter has already of necessity been sufficiently
complex in its demonstration that an apparently peripheral theme in the *Troilus*—the "local color" of ancient religious practice—provides Chaucer with
a subject of philosophical weight, that this subject is implicit in individual
instances of ambiguous language within his poem, and that in developing it
Chaucer repeatedly performs acts of creative imitation through which he chan-
nels into his own enterprise the artistic energies of Virgil, Statius, and Dante,
among others. The poetic genealogy of ambiguity, signaled by a single word,

informs and illuminates the artist's construction of his poem and the reader's understanding of it.

Two salient characteristics of the antique world as Chaucer found it in the ancient and modern poets he most admired were captious language and captious love. His own abiding poetical interest in the themes of truth, of love, and indeed of "trouthe in love" would inevitably lead him to explore and in a sense to confront the amatory economy of ancient poetry. Given his poetic agenda, it was indispensable that he examine love as image worship, or what his own Christian world called idolatry. So must we.

THREE | IDOLS OF THE PRINCE

Ambiguity is for Chaucer in the *Troilus* not merely a consciously exploited artistic device or an unavoidable linguistic risk but a principal philosophical theme that unites the poetic past viewed as a historical matter on the one hand and as an artistic tradition on the other. Chaucer is concerned, that is, with the ambiguities of gentile religion and the ambiguities of poets. The preceding chapter had as its chief aim the presentation of lexical genealogy of ambiguity that might help us reconstruct the nature, and the implications, of one significant feature of the poet's literary education. In chapter 4 I shall examine certain aspects of Chaucer's artistic self-consciousness in raising themes of ambiguation. In particular, I must address the artist's handling of the central question inevitably raised by textual ambiguity, which is the question of interpretation.

I shall first seek to examine, however, that artistic crossroads where Chaucer the poetic historian met Chaucer the moral philosopher; for it seems quite certain to me that in the *Troilus* Chaucer has carefully arranged a poetic confrontation of pagan past and Christian present, and that he has done so in a manner that recognizes, and assuages, certain Platonic and Augustinian anxieties about the truth-claims of poetry. Chaucer's considerable investment in the cultural history of Greco-Roman pagan antiquity is best understood in terms of his pursuit of a distinctively Judeo-Christian idea, the idea of idolatry.

This discovery of idolatry must by the nature of things be a somewhat leisurely affair, requiring a filiation of argumentative exploration not entirely unlike the poetic filiation of the *Troilus* itself. I seek first to identify Chaucer's ethical attitude to his poetic ancestry. Then I shall briefly discuss, for their comparative uses, the literary attitudes of two of Chaucer's near contemporaries—Jean de Meun and Nicholas Trevet—who can with more or less conviction display intellectual parallels for his own enterprise. Next I propose to consider two specific "images," the first poetic and the second sculptural, which are the poet's principal means of delineating and exploring his theme of idolatry. Finally, I shall make explicit the ways in which the poem's eroticism is inseparable, thematically and philosophically, from the idea of idolatry.

CHAUCER AND THE POETIC PAST

To appreciate Chaucer's strategy, philosophical and literary, we may make a beginning near the poet's own ending. As the *Troilus* approaches its notorious conclusion, its author offers two formal but markedly different invitations to place his own work within the context of the classical poetic tradition. In a verse paragraph that imitates Statius' homage to Virgil at the end of the *Thebaid*, Chaucer directs that his own book

> subgit be to alle poesie;
> And kis the steppes, where as thow seest space
> Virgile, Ovide, Omer, Lucan, and Stace.
> (5.1790–92)

This "humility topos" has been much discussed. Its complementary "superiority topos" by contrast has been rather neglected. For some few lines later Chaucer again invokes the pagan poetical tradition, and in a very different tone of voice, when he summarizes the drift of his enterprise as an exposure of "payens corsed olde rites" and "thise wrecched worldes appetites" (5.1849–51).

> Lo here, the forme of olde clerkes speche
> In poetrie, if ye hire bokes seche.
> (5.1854–55)

R. K. Root, an editor who saw poetic interpretation as no part of his task, has the following unflinching linguistic gloss on the word *forme* in line 1854: "The context suggests that *forme* is here used in the sense given to *forma* by scholastic philosophy, i.e., 'the essential principle of a thing which makes it what it is.' . . . The meaning of the sentence would then be: 'See what is the essential principle which informs ancient pagan poetry!,' i.e., a set of false gods, and 'thise wrecched worldes appetites.'"[1]

1. Chaucer, *The Book of Troilus and Criseyde*, ed. R. K. Root (Princeton: Princeton University Press, 1926), 563.

The superficially paradoxical attitude that at once honors the artistic achievement of the ancient poets and confidently scorns the "essential principle" of their poems is actually one that characterizes medieval humanism generally. It can be traced to one of the major strands of patristic criticism of a pagan society still a social reality rather than a literary memory, and in a number of the most eminent vernacular poets of the later Middle Ages an attitude that began as a tacit cultural assumption finds expression as a self-consciously developed poetic theme.

Jean de Meun, soon followed by Dante Alighieri, explored the theme with notable learning, variety, and subtlety. These two poets, obviously among Chaucer's important sources of inspiration in the *Troilus*, were likewise the teachers of his immediate and principal source, Giovanni Boccaccio. I shall not here repeat the lengthy argument, developed elsewhere with reference to the *Roman de la Rose*, by which I attempt to demonstrate the interpretive implications of the poetic attitude toward ancient subject matter shared by these poets. But I do conclude that for Chaucer, as for the vernacular poets in whose tradition he elects to place his own work, the differences between pagan and Christian are matters of central poetic meaning rather than of subordinate and accidental historical fact. It is my view that what is usually called the pagan "background" in the *Troilus* would be better called the foreground.

I take the phrase "payens corsed olde rites" to refer primarily to what Christians would have regarded as the idolatrous and superstitious practices that crowd the pages of Latin epic, and the phrase "thise wrecched worldes appetites" to refer in context to the appetite for love viewed from a certain moral perspective. The narrative voice of the ending of the poem thus links quite specifically, through their common involvement with the "rascal gods," pagan idolatry and pagan love. Here we have the "forme of olde clerkes speche / In poetrie," now faithfully translated from the original tongue by a modern Christian with a strict objectivity that licenses a few final censorious remarks of a personal and subjective nature in what is in effect a discrete editorial appendix that no reader would confuse with the original "pagan" text.

Love in the *Troilus*—that is to say the love of Troilus and Criseyde—is presented within the poem in relationship to an ancient theological system abstracted from the poetry of Virgil, Ovid, and Statius, a system of which it is indeed an integral part. The poet of the *Troilus* is, in Minnis's nice phrase, "a Christian historian," nor does he abandon his historical stance when he approaches his principal subject, love. He writes about ancient love in an ancient world. It would be theoretically possible to do so with an absolute objectivity, free of contemporary moral judgments of any kind; but Chaucer is far from exploring this theoretical possibility. The *idolatrous* nature of Troilus' love for Criseyde is presented not as a neutral matter of historical fact, but as a morally engaged poetic theme. For what is made morally explicit in the censorious appendix that the Christian historian adds to his "translation" is morally implicit in the prominent initial scene in which we view the origins of Troilus' love for Criseyde.

It is at the feast of the Palladium, a "relic" in which the Trojans put "hire trust aboven everichon," that Troilus first sees Criseyde. As he wanders through the temple of Minerva with his fellows, he has no thought for the goddess or for her simulacrum worshiped by the crowd; his attention is drawn to no divine female but to "the ladyes of the town," but even to them he had "no devocioun." Any reader can see from a mile away that he is riding for a fall, and under Cupid's tough tutelage he soon enough gets religion. Within a hundred lines he will have an image of his very own to adore, the "figure" of Criseyde, called up as by a catopromancer, in the "mirour of his mynde." One form of idolatry has given way to another.

The line of analysis here sketched is of course not my original discovery. The claim that Troilus' love is presented as idolatry in a morally serious way by Chaucer was first made by D. W. Robertson, and it has been elaborated in varying degrees by several other scholars.[2] Recently, however, it has been emphatically repudiated by Alastair Minnis in his important and pioneering study of Chaucer's attitudes toward classical antiquity.[3] Minnis's book is characterized by a wide and generous learning, by a clearly stated argument, and by a genuine engagement with other scholars. These excellent features, among several others, will commend it to any reader attempting to approach Chaucer from a historical point of view, but they present me with a strategic problem in the present circumstances.

No writer on Chaucer's attitude to the pagan past can ignore Minnis's essay; but since I find some of the literary conclusions he draws from his "historical" analysis unconvincing and even perverse, my own engagement of his argument, as it bears on the theme of idolatry in the *Troilus*, does not begin to

2. See, e.g., John Frankis, "Paganism and Pagan Love in *Troilus and Criseyde*," in *Essays on Troilus and Criseyde*, ed. Mary Salu (Cambridge: Boydell and Brewer, 1979), 57–72.
3. A. J. Minnis, *Chaucer and Pagan Antiquity* (Cambridge: Boydell and Brewer, 1982).

suggest my genuine appreciation of his imaginative formulation of the scholar's task. Since Minnis has so explicitly addressed certain questions central to my own study, it simply will not do either to pass over his views in silence or to express simple disagreement without giving specific causes founded in textual analysis. We shall in due course return to our discovery of idolatry in Chaucer's poem, after a consideration of our theoretical grounds for doing so.

Minnis's argument has multiple strands, but insofar as it relates to the principal concern of this chapter—the *theme of love as idolatry* in the *Troilus*—it might be summarized thus. Chaucer's artistic stance toward his ancient subject matter differs markedly from that of earlier medieval writers on the Troy legend but does reveal some striking parallels with the attitudes of a number of his more forward-looking contemporaries and near contemporaries in the fields of scriptural exegesis and Latin textual criticism—such men as Robert Holcot, Trevet, and John Ridewall. In their approach to ancient historical and literary materials, these men typically eschew old-fashioned allegories and labored moralization to engage in straightforward historical annotation and philological explanation. So does Chaucer, whose narrator adopts the role of a poetical historian who publicly acknowledges his responsibility to anterior textual tradition and who publicly eschews offering his own comment and interpretation on the action described. Thus pagan idolatry is simply a historical fact of the antique setting and, to the considerable extent that the narrator remains true to professional objectivity, a neutral one. Chaucer's interest is in reporting pagan religion, not in moralizing about it.

Chaucerians will recognize that Minnis, basing his argument to a large extent on primary materials first drawn prominently into the Chaucerian context by Robertson, has arrived at very different interpretive conclusions. It is indeed his impressive familiarity with the exegetical and historical scholarship of the fourteenth-century friars that allows him to appreciate the plausibility of the Robertsonian argument. Playing the role of "devil's advocate," Minnis draws attention to the special importance of the fourteenth chapter of The Wisdom of Solomon in the formation of medieval commonplace ideas about idolatry and to the special interest of Robert Holcot's influential fourteenth-century commentary on Wisdom for Chaucer's possible understanding of the subject.

He notes that "Holcot's exegesis contains many ideas which seem very relevant to Chaucer's poem" and goes on to catalog some though by no means all of them. He notes the close parallel between Holcot's account of the process of mental idolatry and Troilus' meditation on the "figure" of Criseyde: "Here Troilus may be making to himself an idol (in the imaginative manner which Holcot warned against), and in the process preparing his own downfall. Having gazed upon another's beauty, he has fallen into the snares of a woman who, as it transpires, has a mind for many. What a pity that Ecclesiasticus was written long after the time of Troilus."[4]

He even mentions the Palladium. "Certain details in the text of *Troilus* lend some credibility to this approach. It is interesting that Troilus should first catch sight of Criseyde in a pagan temple during the service of an idol and relic, the Palladium, and that on his first night of love with her he is (the excuse goes) supposed to be performing his sacrifice to Apollo." The argument seems promising, but Minnis, not unlike Chaucer himself, does a sudden volte-face. "It is precisely because I find this alternative interpretation so (superficially) attractive that I have been able to play devil's advocate as such length. But reject it I must, because in my opinion it does not fit all the facts of the text. It would be perverse to read into Chaucer's poem a moral framework which he systematically sought to avoid."[5]

So indeed it would be, and likewise perverse to reargue a case that so learned a colleague as Minnis had successfully refuted. But I do not find that Minnis has done so. If devil's advocacy were always so effective, there would surely be far fewer saints. For unfortunately Minnis does not fulfill the implied promise to engage the Robertsonian argument, and he provides no "facts of the text" that would lead me to hesitate in identifying the prominent theme of sexual idolatry in Chaucer's poem. Even less, in my view, does he demonstrate that Chaucer "systematically avoids" a critique of pagan idolatry. What he does do,

4. Minnis, *Chaucer and Pagan Antiquity*, 87. With the last sentence quoted, the cat is out of the bag. Minnis thinks that the invocation of scriptural criteria is in this context *unhistorical*. The "pity" is rather attenuated, in my view, by the fact that Pandarus has read and quotes from Ecclesiastes at 1.694–95. What leads Minnis to the notion that "Ecclesiasticus was written long after the time of Troilus" I cannot say. I find Chaucer's textual witticism one of several indications that, following a general medieval belief fostered by Augustine in the *De civitate Dei*, he imagines the cultural and moral ethos of the regal period of Israelite history as parallel to that of its contemporary Trojan society. The most striking of these is his invention of Troilus' fake illness after the biblical story of Jonadab and Amnon (discussed in chapter 4). Chaucer's imagined chronology is generally consistent with the compilation of Eusebius and Jerome, the standard patristic authority, and with Dante, who wrote "E tutto questo fu in uno temporale, che David nacque e nacque Roma, cioè che Enea venne di Troia in Italia" (*Convivio* 4.4.6).
5. Minnis, *Chaucer and Pagan Antiquity*, 87–88.

perhaps, is to exemplify Robertson's theory of "courtly love as an impediment to the understanding of medieval literary texts"; for he invokes the concept as one of critical and *historical* weight to explain the ethos of the poem.

Thus according to Minnis, "Chaucer was even more interested in *fin' amors* than was Benoît. Troilus and Criseyde conduct their affair in accordance with the code of fashionable behaviour in vogue in Chaucer's day." The poem becomes, accordingly, "to some extent . . . a work designed to demonstrate to its immediate audience the rules of the game of love."[6] With all due respect I wonder precisely what features of fashionable Riccardian social life Minnis has in mind: Palladium parties? gutter crawls? matutinal incest? suicide pacts? long and muddled Boethian monologues? Surely it is the "alterity" of the lovers' social behavior in this poem that is remarkable, not its conformity to contemporary social fashion.

This I take to be the point, or part of the point, of the narrator's famous comparison between linguistic change and change in amatory custom over the period of a millennium (2.22–28). The love conventions he describes differ as decidedly from those of his own society as the language of Alfred, King of Wessex, differs from that of Alfred, Lord Tennyson. My further opinion is that any of Chaucer's contemporaries simple enough to read *Troilus and Criseyde* as "a work designed to demonstrate to its immediate audience the rules of the game of love" would nonetheless be shrewd enough to conclude that, given its rules, the game of love was best pursued strictly as a spectator sport.

It is Minnis's view that the application of moral categories abstracted from the Latin theologians and humanists of the fourteenth century to a critical analysis of the *Troilus* involves an embarrassing generic solecism, for *Troilus* is what he calls a "courtly romance," a phrase he nowhere defines but nevertheless uses as a term of critical weight as though it determined in and of itself what ideas could or could not be in Chaucer's poem. Yet the narrator of the *Troilus* has gone to elaborate lengths to pretend that he is presenting us with an antique rather than a modern (which is to say, medieval) fiction; and even his apparently disingenuous suppression of the name of Boccaccio in favor of that of Lollius is in part an attempt to out-Boccaccio Boccaccio in this regard; for whereas Boccaccio gives us a narrator who merely writes as though he were an antique pagan, Chaucer has found the empirical antique pagan himself.

Under these circumstances I find Minnis's vague appeal to the "genre" of the

6. Ibid., 90.

"courtly romance" as the apparently final arbiter of moral vision in the *Troilus* rather bemusing. The "courtly romance" is in the first place a generalization of dubious substantiality that is nearly irrelevant to Chaucer's poem except insofar as it may denote certain medievalized transformations of his actual classical models, such vernacular *romans d'antiquité* as *Thebes* and *Troie*. These models, as I have implicitly argued in this book, seem to me sufficiently clear: Ovid in matters of love, Boethius in matters of philosophy, and Augustine in the matter of the stance toward pagan antiquity. One of Chaucer's principal modern models, Jean de Meun's *Roman de la Rose*, in which the Ovidian, the Augustinian, and the Boethian were conspicuously blended, is a "courtly romance" only if we stretch the definition of that genre even beyond its already remarkable elasticity. Just as I think that the phrase "Ovidian love" would better serve the erotic history of Troy in the Middle Ages than does the phrase "courtly love," so also do I think that the phrase "antique romance" better serves the general phenomenon of the *matiere de Troie* in medieval Europe than does the phrase "courtly romance."

Though one may dispute the conclusions C. S. Lewis came to in addressing the question of what Chaucer "really did" to Boccaccio's *Filostrato*, he was certainly right to concentrate on the twin issues of Chaucer's attitude toward history and his attitude toward love. But the fact of the matter, a fact perhaps overlooked in many traditional accounts of the *Troilus*, is that the impulses to "historicize" Homer and to "romanticize" him—which is to say the impulse to transform epic to romance—are markedly present in the late antique pseudo-histories that became the indispensable "sources" of serious writers about Troy. When Chaucer directs his readers to Dares and Dictys, he is directing them to authors implicitly or explicitly presented as superior to Homer precisely in their possession of firsthand, eyewitness, historical *truth* impossible to find in a *poet* writing long after the events he celebrated. These identical authors, in appropriating a spurious but insistent historicity, are at the same time the founders of the *romance* tradition that would make Achilles a heroic lover no less than a heroic warrior and, indeed, eventually give the boudoir top billing over the battlefield as an arena of the reader's interest.[7]

According to Minnis, "religious imagery of veneration and worship is a stock feature of the language in which literary lovers describe their feelings toward

7. Cf. the chapter "*Heroikos e romanzo di Troia*" in Teresa Mantero, *Ricerche sull'Heroikos di Filostrato* (Genoa: Istituto di filologia classica e medioevale, 1966), 198–224.

their ladies; its use in *Troilus and Criseyde* need not carry the implication that Troilus is doubly reprehensible as an idolator in love and in religion." It seems quite true that it "need not"; but Minnis's entirely circular argument does nothing to prove the point one way or the other. The only texts known to me in which religious imagery of veneration and worship is used by literary lovers to describe their feelings toward their ladies with anything like the protraction and historical specificity of Chaucer's *Troilus* are certain works of Latin Ovidiana, the *Roman de la Rose* and its immediate progeny, the "pagan" romances of Boccaccio, and the *Canzoniere* of Petrarch. These texts cannot be unified by an appeal to a spurious genre, but they do make up a tradition of a sort: a tradition in which we find precisely an insistence upon complicating the "idolatrous" imagery of vernacular love poetry with inescapable allusions to the Christian theology of idolatry. I fully accept the argument, in part based on the excellent work of Douglas Kelly, that "the function of the imagination, the image-making faculty of the mind, is commonly emphasized in medieval love poetry without possessing the moral significance which Holcot gave to it in his account of the idol of incontinence and enticing disposition."[8] But that hardly proves that there are not examples of medieval love poetry in which precisely the opposite is true, that is, in which "the moral significance which Holcot gave to it" *is* conspicuously present. But its presence or absence can be successfully argued only by a close examination of texts, and not by the mere appeal to Minnis's "genre" or to my "tradition." I am convinced that the examination of textual detail in the *Troilus* makes it certain that such implications are clearly intended, that indeed sexual idolatry is for Chaucer a central poetic theme. I accordingly want to shift the focus of my own discussion from a general engagement of Minnis's argument to an analysis of a specific textual moment within the poem.

Minnis is concerned, and of course rightly concerned, with questions of literary genre; and one of his most impressive contributions is the demonstration of the relationship of *Troilus* to the Anglo-French "historical novel," the *roman d'antiquité*. He notes that Robertson and others, in advancing their "idolatrous" reading of *Troilus*, make use of a moral analysis of erotic behavior "taken from scholastic discussions of love and marriage, with a preponderance of antifeminist and antimatrimonial texts. Of course, judged by these standards, which

8. Both quotations are from Minnis, *Chaucer and Pagan Antiquity*, 90. In the latter, Minnis alludes, of course, to Holcot's exegesis of Wisd. of Sol. 14.12.

to some extent are reflected in Holcot's exegesis of Wisdom 14.12, Troilus and Criseyde are reprehensible. The question is, are these standards appropriate, that is, did Chaucer mean his audience to have such criteria in mind when listening to or reading his poem?"[9]

That indeed is the question, or at least *a* question, but before attempting an answer of my own, I must review Minnis's. He finds that Chaucer departs significantly from earlier medieval treatments of the story by "the Latin clerical group of writers on the Trojan war" in excising their distracting moral kibbitzing on the action and their vociferous railings against female wiles and female sexuality generally. Chaucer, it is claimed, has a sympathetic, largely positive attitude toward Criseyde. In a memorable sentence Minnis puts it thus: "In book V of Troilus and Criseyde, Criseyde the fearful pagan found two protectors, Diomede and the narrator—one for the time, the other for posterity."[10]

The idea of fear is central to Minnis's conception of her character. He convincingly notes the many textual references to her fearfulness in the poem, and he maintains that many Christian writers regarded fear as the dynamic force behind paganism. Criseyde behaves as she behaves because—that is the way people behaved. "Chaucer seems to regard this failing primarily as an historical fact to be recorded objectively rather than as a moral fault to be condemned. . . . The narrator of *Troilus* ostentatiously suspends his moral judgments in the face of the historical fact."[11]

The narrator of the *Troilus* does indeed suspend his moral judgment, or at least he reserves it, but does he do so "in the face of the historical fact"? Unique among the many medieval poetic narrators of the Troy story, Chaucer's pretends to be first and foremost a responsible translator of an antique Latin text, an intermediary who speaks only when and only what his author spoke before him. As a matter of historical fact, this pose is an elaborately unhistorical fiction of markedly subversive tendency that allows him to authorize, in the name of anterior authority, the considerable liberties he has taken with anterior authorities. One historical fact of his literary tradition (i.e., Boccaccio) is an explicitly censorious attitude toward Criseyde; in largely removing this from his own poem, he is surely motivated not by fact but by fiction.

9. Ibid., 88.
10. Ibid., 93.
11. Ibid., 92.

I cannot be certain whether Minnis is arguing that Chaucer actually believed (on the basis of his readings in various friar-antiquaries and elsewhere) that fear was a morally neutral "historical fact" of pagan anthropology or whether he is supposed to have posited the idea as an interesting functional fiction of his imagined world, but the one is as unlikely as the other. If fear—and by extension treacherous behavior motivated by fear—was not "a moral fault to be condemned" in pagan society, why is it so clearly held to be despicable by the pagan epic poets? Why did the greatest pagan philosopher establish fortitude as one of the cardinal virtues? Why did the Stoics excoriate fear as a principal strand of the miserable "tetrachordon" of human moral failure? [12] Why do the most influential Latin moralists, Cicero and Seneca, repeatedly identify fear as among the basest and most destructive of human passions? Can any reader of the *Tusculan Disputations* or the *De constantia sapientis* think that fear is a "morally neutral" fact of antique anthropology? Within the text of the *Troilus* itself both of the lovers repeatedly express the idea that valor is morally admirable and pusillanimity base. If Chaucer's pagan characters do not suspend their moral judgments of the virtue of courage and the vice of cowardice, it is difficult to believe that Chaucer would do so on the grounds adduced.

Actually, of course, there are cultural and social factors concerning the condition of women—whether in antiquity, in the Middle Ages, or in antiquity as reflected in medieval literature—that might indeed be responsibly invoked to defend the literary plausibility of Criseyde's fearfulness. She is a widow. She is abandoned by her father, whose perceived treachery likewise puts her in a difficult situation. She is among that group of socially vulnerable people whom the theorists claimed the institution of chivalry was meant to protect. But these are not the kind of considerations that Minnis's "historical" explanation of her character raises, and I shall not pursue them either.

What concerns me is not whether, at the theoretical level, Criseyde may or may not be fearful with impunity. The theoretical difficulties inherent I find in Minnis's account of Chaucerian paganism become of practical critical con-

---

12. Max Pohlenz, *Die Stoa: Geschichte einer geistigen Bewegung*, 2d ed. (Gottingen: Vandenhoeck, 1959), 1:148. The Stoic analysis, classically summarized in a famous Virgilian line (*Aeneid* 6.733)—a line cited verbatim no less than ten times in the works of Augustine, according to K. H. Schelkle, *Virgil in der Deutung Augustins* (Stuttgart: W. Kohlhammer, 1939), 127—is still current in fourteenth-century moral philosophy; see Klaus Heitmann, *Fortuna und Virtus: Eine Studie zu Petrarcas Lebensweisheit* (Cologne: Böhlau, 1958), 89–90.

cern only in view of the specific acts of interpretation with which they are implicated. That is, how does a particular "historical" view guide poetic interpretation? I shall attempt to amplify my criticism in relation to a single passage of text, the scene (4.1366–1414) in which Criseyde explains to Troilus how she intends to deceive her father in order to return to Troy. We have already touched upon it briefly in our examination of its specialized pagan vocabulary; what concerns me now is its literary genealogy. In it Criseyde predicts that she will be able to lie to her father successfully because he will be blinded by his own cupidity, and that even should he put her word to the test of divination she will be able to manipulate the *sortes* (in the accuracy of which she apparently believes) by fraud. So far as our reading of the poem is concerned, Criseyde would appear to be lying in the present about lies she intends to tell in the future; for there is no evidence that she ever tries to act upon her plan once she has met Diomede. It is the extraordinary disjuncture between what she says will happen and what actually happens, I take it, that accounts for the narrator's explicit assurances, against the silent incredulity of his readers, that she really meant it at the time.

In general Minnis finds the episode a particularly significant one, and one that throws a *positive* light upon Criseyde's character, demonstrating her to be practical, efficient, and sensible. He argues, furthermore, that the passage links Criseyde "the fearful pagan" with the wider theme of pagan fear generally; for among the things Criseyde plans to say to Calchas is "Ek drede fond first goddes, I suppose" (4.1408). "The statement that fear first caused the gods to exist in the world—probably based on Petronius' *Primus in orbe deos fecit inesse timor*—echoes the belief of Holcot, Ridevall, and others that human fear was a major cause of the origin and survival of idolatry. . . . A pagan has uttered what is virtually a condemnation of paganism; for a moment Criseyde speaks out of character, with a degree of insight which exceeds her usual abilities."[13]

Yet, as it happens, the sentence "Primus in orbe deos fecit timor" is to be found in the *Thebaid* of Statius (3.661), and common sense suggests that Chaucer probably took it from Statius rather than from Petronius by way of Robert Holcot. The suggestion that Petronius ever wrote the line in the first place is almost certainly mistaken, even though it was copied from one scholiast after another beginning with Lactantius. It probably appears in the

13. Minnis, *Chaucer and Pagan Antiquity*, 82; cf. 39.

Petronian fragment as a misplaced gloss from Statius.[14] There are a number of good reasons to believe that the sentence—commonplace though its idea be— is original with Statius.[15] I am not concerned to argue technical points relating to the textual transmission of antique Latin poetry in the Middle Ages, points that may have no practical implications for the nature of Chaucer's erudition, but I do want to insist that the *Troilus* is much more likely to bear the impress of major primary texts that we know Chaucer read than of secondary texts which we do not know whether he had read or not. Minnis's argument typically implies the opposite by aggrandizing the importance of secondary writers (Trevet and Holcot in particular) at the expense of the major classical poets themselves.

In other words my argument is that Chaucer first learned about paganism from reading pagan poets—Virgil, Ovid, and Statius in particular—and not from fourteenth-century commentators. He read as a poet, not as a grammarian, scholiast, preacher, or censor. The friar-scholars of the fourteenth century are often highly relevant to the study of Chaucer's intellectual world, and Robertson certainly did scholarship a service by introducing them to the general Chaucerian community; but they cannot have taught the poet much, if anything, about *poetry*. As uncongenial as friar bashing is to me, I do have to point out certain *literary* limitations to the authorities invoked by Minnis as normative. Trevet could write a lengthy commentary on the *Consolation of Philosophy* without betraying the slightest interest in the fact that Boethius' meters are among the great masterpieces of late antique verse; he could undertake "learned" commentaries on Seneca's tragedies without even mastering their plots.[16] I suggest that what we have in Criseyde's speech is not an ornament of scholastic commentary but a quotation of Statius—a quotation that signals a poetic *aemulatio* of a textual moment.

Why does Criseyde propose to say to her father "Ek drede fond first goddes, I suppose"? We must submit the "proverb" to contextual examination, for as B. A. Wise correctly noted in 1911, Chaucer's quotation of Statius is part of his imitation of a scene from the *Thebaid*.[17] The third book of that poem is

14. See A. Ernout's edition of Petronius, *Le Satiricon* (Paris: Belles Lettres, 1962), 190.
15. See H. Snijder's edition of Statius, *Thebaid/A Commentary on Book III* (Amsterdam: Hakkert, 1968), 251.
16. See Seneca's *Agamemnon*, ed. R. J. Tarrant (Cambridge: Cambridge University Press, 1976), 81–82.
17. Wise, *Influence of Statius*, 15–17.

given over in large measure to the impressive scene of the augury at Argos, in which the priests Amphiaraus and Melampus read the terrible destruction of the enterprise of the Seven against Thebes in the ornithological horrors revealed to them in the skies. The prognostications, it is important to note, are specific, accurate, and devastating. Against the decrees of the immortals so clearly revealed to the augurs Capaneus madly rails. Amphiaraus, he claims, is a coward and a fraud. He taunts and insults the *vates* and riles the mob with a bombastic speech (3.668–69) advancing the idea that military valor is the only true priestcraft: "illic augur ego et mecum quicumque parati / insanire manu" (Then shall I be augur, and with me those ready to go crazy in battle.) It is in the course of his rabid harrangue that Capaneus utters the opinion that "primos in orbe deos fecit timor."

Classicists who have discussed the line agree on its intentionally trite character.[18] If Criseyde has actually spoken "out of character, with a degree of insight which exceeds her usual abilities" in order to achieve classical banality, it can hardly be Chaucer's intention to signal her inspired moment of illumination. What we see instead is another "creative imitation." For this textual moment Criseyde is being cast as Statius' Capaneus; and for all the difference between Statius and Chaucer, the two scenes reveal extensive parallels. In each we find a *vates* who has correctly foretold the future on the basis of divination, and in each instance the veracity of the augur is impugned by a rash agnostic. It is impossible to read the *Thebaid* with poetic sympathy without seeing in Amphiaraus a true moral grandeur and tragedy or in Capaneus a mad and self-destructive arrogance. And it is certainly arrogance, not heroic mental liberation from superstition, that motivates the lines "Primos in orbe deos fecit timor." From the point of view of medieval Christianity, atheism was no more admirable in the ancients than in the moderns.

My presumption is that Chaucer was a careful and gifted reader of poetry, and that the whole enterprise of the *Troilus* rested upon a complicated perception of his own relationship with the classical poetic tradition. If we seek to know what dull Dominicans made of the classical tradition, we may indeed read Trevet with profit; but if we seek to know what brilliant poets made of it, we are safer with Dante, Petrarch, and Geoffrey Chaucer.

Chaucer cannot have missed the sense of genuine religiosity that often

18. Thus Vessey (*Statius*, 158n.) writes that "the idea is recognisably trite. . . . Statius' Capaneus is a warrior, not a philosopher."

attends Virgil's treatment of the Roman cult in the *Aeneid*. Like other readers after him, he would have no doubt noted and appreciated the quite different tone of the epic poets of the Silver Age, Lucan and Statius. They lack Virgil's archaic piety, but they are nonetheless deeply conservative thinkers for whom the traditional Roman religion has been clarified by the high thinking of Stoicism. Both poets have a complex but committed interest in divination.[19] The attitude expressed by Capaneus in the *Thebaid*—that of atheism or at least truculent agnosticism—is essentially an Epicurean one. As Snijder points out, Statius seems to have gone out of his way for thematic effect to develop Capaneus as an "Epicurean," even at the expense of anachronism.[20] The religious sense conveyed by the character Amphiaraus in the *Thebaid* is one of tragic piety, and there is something of this still in the Amphiaraus of Dante in the twentieth canto of the *Inferno*.[21]

Wetherbee has taught us to see that, for Chaucer, Dante's Statius is as important as Statius himself, and in this regard the tonal difference between Dante's presentation of Capaneus and that of Amphiaraus is eloquent. I find in Statius' Capaneus, amidst the rabid and grotesque disorder, a baroque titanism that commands a certain awe if nothing more. This faint tint of authorial admiration has been wholly bleached out of Dante's Capaneus, presented in his moral nakedness as a ranting blasphemer who merits one of the most explicitly censorious judgments uttered from the mouth of Virgil in all the *Inferno* (14.63–66). His lese majesty against Jove is a blasphemy against God (69–70).[22] Medieval Christian readers could indeed find within the pagan poets models of intellectual and spiritual probity, but Capaneus is far from being one of them. The antidote to the evils inherent in the pagan tragedy of divination—to use Hollander's phrase—is not mad, ranting blasphemy but the

19. See the discussion of Henri Le Bonniec, "Lucain et la religion," in *Lucain* (Geneva: Fondation Hardt, 1970), 189–90; on Statius see Vessey, *Statius*, 156.

20. Snijder, *Book III*, 250–51.

21. See the penetrating essay of Robert Hollander, "The Tragedy of Divination in *Inferno* XX," in his *Studies in Dante* (Ravenna: Longo, 1980), 131–218.

22. Dante's treatment of Capaneus chiefly reflects Statius' remarkable scene (*Thebaid* 10.907–39) in which Jove blasts him with a lightning bolt as he attempts to scale the wall of Thebes; but as Ugo Bosco points out (*Nuove letture dantesche* 2 [1966]: 59), Virgil's condemnation of his disdain for God responds to the atheism of his taunts to Amphiaraus in the third book—including the taunt "Primos in orbe deos fecit timor."

monotheistic confidence of the Stoic Cato at the oracle of Hammon (Lucan, *Pharsalia* 9.564–88).

Chaucer's thematic quotation from the third book of the *Thebaid*, one of hundreds of such quotations from the poets, does not of course posit an uncomplicated equation of Capaneus and Criseyde; but it makes it difficult to believe that Chaucer here presents Criseyde's actions and words as either admirable or wise, let alone that he is presenting them as the morally neutral and historically normative actions and words of a "fearful pagan."

Perhaps he is instead showing us the actions and words of a "lying pagan"? It surely is of some significance that Criseyde never for an instant entertains the possibility of telling the *truth* to her father, a man whose crime toward her is to have remorsefully repented of having abandoned her in Troy, a city whose certain destruction the Delphic oracle has truthfully foretold. In fact, Chaucer no more believed that "pagans are liars" than he believed that "pagans are cowards." We can safely leave that sort of generalization to the *Chanson de Roland*. The more interesting and unsurprising reality revealed by the great Latin poets whom he read and admired was that some pagans were liars and others were not, some cowards, some not. And between the poles of black and white there were even discernible shades of gray.

Most readers would surely regard as unconvincing the argument that Chaucer denied moral seriousness to his poem by positing a "pagan truth" or a "pagan courage" to which the concepts that his contemporaries called truth and courage were historically irrelevant. But what of *idolatry* in this context? Let us return to Minnis's question: are the standards of Holcot's indictment of idolatry appropriate to the pagan world of the *Troilus*? And "did Chaucer mean his audience to have such criteria in mind when listening to or reading his poem?" My answer to these questions must be "Yes, certainly." For Holcot's "criteria" for the moral analysis of idolatry are no different from those of the Wisdom of Solomon which he glossed. The biblical condemnation of idolatry does not make its appeal to the revelation of Hebrew religion but to the rational nature of human beings. All men and women have reason; reason indeed defines their humanity. Reason is not a theological "grace," nor is it a historical development that appeared on the scene sometime after the Trojan War.

It is a commonplace of Hellenistic ethics that idolatry is an insult to the natural religion of reasonable beings, since God has sufficiently revealed himself in Nature to be known as spirit rather than as a stick or stone. This is the burden of the famous passage (Wisd. of Sol. 13.1–9) that introduces the sapiential attack on idolatry, and the burden of the even more famous remarks on the subject by Paul (Rom. 1.18–32).[23] When Paul writes that idolators are "without excuse," it is precisely the excuse of historical accident that he precludes; for idolatry is naturally repugnant to all men who follow right reason. Indeed, the Pauline argument was common among the pagan philosophers themselves.[24] And like the sapiential author, Paul goes on to link idolatry with disordered sexuality.

When Wetherbee writes that Pandarus is "the artist and in a sense the god who oversees Troilus's innocently idolatrous pursuit of Criseyde," he invokes a concept, "innocent idolatry," which I believe quite simply could not have existed in Geoffrey Chaucer's intellectual universe.[25] To say that Chaucer was not primarily a theologian or a philosopher is not to say that he had no theological or philosophical ideas. He clearly had quite a few, and they are just as clearly the cultural commonplaces, by and large, appropriate to a man of his time, his education, and his particular social grouping. There seems to be abundant evidence within his poetry that he believed as a theological and scientific fact that human beings were endowed with reason.

It is quite true, and usefully emphasized by Minnis, that the censorial tone of theological criticism so apparent on the surface of a number of Chaucer's obvious "sources"—Minnis's "clerical group"—is almost wholly absent from the *Troilus*. In Guido the textual appearance of the Palladium brings with it an explicit polemic against pagan idolatry. That is the way Guido wrote, and that is exactly the way Chaucer, for artistic purposes refuses to write. This is an exciting fact about the nature of Chaucer's poem, but it tells us nothing about whether Chaucer did or did not believe that the worship of sticks and stones was reasonable human behavior.

If we find the theme of idolatry prominently present in his poem, we cannot safely regard that fact as morally irrelevant because Troilus is an "idolatrous pagan" or because he is a character in a "courtly romance"; nor is there any

23. See A. Feuillet, "La Connaissance de Dieu par les hommes d'après Rom. 1, 18–23," *Lumière et Vie* 14 (1954): 207–24.

24. K. H. Schelkle, *Paulus Lehrer der Väter: Die altkirchliche Auslegung von Römer 1–11* (Dusseldorf: Patmos, 1954), 54.

25. Wetherbee, *Chaucer and the Poets*, 75. Wetherbee here builds on the idea of John Fyler, "The Fabrications of Pandarus," *MLQ* 41 (1980), 115–30, that Pandarus in his role as liar imitates the creative activity of the divine Artificer.

reason to believe that Chaucer intends his readers to be less willing to recognize mental idolatry than, say, Pandarus (5.384–85). The issues raised in his poem include several—the human appetite for love, the nature of truth, and the freedom of the will, for example—that were at the very heart of the classical and the Christian philosophical enterprise alike. Far from isolating them from contemporary relevance in a fenced preserve of the historical imagination, he took a revolutionary literary initiative to guarantee their availability within a well-established context of Christian philosophical poetry.

We are forever talking about the oddness of the end of the *Troilus*, with its explicit intrusion of a censorious Christian voice silenced until nearly the last moment by the higher claims of objective scholarly fidelity to an "auctour." I wonder if perhaps we are not squandering our astonishment on the wrong poem. Surely it is less surprising that a fourteenth-century courtly poet should write as though he were a conventional Christian than that he should write as though he were an antique pagan of the early empire. For that is what Boccaccio did from beginning to end of the *Filostrato*.

Boccaccio's device allowed him to pursue the theme of idolatry quite openly as a radical part of his design; we may indeed be offended by his heavy-handedness in this regard. His narrator is not merely a pseudoantique worshiper of pagan gods but a cheerful blasphemer and sexual idolator, as he makes abundantly clear in his second stanza.

Tu, donna, se' la luce chiara e bella
per cui nel tenbroso mondo accorto
vivo, tu si' la tramontana stella
la quale io seguo per venire a porto;
ancora di salute tu si' quella
che se' tutto 'l mio bene e 'l mio conforto;
tu mi se' Giove, tu mi se' Apollo,
tu se' mia musa, io l'ho provato e sollo. (*Fil.* 1.2)

(Thou, lady, are the clear and beautiful light under whose guidance I live
in this world of shadows; thou are the lodestar which I follow to come to
port; anchor of safety, thou art she who art all my weal and all my
comfort; thou to me art Jove, thou to me art Apollo, thou art my muse; I
have proved it and know it.)

Though Boccaccio has a sharp enough conception of the pagan ethos of the *Filostrato*, he lacks Chaucer's interest, or perhaps skill, in creating a taut fictional world beyond the slovenliness of historical anachronisms. His lover/ narrator is at once an ancient pagan and the contemporary suitor of Maria d'Aquino. He can quote by name the Lamentations of Jeremiah in his introduction, and in the passage just cited he complicates his "ancient" idolatry with obvious echoes of a revered title of the Blessed Virgin, the *Stella maris*. There are many other such examples throughout the *Filostrato*. In all this he is closer to the authors of the *Roman de la Rose* than to the author of the *Troilus*. Guillaume had in effect dedicated his book to one who "tant est digne d'estre amee / qu'el doit estre Rose clamee" (is so worthy of being loved that she ought to be called Rose; *RR* 43–44), and as we shall see, Jean is happy enough to bring paternosters and crucifixes into the world of Venus and Adonis to underscore a moral dichotomy.

Boccaccio obviously had the *Roman de la Rose* rather vaguely in mind throughout the course of the *Filostrato*, and his mind returns more precisely to the French poem at cardinal moments in his own enterprise. Thus as he comes to the end of his poem, he rounds off its tragic action by closing the maritime metaphor with which he had begun: "Noi siam venuti al porto" (We have arrived at port). But the end of the journey is also the end of a pilgrimage, and the pilgrim-lover must give thanks to those who have guided him safely:

> Estimo dunque che l'ancore sieno
> qui da gittare, e far fine al cammino,
> e quelle grazie con effetto pieno
> che render dee il grato pellegrino,
> a chi guidati n'ha qui rendereno . . . (9.4)

> (Here then, I think, the anchors are to be cast and an end made of the voyage; and here with full warmth shall be offered those thanks that the grateful pilgrim must pay to him who has been our guide . . .)

This, as David Wallace has pointed out in a perceptive essay, is surely an echo of the end of the *Roman*, where pilgrim Amant thanks those—Cupid and Venus in particular—who have so successfully aided him.[26] Thus the gross sexual idolatry of the *Roman de la Rose*—in which the Lover worships at a genital reliquary—lies just beneath the surface of the text of the *Filostrato* as well. Chaucer was the translator of both works. He knew what was in them, and what the one owed to the other. One of his most crucial artistic decisions

26. Wallace, "Chaucer and Boccaccio's Early Writings," 141–62.

as he framed the *Troilus* was that Boccaccio's story had too little Jean de Meun in it, and one of his greatest artistic triumphs was the manner in which he redressed the balance.

The transformations wrought by Chaucer on his primary sources for the story of Troilus and Criseyde were many and varied; but in my opinion the principal originality of his poem entirely unanticipated by his predecessors is its formal philosophical seriousness commanded by the extensive and often explicit presence of Boethian language and themes. So far as Chaucer's literary strategy was concerned, the *Consolation of Philosophy* was the absolutely indispensable catalytic agent that could make the subject of Ovidian eroticism both philosophically and morally weighty.

Here was the Christian criticism of the false goods of "love," a criticism powerfully advanced not from the cultural perspective of biblical theology but in the commonplace terms of the most venerable traditions of pagan moral philosophy, a book so apparently pagan in its assumptions and procedures that several distinguished scholars have denied that its author could possibly have been a Christian. Chaucer had no such doubts, of course; but in inviting his readers to make moral adjudications within the world of the *Troilus*, his implicit appeal is not in the first instance to the Pentateuch or to Pennyfort but to Socrates and to Cicero. Thus he needs must inscribe within his own book the book of Boethius, and this he does with panache as well as with reverence.

If I try to answer the question famously implied by C. S. Lewis—"What did Chaucer really do to *Il Filostrato?*"—I find that I cannot agree with its poser that what he chiefly did was to correct certain errors that Boccaccio had committed against the code of courtly love. I reckon that what he chiefly did was to complicate the eroticism of Boccaccio's ancient pagan story by superimposing upon it the structure, the principal philosophical themes, the verbal iconography, and several hundred lines translated from the greatest Christian fiction of the patristic period, the *Consolation of Philosophy* of Boethius. Thus before I can be persuaded by those critics who find it inappropriate to apply Christian "answers" to the moral issues raised by Chaucer's text, I must know why the author went to such unlikely lengths to make his text ask distinctively Christian questions.

Only slightly less important than an appreciation of Chaucer's Boethian strategy is an appreciation of his vernacular model for it: the *Roman de la Rose* of Jean de Meun. Jean was the pioneer whose invention, as obvious and even as crude as it must now seem when compared with Chaucer's refinement of it, alone offered the English poet an accessible path to his desired end: a fiction responsive both to the demands of the historical imagination and to the impulses of the socially responsible moralist, a fiction that could transform the problem of the disjunctions of ancient and modern, pagan and Christian, into a central poetic theme.

Jean had inherited, in the poem of Guillaume de Lorris, a major if incomplete monument of thirteenth-century Ovidiana, a work in which the author did his best to maintain the façade of an allegorical world secular and erotic to its core, in which the only social concerns were those supplied by Ovidian decorum or stratagem (such as the way lovers should behave) and the only history was Ovidian history (such as the story of Narcissus). Guillaume's thirteenth-century Christian culture is, of course, the very backdrop against which his Ovidian miming was played out, but throughout his poem it maintains the courteous unobtrusiveness of the obvious.

Things are very different with Jean de Meun, for among the many differences between the two parts of the *Roman*, Jean's vast increment of ambition is conspicuous. What has usually been taken by scholars to be his critique of Guillaume de Lorris is more accurately described, in my view, as his critique of Ovid, or rather of one voice of Ovid, the deadpan pedagogue of the *Ars amatoria*, the book that Guillaume had explicitly identified as the model for his own enterprise. Jean's first and most powerful move is to subject this "Ovid" to the scrutiny of Boethius, which is the effect of the long dialogue between Reason and the Lover with which his continuation of the poem begins. He thus examined sexual love from the perspective of a Boethian analysis, treating love as one of the goods of Fortune.

The literary possibility thus exploited was already explicit in the *Consolatio* itself, in the second prose of the third book, and it had found embryonic development in the Latin school-poetry of the twelfth century. From the introductory portrait of Reason in the *Roman de la Rose*, a portrait that conflates scriptural Wisdom with Boethian Philosophy, we may licitly deduce that Guillaume de Lorris himself was entirely aware of it, as Chrétien, among others of his vernacular forebears, had been before him. But to Jean de Meun must go the credit, or perhaps the blame, of being the impressario who arranged the pugilistic contest between Love and Reason that was to be the main event in a good deal of European erotic poetry until the time of Shakespeare's sonnets and beyond.

For Jean as for his readers, Boethius was a Christian theologian of nearly unimpeachable authority, the most happily literary of the Fathers of the Church, even if he had chosen to write his *Consolatio* not as a dogmatic theologian but as a "philosopher," a lover of wisdom. Jean could thus internalize within his poem the Christian corrective to Ovidian erotic doctrine, and he did so in a manner decorously appropriate for a poem ruled over by the Ovidian deities, Venus and Cupid. Boethius had written a book in which the moral theology of the Christians was submerged in the wisdom of the antique philosophers, a book that made obligatory claims not merely on the baptized but on all people endowed with reason. Jean transposed its claims to the Ovidian never-never land of Guillaume's dreamscape. Amant, vassal to Cupid and votary to Venus, is nowhere held accountable for his ignorance of the book of Leviticus or the Epistle to the Galatians; but he is repeatedly and schematically lampooned for his unwillingness to accept the literary lessons of Lady Reason, a guide as highly esteemed by the pagan world of Socrates or Cicero as by the Christian world of Thomas Aquinas.

Chaucer grasped that Jean's winning strategy could work for him as well, and he set out to correct the Ovidianism of the narrative voice of the *Filostrato* in precisely the fashion that Jean had set out to correct Guillaume's Ovidianism. Thus following in Jean's footsteps, Chaucer "translated" the *Consolation of Philosophy* twice, once straight, once decidedly crooked. It is no coincidence that when we see Chaucer playfully or self-consciously thinking about his career we see him linking the *Troilus* with the *Consolation* on the one hand and with the *Roman* on the other.

I believe that there is in the text of the *Troilus* significant evidence both of Chaucer's appreciation of the power of the *Consolatio* to transform the moral basis of an erotic fiction and of his appreciation of the particular achievement of Jean de Meun in the *Roman de la Rose*, for he has taken one crucial episode from the *Filostrato* and rewritten it twice, first as the *Consolatio* and then as the *Roman*.[27]

One of the commonplaces of Chaucerian criticism is that there is a certain likeness between the narrator of the *Troilus* and Pandarus; but the fact that the relationship has been so often noted makes it no less important or suggestive. Both are self-confessed erotic failures, yet both are called upon—admittedly in

27. I have published part of this argument in an essay entitled "Smoky Reyn: From Jean de Meun to Geoffrey Chaucer," in *Chaucer and the Craft of Fiction*, ed. Leigh Arrathoon (Rochester, Mich.: Solaris, 1986), 1–21.

different ways—to order the same love affair. Both men have bookish natures, and each displays a tendency instinctively to dispose the ostensibly historical materials with which he deals into the discernible categories of classic literary fictions. Both, that is, are born storytellers, and what might be called their fictional tastes for actual fictions points to a factual truth about Geoffrey Chaucer's literary education. I shall try to demonstrate the implications of their kinship in an examination of a twice-told tale, the single fiction within the poem that links the narrator and Pandarus in explicit competition.

Troilus has fallen in love, if we may stretch that phrase somewhat beyond the breaking point, but his love is secret, known to Troilus alone, and of course to Cupid, who knows of it only too well. The first energetic deception of the poem—a poem in which untruth in all its forms from the verbal quibble to the bald-faced lie commands the discourse—is the dissimulation involved in keeping Troilus' love from the world at large (1.279–80, 320–22, 351–57). The resulting erotic impasse is hardly more satisfactory for the reader than it is for Troilus himself, for neither the affair nor the fiction is likely to advance unless, at the very least, Criseyde finds out that Troilus loves her. The revelation of Troilus' love, accordingly, is a moment of cardinal drama within the poem, though the revelation comes in the first instance not to Criseyde, but to her uncle Pandarus.

The *Filostrato* of Boccaccio, which fully honors the theme of occult love, handles this revelation in what we may regard as a slightly brusque way. Young Pandaro strolls into Troilo's bedroom, finds him in the dumps, discovers the cause of his distress without elaborate divagation, and in fairly short order sets out to begin suborning Criseida. The scene is characterized by much of the shallow and maladroit ellipticism of the Italian popular verse romance, and there is little serious attempt to create a convincing psychological flavor for the scene.

The narrator of the *Troilus*, translator of Lollius, honors the immutable facts of the plot but greatly improves them in the retelling. In the first place, he dilates the narrative, more than doubling the number of lines between the opening of the scene and the articulation of the fatal name "Criseyde." And though the reader would be hard pressed to explain this delay more adequately in terms of Troilus' diffidence than of Pandarus' sententious loquaciousness, one nevertheless has the sense of a man seriously trying to keep a secret and revealing it only under a credible duress of inner anguish and outer coaxing. The second and more remarkable fact about the narrator's retelling of the story is its forced submission to an easily identifiable (not to say ostentatiously coercive) anterior text, the *Consolation of Philosophy* of Boethius. The narrator casts Troilus as "Boethius" and Pandarus as Lady Philosophy, thereby introducing in a single brilliant stroke levels of sophisticated comedy and of high philosophical seriousness of which the *Filostrato* is entirely innocent.

Two passages in particular (1.729–53, 841–49) so establish the *Consolatio* as an inescapable complication in the text of the *Troilus* that they demand a special attention. The first identifies the pathological nature of Troilus' situation by the presence of the privileged medical term *litargie,* and the second introduces the specifically Boethian notion of Fortune so central alike to the military history of the Trojan War and the amatory adventures of the Trojan prince Troilus. The narrator's handling of Troilus' first confession to Pandarus of his love for Criseyde quite clearly signals his intention of examining his erotic fiction in the light of the philosophical fiction of Boethius. And whether we think of the two texts as being wired in parallel or in series, so to speak, it is their conjunction that is Chaucer's essential novelty in the treatment of the history of Troilus. But the idea of subjecting an extended erotic adventure to an intermittent Boethian critique was of course not original with him. As we have seen, it was the happy initiative of Jean de Meun in the *Roman de la Rose*.

The twice-told tale of Troilus' erotic confession makes its second appearance in book 2, and this time the teller is not our narrator, but Pandarus. Pandarus has made good progress. He has found Criseyde and found her to a degree pliable; he has interested her in Troilus through a combination of lying, bullying, and coaxing. In a passage that marks a crucial transition from a plausibly apprehensive defensiveness to a subliminally flirtatious availability, Criseyde asks her uncle to tell her how he first learned that Troilus had fallen in love with her.

> "O good em," quod she tho,
> "For his love which that us bothe made,
> Tel me how first ye wisten of his wo;
> Woot noon of it but ye?" He seyde "no."
> "Kan he wel speke of love," quod she "I preye
> Tel me, for I the bet me shal purveye." (2.499–504)

Pandarus, though he "a litel gan to smyle," is solemn enough in his reply. He prefaces his fantastic cock-and-bull story with the oath "By my trouthe," a concept that he nearly always invokes when he is lying. Those of us who have heard the narrator's version of the interview in Troilus' bedroom will hardly be prepared for Pandarus' account of the same event.

The story he tells Criseyde is this. Pandarus and Troilus passed several hours together next to a well in a garden. Tired by calisthenics and javelin practice, Troilus announced his intention of sleeping on the grass while Pandarus took a walk. But when Troilus began groaning, Pandarus sneaked behind him and heard an elaborate act of contrition to the god of Love, including the information that he had been erotically wounded by a woman in a black dress. Pretending that he had heard nothing, Pandarus called Troilus to wake up, and Troilus, likewise pretending, tried to mask his erotic depression with a cheerful façade. Only at this point, and then very briefly and in a manner entirely inconsistent with what we have heard before, does Pandarus mention the bedroom scene.

Though Pandarus proves himself a cheerfully gratuitous liar time and again in the poem, we can, with regard to this elaborate fabrication, credit him with plausible motivations or at least extenuations in the psychology and the sociology of the literary moment. Criseyde's question concerning Troilus—"Kan he wel speke of love?"—may have drawn to Pandarus' attention the embarrassing fact that except when he is paraphrasing the *Rime sparse* of Petrarch, Troilus speaks not all that well and that, indeed, he could use a ghost-writer. We note further that Criseyde's question echoes one asked by Pandarus at the very beginning of their interview when he discovered her with her friends listening to "a mayden reden hem the geste / Of the sege of Thebes." Of this book Pandarus says:

> "For goddes love, what seith it? Tel it us;
> Is it of love?" (2.96–97)

To this question "Is it of love?" Criseyde gives no explicit answer, though the matter of Thebes is hardly auspicious for Pandarus' embassy. In their brief exchange about the book the two act out their decorous gender roles as literary critics. "This romaunce is of Thebes that we rede" says Criseyde, signaling with the word *romaunce* her immersion in a vernacular world of the mother tongue. "Herof ben there maked bookes twelve," counters Pandarus, just as clearly signaling the Latinity of Statius and the masculine world of clerks and poets. As he comes to frame a story of his own, Pandarus may fairly suspect his neice of the well-attested female weakness for softheaded romantic fiction.

She is, after all, just a bit like Emma Bovary; and the story he tells her is, after all, just as true as is the book of Lancelot de Lake.

The two "texts," the narrator's and Pandarus,' are radically different but also firmly bound together, lexically sutured along thematic seams of waking and sleeping and of Troilus' dullness. In the first book Pandarus cries out

> "Awake," ful wonderlich and sharpe,
> "What? slombrestow as in a litargie?
> Or artow lik an asse to the harpe,
> That hereth sown whan men the strenges plye;
> But in his mynde of that no melodie
> May sinken, hym to gladen, for that he
> So dul is of his bestialite?" (1.729–35)

That is the Boethian text. In the romance text of book 2 this becomes

> "Awake! ye slepen al to longe;
> It semeth nat that love doth yow longe,
> That slepen so that no man may yow wake.
> Who sey evere or this so dul a man?" (2.545–48)

Boethian dullness, a manifestation of pathological *litargie,* is an emblem of a wounded human nature reduced by unreason (cf. 1.764) to bestiality. In the romance world as whimsically painted by Pandarus, the chief "meaning" of lethargic stupor is exemption from love, not immersion in it. That Troilus cannot "wake up" is taken disingenuously by Pandarus to mean he is not in love. I say disingenuously, of course, because at this point Pandarus has already eavesdropped on Troilus' alleged confession to Cupid. The intentional status of Troilus' erotic contrition, incidentally, is wonderfully unclear, confused as it is by the studied ambiguities of sleeping and waking. As part of an outrageous lie told by an outrageous liar, the story of Troilus' submission to Cupid can make no claim on us as fact; but as fiction it is powerfully intriguing.

The question is whether Troilus is ever actually asleep and, hence, whether the erotic mea culpa is a projected dream vision or the insomniac mutterings of a man whom Love will not grant sleep. The evidence is ambiguous. Troilus lies down to sleep on the grass, and the "mode of discourse" in his address to Cupid is at least arguably somnambulistic; that "he smot his head adown anon, and gan to motre" does not much aid this tentative interpretation, but it does not entirely undermine it. On the other hand, the obvious phoniness of Pandarus' attempt to wake Troilus seems clearly to show that he was never asleep in the first place.

Now the canonical poem in the romance tradition that makes the most of the themes of sleeping and waking, to which Chaucer manifestly turned when he wished to explore these themes in depth in the "Book of the Duchess," is of course the *Roman de la Rose*. The *Roman* begins with an explicit citation of Macrobius, who provided the Middle Ages with its vocabulary of somnology and who had defined the erotic dream as a nightmare, a fiction that occupies the dreamer's sleeping hours only because it first occupied his waking hours. Whether the narrator of the *Roman de la Rose* is more "awake" in the narration of his dream than in the actual dreaming of it is, or should be, an open question for us as it was for Petrarch:

Somniat iste tamen, dum somnia uisa renarrat
Sopitoque nihil vigilans distare videtur.[28]

(This one [Amant] dreams; and when he retells his dream, one can see no difference between sleeping and waking.)

We are hardly likely to miss the specific literary connections of the romance world economically conjured up by Pandarus the poet. The setting is a garden with a well, and it is the habitat of the god of Love. The most famous such garden by far is that of the *Roman de la Rose*, and Pandarus thickens his allusiveness to that poem with a number of specific elements—"leaping," dart throwing, silent stalking, and sleeping on the grass—taken from Guillaume de Lorris and redistributed for his own fictive purpose.

For a moment, as the silent stalker of an unwary lover, Pandarus casts himself in the role of Cupid—thus honoring Chaucer's own more complex transformation by which Pandarus' doctrines echo at different times nearly all of Love's preceptors from the *Roman de la Rose*, including Cupid, Lady Reason, Friend, La Vieille, Nature, and Genius. But in the main set piece of his miniromance, "L'Homage de l'Amant devant Amours," he is rather a witness (not to say a voyeur) than a principal actor, even as he will be a voyeur of a distinctly literary kind in the boudoir scene of the third book:

28. These lines are a summary judgment on the *Roman* in Petrarch's letter to Guido Gonzaga of Mantua, *Opera* (Basel, 1554), 3:1371.

And with that word he drow hym to the feere,
And took a light, and fond his contenaunce
As for to looke upon an old romaunce.
                    (3.978–80)

The reader can be pretty sure about what "old romaunce" Pandarus pretends to be reading, or rather rereading. One can also suspect—I say no more than suspect—that Pandarus is telling Criseyde somewhat more than he is aware of when he says near the beginning of his tale: "And I afer gan romen to and fro," a line in which a possible pun (*romen/roman*) suggests to me something of that fruitful confusion between aimless or ambagious wandering and aimless fiction lurking so happily in the Latin word *error*.[29]

JEAN DE MEUN AND MORAL ALLEGORY

Chaucer's vast debt to the *Roman de la Rose* of Jean de Meun remains one of the unexplored and inviting horizons of "Chaucer studies." How does Jean's art enrich his English disciple's poetic treatment of the theme of idolatry? My claim so far is that Chaucer's attitude toward pagan antiquity, far from being that of objective and "value-free" anthropological description, is fully committed to the Christian moral consensus concerning the cursed rites of the pagans shared by such clerical historians of the matter of Troy as Guido delle Colonne and Joseph of Exeter. Except in one famous passage (*TC* 5.1849–55) he is much less *moralistic* than they, but this is a different matter, one of artistic strategy.

Here Chaucer follows a clerical authority of a very different sort—that of the historical satire of Jean de Meun. It is my opinion that what Chaucer found most useful in the *Roman de la Rose*, so far as his plan for the *Troilus* was concerned, was Jean's anthology of devices for harnessing the energies of numerous earlier writers, Boethius conspicuous among them, to the purposes of his moral allegory; but even before I can put terminal punctuation to my opinion I once again run afoul of the authority of Alastair Minnis, who is of the opinion that Chaucer is not much interested in that sort of thing.

29. On the implications of the Augustinian play on *error,* see Bortolo Martinelli, *Petrarca e il Ventoso* (Bergamo: Minerva Italica, 1977), 278–79.

Indeed he goes so far as to say that "moral allegory held no attraction for him, save as an object of humour and irony."[30] The context of this remark is a broad-brushed survey of exegetical ideas in the late Middle Ages in which he expresses surprise at "the surprising tenacity" of the "oft-refuted" ideas of D. W. Robertson, which he counters with an affirmation of the primacy of various kinds of literalism and the infirmity of various kinds of allegory among the scriptural exegetes, the secular scholars, and the poets who most clearly define the progressive tendencies of Chaucer's intellectual world.

Were I persuaded that it really is the case that moral allegory was of little relevance to the late fourteenth-century literary climate, the decent thing to do would be to find another topic, or perhaps another profession, from the one I currently pursue. I am not so persuaded, but I again defer the invitation to any broadly based theoretical dispute about the issue. My ambitions are strictly limited: I seek to construct the foundation for an examination of the theme of sexual idolatry in the poem by an empirical examination of specific texts. Minnis invites us to see Chaucer's essential literalism in the poets and classical scholars from whom he learned. "These attitudes of Chaucer's may emerge very clearly," he writes, "if they are considered in relation to the similar views held by two writers who influenced him considerably, Jean de Meun and Nicholas Trevet." Let me begin with Jean de Meun and his probable attitude to the traditional moral exegesis of classical fable. According to Minnis, Jean's "own attitude was unflinchingly literal, and on occasion we may even detect him regarding the procedure of moralization with amusement."[31] The particular passage in which we are invited to observe Jean's unflinching literalism and his possible amusement at the moral interpretation of classical fable comes at the very end of the *Roman de la Rose* in the veiled description of sexual intercourse that concludes the Lover's quest.

Paraphrasing and condensing somewhat, I find that the Lover says roughly this: "I kissed the statue. Then I tried to ram my pilgrim's staff into the aperture in the wall between the pillars. I worked very hard to get by an obstruction blocking the path—rather as Hercules worked hard to get past the stone blocking the way to Cacus' cave. When I got in, I shook the rose." Now in order to believe that this is an unflinchingly literal description of sexual coition one would have to hold, I suggest, rather peculiar notions about the nature of

30. Minnis, *Chaucer and Pagan Antiquity*, 16.
31. Ibid.

language or even more peculiar notions about the mechanics of sexual intercourse. But that is not Minnis's point. The point is that "like Chaucer after him, Jean eliminated the 'wonder-element' of the story of Hercules, ignored any possible allegory which could be derived from it, and related its incidents in an earthy way." Minnis contrasts the treatment of the story of Hercules and Cacus as he finds it in the Boethius commentary of William of Conches, where it "formed part of an elaborate allegory about the moral progress of the wise man."[32]

I want to suggest a fundamentally different approach. Let us recognize that Jean de Meun is writing a *poem,* not a philosophical commentary, and that his techniques and strategies are in the first instance more likely to be illuminated by the practice of poets than by that of scholiasts. To begin with, Jean de Meun and his narrator (the Lover) are two very different people. That the Lover is at times (though not at this time) unflinchingly literal is certain. This is the principal point of his truculent ignorance of poetic integuments:

> Mes des poetes les sentances,
> les fables et les methaphores
> ne bé je pas a gloser ores. (*RR* 7160–62)

> (But as for the sentences, fables, and metaphors of the poets, I do not now hope to gloss them.)

As all major commentators of this passage agree, the words *sentances* and *methaphores* refer to what Reason has called the *integumenz*—which in turn is defined in Félix Lecoy's glossary as "interpretation allégorique des poètes." Hence, no less apparent to me than the fact of his attitude of unflinching literalism is its poetic meaning. The Lover's attitude, which is jovially stupid in its context, stands in stark opposition to the literary attitudes of Reason. Common sense alone would suggest that the authorial Jean de Meun, a poet, is more likely to mock than to embrace it; but of course there is considerable contextual evidence to demonstrate the same truth.

When we examine the Lover's invocation of the story of Hercules and Cacus in its context, we find he says this:

> Se bohourder m'i veïssiez,
> por quoi bien garde i preïssiez,

32. Ibid., 16–17.

d'Herculés vos peüst mambrer
quant il voust Cacus desmambrer:
.iii. foiz a sa porte asailli,
.iii. foiz hurta, .iii. foiz failli,
.iii foiz s'asist en la valee,
tous las, por ravoir s'alenee,
tant ot soffert peine et travaill.
(21589–97)

(If you had seen me jousting—and you would have had to take good care
of yourself—you would have been reminded of Hercules when he wanted
to dismember Cacus. He battered at his door three times, three times he
hurled himself, three times fell back. His struggle and labor were so great
that he had to sit down three times in the valley, completely spent, to
regain his breath.)

I find nothing notably "earthy" in Jean's mode of narration here, any more than
in the Virgilian text he certainly had before him as he wrote.

Ter totum fervidus ira
lustrat Auentini montem, ter saxea temptat
limina nequiquam, ter fessus ualle resedit.
(*Aeneid* 8.230–32)

(In a boiling rage he circled the Aventine Mount three times. Three times
he tried the stone-blocked entrance way, but in vain. Three times down in
the valley he sank back in weariness.)

There is a fine metaphysical—or, perhaps, Pythagorean—wit in the Virgilian
passage that describes Hercules' triplex assault with three uses of the adverb
ter in three lines. Jean acknowledges his appreciation of Virgil's wit even as the
Lover, with an excess decorous to his poetic character, adds a fourth "trois
fois," thus violating the text even as he violates the woman.

That we here discover Jean de Meun regarding the procedure of moralization with amusement strikes me as most unlikely, except insofar as the Lover's
mock heroics amusingly deflate his pretentions. Jean depends upon his reader
—at least any reader learned enough to be worried about whether Jean is
or is not moralizing classical fable in the first place—to recognize and apply
the Virgilian context. Aeneas has arrived in Latium, where he finds his way

challenged by Turnus. At an appropriate narrative point Virgil describes how Aeneas assisted at the festival established by the grateful Arcadians in honor of Hercules' triumph over Cacus, a three-headed, fire-breathing monster who had ravished their countryside. It is nearly impossible to read the eighth book of the *Aeneid* without seeing in it the "procedure of moralization": there is an obvious thematic and moral parallel between the heroes Hercules and Aeneas, both of whom arrive from foreign parts to cleanse Italy of malign forces.

Many critics have sought to discover more or less specific allegories, the most obvious and tropological of which depend upon the observation that "Cacus" is a Latin form of the Greek word meaning "evil." This etymological observation was not the inspiration of the twelfth century; it came from the ancient schools, as of course did the long tradition of the "moralized" Hercules, of which the philosopher Seneca was a powerful advocate.[33] It did not require the academician William of Conches to "allegorize" Boethius' treatment of Hercules in *CP* 4m7; it should be obvious to any reader that Boethius had already "allegorized" the hero himself.[34] For Boethius, Hercules is indeed the just mythological analogue for the *vir sapiens* which Lady Philosophy would have "Boethius" become in 4p7—the man, that is, who is not a cat's-paw to Fortune. (This meter, incidentally, is noisy with echoes of Seneca's *Agamemnon*.)[35]

Are we really to believe that Jean de Meun chuckled with secular amusement over the folios of William of Conches that dealt with *Hercules sapiens*? In that case, one presumes, he absolutely howled with laughter at the tragedies of Seneca. I must say I doubt that he did either. Whether he agreed with Seneca that Hercules was a moral philosopher of the caliber of Cato (*Dialogues* 2.21.1)

33. On "Cacus," see, e.g., Gerhard Binder, *Aeneas und Augustus: Interpretationen zum 8. Buch der Aeneis* (Meisenheim: A. Hain, 1971), 141–47. "Novimus autem malum a Graecis kakon dici"; Servius 2:227. Servius' gloss, incidentally, is both "demythologizing" and "allegorizing" at once. Salutati quotes it at length in *De laboribus Herculis*, ed. B. L. Ulmann (Turin: Thesaurus Mundi, n.d.), 335–43. This book, usually regarded as one of the great works of classical scholarship of the Italian Renaissance, would be rendered old-fashioned and retrograde by the phantom demise of moral allegory and "fable moralization" in the late Middle Ages.
34. See Joachim Gruber, *Kommentar zu Boethius de Consolatione Philosophiae* (Berlin: de Gruyter, 1978), 372–74.
35. See Seneca, *Agamemnon*, 324n., where, however, the relationship seems to me to be too cautiously suggested.

I cannot say, but he certainly presents Seneca himself as a philosopher of the caliber of Socrates, a *preudhom* untouched by the treachery of Fortune (*RR* 6145–55).

I am far from believing that Jean wants an amused attitude as he writes this passage or that he would deprive the reader of amusement in its perusal; but I conclude that the objects of amusement are not the procedures of allegorical moralization but the Lover's sexual and rhetorical grotesqueries. Once again the critic is aided by poetic context. Jean's introduction of the myth of Hercules and Cacus at the end of his poem is in fact a thematic reprise. The story is first introduced midway through the formal psychomachia that is the poem's military centerpiece and which prepares the definitive rout of the forces of Chastity. Braggadocio Seurtez takes on Paor in single combat and derides her for her cowardice:

> Avec Chacus vos anfoïstes,
> quant Herculés venir veïstes
> le cours, a son col sa maçue;
> vos fustes lors toute esperdue
> et li meïstes es piez eles,—
> qu'il n'avoit onques eu teles
> por ce que Chacus ot emblez
> ses beus et les ot assemblez
> an son receit, qui mout fu lons,
> par les queues a reculons,
> que la trace n'an fust trovee.
>   (15543–53)

(You fled with Cacus when you saw Hercules come running, with his club at his neck. You were quite completely distracted then, and you put wings on his heels, wings such as he had never had before. Cacus had stolen Hercules's cattle and brought them together into his cave, a very deep one, by leading them backward by the tail, so that no trace of them was found.)

This part of the story prepares and complements its fugal reprise at the end, but even so it anticipates its audience's independent awareness of the Virgilian text. (If we do not realize that Cacus' "door" is in fact a huge boulder we shall not fully appreciate the Lover's sexual stamina in breaking through a maidenhead.)³⁶ Of the several amusing aspects of Jean's text, one of the most delightful is that Fear is not the least bit fearful in taking on the forces of lubricity, which she does so effectively that Cupid fears he is about to lose the whole campaign. In this situation Jean de Meun orchestrates an elaborate mythographic joke. Cupid treacherously arranges a truce to give him time to send off for his Doomsday Weapon, Venus Cytherea.

It is on Mount Cytheron that Cupid's messenger discovers Venus, who has just returned from a tumble in the hay with Adonis down below. (I think that this approximates Jean's tone: "Li un se geue a l'autre et deduit.") Jean prepares the meeting with a summary precis of the story of Venus and Adonis from the *Metamorphoses* of Ovid, followed by a brief but memorable *moralization* of the same from the Lover. The story, briefly, is this. Young Adonis loved to hunt. Venus loved young Adonis and feared lest a hunting accident do him a damage and hence deprive her of her own sexual pleasure. She therefore instructed him never to hunt *audaces* (bold animals that defend themselves against the hunter) but only timorous *fugaces* (Robertson's "little, furry creatures"). Adonis ignored his lover's warnings, however, and he was killed in the chase by a ferocious boar.

Now is is true that the critical tradition of the Middle Ages and the Renaissance is unanimous in attributing to Adonis a moral heroism in his preference for the "hard hunt" over the "soft hunt." Once again, however, such "moralization" is clearly enough continuous with ancient tradition as we find it for example in the amusing verse epistle of Ausonius called the "Cupido crucifixus." Jean's own Lover is far from regarding the story "simply as a story," and he offers the following moralization of it:

> Biau seigneur, que qu'il vos aviegne,
> de cest example vos souviegne.
> Vos qui ne creez voz amies,
> sachiez mout fetes granz folies;
> bien les deüssiez toute croire,
> car leur diz sunt voirs conme estoire.
> S'el jurent: "Toutes somes vostres,"

36. Individual lines once again show that Jean has the Virgilian text specifically in mind: "fugit ilicet ocior Euro / speluncam petit, pedibus timor addit alas." Cf. "et li meistes es piez eles."

creez les conme paternostres;
ja d'aus croise ne recreez.
Se Reson vient, point n'an creez;
s'el vos aportoit croicefis,
n'an creez point ne quel je fis.
Se cist s'amie eüst creüe,
mout eust sa vie creue.
                    (15721–34)

(Fair lords, whatever happens to you, remember this example. You who do
not believe your sweethearts, know that you commit great folly; you
should believe them all, for their sayings are as true as history. If they
swear "We are all yours," believe what they say as if it were the *paternoster*.
Never go back on your belief in them. If Reason comes, do not believe her
at all. Even if she brought a crucifix, believe her not one bit more than I
do. If Adonis had believed his sweetheart, his life would have grown much
longer.)

That we have here unflinching literalism I take to be obvious; that it is Jean
de Meun's I utterly deny. This passage, too, is a thematic reprise, and in it the
Lover plays out his deadpan and doltish role of one who explicitly despises
the *sentances,* the *fables,* and the *methaphores* of the poets. In proposing as the
moral of the story of Venus and Adonis that the whole duty of man is the absolute credence of woman (except for the woman Dame Reason, *bien entendu*),
the Lover echoes, thematically and verbally, his earlier and equally preposterous opinion (in Guillaume's part of the poem) that the moral of the story of
Narcissus is that the whole duty of woman is sexual generosity to man:

Dames, cest essample aprenez,
qui vers vos amis mesprenez;
car se vos les lessiez morir,
Dex le vos savra bien merir.
                    (1505–8)

(You ladies who neglect your duties toward your sweethearts, be
instructed by this exemplum, for if you let them die, God will know how
to repay you well for your fault.)

Thus where Minnis finds in the *Roman de la Rose* an amused rejection of
"the procedure of moralization," I find artistic manipulations made possible by

the stability of the traditional exegetical associations of Virgilian and Ovidian myth. My view must be that, far from following Jean de Meun into alleged attitudes of literalism, Chaucer followed him into a number of the more sophisticated techniques of Gothic allegory. What we often detect in Jean de Meun and in Chaucer is a certain surface inappropriateness or incongruity of what we too simply call "classical allusion." The adjective that best describes the phenomenon is, I think, "Ovidian." The great secular writers of the vernacular Middle Ages learned so much from Ovid's grandeur and his high style that we may neglect the fact that they learned also from him much of their impishness. When Jean de Meun reports the labored progress of his Lover's penis in the language of Virgilian epic—

.iii. foiz a sa portes assaili,
.iii. foiz hurta, .iii. foiz failli,
.iii foiz s'asist en la valee

—he exercises his taste for robust and baroque parody, not an unflinching literalism. One distinguished classicist has written thus of Ovidian parody: "Parody is of two kinds: in one the writer derides the thing parodied, in the other himself or his theme. Parody of the second kind delights by its incongruity: when Ovid writes hoc opus, hic labor est, primo sine munere iuni (*Ars amatoria* 1, 453) he is mocking not so much Virgil (*Aeneid* 6, 129) as his own pretentions."[37] Thus also does Jean de Meun deride "himself" (that is, his first-person narrator) and his theme—the pursuit of sexual gratification as an idolatrous religion.

NICHOLAS TREVET AND THE ENERGIES OF ART

Jean de Meun is indeed a major influence upon Chaucer's poetic conception of the *Troilus*. He did not teach him how to avoid moral allegory, of course, but how to pursue it cleverly. In the specific terms of the inquiry of this chapter he offered Chaucer one model of a "humanistic," poetic attitude toward sexual idolatry. Nicholas Trevet is someone and something else. That Trevet should be mentioned in the same breath with Jean de Meun as

37. E. J. Kenney, "Nequitiae Poetae," in *Ovidiana*, ed. N. I. Herescu (Paris: Belles Lettres, 1958), 201.

an influence on Chaucer strikes me as curious, for Trevet's scholarly intentions, techniques, and enterprises are fundamentally different from the poetic intentions, techniques, and enterprises of Jean de Meun and Geoffrey Chaucer.

Trevet was a kind of cultural entrepreneur in precious raw materials, Jean de Meun and Chaucer lapidary artists or jewelers, diamond cutters as opposed to diamond miners. Even so, I find little more in Trevet's intellectual and literary attitudes than I do in Jean de Meun's to support Minnis's argument. Minnis has done pioneering work with him and many other neglected Latin writers who have much to teach us about late medieval literary culture, and all medievalists are in his debt, a debt I happily acknowledge even in maintaining my distance from some of his conclusions. Since Trevet has been explicitly invoked as an index of Chaucer's mental habits, the issues involved become, of course, strictly relevant to our understanding of the *Troilus*.

Trevet's best-known work, indeed his only well-known work, is his still unpublished commentary on the *Consolation of Philosophy* of Boethius, and it is this work that Minnis draws into his discussion of *Troilus* and the "Knight's Tale." He compares Trevet's academic agenda with that of his predecessor William of Conches. "William of Conches gives the impression of having been interested in pagan mythology in so far as he could moralize it. By contrast, Nicholas Trevet . . . was more concerned with explanations which were literal and historical." With this eminently just statement of the case it would be rash to disagree. One can even agree that for Trevet "moralization has receded before narration."[38] But why agree with the non sequitur that the phenomenon thus identified is evidence of a general disappearance of an interest in or practice of moral allegory by late medieval *poets*?

The unwavering dullness of Nicholas Trevet would be difficult to convey to anyone who has not experienced firsthand the aridity of his plodding pages. Trevet's great student and editor, Ezio Franceschini, perhaps understates the matter when he describes Trevet's scholarly achievement as one of "imperturbable monotony."[39] That is what Trevet's *friends* say about him. That such a writer should be taken to exemplify the cutting edge of literary sophistication in the world of Chaucer's youth I find a most dubious procedure. But even

38. Minnis, *Chaucer and Pagan Antiquity*, 17.
39. Trevet, *Il Commento di Nicola Trevet al Tieste di Seneca*, ed. E. Franceschini (Milan: Vita e Pensiero, 1938), ix.

if he did have the representative value that Minnis wishes to assign to him, his claims on our reading of the great imaginative writers Jean de Meun and Geoffrey Chaucer would remain incidental at best.

Jean de Meun and Geoffrey Chaucer did not face the simplistic choice of being either old-fashioned, "moral," and "allegorical" or being progressive, "historical," and "literal." Rather they were both poets who greatly enriched their inherited traditions of moral allegory through what was, for their time, advanced study in the humanities. When one says that William of Conches and Nicholas Trevet wrote rather different kinds of books about the *Consolation of Philosophy*, one has said nearly all. Fredson Bowers and G. Wilson Knight, say, bring rather different agendas to the text of Shakespeare; but a scholarly reader of Shakespeare is not forced to choose between the literal and historical concerns of Bowers and the moral and allegorical concerns of Wilson Knight. We can, and should, have both.

To read Trevet on Boethius is a good if joyless thing, but if we are interested in elucidating Chaucer's Theban/Trojan poems surely we should not fail to examine his commentaries on the Theban and Trojan plays of Seneca, a writer whose own influence on the *Troilus* has been much neglected. In Seneca, Trevet has a genuine pagan author—not a Father of the Church using pagan myths for allegorical Christian purposes—and a genuinely secular body of texts. His attitude toward them is accordingly all the more interesting with respect to the secular literature of the later Middle Ages.

Trevet is frequently called a "humanist," and he certainly was one of sorts, though he is not free of that suspicion of humane letters common among academic theologians of the fraternal orders and so unpleasantly manifested by some later and better known Dominicans, Johannes Dominici and Vincent Ferrers. Both the ambivalence of his attitude and the means used to circumvent intellectual difficulties recall his master Augustine who, in the *De doctrina christiana*, had definitively authorized the notion that pagan letters, like the silver and gold ornaments of the Egyptians, could rightly be appropriated for Christian use.

The image that Trevet used in the scholia to Seneca's *Thyestes* was not that of "Egyptian gold" but another from the Pentateuch—that of the land of Canaan before the conquest. Christian readers approach the Senecan text as the spies sent out by Moses and Aaron (Num. 13); the land flows with milk and honey in very deed, but it is inhabited by "certain monsters of the sons of Enac, of the giant kind." Surely this is not the attitude of a man for whom classical archaeology everywhere supplants the search for tropological application or for whom "fable moralization" has nothing to do with scriptural exegesis.

What Trevet means by invoking a scriptural text with an allegorical meaning simply taken for granted is, I think, sufficiently clear. Seneca's plays are great warehouses of Christian moral verity once they have been expurgated of certain cultural flaws. The "sons of Enac" that he had in mind were almost certainly testimonies to polytheism, idolatry, and divination, concerning which Seneca's attitude can at times be matter-of-fact and noncommital, rather than the plays' erotic doctrines. I nowhere find in Trevet evidence of genuine literary sensitivity; but he was an intelligent man, and for his time widely read in the classical authors. On that basis alone I presume he would have agreed with Seneca's first English translator, one Thomas Newton: "I doubt whether there bee any among all the Catalogue of Heathen wryters . . . that more sensibly, pithily, and bytingly layeth doune the guerdon of filthy lust, cloaked dissimulation and odious treachery: which is the dryft, whereunto he leueleth the whole yssue of ech one of his Tragedies." That certainly is the "drift" of the tragedy of *Troilus* in the narrator's notorious summation—"Swych fyn his lust!"—and it seems probable to me that the distinctive five-book structure in which Chaucer has recast the materials of the *Filostrato* owes something to the structure of Senecan tragedy even as it does to Boethian dialogue.[40]

In his general preface to the Senecan corpus Trevet identifies the genre as tragedy written within the general category of "fabulous theology," a phrase that should make it nearly impossible for us to believe that he writes as a value-free scholar who has no interest in subjecting antique religious beliefs to the moral corrective of Christian revelation. For he explicitly acknowledges the source of his analysis—the sixth book of Augustine's *City of God*—and to understand his intellectual agenda we must read back through his essay to the controlling passages in his master. Varro's taxonomy of the "three theologies" is taken from *De civitate Dei* 6.5; but this Trevet collates with the testimony from Seneca's lost *De superstitione* in 6.10, a testimony that pillories "gods" who would honor themselves in human agony and blood.

Trevet implies that Seneca's scathing criticisms of certain popular religious customs, criticisms warmly approved by Augustine, will be found in his dramatic works as well. Diomede prophesies that the fall of Troy will occasion

---

40. See Norton-Smith, *Chaucer*, 169.

such atrocities as would make the Furies themselves weep for pity (*TC* 5.890–
96). Chaucer of course knew what they were. The central subject of Seneca's
Trojan play, the *Troades*, is the ordeal of the Trojan women, Hecuba and Andromache, caused by the ritual murders (blood sacrifices) of their children—
the innocent virgin Polyxena, daughter of Hecuba and Priam, and her prepu-
bescent nephew Astyarax, son of Hector and Andromache and grandson of
Hecuba. The child Astyarax is hurled by the villain Ulysses from the highest
rampart left standing in Troy, his brains splattered on the jagged rocks below.
Polyxena is butchered by Pyrrus in a necromantic wedding atop the tumulus
of his father Achilles, whose grave sucks in her blood.

This is the kind of Grand Guignol that has given Seneca a bad name in some
quarters, but within the text of the *Troades* as glossed by Trevet it is clearly
accurate historical anthropology—payens corsed olde rites, indeed—requiring no superimposition of Christian "fable moralization" to make its moral
point. The grisly sacrifice has been demanded by the shade of Ulysses as his
share of the Trojan booty and as a prerequisite for a favorable wind for the
Greek fleet's departure. Even Agamemnon, who we recall murdered his own
daughter in exchange for a favorable wind on an earlier occasion, gags at the
suggestion of the cruel slaughter, and he is willing to proceed only on the basis
of an expensive theological consultation. He sends for Calchas, mouthpiece
of the gods (*interpres deum*) to learn "what the god commands." Calchas' unwavering and immediate response is that the Fates demand what they usually
demand—gore—and Seneca reminds us with his use of the verb *solere* that
this sort of thing happens all the time. This is the kind of "fabulous theology"
that Varro would have banished from Rome and which encouraged Augustine
in his opinion that the behavior of your average literary "god" would scandalize
a self-respecting demon.

There is absolutely no reason to suspect that Geoffrey Chaucer had a less
censorious attitude toward "fabulous theology" than did Varro, Seneca, Augustine, or Nicholas Trevet—even if, with Seneca, he chose to explore the theme
as a poetic anthropologist. The *Canterbury Tales* are full of gods behaving as
the *rascaille* such writers took them to be—that is, depicted (to use Augustine's language) in a manner "contrary to the dignity and nature of immortal
beings." In the "Knight's Tale" the gods squabble, quibble, and mislead; in the
"Merchant's Tale," Pluto and Proserpina become involved with the pear-tree
coitus of Damyan and May; in the "Manciple's Tale" Phoebus Apollo murders
his wife in a squalid drama of lover's jealousy. Such episodes, Homeric and

Lucianic in their irreverence, echo Jean de Meun's style of "fabulous theology" in the *Roman de la Rose*. In the *Troilus*, to be sure, there is a certain decorum in such matters, but it is the double-edged high seriousness of Virgil and Ovid. As I shall explore in some detail later, the scene in which Troilus falls in love with Criseyde has its obvious parallels with the story of Daphne and Apollo, a story in which a "god" is punished for his pride. The entire action of the *Aeneid*, the central epic of medieval Latinity, is animated by the "fabulous theology" of the wrath of Juno.

Trevet's glosses to Seneca are, as several classical scholars have pointed out, elementary in character. Their principal purpose seems to be to paraphrase into straightforward prose the sometimes difficult verse of the poetic text in the fashion of a school edition. To the considerable extent that Trevet is simply a pedestrian simplifier of vocabulary and syntax, he is indeed, as Minnis suggests, a literalist. As the glosses become more ambitious they become also more errant; I have already observed that Trevet could not even get Seneca's plots straight. Yet though they have limited value from the perspective of modern classical philology, they reveal attitudes of middle-brow medieval scholarship of the kind exemplified by a wide range of fourteenth-century scholars and, I would add, by Geoffrey Chaucer in his researches into the Troy story. Though Trevet engages sympathetically with his ancient materials, as most good historians do, he is far from being unwilling to judge the past from a "modern" (that is, a Christian) perspective. Neither he nor any of his contemporaries were yet able to do so without turning their backs on what was the very model of their enterprise, the *De civitate Dei* of Augustine, a work in which the learned examination of paganism was inseparable from its censorious judgment.

In particular Trevet brings to bear upon Seneca the text of the Bible on rare but significant occasions when he seeks historical illumination. Of the numerous scholia that seem to me to offer real illumination on Chaucer's Trojan text I offer two brief examples. Agamemnon pointedly notes that he pays well for the services of Calchas; and Trevet, in turn, is quick to point out a biblical parallel for the mercenary nature of idolatrous priestcraft in the story of Balaam, hired by the Moabites to curse Israel. "And the ancients of Moab . . . went with the price of divination in their hands" (Num. 22.7). This text is repeatedly used by medieval moralists to excoriate both simony and idolatry. Criseyde is no less aware than is Agamemnon of the relationship between greed and the profession of augury, and her plan to deceive her father depends upon her assumption of his "coveytise" (4.1369).

A second example, concerning the ambiguity of dreams, comes from a central chorus of the *Hercules Furens*. Sleep, we are told, mixes the false with the true. Seneca's precise phrase is *miscens falsa veris,* and to its precise meaning I shall return in the next chapter. Its general meaning is that some dreams are true, others not; and Trevet does not miss the opportunity to explicate the passage in scriptural terms. He cites an example of a truly prophetic dream (that of Joseph in Gen. 37.5–7) and another (from Gerald of Wales), which proved to be truly deceiving. Thus does Trevet draw together scriptural and poetic texts for purposes that are neither exclusively historical nor exclusively moral, but both. In this regard, at least, we can safely speak of the common ground he shares with Geoffrey Chaucer, the moral historian of the *Troilus.*

TROILUS, PARIS, AND APOLLO

My aim thus far has been to attend and to answer specific objections that have been raised *in principle* against the discovery of the theme of amatory idolatry in the *Troilus,* and to do so in a fashion that builds as it razes. Simply to appreciate the extent to which Chaucer has apprenticed himself to Jean de Meun is to be authorized with the search warrant to look for the theme; but what is most surprising in the actual finding is the depth of Chaucer's study of ancient as opposed to modern poets. Chaucer develops the theme of sexual idolatry in his poem in the most *historical* fashion available to him; but his sense of the historical past is richly informed by his response to the mythic past. We can trace his imaginative vision in his opening scenes, which invite into his poem the thematic presence of two mythological stories that come early and stay late: the story of the Judgment of Paris and that of Apollo and Daphne.

In the first paragraph of his narrative (as opposed to its proemium) Chaucer, following Boccaccio, reminds us of the motive of the Trojan War: "The ravysshyng to wreken of Eleyne, / By Paris don" (1.62–63). He adds the detail, distinctive to the Ovidian and Virgilian treatments of the subject as opposed to those of other medieval authors—that the Greek army came with a thousand ships.[41] Chaucer thus focuses quite precisely on the fatally compromised

41. See Windeatt's helpful note to 1.58 (*Troilus & Criseyde* [London: Longmans, 1984]). For the most part Chaucer prefers the authority of Virgil and Ovid to that of all his

Trojan past as it was understood by the greatest of Roman poets. For them the immediate cause of the Trojan War was the reckless pursuit of a woman —or, as we have already seen Horace indelicately suggest—part of a woman. It was a war that began in comedy and ended in utter disaster, and neither its beginning nor its end was very flattering to the Olympians. The beauty contest on Mount Ida perhaps reflected even less credit on its divine contestants than upon its human judge. The whole affair was a triumph only for Discord, and Ovid's repeated allusions to it are typically couched in terms that honor both the solemnity of tragedy and the ludicrousness of farce. Even without the explicit presence of the fifth *heroid* (Oenone to Paris) in his text, Chaucer's tone would be sufficient to demonstrate the Ovidian inspiration of his conception of the Judgment of Paris. It is true that medieval and Renaissance poets and commentators saw in the story of Paris' choice a moral emblem of the sorry triumph of sensuality over rationality; but in this elementary critical response they follow the continuous tradition of the ancients.[42]

The action of Chaucer's poem begins with a scene in which Troilus appears at the Festival of the Palladium, a feast of Pallas Athena, goddess of Wisdom. Quite apart from his dangerous amatory pride, he exhibits an attitude far from reverential. "Withinne the temple he went hym forth pleying" (1.267). This is a line that describes the activity of the poet no less aptly than that of the hero; for the poet too is playing, in the fashion of his master Ovid, with the sacred and the solemn. The crucial difference is that the poet knows what he is doing, while Troilus does not. Struck down in his pride by Cupid's arrow, he falls madly—I choose the word with care—in love with Criseyde who throughout the poem is textually and thematically linked with Venus, whose client he becomes. In short, his behavior echoes that of his brother and contributes to the same disastrous result.

Let me here anticipate one certain objection. A passage sometimes invoked to deny the parallel between Troilus and Paris has in my opinion been misread: Troilus' rejection of Pandarus' advice that he take Criseyde by force to

---

later authorities on the matter of Troy. Furthermore, Ovid is particularly important to Chaucer, as much of his Virgilian materials have already been mediated by him.

42. See Turk in W. Roscher, *Ausführliches Lexikon der griechischen und romischen Mythologie*, 6 vols. in 9 (Leipzig: Teubner, 1897–1909), 3.1:1591–92. The story is an ironic version of a well-established type in which a hero/sapiens overcomes carnal temptations. Karl Reinhardt cites the parallels of Hercules at the crossroads and Jesus in the desert, *Das Parisurteil* (Frankfurt: Klostermann, 1937), 5–6.

keep her from being expelled from Troy (4.526–39). The passage is rich with reminiscences of Troilus' sexual timidity of the third book and with Pandarus' therapeutic efforts to get Troilus up. "Go ravysshe hire," he advises, taking the direct approach:

> "Artow in Troie, and hast non hardyment
> To take a womman which that loveth the? . . .
> Ris up anon, and lat this wepyng be,
> And kith thow art a man . . ."
>
> (4.533–34; 537–38)

The casual implication that Troy is Rape City must remind the reader, as it reminds Troilus, of Paris.[43] Troilus tells Pandarus that he has certainly considered *raptus* but rejected it for several reasons, the first of which is that "this town hath al this werre / For ravysshyng of wommen so by myght" (4.547–48). Several scholars have seen here a clear act of virtuous, heroic, or rational behavior, accepting Troilus' own moral analysis of the action as a triumph of reason over desire.[44] However, somewhat earlier, in transforming pandering to gentilesse, Troilus invoked the useful principle of distinction between things superficially similar:

> for wyde wher is wist,
> How that ther is diversite requered
> Bytwixen thynges like, as I have lered.
>
> (3.404–6)

What of the actual rape of Helen and the proposed rape of Criseyde? In carrying off Helen, Paris violated a lawful marriage and the sacred laws of hospitality with the unwitting result of the utter ruin of Troy. In the context of the *Troilus* it is the exchanging of Criseyde rather than the keeping of her that is the unjust and immoral course. Her exchange is staunchly opposed by Hector, the poem's single internal emblem of true pagan virtue, who rightly points out that she is not a prisoner, thus casting doubt on the plan's legality as well as its morality. It is not rational argument but the "noyse of peple"—always

43. In case the reader does not get the hint, Pandarus makes the point obvious a few stanzas later: "Thenk how that Paris hath, that is thi brother, / A love; and whi shaltow nat have another?" (4.608–9).

44. See, e.g., Monica McAlpine, *The Genre of Troilus and Criseyde* (Ithaca: Cornell University Press, 1978), 160–61 and cited bibliography.

bad in a Chaucerian context—that carries the day; and it has been credibly suggested that in painting the Parliament scene Chaucer consciously alludes both to Pilate's surrender of Christ to the mob and to the violent disorders of the Peasants' Revolt.[45] Finally, it is the exchanging of Criseyde for Antenor, rather than the refusal to enter into such an exchange, that has the unforeseen result of destroying the city—as the narrator, in a rare moral intervention into his antique story, angrily points out (4.185–86; 197–210). This reality makes ironic the next reason Troilus adduces for inaction:

> I sholde han also blame of every wight,
> My fadres graunt if that I so withstoode,
> Syn she is chaunged for the townes goode.
> (4.551–53)

Troilus nexts says that he would simply explain the situation to his father, were it not too late.

> For syn my fader, in so heigh a place
> As parlement, hath hire eschaunge enseled,
> He nyl for me his lettre be repeled.
> (4.558–60)

What he has written he has written. We have no way to knowing whether this is true or not. Certainly the exchange requires the dishonoring of explicit assurances made to Criseyde by Hector (1.117–23). Taken as a whole, this episode in Chaucer's poem serves the general purpose of underscoring Troilus' sense that fatal coercion limits or abrogates his freedom of action. To the reader familiar with the history of the Palladium it may also suggest that "little Troy" can hardly look for redemption to the woman whom he himself will not redeem.

This passage of the *Troilus* for the most part follows the *Filostrato* quite closely, but there are at least two independent Chaucerian initiatives that indicate Chaucer's differing design. Troilus reorders Troilo's speech to make it clear that for him the most telling argument against decisive action is the protection of Criseyde's "name" and her "honor." In the *Filostrato* there is a plausible

---

45. See Carleton Brown, "Another Contemporary Allusion in Chaucer's Troilus," *MLN* 26 (1911): 208–11; Ann M. Taylor, "A Scriptural Echo in the Trojan Parliament of Troilus and Criseyde," *Nottingham Medieval Studies* 24 (1980): 51–56.

social explanation for why the lovers cannot legitimate their union: Criseida's social inferiority. Chaucer excludes this fact from his poem, greatly dignifies her aura of moral and social authority, houses her in a "palace," and supplies her with a number of waiting-women.

Under these circumstances we are entitled to wonder in what way the public knowledge that she is beloved by a prince of Troy would be "disclaundre to hir name." There is no explanation of this presumption, any more than there is an explanation for the fact that the lovers never so much as talk about marriage, that is consistent with a prima facie understanding of the moral vocabulary of the poem. To avoid the conclusion that there must then be some moral distance between the lovers' words and their deeds, sympathetic readers find themselves bullied into some very odd theories—such as that Troilus and Criseyde *are* married but do not tell anybody about it.

A second addition, one that has no precedent in Boccaccio, has Troilus analyzing his own situation in terms of an explicit conflict between Love and Reason: "Thus am I with desire and reson twight." This central psychomachic bifurcation of the *Roman de la Rose* is posited repeatedly in the fourth book.[46] The lovers themselves, and many of the poem's readers, present the action of this book as the plain triumph of virtuous rationality over self-indulgence, an interpretation most conspicuously internalized in the extraordinary speech of Criseyde with which the book ends in which she tells Troilus that she fell in love with him on account of his moral virtue and because "your resoun bridlede youre delit." A woman who can believe that can believe anything including, I presume, the entirely worthless vows of fidelity that go with it; but the critic who believes it exchanges credibility for credulousness.

Rationality is not synonymous with rationalization. In the fourth book of the *Troilus* it is the latter that triumphs, as the lovers rewrite their history in comfortable words such as "truth" and "honor," words that are by this point in the poem so debased as to have the value of bills of small denomination in a wildly inflated currency. The book is thick with lovers' lies. For the most part they lack the moral clarity of the lies of Pandarus, their sharpness of intention, and their intelligible functionality. The lovers' language serves a different and sadder sort of deception, self-deception.

The self-deception of lovers is of course a central Ovidian theme that sits

---

46. The texts are gathered by Siegfried Wenzel, "Chaucer's Troilus of Book IV," *PMLA* 79 (1964): 542–47.

uneasily on the frontier between the lightheartedness of social satire and the solemnity of tragedy. Chaucer is by no means unappreciative of the Lucianic perspective on the Judgment of Paris; but the tragic burden of epic that he hurries to take up in the opening lines of his poem, the oppressive memories of a king slaughtered among his household gods, a great city torched, an innocent lad hurled from the ramparts of its ruins, do not allow the thoughtful reader to be amused at the parallel between the behavior of Paris and that of his brother Troilus.

A second and cognate myth is also decisively present in Chaucer's opening scene, and likewise denied the free run of its comic potential: the myth of Apollo and Daphne. Many readers of the *Troilus* have noted how Chaucer's design, when compared with that of Boccaccio, stresses Troilus' culpable pride as a motive for Cupid's attack. Troilus' initial scorn of lovers, though objectively sound as his own story is about to prove, is fatally contaminated with spiritual pride.

> "I have herd told, pardieux, of youre lyvynge,
> Ye loveres, and youre lewed observaunces,
> And which a labour folk han in wynnynge
> Of love, and in the kepyng which doutaunces;
> And whan youre preye is lost, woo and penaunces.
> O veray fooles! nyce and blynde be ye;
> Ther nys nat oon kan war by other be." (1.197–203)

Thank God, he in effect says, that I am not like that Pharisee. The final line of his speech has a particularly sardonic irony, since even as he utters it he himself fails to attend the most famous exemplary warning in Western literature.

> And with that word, he gan caste up the browe,
> Ascaunces, "loo! is this naught wisely spoken?"
> At which the god of love gan loken rowe
> Right for despit, and shop for to ben wroken;
> He kidde anon his bowe nas nat broken;
> For sodeynly he hitte hym atte fulle,
> And yet as proud a pekok kan he pulle. (1.204–10)

The *Metamorphoses* of Ovid, "Great Ovid" as medieval scholars called it in distinction to the amatory works written in elegiac meter, "the Bible of the poets" as others would call it in the Renaissance, was the repertory of gen-

tile myth shared by Chaucer and his audience alike. In the first book of the
Metamorphoses—indeed in the very first metamorphosis of a human body to
another form—Ovid placed, in the position of the keystone, the history of the
first recorded instance of destructive sexual passion, the story of Apollo's mad
love for Daphne. The story is this: From the slime of the primeval creation was
born a frightful and malign serpent, the Python, the scourge of earth's inhabi-
tants. This loathsome beast the archer god Apollo slew and, to commemorate
his exploit, established the Pythian Games in its celebration. However, toxo-
phile prowess fostered in Apollo a dangerous and mocking pride; when he saw
Cupid with his bow and arrows he mocked him, saying that he should stick
to his torch (*faex*), and leave the weapons of war to real men:

> "Quid" que "tibi, lascive puer, cum fortibus armis?"
> Dixerat "ista decent umeros gestamina nostros . . .
> Inritare tua, nec laudes assere nostras."
> (*Met.* 1.456–57, 462)

> ("You naughty boy, what have you to do with warrior's arms? Weapons
> such as these are suited to my shoulders . . . do not aspire to praises that
> are my prerogative.")

Here, I believe, is Chaucer's model; but as so often his Ovid comes to him
in different strengths, so to speak, some straight, some in vernacular dilution.
Troilus' reponse to Love is distinctly literary, not merely in the sense that his
behavior reflects certain discernible literary traditions but in the sharper, more
explicit sense that it is controlled by specific and identifiable literary texts.
The most important of these in terms of Chaucer's philosophical ambitions is
of course the *Consolation* of Boethius; but the first in the priority of its explicit
introduction into Chaucer's own poem is the *Canzoniere* of Petrarch, from
which the "Canticus Troili" is cited in an expanded translation.

Its ostentatious presence, explicitly linked as it is with the name of Lollius
and made conspicuous by the narrator's self-conscious remarks about the excellence of its translation, is a complicating fact of Chaucer's poem; and while
we shall never be sure which of the many and complex Petrarchan associations
led him to make such a decisive intervention in Boccaccio's narrative, our best
hope as always lies in the examination of poetic context—Petrarch's no less
than Chaucer's. "That the Canticus so closely imitates its Petrarchan model
suggests that Troilus's experience is determined by his innocent responsive-

ness to a preconceived pattern of conventional behaviour—an idea we may sense again in such gestures as Troilus's submission to the lordship of love, which immediately follows the Canticus (1.422–24)."[47]

I myself would question whether Troilus' overweening pride is in fact "innocent," as opposed to disastrously ignorant, but it is still perhaps possible to build upon Wetherbee's keen perception; for I think that just as Chaucer has already suggested Troilus' repetition of the patterns of Paris and Apollo, he now suggests his repetition of the pattern of Petrarch/Lollius, the "io" of the *Canzoniere*.

When we look at Chaucer's context in detail, it seems legitimate to conclude that one of the effects of his method, conscious or unconscious, is to pick out the already articulate Ovidianism of Boccaccio's description of Troilo's falling in love with highlights from more contemporary Ovidian texts, particularly the *Roman de la Rose* and the *Canzoniere*. Thus Troilus, like Troilo before him, is wounded through eye contact with the beloved. He "Was ful unwar that love hadde his dwellynge / Withinne the subtil stremes of hire eyen" (*TC* 1.304–5). This is, of course, pure "conventional" Ovid.[48] But Chaucer's narrator, unlike Boccaccio's, comments upon the action: "Blissed be love, that kan thus folk converte" (1.308). Commenting on the comment, Windeatt notes that this exclamation is not in the *Filostrato*. But its model is in the *Roman de la Rose* (2615–16), and in a context disquieting for its benign interpretation. The disaster comes upon Troilus, as upon Troilo, while he is ostensibly participating in a religious gathering. This, too, is orthodox Ovid, who teaches that the temple is a good place to pick up girls.[49]

Yet once again Chaucer further modernizes Boccaccio's Ovid. Boccaccio's Troilo is unambiguously in a pagan temple ogling Criseida "quanto duraro a Pallade gli onori." Chaucer makes the image vaguer, as Troilus steals glances at Criseyde "while that servyse laste." We are to be sure in the Athenaeum of Troy, but the word "servyse" makes it easier for us to imagine that we are also in the church of Saint Clare in Avignon where, on April 6, 1327, Francis Petrarch neglected his prayers to look upon the face of Laura. I suggest, in other words, that in the *Troilus* Chaucer is fully conscious of the fictive erotic

47. Wetherbee, *Chaucer and the Poets*, 66.
48. See, e.g., *RA*, 615–16.
49. *AA*, 1.75–78.

biography of the *Canzoniere* no less than he is aware of that of the *Roman de la Rose*. There are few medieval poems more complex than the *Canzoniere*, and it would be unconvincingly facile to identify this or that among its rich treasury of poetic images as its primary structural myth; yet I have to say that the myth of Apollo and Daphne is as near its center as any. In Apollo, patron of poetry and *philostratus,* are united inseparable impulses of Petrarch's first-person voice. In the transformed Daphne is the *laura* that is his poetic and erotic quest.

It is the detailed thematic justice of the "Canticus Troili" within the *Troilus* that makes me shun the idea that Chaucer really did not understand the Italian original very well or that he knew it only as an isolated sonnet circulated independently of the rest of Petrarch's verse narrative. The "Canticus Troili" is the 132d poem of the *Rime sparse;* the incipit of the next poem is "Amor m'a posto come segno a strale" ("Love has set me up like a target for arrows"). "Love" is here of coure the god Love, Cupid; but Petrarch's commentators have not missed the syncretizing biblical quotation from the Lamentations of Jeremiah (3.12) "Tetendit arcum suum, et posuit me quasi signum ad sagittam" (He has taken his bow, and he has set me up like a target for arrows). Recent studies of the *Troilus* have brilliantly demonstrated that the extraordinary care of Chaucer's writing is directly connected with the extraordinary care of his reading. In Petrarch's smooth melding of sacred and secular text Chaucer would have seen a particularly sophisticated refinement of a technique widely used by his great vernacular teachers—Jean de Meun, Dante Alighieri, Guillaume de Machaut, among others—a technique of accommodating secular pagan mythology to a Christian moral vision as remote from naive storytelling as it was from Minnis's "fable moralization."

If we wish to give a name to the Chaucerian theme here, it is, I suppose, "divine archery." Apollo was its victim at the beginning of the world's history and at the beginning of one of the world's most famous poems; Troilus is its victim now. In neither instance is divine archery a phenomenon of blind fate working outside the framework of a coherent moral system; in each instance, instead, it is linked with the moral opacity of pride. In Ovidian myth Apollo could be its agent as well as its victim so that, for example, when Niobe violated the supernal economy with her inordinate pride in the beauty of her children, it was Apollo who killed them all with his longbow. But as Troilus says of the "veray fooles" of love: "Ther nys nat oon kan war by other be." This I take to be the chief import of the textual references to Niobe that have seemed to some merely decorative. Silently quoting the Old Testament like Petrarch before him, Pandarus thus counsels Troilus:

> "The wise seith: 'wo hym that is allone,
> For, and he falle, he hath non helpe to ryse' [Eccles. 4.10]
> And sith thow hast a felawe, tel thi mone;
> For this nys nat, certein, the nexte wyse
> To wynnen love, as techen us the wyse,
> To walwe and wepe, as Nyobe the queene,
> Whos teres yit in marble ben yseene."
>   (1.694–700)

In the ensuing stanzas Ovid yields to Boethius, but Chaucer has not forgotten Niobe. Like "Boethius," Troilus does not want to take his "medicine," and he dismisses Pandarus' "proverbs"—that is, biblical and Boethian wisdom—by saying that he does not want to be cured.

> "Ek I nyl nat ben cured, I wol deye.
> What knowe I of the queene Nyobe?
> Lat be thyne olde ensaumples, I the preye."
>   (1.758–760)

Naturally Troilus knows nothing of Queen Niobe, for "ther nys nat oon kan war by other be." As we shall see in the next chapter, Troilus' repeated failure to understand his implicit and explicit literary experience becomes for Chaucer one of the most amusing, and the most serious, means of exploring his hero's tragic moral limitations. We can see both the comedy and the pathos in yet another explicit reminiscence of through-shotten and through-darted Apollo in the first book.

In a very funny passage in which Pandarus boldly states the often covert assumption of the teaching profession—namely, that practical incapacity should be no impediment to theoretical authority—suggesting in so many words that a fool can be a fine guide for a wise man, he compares his situation to that of Oenone as described in her letter to Paris. The reference is certainly to the fifth *heroid*, wittily treated as a piece of domestic mail just arrived by the afternoon post. But of course Troilus has no more read the *Heroides* than he has the *Metamorphoses*.

"Ye say the lettre that she wrot, I gesse?"
"Nay, nevere yit, ywys," quod Troilus. (1.656–57)

Textual naïveté is dangerous in this poem, whether embraced by Troilus himself or by his editors, who have been as dependent as the hero himself on Pandarus' quite peculiar summary of its alleged contents.

" 'Phebus, that first fond art of medicyne,'
Quod she, 'and couthe in every wightes care,
Remedye and reed by herbes he knew fyne,
Yit to hym self his konnyng was ful bare;
For love hadde hym so bounden in a snare,
Al for the doughter of the kyng Amete,
That al his craft ne koude his sorwes bete.' "
                                              (1.659–65)

That, says Pandarus, is just how it is with *me;* though I cannot cure my own love-sickness, I can cure yours. All editors of the poem agree that Pandarus does indeed paraphrase a section of the letter of Oenone. [50] That is what Pandarus wants us to believe, but not, I think, what Chaucer does. Though they do indeed have a cognate in the fifth *heroid,* these lines actually come from the first book of the *Metamorphoses,* where, significantly, they describe the situation of the male Apollo rather than of the female Oenone. Quite apart from the marked dubiousness of Pandarus' logic, we see here in his textual manipulation the deconstructive legerdemain by which he deflects the exemplary moral weight of the passage from a proper to an improper referent. An extended consideration of Pandarus' role as an "interpreter" in this passage must await another chapter; my purpose here is simply to identify the fashion in which Chaucer repeatedly alludes to the history of Apollo in his own first book.

It is important to appreciate that Chaucer's strategic options for the use of his classical materials were rather broader than has sometimes been suggested. In particular he was not faced with a simple and stark choice between "fable moralization" on the one hand and morally neutral "narration" on the other, as though his Ovid must mean what it meant in the *Ovide Moralisé* or mean nothing at all. Rosemond Tuve was certainly right to take that work as her

50. Thus also John Fyler, *Chaucer and Ovid* (New Haven: Yale University Press, 1979), 115, who characterizes the passage as "a few innocuous lines from the *Heroides.*"

model of "imposed allegory," and right too to distance from it the attitudes of Jean de Meun and other great vernacular allegorists of the secular tradition.

What must strike many readers as the oddest thing about the very odd exegetical tradition represented by the *Ovide Moralisé* is the relentless determination to find philosophically positive meanings in erotic histories in which Ovid highlights the raw destructive power and the pathos of love.[51] The interpretations *in bono* of Apollo's mad pursuit of Daphne seem particularly perverse in this regard.[52] But Chaucer did not have to abandon moral allegory when he abandoned Frère Lubin. For the moral and emblematic "use" of the Apollo legend he had other, poetic, models, beginning with that of Ovid himself, who adopted, as the first first-person voice in the *Amores*, the voice of Apollo. If Ovidian tradition—or one of a plurality of medieval Ovidian traditions—provided an analogue for Chaucer's hero, so did it offer a surprising literary analogy for his heroine Criseyde: the Palladium of Troy. The lyre of Apollo was a poetic image, but the Palladium was an artifact of history. For a poet who insisted that he was writing history, the Palladium had a special poetic usefulness that Chaucer's medieval predecessors in the *matière de Troie* had, astonishingly, left unrealized.

THE PALLADIUM

"**B**ut how this town com to destruccion" writes the narrator, "Ne falleth naught to purpos me to telle; / for it were here a long digression" (1.141–42). Like so many other of the narrator's self-conscious and "literary" comments—he goes on to refer the reader to primary historians, Homer, Dares, and Dictys—this one covertly encourages us to think along the very lines that he now dismisses as digressive. How *did* the town come to destruction? That is a question that can be diversely answered, depending upon which link in the tragic chain of Trojan history happens to capture our attention, but the image most likely to come to mind, surely, is that of a huge wooden simulacrum of a horse. That image is not itself in the poem, for, as the narrator says, it is not

51. See the remarks of Paule Demats, *Fabula* (Geneva: Droz, 1973), 109–11.
52. For a collection, see Wolfgang Stechow, *Apollo und Daphne* (Leipzig, 1932), 66–70; cf. the excellent remarks of Yves Giraud, *La Fable de Daphne* (Geneva: Droz, 1969), 95–96.

in his historical matter, which must end when Troilus ends. But we do get an image of another wooden simulacrum:

> But though that Grekes hem of Troie shetten,
> And hir cite bisegede al aboute,
> Hire olde usage nolde they nat letten,
> As for to honoure hir goddes ful devoute;
> But aldermost in honour, out of doute,
> Thei hadde a relik heet Palladion,
> That was hire trust aboven everichon.
>   (1.148–54)

On the page of the *Filostrato* that lay open before him as he wrote of "Palladions feste" he would have read the following lines:

> i Troian padri al Palladio fatale
> fer preparare li consueti onori . . .
>   (*Fil.* 1.18)

(The Trojan elders went to make ready the wonted honour to the fateful Palladium . . .)

Chaucer avoided the loaded word *fatale,* and with it the whiff of censoriousness present in Boccaccio's text, unless, that is, we are prepared to see that censoriousness transferred to the adjective "olde":

> In sondry wises shewed, as I rede,
> The folk of Troie hire observaunces olde,
> Palladions feste for to holde. (1.159–61)

The tone appears to be that of objective historical description, not of anti-ethnic polemic, and another of Minnis's instances, perhaps, of moralization receding before narration. Yet, if so, the moralization eclipsed was not that of Christian scholiasts but that of the greatest pagan poets of Latinity. For Chaucer certainly knew why the word *fatale* was there in Boccaccio's text in the first place; it was there because it was the canonical word to describe the Palladium, the word used thrice by Ovid and, more important still, the word copied by Ovid from his own great authority, Virgil:

> Omnis spes Danaum et coepti fiducia belli
> Palladis auxiliis semper stetit. impius ex quo

Tydides sed enim scelerum inventor Vlixes
fatale adgressi sacrato avellere templo
Palladium . . . (*Aeneid* 2.162–66)

(From the start of the war the only hope of victory which the Greeks ever
had lay in help from Pallas. But there came the night when sacrilegious
Diomede and Ulysses, always quick to invent new crimes, crept up to
wrest Troy's fatal talisman, the image of Minerva, from your hallowed
temple . . .)

It is easy enough to demonstrate, I think, that it was this Virgilian passage that made medieval "antiquarians" aware of the Palladium, especially, as
we shall see, since it was prominently enshrined in what was for medieval
"historians" the most authoritative book ever written about ancient Roman
religion.

It is worth looking at a couple of Ovidian references to the Palladium which,
though they may well originate in Virgil, may help us understand how Chaucer
could so easily accommodate the image to his *semiotic* theme. Virgil does not
actually say what the Palladium was. He simply assumes his reader will know.
Ovid alludes to the object as a *signum*. At *Fasti* 6.421 it is the "heavenly sign
of an arms-bearing Minerva." At *Met.* 13.381, with the Virgilian passage more
clearly in control, it is "the fatal sign of Minerva." Elsewhere (*Met.* 13.337)
Ovid uses another phrase, *signum penetrale Minervae*, where *penetrale* means
a religious shrine, and by extension the cult object within it. Ovid's words
signum and *penetrale* will in due course offer commodious ingress to patterns
of serious philosophical theme and of blithe, lexical whimsy, within Chaucer's
poem.

The pagan grammarian Servius, by far the most influential of the early commentators on the *Aeneid* and for all practical purposes a part of the medieval
reading of the poem, has a lengthy explanatory note on the word *Palladium*
at 2.166.[53] He is quite aware of the diverse, and in some ways contradictory
legends surrounding the wonderful image, but his summary remarks, designed
to help Latin readers understand the prehistory of Virgil's epic, touch upon
the points of chief relevance to the *Troilus*. The Palladium was a wooden likeness of Pallas Athena, of mysterious but supernatural origins, which fell from

53. See Servius, *Servii Grammatici . . . commentarii*, 3 vols. ed. G. Thilo and H. Hagen
(Leipzig: Teubner, 1881–1902), 1:247–48.

heaven into Troy as a token of the goddess' patronage of the city. She gave the Trojans the absolute guarantee that the city would remain secure so long as the Palladium remained within its possession. The Greek spies Ulysses and Diomedes, aided by the treacherous Antenor, penetrated the city, bribed the Palladium's corrupt guardian, and seized the image. It was Diomedes who actually succeeded in removing it from Troy.

Considerably more is of interest in the history of the Palladium, and I shall have occasion to mention other aspects of its legend; but Servius' notes certainly explain the meaning of the word *fatale* as Chaucer would have found it in Boccaccio, in Ovid, and in Virgil. The fate of Troy, the very life or death of the city, was radically contingent upon a graven "image" or "sign." Chaucer can excise the word, thus keeping at least at some distance the hints of the fall of the city that it underscored in earlier texts, because as the narrator explicitly says the theme is not the destruction of Great Troy but the destruction of *little* Troy, the man Troilus. The folk of Troy, says the narrator following Virgil and Boccaccio, made of the Palladium "hire trust aboven everichon" (1.154). Troilus' fatal "trust," as the reader has learned a hundred lines earlier still, was in Criseyde. There is a remarkable parallel between the Palladium and Criseyde, and one that astonishingly remains unremarked. The first is the idol of Great Troy, the other the idol of little Troy. The loss of Criseyde heralds Troilus' destruction, just as the loss of the Palladium will herald Troy's. Diomede, who carries off the one, will carry off the other.

An awareness of the parallel idolatries of great and little Troy, incidentally, may help us to resolve even certain philological problems presented by the poem. Following Virgil, Chaucer calls Diomede "sone of Tideus" at important moments in the text, forcing us to bear, as the characters in the poem themselves must bear, the oppression of a tragic past that controls the present. In the first chapter I alluded to the fact that Chaucer's "translation" of the Italian word *casa* as *paleys* in Troilus' address to Criseyde's empty house has invited various scholarly speculations. To them we can now add another. Among other reasons, the word allows Chaucer to pun against "Pallas" in Troilus' idolatrous prayer before the "shryne": "O paleys [Pallas] desolate."

Chaucer's triumph over Boccaccio, one that could never have been dreamed of in the 1380s, is that he made the *Filostrato* a poem destined to be studied almost exclusively in terms other than those established by its author. The only gift required of the critic of an ugly duckling is patience; he must await the emergence of the graceful swan. Nearly every discovery of subtlety in the

Troilus—and is there a subtler poem in the language?—may seem to discover a corresponding awkwardness in the *Filostrato*. It is thus only fair now and again to point out some of the diamonds so generously present in the gangue of Boccaccio's text. One of them, surely, is this witty idea of linking Criseyde and the Palladium.

It was Boccaccio who returned to its proper realm of poetic fact what for Guido and Benoît was simply an archaeological fact. As usual, Chaucer, the jeweler, makes Boccaccio seem a mere miner. He picks up Boccaccio's diamond, polishes it. Between Chaucer's actual narrative beginning of his story at 1.57 and the narrator's self-conscious *occupatio* starting at 1.141, there is but a single passage in the *Troilus* that significantly departs from Boccaccio's text. It is the description of Criseyde. Boccaccio speaks of her heavenly beauty in the tired jargon of the love poets:

> si bella e si angelica a vedere
> era, che non parea cosa mortale.
> (*Fil.* 1.11)

(She was so fair and so like an angel to look upon that she seemed not a mortal thing.)

Chaucer's augmented version is this:

> So aungelik was hir natif beaute,
> That lik a thing inmortal semed she,
> As is an hevenyssh perfit creature,
> That down were sent in scornyng of nature.
> (1.102–5)

To be sure, the Chaucerian passage too can be taken at the level of unambitious cliché; but even while saying the same thing it manages to say something different.[54] Criseyde is not merely angelic; she is like a celestial "creature" sent by supernatural agency from heaven to earth. The language accommodates the legend of the Palladium without abandoning the cover of the convention.

The genuine classicism of the great vernacular poets of the later Middle Ages is nowhere more striking than in their elaborate and ambiguous deference to

---

54. See Ian Bishop, *Chaucer's Troilus and Criseyde: A Critical Study* (Bristol: University of Bristol Press, 1981), 19.

anterior models. The *Roman de la Rose* is an assumed fact in the composition of the *Troilus* in precisely the way that the *Aeneid* is an assumed fact in the composition of the *Metamorphoses*. It is of course technically possible to read Ovid and Chaucer without having first read Virgil and Jean de Meun, but it is not easy to believe that the authors themselves will have imagined that anyone would ever actually do so. To catalog the playful, often capricious, migration of images among the poets is no easy or certain task; but the attempt, even if doomed from the start to partial success at best, must in my opinion be vigorously prosecuted if we wish to appreciate the nature of poetic imagination as it operates in several late medieval narrative poems.

I have already demonstrated that as he wrote his nonparaclausithyron Chaucer's imagination returned repeatedly to what is at face value presumably the filthiest passage of verse in the vernacular canon, the ending of the *Roman de la Rose*, where Jean developed at some length in the distinctive features of the Gothic grotesque, an intellectual fantasy on the female sexual organs as religious shrine. It would not be easy to say which is more unlikely—Jean de Meun's invention, or Chaucer's *aemulatio* upon it; but I think that Chaucer's larger conception of "erotic idolatry" in the *Troilus* is related to his intellectual intuitions of the origins of Jean's quite visceral imagery.

A serious study of the classicism of Jean de Meun remains to be undertaken, but my own reading of his poem has convinced me that he was a careful reader of Latin and that his interest in Ovid and Virgil went far deeper than mere narrative. To give a single and unnoticed example, Genius, speaking of the notable irascibility of women, cites Virgil:

> Virgiles meïsmes tesmoigne,
> qui mout connut de leur besoigne
> que ja fame n'iert tant estable
> qu'el ne soit diverse et muable.
> Et si rest trop ireuse beste . . .
> (16295–99)

(Virgil himself bears witness—and he knew a great deal about their
difficulties—that no woman was ever so stable that she might not be
varied and changeable. And thus she remains a very irritable beast.)

The specific source of this misogyny is the notorious sententia "Varium et mutabile semper / Femina" (*Aeneid* 4.569). In "translating" it, Jean has not failed to notice the dehumanizing force of Virgil's neuter adjectives, and he achieves the same shocking end by calling her a "beast."[55]

This is by way of prefacing my belief that Jean's grotesque image of the sacral pudendum, if one may call it that, is of classical and philological origin. It arises, I suggest, from a playful meditation on the Latin words *penetro* and *penetrale,* as the latter word would recur in the reading of the major Latin poets. To "penetrate" is to force entry to the inner sanctum, the shrine, the cult image in the innermost recesses of the house or temple. For medieval Christian clerks, the theological connection between disordered sexuality and idolatry was explicit in the famous Solomonic text, "Initium enim fornicationis est exquisitio idolorum" (For the beginning of fornication is the devising of idols; Wisd. of Sol. 14.12). Exercising a mental habit that typically links passages from Scripture with passages from the classical poets (as, e.g., at 16293–316), Jean seems to have taken Ovid's *signum penetrale* and its common cognates in the *Aeneid* and the *Metamorphoses* to authorize an etymological allegory of alarming surface ribaldry but unexceptionable moral content. This is a critical speculation in which I should wish to invest no capital of probative argument, but I find it consistent not merely with Jean's general mental habits but with his use of the more objectively demonstrable classical text out of which this passage in the *Roman* grows.[56]

What I mean, specifically, is Jean's prominent use of the Ovidian story of Pygmalion. Whether Jean's subliminal Latin pun (if it existed) penetrated Chaucer's poetic consciousness or not, the English poet certainly knew that the image of the sexual "shrine" at the end of the *Roman de la Rose*—in a text demonstrably present in the *Troilus*—was intimately and elaborately connected with the statue carved by Pygmalion. I shall not repeat my extended argument, published elsewhere, that the principal thematic function of the Pygmalion episode in the *Roman de la Rose* is its delineation of sexual idolatry. There are

55. Cf. Petrarch, *Canzoniere* 183.12: "Femina e *cosa* mobile per natura."
56. According to J. N. Adams, *The Latin Sexual Vocabulary* (Baltimore: Johns Hopkins University Press, 1982), 151, "*Penetrare* does not occur in a sexual sense in the Classical period." There remains an obvious possibility of play on *penetralia* nonetheless. For instance, in one of his poems Marbod of Rennes uses the word *penetralia* as a synonym for "genitalia"; see *Marbodi Liber decem capitulorum*, ed. Rosario Leotta (Rome: Herder, 1984), 82. Jean, who had apparently thought more than most of us about the nomenclature of the sexual organs, may also be toying with the obvious potential wordplay on *penis* and *penus*.

fortunately now available detailed studies which, arriving at nearly identical conclusions from the differing perspectives of art history and literary history, provide a context for the conclusion arrived at.[57]

I am not unaware, of course, that not all Chaucerians who have considered the idea find it as convincing as I do, so that it is necessary to consider objections.[58] The chief difficulty is that the principal medieval moralization of the Pygmalion legend has been supplanted by a modern moralization that sees Jean's focus on the link betweeen *artistic* and *sexual* generation. It is a cultural fact worthy of reflection that readers of Ovid disposed to dismiss medieval "moralization" of Pygmalion are often enough eager to embrace modern ones. For Etienne Falconet and G. B. Shaw are certainly in their way just as much mythographers as is Arnulf of Orleans.

There are even in the mythographic traditions of the Middle Ages and the Renaissance interpretations *in bono* of the Pygmalion story, but there is no commentator known to me before the Romantic period who suggests that the story is about the vivifying or fecundating powers of *art*. That in and of itself is inconclusive but hardly insignificant, since Jean's forte is quite clearly the elegant, forceful, witty, surprising, or simply tedious expression of what oft was thought.[59] Until quite recently, no reader of Ovid's text suggested that it is principally about the vivifying powers of artistic creation.[60] Art (*ars,* technical

---

57. My discussion of Pygmalion is in *The Roman de la Rose: A Study in Allegory and Iconography* (Princeton: Princeton Univ. Press, 1969), 228–37. See H. Dörrie, *Pygmalion: Ein Impuls Ovids und seine Wirkungen bis in die Gegenwart* (Opladen: Westdeuscher Verlag, 1974); and Annegret Dinter, *Der Pygmalion-Stoff in der europäischen Literatur* (Heidelberg: Winter, 1979). Michael Camille informs me that in a forthcoming study of the idol in Gothic art he arrives at conclusions differing from mine.

58. Cf. Donald Rowe, *O Love, O Charité! Contraries Harmonized in Chaucer's Troilus* (Carbondale: Southern Illinois University Press, 1976), 190: "Though the allegory of Pygmalion may indeed reveal the self-love inherent in cupiditas, it has more important functions in the poem, ones that relate to Jean's conception of how both the artist and the lover create."

59. See Luis Cortes Vasquez, *El Episodio de Pigmaglión del Roman de la Rose* (Salamanca: Universidad de Salamanca, 1980), 55.

60. Among classicists the view has been most elaborately argued by Douglas F. Bauer, "The Function of Pygmalion in the *Metamorphoses* of Ovid," *TAPA* 93 (1967): 1–21. What this author calls the "improbability" of his own interpretation has been criticized by (among others) Brooks Otis, *Ovid as an Epic Poet*, 2d ed. (Cambridge: Cambridge University Press, 1970), 419.

skill) is indeed dramatically powerful in Ovid's story, but its power is the dangerous power of deception. The artist Pygmalion is betrayed by his art, even as the artist Apollo is abandoned by his.[61] The agency of the metamorphosis, the transformation, is the goddess Venus. John Gower's ostensibly benign moralization of the story in the *Confessio Amantis*—that lovers should be steadfast and forthright in expressing their desires—seems true to the narrative logic of the Ovidian text.

In the *Roman de la Rose* we are confronted not with Ovid's Pygmalion but with Jean de Meun's, and it is on the basis of an internal examination of Jean's text that we must deduce the poet's artistic and moral purposes. Jean's drift seems to me sufficiently clear. He removes all reference to the Propoetides and with them Ovid's moral predisposition in Pygmalion's favor. Then he ostentatiously burlesques—in tones nearer the lower than the higher comic pole—Ovid's conception of the artist's courtship of the statue. He next compromises the Ovidian "story" with covert scriptural allusions and the overt comparison of the Narcissus myth—a myth that by this point in his poem already has been the subject of an explicit, extended, and negative "moralization."

Robert Holcot, perhaps the best known of the classicizing English friars of the fourteenth century, uses Ovid's story of Pygmalion as an evidence of idolatry. Pygmalion's statue was an idol of the "rubricated" sort mentioned at Wisd. of Sol. 13.14. If we must distinguish between the "moral" and the "historical" Holcot's interest here is principally of the latter sort. This is a bit of biblical archaeology; the pagan idolatry abstractly identified by the sacred text is exemplified by a specific detail in the profane text. We find here, incidentally, yet another exemplification of the common medieval assumption of the historical simultaneity of the world of the classical epic and the world of Old Testament history. Guillaume de Machaut, a close reader of the *Roman de la Rose*, in one of his mainly unread poems develops at length a comparison between the idolatry of Pygmalion and that of King Mannasses. That he departs radically from Jean's own poetic agenda is, on the face of it, quite unlikely. There may be less dispute here than meets the eye: I can certainly agree that in the *Roman de la Rose* the story of Pygmalion relates "to Jean's conception of how both the artist and the lover create" if we see that what they both create are "idols."

But if Pygmalion's statue was a notorious "idol" in medieval literary tradi-

---

61. Cf. *Met.* 1.524 ("Nec prosunt domino, quae prosunt omnibus artes" with 10.252 ("Ars adeo latet arte sua").

tion, so also was the Palladium; and it is probable that Chaucer appreciated in Jean's robust conclusion of his *Roman* the evidence that the French poet's silent collation of the two images in his imagination. There was in the first place the happy coincidence that Pygmalion's image—like the twin idols of the Trojan mind, the Palladium and Criseyde—was of a supernal, supernatural beauty; of it Ovid had written "qua femina nasci / nulla potest" (*Met.* 10.248–49). That is a cliché; more eccentric and therefore more suggestive is the curious positioning of the image, which, in an elliptical allegory that defies a literal reduction, is at once the image of a woman and a structural detail of the architecture of the castle keep in which Bel Accueil is imprisoned. The image appears as abruptly and mysteriously in Jean's textual wall as the Palladium appeared mysteriously on the masonry walls of Troy. The first we hear of it is when Venus, in a quaint image, takes aim at "un petitete archiere / qu'ele vit en la tour reposte" (a tiny narrow aperture which she saw hidden in the tower; 20762–63). It is mentioned a second and final time, also in terms of its position in the tower:

> Bien avisa dame Cypris
> cele ymage que je devise,
> antre les pilerez assise,
> anz en la tour, droit ou mileu.
>   (21198–202)

(Dame Cypris looked well upon the image which I have described, the one placed between the pillars, within the tower, right in the middle.)

The English *Recuyell*, translating with full accuracy the Latin of Guido delle Colonne, says this of the construction of Troy: "And what hit was all redy and made saue the tour a meruayllous thynge descendid from the heuen. And that stack in the walle of the temple with the grete Awter."[62] Jean's repeated

62. Raoul Lefevre, *The Recuyell of the Historyes of Troye*, trans. William Caxton, ed. O. Sommer (London: David Nutt, 1894), 659. An illustration of the adoration of the Palladium in a copy of the *Filostrato* (Florence, Bibl. Naz. II. 90, fol. 67) as published by R. S. Loomis, *A Mirror of Chaucer's World* (Princeton: Princeton University Press, 1965), fig. 69, nicely suggests both the mural elevation of the idol and the syncretistic aspect of its veneration. A cognate Palladian "idol"—not of course the Palladium itself —had been found in the Temple of Minerva in the Forum of Nerva at Rome. According to one medieval "archaeologist" it was this idol that was associated with the destruction of the chaste Hippolytus and with the martyrdom of recusant Christians. See the

allusions to the matter of Troy in the *Roman de la Rose*, taken as they are from Virgil, Ovid, and Horace, are for the most part commonplace adornments of medieval erotic and satiric poetry, but insofar as he thinks of the plucking of his rose as involving the burning of a fortified place, the place he seems to have in mind is Troy. We recall the curious fact that the missile that Venus fires is at once an arrow and a torch or blazing brand (*brandon*). According to the Trojan legend transmitted by the Latin poets, Paris' mother Hecuba had dreamed during her pregnancy that a flaming brand came forth from her womb and set fire to the city, all of which was destroyed. The prophecy was hardly obscure in the light of subsequent events. It is a typical Magdunian grotesquerie that combines the brand and its implausible vaginal housing. We may also wish to recall Apollo's imperfect squelch of Cupid: "Stick to your torch."

If we have learned anything about the operations of "classical imitation" in Chaucer's *Troilus* it is that it involves not so much a series of bilateral textual relations as the invocation of large traditions of topical commonplaces. Thus specific details of Jean's description of the castle may reflect (or be reflected in) medieval notions of the extraordinary beauty of ancient Troy to be found in a wide variety of texts.[63] One book of special potential interest in this regard is Benoît's *Roman de Troie*, a poem with substantial claims on Chaucerians yet pending. Benoît's description of the Ilium, the great tower of Troy, includes the details of "images" mounted in it.[64] It is not the fact of these general and conventional reminiscences that draws our attention to Benoît, however, but a deeper textual filiation. Benoît's memorable contribution to the medieval Trojan legend was of course the episode of Briseida, direct ancestress of Criseyde, an episode that in Boccaccio and Chaucer moves from the poet's

---

Narracio de mirabilibus urbis Rome of Master Gregorius, ed. R. B. C. Huygens (Leiden: Brill, 1970), 22: "Huic adducebantur Christicole et quicumque flexis genibus Palladem non adorabat, diversis penis vitam terminabat. Ad hoc ydolum vel simulacrum Ypolitus cum familia sua adductus, quia illud neglexit, equis distractus martirium subiit."

63. E.g., Jean writes of the shrine mounted in the tower, "Cil pilerez d'argent estoient, / mout gent, et d'argent soutenoient / une ymage," which is then compared with Pygmalion's "ymage d'ivuire" (*RR* 20767–69, 20796); cf. the description of the keep of Troy, "le chastel sans per, dont les portes furent d'ivoire et les columpnes d'argent," *Ovide moralisé en prose*, ed. C. de Boer (Amsterdam: North Holland, 1954), 275.

64. "Les batailles a li crenel / Furent tuit orne a cisel. / Images de fiin or entieres / On mout asis par les maisieres / Quant achevez fu Ylion." Benoît de Ste.-Maure, *Le Roman de Troie*, ed. L. Constans (Paris: SATF, 1904–12), 3085f. (I, p. 156).

peripheral vision to the center of narrative attention. Since the story would seem to be Benoît's invention, he merits the lasting honor of having created one of the great love fictions in our literature. But Benoît's version begins quite late in the story as we know it, with the plan to transport Briseida from Troy to the Greek camp.

More important if less remarked is the fact there there is also in the *Roman de Troie* a clear narrative paradigm for the action of Chaucer's first two books (Boccaccio's first three parts). I refer to Benoît's extended account of the mad passion of Achilles for Polyxena. There are cardinal parallels between this story and the story of Troilus' spectacular inamoration. Achilles abruptly falls in love with Polyxena upon seeing her.[65] Nursing his debilitating passion in extended soliloquy, he is discovered by a friend to whom he reveals his secret. The unnamed friend then undertakes to be his go-between in embassies to Hecuba and Priam. It seems quite likely to me that Boccaccio here found, almost thrown away by the centrifugal tendencies of Benoît's narrative method, the bright idea that would eventually and brilliantly illuminate Chaucer's poem through the character of Pandarus; but Boccaccio was not the first writer to build upon Benoît's invention. One of the most arresting passages in the soliloquy of Achilles identifies the erotic folly of the Greek hero with that of Narcissus:

> Narcisus sui, ço sai e vei
> qui tant ama l'ombre de sei
> qu'il en morut so la fontaine.
>   (*Roman de Troie* 17691–93)

(I am a Narcissus—that I know and see—who so much loved his own shadow that he died beneath the fountain.)

It is distinctly possible that this passage was known to Guillaume de Lorris when he wrote his own version of the Narcissus story in the *Roman de la Rose*.[66]

---

65. This episode belongs to the earliest phase of the process by which the Homeric heroes rapidly became "romanticized" in late antique literature. See Mantero, *Ricerche sull'Heroikos*, 206 and cited bibliography.

66. Cf. especially "Qu'il musa tant en la fontaine / qu'il ama son ombre demainne, / si en fu morz a la parclouse" (1491–93). However, Guillaume may instead be remembering a cognate passage in Chrétien's *Cligès*, ed. A. Micha (Paris: Champion, 1957), lines 2726–31.

What I regard as more than possible, as quite probable indeed, is that Jean de Meun drew inspiration from Benoît's passage when he wrote his "Pygmalion." For Jean's Pygmalion, speaking in the first person, compares himself specifically with Narcissus on precisely the grounds that Benoît's Achilles does—the grounds of comparative folly:

> Car, se l'escriture ne ment,
> maint ont plus folement amé.
> N'ama jadis ou bois ramé,
> a la fonteine clere et pure,
> Narcisus sa propre figure . . .
>   (RR 20844–48)

(For, if the text does not lie, many have loved more madly. Did not Narcissus, at the clear, pure fountain in the wood, love his own image?)

We know that among the texts Chaucer knew earliest and best the *Roman de la Rose* was prominent. We know as well that in writing the *Troilus* Chaucer proceeded, in a fashion not unlike that of a careful research scholar, to make a thorough survey of all the principal primary sources written in the languages at his command that dealt with the poetic history of Troy. We have no reason to doubt that he noted, appreciated, and responded to some of the more delicate, complex, and tenuous relationships among the texts of his library-quarry, or even that he did so with as much perspicacity and imagination as modern scholars who have examined those same ruins in the cause of understanding his poem. Thus what may at first blush seem paradoxical and bizarre—the discovery throughout Chaucer's poem of a poetic pattern of sexual idolatry, rich in its textual filiations to a broad spectrum of antique and pseudoantique texts, becomes upon reflection wholly explicable.

PAGAN LOVE AND SPIRITUAL FORNICATION

The unifying image of Trojan idolatry—the Palladium—not infrequently appears as a stage prop in early medieval antipagan polemic. In the constantly surprising *Anthologia Latina*, for example, Riese has published under the title of "Contra paganos" a very old school-poem that perfectly illustrates one essential tension of medieval Latinity—that between an impulse toward explicit theological condemnation of pagan religion and the nearly paralyzing admiration for the classical poets who wrote about it. It is worth quoting its opening lines, as they provide something of an anthology of the religious archaeology of the *Troilus:*

> Dicite, qui colitis lucos antrumque Sibyllae
> Idaeumque nemus, Capitolia celsa Tonantis,
> Palladium, Priamique Lares, Vestaequae sacellum,
> Incestosque deos, nuptam cum fratre sororem,
> inmitem puerum, Veneris monumenta nefandae,
> Purpurea quos sola facit pretexta sacratos,
> Quis numquam verum Phoebi cortina locuta est,
> Etruscus ludit semper quos vanus haruspex . . .[67]

The thematic connection here between idolatry and the sexual licentiousness (the *incesti dei* and *nefanda Venus*) is a biblical and medieval Christian commonplace. So far as Chaucer is concerned, he repeatedly links the ideas of sexual attraction and consummation with specific rites of religious observance —so repeatedly, indeed, that it is impossible to avoid his thematic thrust. Troilus first sees Criseyde at a religious service, the veneration of the Palladium. Pandarus anticipates Criseyde's apprehension of what people might think if they saw Troilus coming to and from her house in the following remarkable fashion:

> "What! who wol demen, though he se a man
> To temple go, that he thymages eteth?"
>   (2.372–73)

I shall spare the courteous reader my speculations concerning the import of those lines. Troilus, when he needs a lie to explain where he is when he is actually in Criseyde's bed, comes up with a real whopper: he is keeping a solitary

---

67. *Anthologia Latina*, ed. Alexander Riese (Leipzig: Teubner, 1894), 1.1:20, p. 20. (Tell me, you who worship sacred groves, the cave of the Sibyl and the holy glade of Ida, the lofty temple of the Thunderer, the Palladium, the Lares of Priam, Cybele's shrine, the incestuous gods, the sister married to her brother, the ruthless boy, statues of obscene Venus, you for whom the purple robe alone makes priests, to whom the tripod of Apollo has never spoken truth, whom the fraudulent Etruscan haruspicator ever deludes.)

vigil at an Apollonian oracle (3.533–46). In the event it turns out that Troilus was not mistaken to imagine his night in bed with Criseyde in the alternative terms of religious experience, for the description of sexual consummation is thick with religious language, prayers, liturgical actions, ceremonial echoes, and the persistently sacerdotal ministrations of the priestly Pandarus.

I conclude that Chaucer's determination to get the theme of idolatry "right" explains the fact that he so thoroughly researched ancient religious practice—more thoroughly, in some instances, than those modern critics who have gone to the trouble of cataloging his supposed confusions.[68] Though the original brilliant invention of collating the Palladium with Criseida was Boccaccio's, it is Chaucer alone who has made the theme of sexual idolatry radically present during all the stages of the love affair, including its aftermath.

Any consideration of sexual idolatry must de rigeur make at least a brief consideration of the decisive "sex scene" of Chaucer's poem, an episode that elicits widely divergent interpretations among Chaucer's most thoughtful readers. I am well aware that I offer nothing new in observing that the text of this scene is bright with threads of religious language and indeed of specifically Christian sacramental and liturgical language. What is at issue is not the presence of such language but its import. Anyone who believes, as I do, that a great deal of our traditional difficulty in understanding medieval poetry reveals our imperfect ability to grasp the intentional ironies of medieval poets must perforce be aware that the critical appeal to "irony" is fraught with dangers; for "irony," like "deconstruction," can devour its own children. I must nonetheless invoke it, even in the full awareness that the ironic criterion is not one that can be empirically demonstrated or satisfactorily proven at the theoretical level. Let me propose as a point of departure a suitably Gothic *questio disputata:* can good sex get you into heaven?

One of the most distinguished of living medievalists, Peter Dronke, pub-

---

68. E.g., Troilus' deceitful account of his planned vigil at the Apollonian shrine speaks of seeing the holy laurel shake "or that Apollo spake out of the tree" (3.543). Both Root and Windeatt irrelevantly cite the first book of the *Metamorphoses*. Root says, "I know of no authority for Chaucer's idea that Apollo speaks from out the tree" (472). Windeatt says, "This line seems an instance of Chaucer's confusing a classical story" (277). The fact is, however, that *the god spoke from a tree.* See Pierre Amandry, *La Mantique apollinienne à Delphes* (Paris: E. de Boccard, 1975), 126–34 and cited texts; Marie Delcourt, *L'Oracle de Delphes* (Paris: Payot, 1955), 73; and H. W. Park and D. E. W. Wormell, *The Delphic Oracle* (Oxford: Oxford University Press, 1956), 1:3.

lished a brief but memorable article in 1964, "The Conclusion of Troilus and Criseyde."[69] His argument—in crude summary but with no intention of misrepresentation—was this. The religious language of the bedroom scene of the third book, particularly the echoes there of the Easter liturgy, signal Chaucer's remarkable valorization of the love of Troilus and Criseyde. Their sexual union is a nearly sacramental act, an emblem of the force of cosmic regeneration which the poet sincerely reverences. Troilus' performance as a lover, here and elsewhere in the poem, is in Chaucer's eyes sufficient to merit for him a kind of salvation, sidereal immortality in the eighth sphere. With astonishing irony Chaucer in the very act of translation overturns the clearly negative implications of *Fil.* 8.28 ("Cotal fine . . .") in his own stanza (5.1828–34) "Swich fyn hath, lo, this Troilus for love! . . . Swych fyn hath false worldes brotelnesse!" The sense of this crucial stanza is something like the following: "Look at what a wonderful and unexpected end Troilus had, saved by the quality of his love from the apparent imperfections and difficulties of his situation."

Of course, numerous other critics have claimed that Chaucer sees in his lovers' sex life a virtue nearly religious in its quality.[70] But I find Dronke's argument particularly fascinating in its implicit reliance on the criterion of irony, that is, an utterance whose actual meaning is the opposite of its apparent meaning. If I may continue for a moment to use "positive" and "negative" as shorthand terms, I find that Dronke's claim is that a stanza actually negative in the Italian original while remaining apparently negative in the English adaptation actually becomes wholly positive. The Italian *fine* is a bad end so to speak, the English *fyn* a good end.

It will not surprise my reader to hear that I think that the English stanza in question ("Swich fyn hath, lo, this Troilus for love!") is both apparently and actually "negative" in its assessment of Troilus' amatory career. On the other hand, I am faced with the difficulty of also believing that certain passages in the poem that appear to be positive in their thrust are actually negative.

For example, Chaucer thus describes Troilus' sexual foreplay:

Hire armes smale, hire streyghte bak and softe,
Hire sydes longe, flesshly, smothe, and white

---

69. Peter Dronke, "The Conclusion of Troilus and Criseyde," *Medium Aevum* 33 (1964): 47–52.
70. See, e.g., Peter Heidtmann, "Sex and Salvation in Troilus and Criseyde," *ChR* 2 (1968): 246–53.

He gan to stroke, and good thrift bad ful ofte
Hire snowissh throte, hire brestes rounde and lite;
Thus in this hevene he gan hym to delite . . . (3.1247–51)

We are so used to extended and explicit descriptions of physical lovemaking
that we may forget just how unusual they are in the literature of earlier centuries. In premodern Europe such passages appear to have been implicitly
reserved for the genre of comedy. There are virtually none in medieval literature outside of the context of ribald and often bitter humor, and certainly none
in the *Filostrato*, written by the allegedly randiest author of his century.

I suppose that in this passage Chaucer is imitating a memorable antique
poem, *Amores* 1.6, Ovid's "Love in the Afternoon." The solitary interesting
addition to Ovid's anatomical catalog of desirable female parts, and consequently the detail most likely to claim our attention, is the syncretistic idea of
a sexual "heaven." To believe that Chaucer thought that sexual intercourse was
the highest earthly good is already for some of us a difficult assignment. Must
we also believe that he thought it was the highest *heavenly* good? Even critics
disposed to a benign and optimistic view of the treatment of sexuality in the
poem may find themselves disturbed or at least pensive at the suggestion.[71] Yet
there seems no prima facie reason to deny that Chaucer is here saying straight
something entirely consistent with what Dronke finds him to be saying with
the obliqueness of irony at the end of the poem.

The solution I propose—though its fuller explication with regard to this
specific passage of text must await another and more appropriate context—is
once again the invocation of anterior poetic tradition; for I think that it can be
demonstrated that in the third book Chaucer's treatment of sexual idolatry (or,
if that term begs the argument, religious sex) continues to be guided by Jean
de Meun's treatment of the same theme in the *Roman de la Rose*. Let us recall
that the equation of sexual satisfaction with the joy of heaven is introduced
into the third book by Pandarus. "Make the redy right anon" he encourages
Troilus, "For thow shalt into hevene blisse wende" (3.703–4). The image does
not come from Boccaccio, but when the narrator uses it again he does so in a
context that hints at its specific ancestry:

Awey, thow foule daunger and thow feere,
And lat hem in this hevene blisse dwelle,

71. See Rowe, *O Love, O Charité*, 102.

That is so heigh that no man kan it telle.
(3.1321–23)

Foul Danger and Fear are not merely abstractions but personified abstractions (hence the pronoun "thow"), and they surely invoke the *Roman de la Rose*, a poem in which Dangiers and Peor ally against the Lover in a doomed attempt to frustrate his quest for sexual intercourse.

The Lover's own most powerful ally is Venus—to whom, we may note, Troilus utters a quick prayer immediately upon being told that he is about to be transported "into hevene blisse" (3.705)—but Venus acts only after the decisive pronouncement of Genius. I know of no other medieval thinker, using that word loosely, from either the historical or the fictional worlds, who actually preaches that you can screw your way into heaven. Fellow admirers of Jean de Meun may agree with me that one such thinker is enough. In his sermon, the metaphor of "heavenly sex," which one might suppose to be a hackneyed metaphor of a tired imagination, takes on a remarkable and memorable vivacity. For Genius claims that it is the religious duty of all men—and though he addresses a mixed congregation, his advice is gender-specific—to use their sexual organs with vigor and with high purpose. The reward of loyal loving is eternal life in a biblical heaven of which the garden of Guillaume de Lorris is merely a deceptive type or shadow; and the appropriate penalties for anything less than a total commitment to uninhibited heterosexual intercourse are brutal castration and eternal damnation. No excuse will do: neither "sexual orientation," as we now call it, nor ascetic aspiration, nor even the inglorious fatigue of the middle-aged. The literary filiation between Genius and Pandarus is by now too well established for me to need to argue it here; it is one of the most astonishing, but also one of the most satisfying, literary relationships in fourteenth-century poetry.

I realize that to invoke the *Roman de la Rose* is not to resolve the irony debate but to change its venue. But at least the philosophical issues are clearer there because in a sense cruder. There the chief issue is quite literally life and death. Genius claims to be on the side of life, but from the point of view of Christian theology he is on the side of death.[72] Jean de Meun was both a genuine scholar and a genuine intellectual. He was much impressed by the philosophical poetry

72. See the excellent essay by Brigitte L. Callay, "The Road to Salvation in the *Roman de la Rose*," *Pascua Mediaevalia: Studies voor Prof. Dr. J. M. De Smet* (Louvain: Universitaire Pers Leuven, 1983), 499–509.

of Alain de Lille, and he tried to build on his predecessor's work. It became his satirical philosophical purpose to explore the limitations of "natural man," by which he understood the human species minus the grace of the Incarnation. Chaucer takes the same journey, though by a different path. He is writing not personification allegory but covertly polemical historical fiction. His device is to create an insistently historical world populated by highly engaging and at times highly admirable pagans who nonetheless fall tragically and culpably short of the spiritual possibilities of their own culture and their own humanity.

A certain level of comedy is easily enough apprehended in this enterprise, but it is important as well to try to appreciate Chaucer's serious, indeed his philosophical purposes, however bizarre their context may seem. We here see Chaucer as pupil to Jean de Meun, a poet preoccupied with the problem of surface and substance, preoccupied by it to a degree far greater than is demanded of any poet who elects to write allegory. Perhaps his greatest single invention was Faussemblant, in Rutebeuf a mere name, in his own *Roman* an invention that allowed him to make poetically visible the vice that walks invisible, except to God alone. A deep and philosophical interest in love, comprehensively considered in its special variety, led Jean to explore from the point of view of the wisdom of his own day some of the more interesting disjunctions, linguistic and otherwise, involved in the pursuit of Ovidian love—love seen as a social ideal presided over by the Cupid of the *Amores* on the one hand or as a cosmic, generative force presided over by the Venus of the *Fasti* on the other.

To the theme of love as elegant social ritual inherited with the poem of Guillaume he added the theme of love as the sexual redress of human mortality, a strain of ancient Epicureanism securely preserved for medieval readers in several of their surprisingly favorite books—patristic theories of virginity. In a series of remarkable scenes, such as the arrival of Faussemblant at the court of Amours and the episcopal vesting of Genius by the hands of Venus, Jean's ungentle satire dramatized the moral sleaziness and the intellectual fatuity implied in an absolute valorization of sexual love. Jean's enterprise involved him in the somewhat paradoxical discovery of obscenity. With Augustine he found that what the world may take to be elegant and courtly may be in fact obscene.[73] And with John of Salisbury he showed that what might be obscene on the literary surface could be most beautiful in its moral substance.[74]

73. See J. V. Fleming, *Reason and the Lover* (Princeton: Princeton University Press, 1984), 24.
74. "Res quoque quae turpis et obscenae est in superficie, honestissimae veritatis quan-

Like Jean's, Chaucer's classicism never strayed far from central Christian philosophical concerns. Certainly we see in his thematic use of the Palladium a happy issue of the marriage of antiquarian and moralist. Benoît and Guido had already treated the Palladium as a representative pagan "idol," and while it is probably impossible to identify with certainty their own historical sources, it is both possible and useful to point to a general pattern. The various references to the Palladium in the apologetic literature of the early Church, in addition to sharing a common theological point of view, seem to share a common reliance on Virgil.[75] The historical mood of *Troilus and Criseyde* is the mood of the christianized Virgil.

It is fitting that the greatest of the Christian exegetes, Augustine, was also an accomplished Virgilian whose complex attitude toward pagan religion was displayed at length in a number of his most widely read books, and in particular in the *City of God*, a work universally admired in Chaucer's world. Merely to mention Augustine's name is substantially to refute the notion that the fourteenth century witnessed the eclipse of allegorical scriptural exegesis or the emergence of a widely shared "value-free" historical attitude that habitually eschewed acts of moral judgment in favor of neutral and objective description. If we know the intellectual climate of an age by what it reads as well as by what it writes, we may well conclude that the fourteenth century was in western Europe an *aetas Augustiniana* unprecedented even in earlier times; for never was Augustine's intellectual authority more profound or more ubiquitous, and never were his major works, including of course his exegetical works, more widely distributed and cited.[76] This is not to say that we do not find writers and thinkers of a different mold; we do, of course. But the discovery that would make Jean de Meun or Geoffrey Chaucer stylistically retrograde by being "Augustinian" could in my opinion be only the result of concentrating on a few selected and probably exotic trees at the expense of the vast forest.

It would be difficult for me to believe that Chaucer is more likely to have

doque substantiam tegit." *Policraticus* 2.16 (Webb 1.95). This citation was drawn to my attention by D. W. Robertson, Jr.

75. Schelkle, *Virgil in der Deutung Augustins*, 91.

76. On the subject of "best-selling" authors in the later fourteenth century, see Joseph de Ghellinck, "En marge des catalogues des bibliothèques médiévales," in *Miscellanea Francesco Ehrle* (Rome: Vatican, 1924), 5:351: "Un nom domine tous les autres, faut-il le dire? c'est celui de saint Augustin."

read secondary commentaries on the *City of God* than the primary text itself. That is, just as I am convinced that Chaucer's knowledge of the Latin poets came from reading the Latin poets, so also am I convinced that he came by his historical information about paganism from reputable primary sources. His researches among the primary sources for the Trojan legend were, as successive editors have incrementally demonstrated, prodigious for his day and age. He would have found, in the very opening chapters of the definitive history of Latin Troy, Augustine's prominent thematic use of the Palladium as an emblem of pagan idolatry generally, as an emblem of Trojan moral and military failure, and as an emblem of the "oldness" of the "City of Man." The a priori assumption that Chaucer reflects these Augustinian attitudes is, given the cultural circumstances, entirely reasonable; when we appreciate the poetic use Chaucer makes of the Palladium, the probability becomes near certainty.

Two related aspects of Augustine's treatment of the Palladium, aspects that suggest the degree to which the "historical" and the "moral" were for him the same side of the same coin, are particularly relevant to Chaucer's *Troilus*. The first is his implicit belief in the idea of the *translatio studii,* the legend of the Trojan origins of the Roman state. Though prepared to identify and on occasion to condemn the fabulous elements in Virgil, he treated the Trojan history of the second book as real history, as medieval readers after him generally would.

It is typical of the revolutionary strategies of the *City of God* that Augustine turns Roman civic history on its head, however. It is not the ancient dignity of Rome that engages him, though he clearly takes that for granted, but the historically demonstrated inefficacy of the Roman gods translated from the banks of the Simois to the banks of the Tiber. Had not Virgil himself said that Aeneas and his companions had carried with them from burning Troy their "defeated gods" (*vinctos deos*)? In this phrase he found an extraordinary indictment of the spiritual debility of paganism. The pagan claim that the calamities of Rome were to be ascribed to Christian apostasy was rendered absurd by the mere invocation of Trojan history, while the military circumstances of the capture of Rome, during which the conquering invaders had respected the sanctity of Christian basilicas, underscored the absolute distinction between the worshipers of Christ and the worshipers of the old gods. That is Augustine's "historical" point, as it were. His "moral" point is to transfer the focus of attention from the incapacities of the allegedly guardian gods to those of their protégés. Here Augustine again quotes Virgil:

corripuere sacram effigiem manibus cruentis
virgineas ausi divae contingere vittas.

(Aeneid 2.167–68)

(They seized the holy figure and actually touched the virgin headband of
our goddess with blood still on their hands.)

It is worth remarking that Augustine simply assumes on the part of his
readers a knowledge of the details of the rape of the Palladium: the treason
of Antenor, the cupidity of the corrupt guardian-priest Thoas, the sacrilege
of Diomedes and Ulysses, the lies of Sinon, and the lethal deception of the
wooden horse, the gift offered by the Greeks in alleged reparation of the out-
rage committed against Athena's sacred image. Every step of this sorry history
involved the moral corruption of Trojans or their inability to hear the truth
even when it was screamed into their faces. With telling sarcasm Augustine
points to the fatuity of believing that the goddess could protect the Trojans
when the Trojans themselves proved incapable of protecting the goddess.

Augustine continues with *Aeneid* 2.169–70, "Ex illo fluere ac retro sublapsa
referri / Spes Danaum" (From that night the prospects of the Greeks receded
like an ebbing tide and trickled away), the last phrase of which, as we have
seen, eventually was reflected in Chaucer's line (1.154) "That was hire trust
aboven everichon." Augustine points out that what actually happened was that
Troy was put to fire and sword and Troy's king slaughtered as he stood at the
altar of his household gods. Augustine does not find it an impressive argument that these things happened only *after* the Palladium had been stolen from
the city, for he sees little efficacy in a guardian who herself needs guarding.
"Neque enim homines a simulacro, sed simulacrum ab hominibus servabatur.
Quo modo ergo colebatur, ut patriam custodiret et cives, quae suos non valuit
custodire custodes?"[77]

Though Augustine was chiefly concerned with what he took to be the *spiritual* fornication, or idolatry, of the old Roman state, the heir of Troy, he was
not wholly unconcerned with more mundane adulteries. His witty remark
silently invokes Juvenal in a fashion that demonstrates a congruence of thematic association in Augustine's and Chaucer's view of the Palladium. Juvenal
had written thus in his sixth satire:

77. Augustine, *De civitate Dei* 1.2, ad finem. Translation: "The idol did not protect the
men; the men protected the idol. How were they to worship it so that it might guard
the city and its citizens, if it was incapable of guarding its guardians?"

Audio quid veteres olim moneatis amici:
"Pene sera, cohibe." Sed quis custodiet ipsos
custodes? (6.346–49)

(I hear all this time the advice of my old friends: "Put on a lock and keep
your wife indoors." Yes, but who will ward the warders?)

The context here is the familiar misogynist argument that marriage is unwise
because all women are sluts simply waiting for the first opportunity to betray
their husbands. Guardians, including eunuchs, are dangerous threats themselves. No one is to be trusted, and no place—however sacred—is safe. "Every
altar now has its Clodius." Clodius was an enterprising lecher who had dis-
guised himself as a woman and penetrated the secret and exclusively female
cult of the Bona Dea to attempt the seduction of Caesar's wife. Such are the
sleazy associations Augustine invokes when he writes of the history of the Palladium. Medieval readers were as happy to believe the worst about what really
happened in the mysterious privacies of ancient religion as they were to read
about the depravities of their own professional religious.[78]

Like Augustine, Chaucer lived in a state that claimed its moral descent from
ancient Troy. The city in which he lived and wrote, London, was known in
civil mythology as Troinovant, or New Troy; and although we shall probably
never be able to reconstruct with any real degree of intellectual sharpness the
thematic connections of old and new that he sought to exploit in his poem,
we can still appreciate the care he takes, once again unique among medieval poetic historians, to bring out the parallels between Great Troy the city
and little Troy the man. Lest any reader mistake his superficial loyalty to the
imagined fatalistic ethos of his imaginary ancient *auctor,* Chaucer has invited
Boethius into the fiction to insist upon an order governed by Providence, in
which the moral initiatives of the free-willed and not the immutable decrees
of fate structure the poetic agenda. Chaucer's pagan history is not pagan at all,
but Augustinian.[79]

78. As, e.g., in the popular exemplary story of Mundus and Paulina, memorialized in
English poetry by John Gower (*Confessio Amantis*, 1.761–1076), in *Complete Works of
John Gower*, 3 vols., ed. G. C. Macaulay (Oxford: Clarendon, 1900), vol. 2.
79. The idea of individual moral responsibility is absolutely fundamental to Augustine's
philosophy of history. The famous maxim expressed in the *City of God* is "voluntate
propria quisque malus est" (2.4), and it is intimately connected with his idea of the
freedom of the will. Just as he is a great believer in and recorder of the virtues of the

It will be immediately apparent to anyone who has spent time over the pages of the fourteenth-century scholar-friars that most of their knowledge of the history and culture of classical antiquity comes directly from the *City of God*. We need not imagine that the capacities of a humanist working in the vernacular sphere were notably inferior to those of various Dominican scholarasters. One of Chaucer's strict contemporaries, the Frenchman Raoul de Presles, undertook in the 1380s the formidable task of making a full translation with commentary of the *City of God*. Though he freely and often silently used the exegetical work of his predecessors, in the style of his age, he could boast of a considerable learning that he brought to bear upon his work in numerous original contributions.[80] His explanation of the Palladium is learned but straightforward in its moral drift.[81] Of it he naturally used the word *idol,* that being the term that most easily explains its presence in the Augustinian text. He had a sophisticated appreciation of the varying versions of its history, and he recommended Dictys as the particular authority whom the interested reader should pursue for information. One point of particular interest, perhaps, is his knowledgeable use of Ovid's *Fasti,* the poetical source that most clearly articulated the continuing Roman history of the Palladium. This was a subject of interest to Geoffrey Chaucer, burgher of Troinovant.

The Roman investment in the myth of the Palladium, in part recorded by the great Latin poets and in part created by them, was substantial. Livy, recording an ancient debate about the possible relocation of the Latin capital away from Rome, represents Camillus as opposing the plan as an impious slight against "the undying fires of Vesta and the statue which is kept in Vesta's temple as a guarantee of success."[82] So great was the importance of the Palladium in the Roman civil religion that the image was kept in the innermost sanctuary (*penus*) of the Vesta and handled by the priestesses on ceremonial occasions.

---

ancient pagan Romans, Augustine is the confident judge of ancient pagan vice. What is being praised or blamed is not, for Augustine, morally netural, historically determined behavior, but the free moral choices of human beings created by God and endowed by Him with reason and freedom of the will.

80. Sharon Dunlap Smith, "New Themes for the City of God around 1400: the Illustration of Raoul de Presles' Translation," *Scriptorium* 36 (1982), 69.

81. Raoul de Presles, *Cité de Dieu* (Abbeville, 1486), A8v–B1r.

82. 5.57.2, cited by R. M. Ogilvie, *The Romans and Their Gods* (New York: Norton, 1970), 90; see further Ogilvie's learned note in his *Commentary on Livy, Books 1–5* (Oxford: Oxford University Press, 1965), 745–46.

The impression given by certain coins of the reign of Galba, which show a seated virgin holding in her outstretched hand the statue of the virgin goddess, is that this Roman Palladium was a miniature, perhaps one-fourth or one-fifth of life-size.[83]

There were several stories, none of which really made sense, to explain the Palladium's presence in Rome.[84] The canonical epic legend, which was at least not contradicted by Virgil's text, was that Aeneas had brought it himself. The theory that Aeneas had in his possession the statue whose theft from Troy precipitated the destruction of the city appears to have seemed plausible to a race for whom the importance of being Trojan was all-consuming. As R. G. Austin perceptively noted, Virgil's own account of the functions and powers of the Palladium is a brilliant "rigmarole" designed by Greeks further to deceive Trojans already self-deceived.[85] In a rather different way this is Augustine's view too. His adversaries were not ancient pagans but modern ones, and his concern is to expose the folly of trusting in the Roman present the gods who have proven themselves untrustworthy in the Trojan past.

It is Augustine's emphatic focus on the disastrous *social* implications of individual irrational passion that I find most arresting. He rails not against idols but against idolaters. This is a healthy attitude with which to approach the vexed question of the character of Criseyde, Troilus' idol. It seems safe to predict that a feminist criticism will one day offer a fresh and satisfying account of aspects of the *Troilus* that continue to be intractable, but I venture to suggest that it must first move beyond the impulse to vindicate Criseyde as a social

---

83. See Henry Cohen, *Description historique des monnaies frappées sous l'Empire Romaine* (Paris: Rollin et Feuardant, 1880–92), 1:339. Apollodorus (*Bibl.* 3.12.3, as cited by Austin on *Aeneid* 2.168) described the ancient Palladium "as a wooden image, 3 cubits high, the feet close together, the right hand holding a spear, the left a distaff and spindle." Ancient visual evidence is analyzed in the still useful dissertation of Fernand Chavannes, *De Palladii raptu* (Berlin: Heinrich & Kemke, 1891), 1–26. Some indication of the way in which Chaucer's contemporaries imagined pagan idols—in a visual tradition unbroken from the time of the Pompeii murals—is afforded by illustrated manuscripts of the *City of God;* see Alexandre de Laborde, *Les Manuscrits à peintures de la Cité de Dieu de saint Augustin* (Paris: E. Rahir, 1909).

84. See Jacques Perret, *Les Origines de la legende troyenne de Rome (281–31)* (Paris: Belles Lettres, 1942), 66–67; Franz Bömer, *Rom und Troia: Untersuchungen zur Fruhgeschichte* (Baden-Baden: Verlag für Kunst und Wissenschaft, 1951), 62–64.

85. See R. G. Austin's note on *Aeneid* 2.163 (p. 85).

victim, an impulse that is simply the equal and opposite reaction to forceful
textual strategies to exculpate the male world at her expense. Antifeminism
was not imposed upon the *matière de Troie* by twelfth-century Christian clerics.
They merely saw there what they believed already—namely, that sexual passion brought disaster to even the strongest, the wisest, the noblest, to Samson,
to David, to Solomon. As Benoît has his Achilles ask in the *Roman de Troie*
(18448), "Qui est qui vers Amors est sage?" (Who is there who is wise so far
as Love is concerned?).

The origins of the male animus against Criseyde are much older than Criseyde herself. Criseyde is, as it were, Helen's younger sister. Trojans are willing, perhaps eager to think the worst of them, and await only the changing
winds of Fortune to do so openly. The Byzantine historian Nicetas Aconima-
tus records the glee with which the offspring of Aeneas, amid sarcastic taunts,
burned a statue of Helen.[86] Here the Christian children symbolically brought
to completion a plan first meditated by the old pagan father himself.

In one of the most remarkable scenes of the remarkable second book of the
Aeneid, Aeneas sees Helen hiding in the Trojan Vesta at the very height of the
battle for the city. For a long, mad moment he thinks of going after her, killing
her, avenging his burning city in her blood. In the purity of its impulse to
blame a victim, Aeneas' meditated plan reflects a wonderfully complex sexism.
The cause of Troy's fall is not the folly of Paris, or the venality of Thoas, or
the universal Trojan idiocy that leaves its prophets without honor in their own
land. It is—a woman. And there she is now, the great Greek slut, and in the
Vesta, the inner sanctum of sexual purity! Aeneas abandons his unheroic rev-
erie only when his mother Venus appears on the scene to rub his face in the
incontrovertible fact that it is not Helen who is destroying Troy, but the gods
themselves:

non tibi Tyndaridis facies invisa Lacaenae
culpatusve Paris, divum inclementia, divum,
has evertit opes sternitque a culmine Troiam.
(2.601–3)

(You must not blame the hated beauty of the Spartan Tyndarid, or even
Paris. It was the gods who showed no mercy, it is they who are casting
Troy down from her splendor and power.)

86. *Nicetae Choniatae Historia*, ed. J. A. van Dieten (Berlin: de Gruyter, 1975), 652–53.

The scene is indeed a weird one. Austin calls it "a fantastic apocalypse, gods in devilry, gloating over their horrid work like demons in a medieval Doom." Among them is Pallas (615–616), no longer a prophylactic totem mounted in the wall but a vengeful harridan astride the rampart, glorying in the destruction of the city of which she has been the special protectress. There has been a great deal of controversy about the authenticity of those lines.[87] According to the Servian commentary, in which they are reported, the lines were excised from the poem by Varius and Tucca, Virgil's literary executors, on grounds fascinating for their explicit awareness of the problematical sexual politics involved: "Turpe est viro forti contra feminam irasci" (It is shameful for a strong man to be angry with a woman). The lines are unworthy of Virgil because they are first unworthy of a hero; yet the rage they express is one of the realest facts of medieval literary culture. Within Chaucer's poem it is a Pandarus, the smooth mechanic of Troilus' destruction, who most explicitly (5.1732–33) voices the wrath that Criseyde fully anticipates (5.1054–55) will be her historical lot.

It is a point often argued in Troilus' favor that he is exempt from this mean impulse (5.1695–96). Herein, we are told, Troilus demonstrates the essential "truth" that defines his character, that determines the "comic" arc of his moral progress, and that merits his spiritual salvation in the afterlife. In my own view this is a fundamental misprision of Chaucer's poetic meaning which testifies to the continuing tenacity of the critical urge to exculpate the male world of Trojan heroism. If it be *turpe* for a strong man to be inflamed with anger against a woman, how much more shameful must it be for him to be destroyed by one? Concerning Aeneas it can at least be argued that the episode comes at an elementary stage of the hero's moral education, that it would no more do to judge him entirely by it than it would do to judge Boethius by the emotional self-indulgences displayed in the first book of the *Consolatio*. In the epic world the journey's end is of greater import than the journey's beginning: therein lies the greatness of Aeneas and the tragedy of Troilus. The last living actions of Chaucer's hero are deeply pathological. Troilus *furens,* consumed with jealous

87. The bibliography of works devoted to the passage is extensive. The best defense of its authenticity is by Austin, "Virgil, *Aeneid* 2.567–88"; the most effective attack on it by G. P. Goold, "Servius and the Helen Episode," *HSCP* 74 (1970): 101–68. That the scene is simply the invention of an interpolator seems to me unlikely, since it may be reflected in Greek art of the fourth century. See Marie J. Delepierre, "Une scene de la prise de Troie decrite par Virgile," *Monuments et Mémoirs* 56 (1969): 1–11.

fury against Diomede, announces his suicidal intention (5.1716–22) with adolescent self-pity. His final and memorable feats of arms, emblems of his "ire" (5.1755) make of him the Trojan Achilles.

Chaucer is interested in idolatry, its invention and its reinvention. We recall that he uses of the Palladium the word *relic,* a privileged word from the Christian cultus, a syncretism that has no source in the earlier "Christian historians" of the Trojan myth. I am tempted to wonder whether he had a more radical justification—in the bizarre fact that the Palladium did indeed become a Christian relic, after a fashion. For the goddess did not suffer the sack of New Troy I; well before Augustine's time she sailed to Byzantium with Constantine to his new eponymous capital. From its very foundation the city was in the process of becoming the great warehouse of religious memorabilia which in the West would eventually command the well-heeled piety of the Sainte Chapelle. The Palladium, along with the adze used by Noah to trim the timbers of the Ark, crumbs left over from the feeding of the five thousand, the crosses of the thieves crucified with Jesus, and selected parts of selected saints, was buried beneath the great porphyry column of Constantine.[88] Such an initiative manifests a certain analogy to other arresting inventions of medieval humanism. We may think of it as an archaeological analogue to the fabricated correspondence of Paul and Seneca, perhaps, or Dante's redemption of Statius —or Chaucer's discovery of Lollius.

At the same time it is distinctly not an initiative that a reader of the *City of God* would be likely to undertake. The chief medieval associations of the Palladium were those that linked the city of Troy with the fatal sin of *pride.* In identifying himself to Dante upon their first meeting in the first canto of the *Inferno*, Virgil says

Poeta fui, e cantai di quel giusto
   Figliuol d'Anchise, che venne da Troia,

---

88. Philip Sherrard, *Constantinople: Iconography of a Sacred City* (London: Oxford University Press, 1965), 11. I have not found a fourteenth-century English document claiming that the Palladium was translated to London after the Fourth Crusade, but it would not surprise me if one turned up. There appears to be some documentary encouragement for my own hope that the Palladium is now in New Jersey, a province much in need of Minerva's influence; see Cyril Mango, "Constantine's Porphyry Column and the Chapel of St. Constantine," *Deltion tes christianike Archaiologike Hetairea* 10 (1980–81): 104.

Poiche il superbo Ilïón fu combusto.
      (*Inferno*, 1.73–75)

(I was a poet, and I sang of that just son of Anchises who came from Troy
after proud Ilium was burned.)

With the phrase "superbo Ilïón," Virgil is, as it were, quoting himself, or rather
his hero, the just son of Anchises, who uses the phrase "proud Ilium" in the
opening sentence the third book of the *Aeneid*. Inscribed within the poetic
history of Troy was the belief that its destruction was the punishment of pride,
a belief assumed as the merest empirical fact in the great Christian work of
philosophical history that taught medieval poets so much of what they knew
about the world of the past and so influenced the frame of their thinking about
it. In the preface to the *City of God,* Augustine paraphrases a biblical text (Prov.
3.34) and cites a Virgilian text (*Aeneid* 6.853) of superficially similar meaning. "God resists the proud, but He gives grace to the humble" is the biblical
paraphrase. The Virgilian line, taken from the peroration of Anchises' imperial
charge to Aeneas the Roman to rule the world is "Parcere subiectis et debellare
superbos" ("Remember thou, o Roman, to rule the nations with thy sway . . .
to crown Peace with Law, *to spare the humbled and to tame the proud in war*").
As Augustine wrote he saw before him the New Troy of Aeneas and Augustus
shattered like the Old Troy of Aeneas and Priam, and for him the irony of
history was that God had visited upon the proud that wrathful chastisement
that human pride would arrogate as its own role. Thus he thought of pride,
and he thought of the Palladium.

Chaucer, too, thought of pride and the Palladium. If the London power-
brokers among whom he lived had invested somewhat less heavily than had
the Augustans in the political mythology of the New Troy, they were nonetheless shareholders of record. They had their idols, and they had their idolatries
of private gratification that warred against the common profit. Chaucer was
first of all a poet, not a theologian or a philosopher of history; so he writes as
a poet.

The opening scene of his poem, in which the young bloods of Troy saunter
through the temple square like so many lambs on their way to Cupid's abattoir,
is pure Ovidianism; it is one of dozens of scenes in his poems in which the
erotic doxography of the *Ars amatoria* has been dramatized within the context
of a larger narrative framework. The god's powerful punishment of Troilus'
pride is likewise Ovidian, echoing the *Urtext* of all such episodes in the first

book of the *Metamorphoses*. What of the great world of Troy, of which Troilus is the little world? What is most arresting in the opening scene of the *Troilus* is the fashion in which Chaucer harnesses his antique Ovidian themes to a theme wholly foreign to Ovid's intellectual universe, and wholly native to Augustine's, the theme of idolatry. Troilus scorns the idol of his tribe only for the private idol of a private erotic desire.

This lengthy chapter has had a simple enough agenda of argument, though one that necessarily has involved complex collateral analysis. I have tried to show that the theme of idolatry is central and substantial in the *Troilus*, not peripheral or merely decorative. My demonstration began with a response to certain explicitly "anti-Robertsonian" claims to the effect that idolatry is not for Chaucer a theme of moral weight, claims that I find to be neither soundly based in fourteenth-century intellectual history nor convincingly related to a reading of such major poems as the *Thebaid* and the *Roman de la Rose,* poems that inform the *Troilus* and can help guide our reading of it. The demonstrated debility of the arguments that we examined, in my opinion, fully authorize further researches into the idolatrous theme; and it is on the basis of new researches that I conclude that Chaucer, improving on the invention of Boccaccio, has constructed a careful and sustained parallel between the Palladium, the most famous literary "idol" of antiquity, and the woman Criseyde.

Chaucer's simple but brilliant construction serves several ends. It invites into the poem the political mythology of the "New Troy" as embraced by Virgil in the *Aeneid* and as criticized by Augustine in the *City of God;* that is, it secures within a stable and coherent poetical framework a historically informed presentation of pagan religion inseparable from its authoritative Christian critique. We may identify in this poetic procedure the twin impulses to adulate and to correct antique culture so characteristic of the phenomenon of medieval humanism taken as a whole.[89] It ministers to Chaucer's certain intention, witnessed by the poem's extensive Boethian overlay, of examining irrational sexual passion as a culpably false philosophical good and as a moral insult to gentile doxography and Christian theology alike. It links the themes of false "love" with the larger falsity of "false gods" characterized by false, incomplete,

89. A procedure wonderfully suggested in the title of a fine book by Paul Renucci: *Dante, disciple et juge du monde gréco-latin* (Paris: Belles Lettres, 1954).

or deceptive utterance. Finally, it stimulates Chaucer to a number of poetic "emulations" of notable intellectual complexity—among them the linking of Troilus and Apollo, the recreation of set pieces from the *Thebaid*, the unlikely echoing of Jean de Meun's yet more unlikely parodic cult of the genitalia. Perhaps the chief interest of the idols of the Trojan prince is in a quite narrow sense "literary." The pervasive theme of idolatry, devotional and sexual, is in the *Troilus* notably bookish, involved far less in an independently imagined fiction of the past than in a rich texture of specific and significant anterior authors.

That Chaucer is profoundly interested in love in this poem is certain, but his announced theme, the double sorrow of Troilus, proves upon examination to be as much about textual as about sexual relations. His narrator disclaims much knowledge about the latter, but he repeatedly reveals an astonishing familiarity with a large library of real and imaginary books. We have seen how Chaucer the Christian classicist has been able to make an artistic virtue of certain cultural anxieties of his calling, anxieties aroused by the relationship of the epic subject matter of antique religious rite to an Augustinian conception of "true religion" on the one hand and to "love" on the other. What remains to be explored, so far as the specific ambitions of my own enterprise are concerned, is the remarkable fashion in which Chaucer makes the decipherment and transformation of the past at once a central subject and a central motive of his poem.

Many of Chaucer's recent readers appear to believe that the poet's greatest achievement of characterization in the *Troilus* is his invention of the narrator. There is perhaps a touch of historical overcompensation in this judgment—few readers before E. T. Donaldson noticed there *was* a narrator, so that we need to make up for lost time—but despite its possibly suspicious fashionableness the idea is genuinely engaging. We know remarkably little about this central character. That the narrator is male is culturally obvious and textually implicit, so that we are reasonably entitled to speak of "him"; beyond that we are on less certain ground.

Of numerous intriguing difficulties that challenge a reader's confidence, two are prominent. The first is that as is common enough in even the most rigorously scheduled first-person medieval narration the distinction between poetic author and fictive narrator pales or disappears altogether at crucial moments in the poem. The second is that the one self-referential statement capable of probation turns out to be a blatant lie: his repeated claim to be the English translator of an ancient Latin poet, Lollius. The problematical aspects of poetic narration inhibit clear answers to two perennial but still pressing questions of intellectual relationship: that between the concluding Christian moralizing and the historical love story, and that between the English poem and the actual literary texts that have been used in its construction.

Are these questions susceptible of an answer, or worth the trouble of one? A recent and thoughtful essay on the narrator claims that we must simply accept the inconsistencies and moral confusions of tone and narrative point of view as a radical truth about the poem, possibly a historical necessity. The narration is confusing because the historical author Geoffrey Chaucer was himself confused as a consequence of his sociological circumstances in a highly con-

155

fused and confusing world.[1] This strikes me as alarming insight or alarming blindness; and in either event it well exemplifies how the durable difficulties of our particular text invite counsels of critical despair that, if accepted, leave the reader with only those options of voluntary redundancy and early retirement which daily become more familiar in professional life.

It will be obvious to any reader who has shown the forbearance to persevere this far in my book that I have a different view, a view in which Chaucer's reader has another vocation—and, to my mind, a nobler one—than to stand in appreciative exasperation before the brilliant incoherence of narrative point of view. *Troilus and Criseyde* is a poem that, far from defying interpretation, insists upon it. Interpretation is itself a major poetic theme, always present and often enough ostentatiously present in formal textual acts of translation and in repeated hermeneutical dramas of reading and misreading.

We may return to one solid fact. We can with some philosophical responsibility say that we know one thing about the narrator: he is an interpreter. We do not know as fact that he is an unsuccessful lover, or that he is donnish, or that he is a "bumbleninny" (whatever that is), or that he likes Criseyde or any other of numerous propositions that he makes about himself or that others have plausibly drawn on his behalf. We do know that he is a translator, and we know this not because he tells us so, though of course he does, but because we have independent, reliable, verifiable access to the texts he has translated. The same texts whose anterior existence proves the truth of his claim to be a translator prove also the radical untruth of the specific terms in which the claim to be a translator are couched. Thus it is that the one fact that we know about the narrator must necessarily encourage the fear that we can know no others.

One fact may, however, be enough, and I begin this chapter with it because it unifies all of the major strands of argument of this book. The fundamental fact about Chaucer's *Troilus* is that it is the work of an *interpres,* to use the marvelously multivalent Latin word most appropriate to the poem's persistently pseudo-Latin context. The word *interpres* means a translator; it may also mean a priest. An *interpres* is a literary critic, also an analyst of dreams. An *interpres* may be a poem; it may also be a pimp. All of the major characters in the *Troilus,* and not a few of the minor ones, perform one or more functions of the *interpres;* but two are preeminent. I refer of course to the poet/narrator

1. Richard Waswo, "The Narrator of *Troilus and Criseyde,*" *ELH* 50 (1983): 1–25.

himself and to his most important original invention, Pandarus. In the following pages I seek to explore the concept of the *interpres* in the *Troilus* as I believe Chaucer invites us to explore it. The task is, admittedly, a somewhat daunting one, for the concept of "interpretation" exists within the poem in depth and astonishing variety. We must trace out the narrow ambages of a vast intertextual labyrinth, hoping that the crimson clews lead us safely away from the bull, rather than toward it in a different guise.

SOME VERSIONS OF INTERPRETATION

We may begin with the most foreign concept, that of the "sexual interpreter," as it appears in one of the most widely read of all medieval fictions. In his lengthy meditation on his good fortune in encountering the corporeal form of the girl Galathea, Pamphilus speaks thus as he dreams and schemes:

> Proficit absque Deo nullus in orbe labor.
> Sit Deus ergo mei custos rectorque laboris,
> Omne gubernet opus propositumque meum.
> Non meus *interpres* fuerit fraterque neposque. . . .
> Hic prope degit anus subtilis et ingeniosa
> Artibus et Veneris apta ministra satis.

> (Without God, no undertaking on earth can prosper. May God be my guardian and the supervisor of my labor, may He guide all my effort and my plan. My go-between will not be a brother or a nephew. . . . There is an old woman around here who is crafty and smart and much experienced in the arts of Venus.)

The humor of the passage, as with so much twelfth-century school-poetry, resides in the moral solecism carefully set up by the rhetorical solecism. The love-struck speaker solemnly places himself and his cause into the hands of God Almighty—and into those of the neighborhood bawd! For the word *interpres* here is an ornament of Ovidian poetic diction denoting the specialized office of sexual mediation undertaken by the stock comic character of the *anus* or *vetula*.[2]

2. *Pamphilus*, ed. Franz G. Becker (Düsseldorf: Ratingen, 1972), lines 272–82. The

I shall in due course argue what I take to be Chaucer's deeper concern in implying an analogy of textual and sexual intermediation, but we may pause for a moment to applaud the brilliance of conceptual design whereby the "old woman" of the antique comic tradition has been transformed into the uncle Pandarus. In this regard Boccaccio wins the merit of the pioneer, but little more; for apart from the sexual metamorphosis itself, all that is most interesting about Pandarus is Chaucer's. His originality conspicuously included an act of "creative imitation" that, quite without violating the pseudoantique ethos of the *roman d'antiquité*, guaranteed that the activities of his go-between might be viewed from a biblical perspective.

I refer, of course, to the episode of Troilus' feigned illness, an episode in which Pandarus is cast in the role of Jonadab from the story of the rape of Thamar (2 Kings 13), a sordid history frequently invoked in medieval moral literature to illustrate the evils of sexual passion and the perversion of true friendship. The biblical citation is no less powerful for its tacit character. Without violating the self-imposed constraints of the historical novelist, Chaucer draws pointed attention—in the common fashion of fourteenth-century religious historians Trevet and Ridewall—to the lamentable congruence of mores to be found in the historical books of pagan antiquity and those of the Old Testament. There is nothing of this in Boccaccio, whose sources of inspiration are more narrowly Ovidian.

The Ovidian history of the go-between naturally impinges on Chaucer's text in interesting ways as well, largely through the mediation of what Thomas J. Garbáty in an important essay calls the "Pamphilus tradition," by which he means the Latin *Pamphilus* and its vernacular adaptations and imitations.[3] This tradition has considerable light to throw on the poem, and perhaps even can help resolve some disputed textual and interpretive questions. In one much discussed passage, for instance, Troilus expresses amazement that Pandarus, who lacks the ability to advance his own love affair, can help *Troilus* with his:

> "This were a wonder thing," quod Troilus;
> "Thow koudest nevere in love thi selven wisse;

---

word *interpres* had no easy vernacular equivalent. The Venetian translator thus includes a gloss: "meu interpretaore, coe mieu conseiro." See Pamphilus, *Il Panfilo veneziano*, ed. H. Haller (Florence: Olschki, 1982), 49.

3. Thomas J. Garbáty, "The Pamphilus Tradition in Ruiz and Chaucer," *PQ* 45 (1967): 457–70.

How, devel, maistow brynge me to blisse?"

(1.621–23)

The passage follows Boccaccio's sense closely enough, but the word *devel*, the word that has caused all the trouble, is Chaucer's own. Alluding to this passage, Robertson said that on one occasion Troilus calls Pandarus his devil. His parenthetic critical observation excited only slightly less protracted philological indignation than that concerning "queynt." Root alone of the poem's editors punctuated the phrase in such a way as to encourage the reader to take the word *devel* as a vocative. All the rest print "how devel," and most of those who had commented on it said it meant "how the devil?" Charlotte D'Evelyn published an article, often cited as an undoubted refutation of Robertson, trying to demonstrate on philological grounds that the meaning "how the devil" was the exclusive meaning.[4] In fact, she could find no other example of the phrase "how devel" in the Middle English language, but was hopeful that the relevant fascicule of the *Middle English Dictionary*, which had not at that time appeared, would do so for her. Although in the event this hope was not realized, it is nonetheless highly likely that *one* meaning of the phrase is "how the devil." The polemical thrust of her argument is wholly deflected, however, if the phrase is a genuine ambiguity, as E. T. Donaldson claims. This possibility D'Evelyn did not even consider.

We may usefully invoke the criterion of context yet again. Does context confirm or deny an association of Pandarus with the diabolical? If we include in our concept of literary context the literary history of the go-between, the answer must surely be that it confirms it. Pandarus is among other things a dramatic transformation of the *vetula* of Latin comedy; among his most memorable literary sisters are Dipsas, La Vieille, and the Celestina. The Wife of Bath is a first cousin. The subject under discussion at this point in Chaucer's text is precisely the unlikeliness of Pandarus' credentials as an *interpres*. How the devil can he achieve for others what he cannot achieve for himself?

The medieval *vetula* is often—indeed, one can say usually—associated with witchcraft and the black arts.[5] Such is clearly the case with Houdée, the go-between of *Pamphile et Galatée*, an important text that I believe to be among the unnoticed sources of the *Troilus*. As a witch she is, metaphorically speaking,

4. C. D'Evelyn, "Pandarus a Devil?" *PMLA* 71 (1956): 275–79.
5. The association is classical. Thus Richard Müller, *Motivkatalog der römischen Elegie* (Zurich: Abhandlung, 1952), 44, associates the *lena* (procuress) and the *saga* (witch).

married to the devil. This is precisely the point of one of the little anecdotes gathered by Thomas Wright called "De vetula sortilega." A *vetula* succeeded in corrupting numerous young women by promising them that by following her advice they would gain rich husbands, but one virtuous girl squelched her as follows: "Your own husband [i.e., the devil] is a wretched beggar; how do you intend to get a fine husband for me?"[6]

Such associations, which become for informed readers a part of the literary context of the passage in Chaucer, obviously support Robertson's suggestion of the presence of an artistic double entendre. It is hardly a major or startling textual "find," and the attention I have already paid to it is incommensurate with both the casual way in which Chaucer tossed it off and the casual way in which Robertson mentioned it. But in a chapter on interpretation this example shows yet another way in which interpretive predisposition, in the borrowed raiment of "philology," can blind a reader to the enriching complexities of Chaucer's language.

If Pandarus is a *devil* to Troilus, he is a *fox* to Criseyde (3.1565). So far as I know there has been no attempt to philologize the latter word away, though in fact it is no whit less devastating than the former in its metaphoric characterization of Pandarus' role. The words *devil* and *fox* apply to Pandarus figuratively, as is the wont of metaphorical language. Neither Troilus nor Criseyde claims that Pandarus has a tail, horns, or red, furry ears; but viewing the same action of *lenocinium* from different points on the temporal spectrum both suggest, in language as superficially ambiguous as Pandarus' view of his office, a quite traditional moral judgment of the drama in which they have allowed themselves to be cast.

The word *devil*, thematically connected with the literary tradition of the sexual *interpres*, is decorously complemented by the word *fox*, which in the specific Chaucerian context of hypocrisy clearly derives from the language of sexual fraud as Jean de Meun remade it after Ovid.[7] In each case the moral

6. "Maritus tuus pauper est et mendicus; quomodo divitem maritum facies me habere, quae tibi subvenire non potuisti in haec parte?" See *A Selection of Latin Stories*, ed. Thomas Wright (London: n.p., 1842), p. 61.

7. See in particular the cynical advice of Amis to Amant concerning Bel Accueil: "Face ses meurs au siens ouniz, / ou autrement il iert honniz, / qu'el cuide qu'il soit uns lobierres, / uns renarz, uns anfantosmierres" (7725–28). The Ovidian *vetula*, incidentally, typically speaks in ambages. See the pseudo-Ovidian *De vetula*, ed. P. Klopsch

insight is imperfect, fleeting, indeed nearly accidental. Troilus never really challenges Pandarus' advice except on those several occasions when it is good, and Chaucer teases us to entertain the belief that Criseyde, a few lines after calling her uncle a fox, makes love with him. For the reader of the *Troilus*, the task of all audiences of moral tragedy, the task of seeing more and more clearly than the tragic principals themselves, is seldom onerous; and it is lightened by the guidance of clearly defined literary traditions.

In another sense it is lightened by comedy. Pandarus is in many aspects a comic character, a very funny man. His frequent joviality is inescapably engaging. All the best laughs in the poem—and few tragedies can have more of them than the *Troilus*—come in his presence and through his agency. In all of this we see Chaucer the literary conformist as well as the literary transformer, for the sexual *interpres* is by tradition a comic type. On the other hand, there is nothing in the tradition to encourage us to confuse the comic treatment of character with moral levity of poetic vision. Even in the deeply and overtly moralistic *Celestina*, which ends in an orgy of violent death and social ruin, the wise-cracking, crafty crone is as fully funny as she is fully awful. This ambivalence—an ambivalence of tonal treatment rather than of moral conception—is also discernible in the Great Mother of all medieval literary bawds, the witch Dipsas of Ovid's *Amores* 1.8.

The peculiar importance of Dipsas for the "Pamphilus tradition," I suggest, lies in the relationship between conception of character and narrative stance. The narrator of *Amores* 1.8 is "Ovid" the lover, an eavesdropper to the cynical tutorial between the old witch and her lovely young pupil, the girl on whom the narrator has designs. The *vetula* teaches her protégée how to make the most out of sex; and her deeply meretricious advice, though it shocks and scandalizes "Ovid" the voyeur, will come as no surprise to readers of Ovid the poetic pedagogue. For the advice that comes from the lips of Dipsas is identical in spirit, and to a large extent similar in content, to the advice that comes from "Ovid" in the *Ars amatoria*. I take the collusion between, and partial melding

---

(Leiden: Brill, 1967), lines 415ff.; and *La Vielle*, ed. H. F. J. M. Cocheris (Paris: n.p., 1861), 143–44. A yet more forceful text is at *RR* 11492–95, where Faussemblant (a good deal of whose character survives rebuilt in Pandarus) boasts of his "renardie" and where Amours exclaims, with precisely the ambiguity used by Chaucer, "Qu'est ce, deable?"

of, pimp and poet to be the most original point of the elegy.[8] Ovid had the germ of an idea around which Giovanni Boccaccio could build a whole literary career and which provoked Chaucer to some of the most lustrous inventions of the *Troilus*.

Pandarus, as we shall come to appreciate, is a textual *interpres* in a double sense; but we may note as well that a text itself can be an *interpres*. Baudri of Borgeuil wrote a matching pair of elegiac epistles in imitation of the sixteenth and seventeenth of the *Heroides*. In the first of them, Paris to Helen, the speaker, or rather writer, expresses envy of his letter which, unlike its sender, will soon be in intimate contact with Helen:

> Carta quidem felix nimium, que tangere uestras
> In scribendo manus meruit, felicior autem
> Hec mea, si recubans Helene sub pectore pauset . . .
> Carta domi remaneret, ego quoque mitterer ad uos
> Essem legatus pro me bonus atque fidelis
> Interpres Paridis Paridisque uicarius essem
> Et propter Paridem tecum causas agitarem . . .[9]

(Most happy is this letter, which had the opportunity to be touched by your hands in the writing of it; happier yet will be mine, should it rest beneath Helen's recumbant breast . . . May this letter that I who remain at home send to you be for me a good ambassador and a reliable intermediary of Paris, may it be Paris' stand-in, and may it press suit with you on behalf of Paris . . .)

Some of these Ovidian extravagances appear in Boccaccio's account of the first letter written by Troilo to Criseida, though not necessarily through a reading of Baudri of Borgeuil, of course. "Lettera mia," says Troilo, "tu sarai / beata, in man di tal donna verrai." Chaucer elaborates with the reference to the signet ring:

> And with his salte teris gan he bathe
> The ruby in his signet, and it sette
> Upon the wex deliverliche and rathe . . .
>   (2.1086–88)

8. See further Ojars Kratins, "The Pretended Witch: A Reading of Ovid's *Amores*, I.viii," *PQ* 42 (1963): 151–58.
9. Baudri de Borgeuil, *Carmina*, ed. K. Hilbert (Heidelberg: Winter, 1979).

This may suggest the idea of the ring as a genital proxy deriving eventually from *Amores* 2.15, the poem that many readers have found the most offensive in Ovid. As we saw in the first chapter it is an idea toward which the double entendres of Chaucer's text repeatedly point.

In Ovid the baroque fantasy of the writer is that, were he the ring he sends to the girl, he could slip off her finger whenever he wished to play with her breasts. The language of Baudri's poem, though sexually attenuated, suggests similar intimacy: "felicior autem / hec mea, si recubans Helene sub pectore pauset." There is little coyness in Boccaccio's Criseida. She takes the letter with a smile, presumably a knowing smile, and slips it into her bodice like the heroine of a spaghetti western she at times becomes. There is some sex in the scene but little sense of sexual invasion. As Chaucer rewrites it he manages to recapture for Troilus the sense of sexual initiative present in Ovid but absent in Boccaccio. For a lady to tuck a letter into her shirt-front is one thing. For a man to cram a letter down a lady's shirt-front is something else. The latter is precisely what Pandarus does:

> "Refuse it nat," quod he, and hente hire faste,
> And in hir bosom down the lettre he thraste . . .
>   (2.1154–55)

Those are funny lines. Clearly, Pandarus' idea of special delivery adds spice to the old game of Post Office. From another perspective, however, they are decidedly unfunny. Chaucer's unique contribution is to impose upon his Ovidian topic a symbolic sexual aggression—if not a sexual violation—that smears its light and playful surface. The metaphoric manipulation of text is common enough in the *Troilus;* its physical manipulation is rather rarer, but the physical manipulation is wholly consistent with Pandarus' role as an amatory "director," the man who places the leading lady in the window to view the staged appearance of the leading man, who leads his charges about "by the lap," who actually tucks his lovers into bed. Chaucer's cameo comedy of the delivery of the letter is a considerable tour de force, for he has presented his themes of sexual and textual "intepretation" in a coherent and credible narrative episode. Pandarus is one kind of *interpres,* and the love letter is another. The poet himself, of course, is yet a third kind, and the literary critic a fourth. And before we proceed with an examination of one modest but consequential act of interpretation in which both Pandarus and Troilus are involved, we may for a moment consider a certain kind of textual collusion between poet and critic.

There are in the *De divinatione* of Cicero two most arresting passages that express a traditional comparison between the diviner and the literary critic, both of whom are glossators whose interpretive powers, at their best, must rival the creative powers of the agencies who provide them with their problematical "texts"—the gods in the case of the mediated oracles, poets in the case of poems. In the first passage, undoubtedly authentic, Cicero's word is *interpretes* (1.34); in the second, which incorporates a paraphrastic gloss, the word is *explanatores* (1.116).[10]

The background of the idea variously expressed in Cicero's text is something of a classical commonplace: the doctrine of poetic inspiration perhaps most famously expressed in Plato's *Ion*. In Plato, of course, the focus of mantic grandeur is on the poet; by Cicero's time, by the logical processes of academic communities, the interpreter, too, had long since been granted the dignity of his independent fine frenzy, though not yet the actual mantic priority recently announced by certain literary theoreticians.

Particularly engaging in the context, perhaps, since it has been written as much by an unknown Ciceronian interpreter as by Cicero himself, is the second passage (*De divinatione* 1.116): "Hic magna quaedam exoritur neque ea naturalis sed artificiosa somniorum Antiphontis interpretatio eodemque modo et oraculorum et vaticinationum sunt enim explanatores, ut grammatici poetarum" (Here is the beginning of the artificial as opposed to the natural interpretation of dreams, after the manner of Antiphon, a method applicable to oracles and vaticinations; they are explainers, as critics are for the poets).

As various commentators have pointed out, the inclusion of the proper name Antiphon insults the elegance of Cicero's style no less than the inclusion of the phrase "sunt enim explanatores, ut grammatici poetarum" violates the suavity of his syntax; but it is the necessary tribute paid by the writer of texts to the writer of commentaries. Expanding upon the analogy already present in Cicero, we can perhaps see in Antiphon, author of a popular system of oneirohermeneutics, the authoritative "theorist" apparently now necessary for the artificial as opposed to the natural interpretation of texts. In any event the word *interpres,* happy enough in the ambiguities of sexual and textual mediation, is happier still with the accretion of the further ambiguities of its human

10. Cicero, *De divinatione*, ed. Arthur S. Pease (Darmstadt: Wissenschaftliche Buchgesellschaft, 1963), 153, 307.

and divine hermeneutics. Each aspect of this many-faced concept will in time be brought to bear on Chaucer's text.

Let us examine a concrete example of interpretation within the poem. We recall that according to the Augustinian theory of speech acts, not every untruth is a lie; a lie is an untruth powered by the engine of intentional deceit. An innocent mistake, though it be a falsehood, is not a lie. Nor, as we have seen, are the falsehoods involved in jokes and games lies. In the final word of his preposterous *Encomium of Helen*, Gorgias, identifying his enterprise as an amusement (*paignion*), discharges the burdens of its sophistical truths; and the ludic aspect of poetry might seem to proffer a strong anti-Platonic defense even to poets of a high seriousness, as Boccaccio recognized in the *De genealogia deorum gentilium*.

In this regard what seems most remarkable about Chaucer's major poetry is its determined and self-conscious irresolution of the registers of "earnest" and "game." The operation of this tension is most obvious in the *Canterbury Tales*, where it rises so frequently to the textual surface, but it is in some ways more interesting in the *Troilus*—or perhaps "more philosophical and significant" in Aristotle's famous phrase about tragic fictions—since it is precisely at the blurred edges of earnest and game that Chaucer often most philosophically pursues his themes of truth and ambiguation. In one of several moments of moral self-reflection within the poem, Pandarus tells Troilus:

> "For the have I bigonne a gamen pleye
> Which that I nevere don shal eft for other,
> Although he were a thousand fold my brother.
> That is to seye, for the am I bicomen,
> Bitwixen game and ernest, swich a meene
> As maken wommen unto men to comen;
> Thow woost thi selven what I wolde meene . . .
>   (3.250–56)

The mean that he means is the mean profession of *lenocinium,* the very art of going between, interpreting, being intermediate, so well established in Latin erotic literature. In his account of things, euphemism and indirection thinly veil the truth that is at the very surface of the corresponding text in Boccaccio ("Io son per te divenuto mezzano, / per te gittato ho 'n terra il mio onore" (For you I have become a pimp, for you I have thrown my honor in the dust), but

the truth is still there in the language. Pandarus is hardly one to call a spayed
a spayed, but at least he refrains from calling her a prize breeder. That kind
of linguistic recklessness is left to Troilus in one of his more amazing acts of
interpretation and "creative philology":

> . . . he that gooth, for gold or for richesse,
> On swich message, calle hym what the list;
> And this that thow doost, calle it gentilesse,
> Compassioun, and felawship, and trist;
> Departe it so; for wyde wher is wist,
> How that ther is diversite requered
> Bytwixen thynges like, as I have lered.
>
> And that thow knowe I thynke nat, ne wene,
> That this servise a shame be or jape,
> I have my faire suster, Polixene,
> Cassandre, Eleyne, or any of the frape;
> Be she nevere so faire or wel yshape,
> Tel me which thow wilt of everychone,
> To han for thyn, and lat me thanne allone.
>   (3.400–413)

Let us allow ourselves to stay with this engaging text for a moment.

The typographical organization of Windeatt's recent edition of the *Troilus* is
helpful for my present purposes, for it forces us to remember Boccaccio and
facilitates our more just understanding of Chaucer's relationship with his Italian original. The testimony to Chaucer's independence, in the form of empty
white half-pages, is as valuable as the textual testimonies to his dependence.
The passage under consideration is one of many in the *Troilus* that repays a
careful comparison with the Italian as much for what it does to Boccaccio's
text as for what it takes from it. At least since the issue was forcefully raised
by Robertson, this passage has been something of a litmus test identifying
two broadly differing understandings of the poem. Robertson believed that
this conversation tarnished the speakers fatally from an ethical point of view;
his censors, on the contrary, have advanced diverse and often ingenious arguments to maintain the traditional interpretations of Pandarus as a true and
noble friend and of Troilus as a noble and generous young man of parts. The

question, of course, is that of how we are to interpret Pandarus' self-advertised role of go-between.

The discussion among Chaucerians not surprisingly reduplicated that of Italianists concerning Boccaccio's Pandaro, though Chaucer's gentler language and his poetic tact perhaps leave the issues less clearly defined than does the Italian text. One distinguished Italianist, Robert Hollander, bemused by the opinion of several Italian critics to the effect that Boccaccio is wholly positive or at least ethically neutral toward his creature Pandaro, writes thus: "In this particular case we are observing highly intelligent scholars trying to decide whether Boccaccio thought being a pander was a good or a bad thing. It is really not a difficult question to answer. It has been made into one in order to protect a bad hypothesis—that Boccaccio thinks carnal love is a perfectly honorable pursuit for a civilized person." [11]

The question raised in the Chaucerian context, though arising from a similar hypothesis, is slightly different. What does it mean, if anything, that Troilus should offer to Pandarus "my faire suster, Polixene, Cassandre, Eleyne, or any of the frape . . . to han for thyn"? I want to examine from a critical standpoint the responses to that question made by two fine and sorely lamented Chaucerians, Donald Howard and Elizabeth Salter. I choose them for their stature and authority, for the fact that they were both writing in part in reproof of Robertson, and because their opinions have now been canonized, or at least beatified, in the very exclusive anthology of Windeatt's interpretive notes. Both critics were constrained to deny that the language means what a native speaker of English is likely at first hearing to think it means. Howard's explanation is that Troilus' offer is an ornament of historical local color, Salter's that it is a *lapsus calami*.

Let us first consider Howard's view, with which I have less quarrel than with the premise from which it is drawn, and that is that "Pandarus represents Chaucer's interpretation of the philosophy, or at least the morality of paganism." [12] I am in no wise disposed to retreat from my view that Chaucer is a Christian poet, but I must deny that he is a Christian bigot. In order for him to present Pandarus as an exemplar of the "philosophy, or at least the morality

11. Robert Hollander, *Boccaccio's Two Venuses* (New York: Columbia University Press, 1980), 104.
12. Howard, *The Three Temptations*, p. 135.

of paganism" Chaucer would either have had to be nearly wholly ignorant of the pagan moral philosophers or to have adopted, for literary purposes, a blind, unhistorical Christian prejudice that makes the invective of Arnobius or Savonarola seem responsibly nuanced.

Pandarus is a real bounder, charmingly wicked at best and diabolically evil at worst, whose fundamental immorality is starkly defined precisely in his studied deviance from *pagan* moral doctrines well known to Chaucer from his readings in Virgil, Ovid, Seneca, Cicero, Augustine, and Boethius, among others. It is particularly illuminating to assess his performance as a friend to Troilus in terms of the moral and philosophical doctrines of the *Laelius* of Cicero, the most authoritative pagan text on the philosophy and morality of friendship known to the Christian Middle Ages.[13]

Having posited Pandarus as Chaucer's *norm* of pagan morality, Howard then considers Troilus' offer to fix Pandarus up with one of his "sisters," which, as he points out, echoes Pandarus' own, earlier offer of *his* sister. Offering the sexual favors of one's sister, according to Howard, is a wholly benign if somewhat extravagant bit of ethnic rhetoric. "To be sure it is a stark and pagan avowal. But it is an avowal of good intentions and loyalty, not of depravity—an exaggerated protestation of friendship which in each case carried the implication that the friend would forbear to ask so much."[14]

I know of no text in the corpus of classical literature—in the reading of which, according to Howard, Chaucer must have constructed his view of ancient times—from which the poet could have concluded that offering one's sister was acceptable, let alone conventional or typical "pagan" behavior.[15] On the other hand, he would have found examples in Roman comedy (which he perhaps did not read) and in Ovid (which he certainly did) of bawds, as morally reprehensible as they are comically engaging, who are in another sense Pandarus' siblings. But there is in my opinion no credible way of explaining away this disquieting passage by invoking its "pagan" character.

Furthermore I can see no textual or contextual evidence that validates an "implication" that Pandarus is anything less than serious in offering his "sister"

13. This is done in an excellent article by Robert G. Cook, "Chaucer's Pandarus and the Medieval Ideal of Friendship," *JEGP* 69 (1970): 407–24.
14. Howard, *The Three Temptations*, 137n.
15. Even Christians, who did occasionally indulge in this sort of thing, would appear to have taken a dim view of it, judging from the fate of Venedico Caccianemico in *Inferno* 18. See the discussion in chapter 1, n.27.

or that Troilus for so much as a moment entertains the idea of rejecting the offer because it would be asking too much. Boccaccio's Pandaro uses the word *sorella* in a general sense; he means by the word any woman relative in general and his relative Criseida in particular. I further doubt that the earth has yet known a society so mellow—even in ancient Phrygia or in Marin County for that matter—as to regard the proffering of one's sister in the fashion of an after-dinner mint as "an avowal of good intentions and loyalty"; but I must leave that matter with the cultural anthropologists.

Howard's argument—Troilus said it, but he did not really mean it—I find unconvincing. So do I find Salter's argument—Troilus said it, but *Chaucer* did not really mean it. Of this passage she writes, "It is a careless adjustment of old and new."[16] The context suggests her meaning: this is one of those bumpy spots in Chaucer's text where the moral and sexual crudity of the *Filostrato* has been but imperfectly transformed to the subtler, more courtly, and more ambiguous design of the *Troilus*. Her suggestion rests on an eminently just assessment of what are the tonal differences between the two works and on the observation of a phenomenon, "careless adjustment," which can certainly be documented in individual textual instances; it accordingly deserves careful consideration.

When we compare *TC* 3.232–460 with *Fil.* 3.4–20, we find the following general pattern. Both passages begin with Pandar commenting on his role as sexual facilitator, but, in the words of Windeatt's annotation, "Pandarus uses more circumlocution and euphemism to describe himself, where Pandaro confesses he has become a *mezzano* ('go-between, procurer') and debased his honour (6/1–2)." Here we see clear evidence of Chaucer's *careful* adjustment from old to new in his normal fashion of softening and ambiguating Boccaccio's moral bluntness. Next comes Pandar's insistence that the woman's reputation must be preserved and, therefore, on the need for secrecy—a need to which Chaucer devotes a dilation of no less than eight stanzas, fifty-six lines. This is followed in both texts by Troilus' offer of his gratitude and his sister, a passage to which I shall return presently. Then, in Chaucer's text alone, follow five more stanzas that stress the absolute secrecy of Troilus' love, his vigorous and successful attempts at dissimulation, his public life as a knight on the

16. Elizabeth Salter, "Troilus and Criseyde: A Reconsideration," in *Patterns of Love and Courtesy: Essays in Memory of C. S. Lewis*, ed. John Lawlor (London: Arnold, 1966), 100.

battlefield and his private erotic reveries in bed at night. Let us now focus on
the two specific stanzas in which Troil(o/us) expresses his gratitude.

> E perché tu conosca quanto piena
> benivolenza da me t'è portata,
> io ho la mia sorella Polissena
> piu di bellezza che altra pregiata
> ed ancor c'è con esso lei Elena
> bellissima, la quale e mia cognata:
> apri il cor tuo se te ne piace alcuna,
> poi me lascia operar con qual sia l'una . . .
>
> (*Fil.* 3.18)

(And that thou mayest know what great good will I bear thee I have my
sister Polyxena, prized above others for her beauty, and also there is with
her that fairest Helen, who is my kinswoman—open thy heart if either is
pleasing unto thee—then leave it to me to work with whichever it be.)

> And that thow knowe I thynke nat, ne wene,
> That this servise a shame be or jape,
> I have my faire suster, Polixene,
> Cassandre, Eleyne, or any of the frape;
> Be she nevere so faire or wel yshape,
> Tel me which thow wilt of everychone,
> To han for thyn, and lat me thanne allone.
>
> (*TC* 3.407–13)

Now it is quite true that neither passage puts the speaker in a particularly
admirable light. Each is grossly insulting in his attitude toward women, who
are implicitly regarded in the crudest possible fashion as male sexual recreation. But it can at least be said of Boccaccio's Troilo that he veils the crudity
with a flimsy tissue of courtly language. He does not here use phrases that are
the tonal equivalent of "any of the frape" or "wel yshape"; and in comparison
with the matter-of-fact and functional attitude toward sex suggested in the
concluding English couplet, Troilo's own phrasing ("apri il cor tuo") seems
almost operatic.

In short a comparison of the two stanzas suggests that Chaucer, in deliberate
contrast to his usual pattern, is quite consciously and quite carefully adjusting
his materials to present Troilus' moral moment as even sleazier than it is in

Boccaccio. He has, in this comparatively rare instance, "traded down." I thus find that it will not do to explain away Troilus' remarkable speech as a bit of fossilized Boccaccio, since its more remarkable features were never in Boccaccio in the first place. The price that critics have been willing to pay to defend Troilus against the revelations of his own language has been too high.[17]

The Stoic logicians were right in claiming that all words are ambiguous; but Augustine was right, too, in insisting that we understand words in context, not in isolation. So long as we think of "gentilesse" as a private personality trait rather than a public virtue we are likely to miss much of the point of this passage. There can be few other words in the Chaucerian lexicon for which the poet has provided so rich a context within which we may judge his intentions. Latin *gentilitas* carried the disparate meanings suggested by the modern English *gentile* on the one hand and *genteel* on the other—heathenness, or good breeding.[18]

As it happens, Chaucer wrote two poems about "gentilesse" which between them fairly clearly suggest both what he probably thought it was, or should be, and what he thought it was not. In "Gentilesse," a moral ballad which by its very genre would make irony or philosophical subversion wholly inappropriate, he defines "gentilesse" as the pursuit of virtue in the imitation of Christ. The tone suggests that the definition is entirely serious, though meant to be something of a surprise to anyone who thinks that "gentilesse" is entailed to high office or to aristocratic paternity.

It is in a sense Chaucer's alternative Christian definition of the concept of "gentilesse" found in the other poem, the "Franklin's Tale," a conception much closer to that implied by Troilus. The Franklin is the one thematically identified "pagan" on the pilgrimage—"he was Epicurus' owene sonne"—and he sets his story in an indeterminate but evidently ethnic antiquity. The tale is

---

17. In Elizabeth Salter's case this was the conclusion that "Chaucer could never have intended his poem to be seen as a unified whole, except in the crudest narrative sense" (Salter, "A Reconsideration," 106). Winthrop Wetherbee would save Troilus' good character by making him extremely (in my view, incredibly) naive. Sex is not even in his mind; he thinks that Pandarus is orchestrating a purely platonic friendship; and his offer of his sister is made with the same purity of heart. If so, I wonder what it is that Troilus "missed" at 3.445.

18. Cf. the entry "gentilitas" in the *TLL*. Further illuminating information will be found in Ilona Opelt, "Griechische und lateinische Beziehungen der Nichtchristlichen: Ein terminilogisches Versuch," *Vigiliae Christianae* 19 (1965): 1–22.

indeed something of a "gentilesse contest," but both its structure and incidental editorial comment make it clear that the Franklin knows approximately as
much about moral philosophy as a hog knows about Christmas. One central
character, the knight and absentee husband Averagus, performs the following extraordinary act of "gentilesse." Having previously undertaken a solemn
matrimonial contract based on the absolute equality of the partners and the
explicit renunciation of his claims to seigneurial "maistrie," Averagus orders
his wife to commit in earnest the adultery proposed by her in jest, adding that
he will have her killed if she ever breathes a word of it, since "Trouthe is the
hyeste thyng that man may kepe." This is to be sure a stark and pagan avowal,
but do not call it *gentilesse*.[19]

DIDO AND THE DARDAN

As we have just seen, Chaucer's text is crowded with "interpreters"—including, among its prominent dramatis personae, a translator, a diviner,
a pimp, and a philologically inventive erotic hero. The poet's strategy seems
to be comic, but not only comic. I find that among Chaucer's likely intentions in the "pimp scene" is the brief evocation, in a somewhat amusing if
not lighthearted context, of one of his most serious themes: the relationship
between moral and linguistic aberration.[20] The thinker most responsible for
the currency of this idea in medieval Christian thought was Augustine, but
I suspect that Chaucer's interest in it arose from his reading of poetry rather
than philosophy or theology.

One promising text, the *Ars amatoria* of Ovid, has a lengthy passage (2.641–
702) expanding on the general advice to "forbear to reproach a woman with
her faults, faults which many have found it useful to feign otherwise." Georg
Luck, who has related the topic to the traditional self-deception of the narrator-

19. " 'When *I* use a word,' Humpty Dumpty said in a rather scornful tone, 'it means just
what I choose it to mean—neither more nor less.' " Lewis Carroll, *Through the Looking
Glass*, cap. vi.
20. This theme is explored in the excellent essay of Adrienne Lockhart, "Semantic,
Moral, and Aesthetic Degeneration in Troilus and Criseyde," *ChR* 8 (1973): 100–117;
and from a deeply informed theoretical standpoint by Eugene Vance, "Mervelous Signals: Poetics, Sign Theory, and Politics in Chaucer's *Troilus*," *NLH* 10 (1979): 293–337.

lover in Latin elegy, summarizes it thus: "Label the fault with a nice name and it becomes a virtue."[21] The *Troilus* is a wonderful unity of classical epic and elegiac elements, and to the demonstrable presence of fourteenth-century French lyric movements in the verse it would be possible to add repeated episodes of Ovidian elegy.[22] But the self-deception of lovers is no less a characteristic of the classical epic, and with particular reference to this moment in Chaucer's poem I should point to a text that had so greatly influenced Augustine himself, the *Aeneid* of Virgil.

The most famous love affair in Latin literature, that of Dido and Aeneas, is echoed and re-echoed in the European poetry of the Middle Ages and of the Renaissance. In an earlier chapter I adduced a passage in which Dante alludes to it in concrete exemplification of ancient religious error. Though highly original in his specific point of view, Dante was by no means unique in touching upon the matter itself. I know of no extended love poem of the Middle Ages that does not in some way pay obeisance to the Virgilian fiction, and I find it difficult to believe that there could be one. What of *Troilus and Criseyde*? Chaucer treats a pre-Virgilian matter from the perspective of self-imposed but nonetheless stringent historical constraints. The narrator might quote Juvenal, but it would never do for Pandarus to do so, at least not by name. So for Chaucer allusions as obvious as those in Dante are out of the question. I am nonetheless convinced that throughout the third book of the *Troilus* Chaucer was imagining his Trojan fiction against the memory, perhaps a subliminal memory, of his reading of the fourth book of the *Aeneid*.

There seem to be several textual suggestions of this fact, but the most striking is his invention of the rainstorm that sets the stage for the sexual union of hero and heroine. This rainstorm is entirely absent from Boccaccio's text, and it is powerfully—that is, insistently and repeatedly—present in Chaucer's.[23] Of course it serves a function analogous to the sudden storm in Virgil, since it provides the specific occasion of sexual consummation.

---

21. G. Luck, *The Latin Love Elegy* (London: Methuen, 1959), 163. Luck documents the serious discussion of the idea by the classical philosophers and rhetoricians.

22. See J. I. Wimsatt, "The French Lyric Element in *Troilus and Criseyde*," YES 15 (1985): 18–32.

23. See my essay "Smoky Reyn," 1–22. The (astrological) collusion of Saturn and Jove with the inconstant moon, suggested as the proximate cause of the storm, may well be a topical as well as a thematic allusion. See Windeatt's note on 3.624–26.

Chaucer is dealing with a theme rather rarer in literature than in life: the Wronged Man. Virgil, followed in a yet more sentimental fashion by Ovid, presents the Wronged Woman. There is no easy meshing of the two plots, but even so Chaucer did not give up entirely, and as a result there are moments in the poem that feminize Troilus and masculinize Criseyde. The most sharply allusive of these (4.1548–54) is the role reversal of Paris and Oenone from the fifth *heroid* of Ovid, but there are others, such as the early comparison of Troilus with Niobe, and Pandarus' imputations of effeminacy.

I do not deny the possibility of conscious thematic design on Chaucer's part, but I am more disposed to think of the feminization of Troilus as the palimpsest or subcutaneous appearance of Dido—another victim of a "double sorrow"— in Chaucer's text.[24] I want to suggest, tentatively and subject to the correction of clerks, that the larger pattern of Chaucer's "translation" of Boccaccio in what I am calling the "pimp scene" reflects a series of ideas suggested to him by Virgil. The pattern involves Troilus' rejection of the appearance of pimping, his redefinition of socially unacceptable behavior in terms of a socially approved word, and a lengthy passage on the subject of Criseyde's public fame.

The extraordinary erotic power of Virgil's fourth book lies in its artistic silences and tacit implications rather than in explicit descriptions of sexual activity. One of the greatest lays in our literature is sung but silently, drowned out by the crashing of thunder.

> speluncam Dido dux et Troianus eandem
> deveniunt. prima et Tellus et pronunba Iuno
> dant signum; fulsere ignes et conscius aether
> conubiis, summoque ulularunt vertice Nymphae.
> ille dies primus leti primusque malorum
> causa fuit; nec enim specie famave movetur
> nec iam furtivum Dido meditatur amorem:
> coniugium vocat, hoc praetexit nomine culpam.
> Extemplo Libyae magnas it Fama per urbes,
> Fama, malum qua non aliud velocius ullum:

---

24. Thus an antique school-poem, summarizing the contents of the fourth book of the *Aeneid:* "Quartus item miserae duo vulnera narrat Elissae" ("Basilii de xii libris Aenidos," in *Poetae latini minores,* ed. A. Baehrens (Leipzig: Teubner, 1879), 4:151.

mobilitate viget virisque adquirit eundo,
parva metu primo, mox sese attollit in auras
ingrediturque solo et caput inter nubila condit
(4.165–77)

(Dido and Troy's chieftain found their way to the same cavern. Primeval Earth and Juno, Mistress of the Marriage, gave the sign. The sky connived at the union; the lightning flared; on their mountain-peak nymphs raised their cry. On that day were sown the seeds of suffering and death. Henceforward Dido cared no more for appearances or her good name, and ceased to take any thought for secrecy in her love. She called it a marriage; she used this word to screen her sin. At once Rumor raced through Africa's great cities. Rumor is of all pests the swiftest. In her freedom of movement lies her power, and she gathers new strength from her going. She begins as a small and timorous creature; but then she grows till she towers into the air, and though she walks on the ground, she hides her head in the clouds.)

In a dozen lines Virgil moves from the prelude to the politically disastrous postlude of coition, and in doing so he raises precisely the same medley of themes to be found in the Chaucerian passage. Dido is not enslaved by the mere appearance and report of things (*nec enim specie famave movetur*); like Troilus, she implicitly believes "that ther is diversite requered bytwixen thyngs lik." This translation in turn requires an actual redefinition, in one of Virgil's finest lines: *coniugium vocat, hoc praetexit nomine culpam*. It is true that neither Troilus nor Criseyde literally tries to hide the deed beneath the name of marriage; that is a task undertaken only by modern critics. But Troilus nonetheless follows the pattern: "Calle it gentilesse," he says, redefining as private virtue what is from the point of view of social convention clearly a vice.

But it is the idea of Criseyde's "good name," elaborately teased out in Chaucer's lengthy additions concerning the need for secrecy in the love affair, that is perhaps of greatest interest. In both the Italian and the English texts Pandar advances the unattractive view that the fault is not in the doing but in the being found out. From the fact that she would be dishonored if her sexual liaison with Troilus were to be discovered I conclude, not unreasonably I hope, that there must be something dishonorable in it; but Pandar centers on the question of public reputation, not that of private honor.

Tu sai ch'egli è la fama di costei
santa nel vulgo, ne si disse mai
da nullo altro che tutto ben di lei . . .
> (*Fil.* 3.8)

For wel thow woost, the name as yit of hire
Among the peple, as who seyth, halwed is;
For nevere was ther wight, I dar wel swere,
That evere wiste that she dide amys.
> (*TC* 3.267–70)

We may note with interest that Chaucer here translates Boccaccio's *fama* as *name;* but this is not always so, for the only appearance of the English word *fame* in the poem is also a translation of Italian *fama*. No sooner had the Trojan Parliament decided on the exchange of Criseida for Antenor than rumors of the plan swept the city, and thus did the unfortunate woman learn of her own fate from common gossip. Here Boccaccio himself seized the opportunity for a Virgilian imitation, and his depiction of rumor rife in Troy is a close translation of Virgil's personification of Fama, who spreads the report of Dido's passion:

Extemplo Libyae magnas it Fama per urbes,
Fama, malum qua non aliud velocius ullum . . .
tam ficti pravique tenax quam nuntia veri . . .
et pariter facta atque infecta canebat.
> (*Aeneid* 4.173–74; 188; 190)

(At once Rumor raced through Africa's great cities. Rumor is of all pests the swiftest . . . for she is as retentive of news which is false and wicked as she is ready to tell what is true . . . repeating alike facts and fictions."

a fama velocissima, la quale
il falso e 'l vero ugualmente rapporta
era volata con prestissime ale
per tutta Troia . . . (*Fil.* 4.78)

I take it to be obvious that Chaucer, author of the *House of Fame*, was entirely aware that in translating Boccaccio he was also translating Virgil:

The swifte Fame, which that false thynges
Egal reporteth lik the thynges trewe,

Was thorughout Troie yfled with preste wynges . . .
                    (*TC* 4.659–61)

Chaucer may also have been aware of what Boccaccio had said concerning this passage in the *De genealogia deorum gentilium*.[25] Boccaccio there finds himself somewhat perplexed by Virgil's use of the word *fama* because, he says, that word should be used of good report rather than of ill (i.e., the effects of Dido's love affair.) Boccaccio has here anticipated modern criticism, though on somewhat different grounds, in finding a textual embarrassment in Virgil's treatment of Fama. The uneasiness of modern critics has centered on the specific details of Fama's report, which is

> venisse Aenean Troiano sanguine cretum,
> cui se pulchra viro digneretur iungere Dido;
> nunc hiemem inter se luxu, quam longa, fovere
> regnorum immemores turpisque cupidine captos.
>   (4.191–4)

> (how Aeneas is come, one born of Trojan blood, to whom in marriage fair Dido deigns to join herself; now they while away the winter, all its length, in wanton ease together, heedless of their realms and enthralled by shameless passion.)

All these details seem to be the mere truth, not truth mixed with falseness, or truth on the one hand, falseness on the other, as we are led to expect by the lines *tam ficti pravique tenax quam nuntia veri* (188) and *et pariter facta atque infecta canebat* (190) ("false thynges / Egal reporteth lik the thynges trewe," 4.659–60). The fact that for three generations some of the world's finest Virgilians have argued the toss about the lines is in and of itself a sufficient demonstration of Fama's remarkable powers of destructive muddle.

But the difficulty can be more specifically disarmed, I am convinced, by turning to the ambiguites in such words as *luxu* and *iungere* and abandoning the search for a simple and adversarial collation of truth and lies.[26] The line "with which man the beautiful Dido found it worthy to mate" can be saved

---

25. See B. Koonce, *Chaucer and the Tradition of Fame* (Princeton: Princeton University Press, 1966), 35n.
26. See Michael Strain, "Virgil Aeneid 4.188–194," *Proceedings of the Virgil Society* 14 (1974–75): 18–21.

as "truth" by taking *iungere* in a purely sexual or a generally social sense ("to go to bed with," "to associate herself with") and stopping short of the implication of marital union. But it is not easy, given the amatory context, to stop short of that implication. We are not told, explicitly, what Iarbas, the rejected suitor, makes of the news in terms of construing the verb *iungere;* but he is furious, and he certainly thinks that an unworthy idler has succeeded where he, a worthy chieftain, has failed. Iarbas represents the vulgar mind, Boccaccio's *vulgo,* Chaucer's *peple.* Dido has perhaps convinced herself that what is not true is true—*coniugium vocat, hoc praetexit nomine culpam*—but her self-deception is charged with subtleties and extenuations beyond the ambition of vulgar gossip.

Pandaro's concern for the girl's "fama" was of course a concern for her "reputation." In translating *fama* to *name* Chaucer did not alter the sense, but he did perhaps have in mind the happy assonance of English *fame* and *name* and, in the back of his mind, the Virgilian collocation of *nomen* and *Fama* in the lines about Dido's reputation. It is quite clear that Pandarus and Troilus —whether in their Italian or in their English manifestations—are not worried that people are going to tell *lies* about Criseyde. On the contrary they are concerned lest they discover the *truth.* Likewise we have seen that Virgil's Fama, although described in terms that make us think of her as a liar, is actually more truthful than Dido or that, putting the matter another way, that the lie which she spreads is the lie that Dido herself has invented. Furthermore, Latin *nomen* (*name* or *noun*) is happily implicated in the suggestion of "the written record" that Chaucer quite self-consciously invokes in connection with the idea of literary fame.

In the much remarked and very complex passage in which we view the transfer of Criseyde's love and loyalties from Troilus to Diomede, the narrator speaks as one absolutely constrained to report a written record (4.1037, 1044, 1051) which he himself implicitly would choose not to repeat and, possibly, not to believe. It is perhaps the most damaging passage to Criseyde in the entire poem, a wholly self-centered expression of remorse in which the focus is on the damage done to her reputation rather than on possible injustice done to Troilus:

"Allas! for now is clene ago
My name of trouthe in love for everemo!
For I have falsed oon, the gentileste

That evere was, and oon the worthieste.
Allas, of me, unto the worldes ende,
Shal neyther ben ywriten nor ysonge
No good word; for thise bokes wol me shende.
O, rolled shal I ben on many a tonge;
Thorughout the world my belle shal be ronge;
And wommen moost wol haten me of alle.

(5.1054–63)

Criseyde here suggests a "reading" of her own poem which—despite the fact that the narrator himself twice rejects it—is prophetic of one major strain of the poem's exegesis: it is the story of a wicked woman who destroys a noble man. This superficial view is to be sure implicit in the antifeminism of Chaucer's ancient and medieval materials alike, but whether man or woman it takes a reader as shallow as Criseyde herself really to believe it. One woman, certainly, Criseyde rightly fears: Fama, Dame Fame. I take it that in this passage Chaucer is remembering her. We have the contrast of the "name of trouthe" with "falsing." Fama sang (*canebat*), as Criseyde fears what will be sung. "Tot linguae, totidem ora sonant," writes Virgil. "O, rolled shal I ben on many a tonge; / Thorughout the world my belle shal be ronge" (5.1061–62). Criseyde correctly predicts her fame—a *poetic* fame, as the references to writing and books make explicit—in the vocabulary of the poetic Fame of Virgil.

LOLLIUS

The oblique nature of Chaucer's "translation" of Virgil in the *Troilus* has implications for the problem of his translation of "Lollius," a subtle and paradoxical problem of the sort that has helped to create the formidable reputation of his narrator. In the discussion between Pandarus and Troilus concerning the need for secrecy to save Criseyde's "name"—a passage that, as we have seen, Chaucer considerably expanded from the Italian—it is clear that the "name" depends precisely upon the truth's remaining unpublished. Fame, on the other hand, means the published story; that is why she publishes it, sings it, rings it out. Within the economy of *Troilus and Criseyde* there are four people and four alone who know the secret of the name and the fame.

There is no reason to believe that any of the three principals reveal it. The

only explicit evidence we have concerning them comes from Criseyde speaking
to Diomede:

> "But as to speke of love, ywis," she seyde,
> "I hadde a lord, to whom I wedded was,
> The whos myn herte al was til that he deyde;
> And other love, as help me now Pallas,
> Ther in myn herte nys, ne never was."
>   (5.974–78)

The best hope of the reader sympathetic to Criseyde is that she, like Fama
herself, here mixes truth with falsehood; but the dreadful possibility remains
that the last sentence too may be the truth that simply confirms other and far
crueler lies. In neither case is it the publication of the secret affair that has
controlled so much misery. It becomes obvious that it is the narrator alone,
the poet-*interpres,* who does Fame's work. Like Troilus himself this man would
anticipate the reproach of not having done otherwise with a plea of necessity—
for Troilus fatal necessity, for the narrator, textual. Here I believe, we approach
a genuine anxiety of Chaucer's text.

In the *Ars poetica* Horace, who takes Homer as his model of the poet, gives
the following advice to those who, like Jean de Meun, Dante, Boccaccio, and
Chaucer himself, would aspire to a place in the poetic academy:

> aut fama sequere aut sibi convenientia finge
> scriptor. (119–20)

> (Either follow tradition, or, if you invent, see that your invention be in
> harmony with itself.)

In its context this is advice both about the subject for poetry and the manner
of treating the poetic subject chosen. *Fama* here means in essence "history,"
poetic tradition regarded as true and stable, and in particular the Homeric
anthology of poetic subjects. The phrase *sibi convenientia* refers to original invented fictions treated in a verisimilar and internally consistent fashion. The
Greek terms were "myth" and "hypothesis."

There is accordingly a certain alternative between one kind of truth and
fiction (*aut fama sequere aut . . . finge*), followed by the observations that the
invention of original fictions is a difficult matter and that it is better to follow
tradition. To follow "fame" is, furthermore, to be true to the spirit as well as

the letter. Achilles must be bold and wrathful, Medea savage, Orestes lugubrious. There is no room in Horace's theory for a sympathetic Grendel or for a dithering Arthur—for, in sum, the bold, witty, or daring remaking of the classical tradition that is one of the great glories of our literature since at least the time of Ovid.

Horace's theory of poetry might be called one of qualified imitation. The poet is wise in choosing a traditional and approved subject, specifically a subject from the myth of the Trojan War, and in treating it, he is wise to subscribe to traditional ways of viewing character. On the other hand, he should avoid slavish imitation, the work of what Horace in a memorable passage calls the "faithful interpreter."

nec verbum verbo curabis reddere fidus
interpres, nec desilies imitator in artum
unde pedem proferre pudor vetet aut operis lex.
(133–35)

(Nor trouble to render word for word with the faithfulness of a translator; nor by your mode of imitating take "the leap into the pit.")

It may be jarring to realize that the phrase *fidus interpres* is in the Horatian critical vocabulary a negative one, but so it is is, and so it was taken to be by medieval witnesses.[27] Boethius goes so far as to speak of "the vice of the faithful interpreter," a phrase seasoned with the irony of his own practice as a translator. Horace uses the word *interpres* in a second and strikingly different sense in the *Ars poetica*, and I shall return to that usage; but it is first necessary to examine the position of the *Troilus* itself with regard to the notion of the *fidus interpres*. What kind of a translator is Chaucer himself, and what kind is his narrator, so far as they can be meaningfully distinguished?

On the one hand, he embraces, rather elaborately, the pretense of "following fame"—that is, of faithfully reporting, even against the grain of personal preference and temperamental inclination, the "written record." On the other hand, what he actually does to the "written record," taking that for the moment to be the *Filostrato* of Boccaccio, is to reframe and thus to "refame" the central characters even while, more or less, he follows the story. Since it is

27. W. Schwarz, "The Meaning of *Fidus Interpres* in Medieval Translation," *JTS* 45 (1944): 73–78.

precisely on the question of consistency of character that Horace's thought focuses, Chaucerian practice strains against the leash of Horatian precept.[28]

What Chaucer does, in effect, is to superimpose his own fictional imagination upon the "facts" of the poetic tradition. But surely, we are tempted to say, that is what all historical poets must do, as Horace himself seems to recognize when, writing specifically of Homer, he approves the fashion in which the poet "lies" (151): "atque ita mentitur, sic veris falsa remiscet" (thus he lies, and mixes the false with the true). There is no inconsistency in Horace's thought if we grasp and accept the constraints established upon the exercise of originality in the delineation of character. The "falseness" that the poet adds to the "truth" of tradition is to be seen in terms of verisimilar inventions consistent with poetic fame: "what oft was thought, but ne'er so well expressed." The mingling of truth and fiction creates not a monstrous hybrid like the famous "human head on the neck and shoulders of a horse," but a moral and poetic unity. I have thus far spoken of "Chaucer." What of the "narrator"? He will, I believe, vindicate our hypothesis that the Horatian conception of the *fidus interpres* is highly relevant to the *Troilus*.

At two points the narrator seems to comment, obliquely but no less pointedly, on the options and obligations of the poetic translator. The first of the passages introduces the "Cantus Troili":

> And on a song anon right to bygynne,
> And gan loude on his sorwe for to wynne;
> For with good hope he gan fully assente
> Criseyde for to love, and nought repente.
> And of his song nat only the sentence,
> As writ myn auctour called Lollius,
> But pleinly, save oure tonges difference,
> I dar wel seyn, in al, that Troilus
> Seyde in his song, loo, every word right thus
> As I shall seyn . . . (1.389–98)

These lines, among the most disingenuous in the poem, have been much discussed in the context of the "Lollius problem." The narrator says that he will provide the reader not merely with the gist of Troilus' song, as Lollius did, but

28. Horace, [Ars poetica] Horace on Poetry [vol. 2]: The 'Ars Poetica', ed. C. O. Brink (Cambridge: Cambridge University Press, 1971), 197–208.

with every word of the song's text, fully and accurately. Of the three ways in which these claims are intentionally misleading, only the first and most obvious has been fully appreciated: that the text translated is not that of Lollius (either as an ancient Latin author or a stable proxy for Boccaccio) but that of Francis Petrarch. The second point is that there is no way in which the text translated actually accords with the sentence as reported, or at least implied, in the *Filostrato*, or with the motive ascribed in the Middle English. Troilo

> lieto se diede a cantare
> bene sperando, e tutto si dispose
> di voler sola Criseida amare,
> nulla pregiando ogni altra che veduta
> ne gli venisse, o fosse mai piaciuta.
> (*Fil.* 1.37)

(Full of high hopes and light of heart, he fell to singing and was wholly resolved to love none but Criseida, for he held as worthless any other lady he might see or whom he had ever found pleasing.)

With his song Troilus

> gan loude on his sorwe for to wynne;
> For with good hope he gan fully assente
> Criseyde for to love, and nought repente.
> (*TC* 1.390–92)

I suggest that any reader who thinks that Petrarch's sonnet 132 an ejaculation of "good hope," or that its tune is one a lover might well whistle to keep his pecker up, shows little promise as a student of poetry. That stricture, sadly, does consistently apply to Troilus in this poem. The "Cantus Troili" is deeply subversive of the superficial erotic optimism that defines the ethos of the early sections of the *Filostrato* and that reappears in the more jovially immoral behavior of Chaucer's Pandarus. What Chaucer has in effect done is to have invoked the profounder Petrarch to redress the amatory puerilities of Boccaccio, just as in a larger sense he invokes throughout the poem to the mature, Latin Boccaccio himself to redress the apparent superficialities of the young, vernacular Boccaccio.

The claim to have translated the song "pleinly, save oure tonges difference . . . every word right thus" likewise turns out to be false, or at the very least misleading. Chaucer has transformed Petrarch's fourteen lines to twenty-one, giving a full stanza to each of the quatrains and to the sestet. To increase the size of the text by half required an effort of emulative invention as well as of expansive translation, and Chaucer's version of the "Canticus Troili," while indeed true to the "sentence" of its original, is no monument to the *fidus interpres*.

One of the fascinating achievements of the *Canzoniere* as a whole is its distinctively humanistic syncretism. Petrarch builds an erotic fiction based in Ovidian myth on the one hand and the Augustinian doctrine of the two loves on the other. Chaucer honors this achievement in his own competitive addition in line 405, "For ay thurst I the more that ich it drynke." The idea brings together Ovid's frequently quoted line about Narcissus with Jesus' riddling remarks to the Samaritan woman about "living water"—a collation already established in a courtly and amatory literary context in the speech of Genius in the *Roman de la Rose* of Jean de Meun.[29] Chaucer's addition is in the spirit of the initial line of Petrarch's *next* sonnet (133), "Amor m'a posto come segno a strale," where an Ovidian cliché is formulated in the language of a Bible text (Lam. 3.12).

A second passage in which the narrator speaks explicitly about his function as translator (3.491–504) likewise disingenuously suggests that he is a *fidus interpres*. He claims to be unable to give the contents of a long letter that passed between the lovers:

> For ther was some epistel hem bitwene,
> That wolde, as seyth myn auctour, wel contene
> An hondred vers, of which hym liste nat write;
> How sholde I thanne a lyne of it endite? (3.501–3)

Since there is no mention of a letter at this point in the auctorial text and consequently no possibility that it is the auctor rather than the narrator/translator who controls its simultaneous presence and absence, these lines are of course the purest fiction. Yet when it becomes a possibly signficant critical act to discover that Chaucer's fiction is fiction, we may be reminded how powerfully and perversely his text manages to suggest otherwise. Here we discover

29. See my essay, "The Garden of the *Roman de la Rose*: Vision of Landscape or Landscape of Vision," in *Medieval Gardens*, ed. E. Macdougall (Washington, D.C.: Dumbarton Oaks, 1986), 223, n. 42.

that the two passages in his poem that most clearly imply on the surface that the narrator has adopted for himself the role of the *fidus interpres* actually distance him from that office, furtively but decisively. Taken in its totality, the relationship between the *Troilus* and the *Filostrato* is true to the second rule of "creative imitation": it avoids the vice of the *fidus interpres* in translating the spirit of the original rather than its letter. Chaucer could hardly have done this more wittily than by inventing a letter and then denying himself access to it.

The "vice" involved in the vice of the *fidus interpres* is a lack of poetic self-confidence. "The poet in question, unlike the Horatian poet, has 'trusted' another person, not himself. . . . Use of traditional theme must be original."[30] It is obvious that for the poet to place faith in himself is not the same thing as for the poet to break faith altogether with his original text; and Horace nowhere seems to entertain the possibility of truly infidel interpretation. That is a conception, and a poetic reality, that exists in Chaucer, however. When Chaunticleer, interpreting the Latin "in principio, mulier est homis confusio," says

Madame, the sentence of the Latyn is
Woman is mannes joie and al his blisse

he traduces rather than translates his original text. The comedy of the moment depends upon the possibly unpleasant clerical assumption that good-looking chicks are more conspicuous for their sexual than for their textual potential. Chaunticleer thinks it safe to commit treason against the text because Pertelote should be illiterate. Chaunticleer is an *infidus interpres;* Pandarus, as we shall presently see, is another.

For the moment it is Horace's language rather than his doctrine that engages the attention. The poet "lies"; *sic veris falsa remiscet* (thus does he mingle things false with things true). Horace's description of the practice of Homer seems strikingly similar to Virgil's description of the practice of Fama: "tam ficti pravique tenax quam nuntia veri." That is one Virgilian connection. There is another that will immediately leap to mind: the description of the mode of operation of the Cumaean Sibyl, who from her cave sings out her horrid ambages, "wrapping the truth in darkness," *obscuris uera involvens* (*Aeneid* 6.100). The connection between oracular and poetic language is radical, not accidental; it is rooted in the mythical conception of Apollo as the inspirer

30. Brink, in *Ars poetica*, ed. Brink, 211.

of oracles and poets alike.[31] The ambiguities of oracles and the obscurities of dream-revelations[32] on the one hand, and on the other the operations of Fama considered either as vulgar report or as poetic tradition, share a common descriptive vocabulary.

The most extraordinary claim of the *Ars poetica*, and one that continues to be the subject of lively and fruitful controversy, is that relating to the poet's role as *vates*. Horace presents the wholly positive images of the archpoets Orpheus and Amphion. The former is the tamer of savage nature (lions and tigers), the latter the builder of a city—Thebes. Thus the poet's art is the very foundation of civilization. If for Shelley poets were the unacknowledged legislators of the world, for Horace they were the very authors of law and every civil custom:

> Fuit haec sapientia quondam,
> publica privatis secernere, sacra profanis
> concubitu prohibere vago, dare iura maritis,
> oppida moliri, leges incidere ligno.
> sic honor et nomen divinis vatibus atque
> carminibus venit. (396–401)

(This was what men meant by "wisdom" in old days—to separate the rights of one from the rights of all, divine things from common, to forbid lawless love and prescribe rules of wedded life, to build cities and grave laws on wooden tables. 'Twas so that poets and their song won the honor and the name of divine.)

The connection between poetry and augury is likewise explicit. Orpheus is the *sacer interpres deorum* (391), and Horace alludes to the fact that the oracles of Delphi and the Sibylline books were written in hexameters:

> Dictae per carmina sortes
> et vitae monstrata via est et gratia regum . . .
>   (403–4)

(In song oracles were given, and men were guided in the ways of life . . .)

---

31. The Sibyl's *adytum* and the verb *canit* underscore the connection. See A. Kambylis, *Die Dichterweihe und ihre Symbolik* (Heidelberg: Winter, 1965), 164–68.
32. Thus the chorus in Seneca's *Hercules Furens* invokes personified sleep (Somnus), the brother of Death: "[tu] veris miscens falsa, futuri / certus et idem pessimus auctor" (1070–71).

My brief discussion of certain themes in the *Ars poetica* of Horace, modest though it is, does intend to suggest that there is a definite presence of Horace in Chaucer's conception of *Troilus and Criseyde*, a presence that can help us understand his poetic agenda in both its formal and its moral dimensions. Chaucer's commerce with Horace, one of the many aspects of his "classicism" that still await adequate exploration, has not seemed a very promising line of inquiry except to that series of eminent Chaucerians who have argued either than he never read Horace at all or that his only demonstrable Horatian allusion is a blundering misreading.

Not all aspects of this episode of Chaucerian scholarship are relevant to the argument, and I shall enter it, in the epic fashion approved by Horace, *in medias res*. In 1923 the young C. L. Wrenn, writing from Dacca without the benefit of an extensive library but with the compensating advantage of a traditional English classical education, conclusively refuted the opinion of T. R. Lounsbury that there were no certain Horatian quotations in Chaucer at all.[33] He demonstrated that three passages from the *Ars poetica* are unquestionably reflected in Chaucer. One was the reference to Amphion of Thebes just mentioned; it appears in Chaucer in the "Manciple's Tale" (116–17) The other two are both in the *Troilus*. Wrenn compared *TC* 2.22f. (on linguistic change) with *Ars poetica* 70–73 and *TC* 2.22–28 (on the need to eschew grotesque disjunction in writing) with Horace's opening lines. Root's notes, published in 1926, attest to his independent arrival at the same conclusions about the same time.

There can be no doubt that the *Ars poetica* is "in" the *Troilus*, but as always the legitimate question does remain as to whether it is significantly or only ornamentally there. That is, do we have actual firsthand quotations or merely vague reminiscence or a decoration taken from a florilegium or some intermediary author? This question is a frontier separating textual observation and textual interpretation, realms of greater and less probative certainty, respectively, but it seems to me that at least one of the Horatian passages must surely be a pointed contextual quotation.

Pandarus' advice to Troilus concerning the letter he is to write occupies the final three stanzas of an eight-stanza speech (2.898–1043) in which Pandarus presents himself as a *praeceptor amoris* in the school of Ovid and in the department of Jean de Meun. It is a particularly dense "literary" passage. In the concluding three stanzas Pandarus is specifically a literary critic and

33. C. L. Wrenn, "Chaucer's Knowledge of Horace," *MLR* 18 (1923): 286–92.

a teacher of writing. The pose is that of the older expert who gives advice to the young writer—precisely that, of course, adopted by Horace toward the Pisones. In other words, Pandarus concludes his own abbreviated *Ars poetica* with an obvious echo of the beginning of Horace's:

> "Ne jompre ek no discordaunt thyng yfeere . . .
> For if a peyntour wolde peynte a pyk
> With asses feet, and hedde it as an ape,
> It cordeth naught; so nere it but a jape."
>   (2.1037–43)

There is, furthermore, reason to suspect that Chaucer's attitude toward Horace is not that of the unquestioning acolyte. The "Nun's Priest's Tale"—in my view that closest thing to an *ars poetica* that Chaucer himself wrote—precisely concerns itself with literary grotesques, humanoid chickens who quote Latin authors to each other.

What Pandarus advises is certainly a kind of *aurea mediocritas*. The letter should be neither "dygneliche" nor "scryvenliche" written. It should avoid monotony on the one hand and disjunctive variety on the other. To illustrate the vice of monotony, Pandarus conjures up the image of the best harper in the world who lavishes all his energies on playing a single note. Here the editors have seen, correctly in my view, an allusion to another part of the *Ars poetica* (355–56). To exemplify the vice of grotesque disjunction, Pandarus gives two examples: the verbal collation of "terms of phisik / In loves termes," and the picture of a fish with the feet of an ass and an ape's head. This is a version, certainly, of the Horatian "human head on a horse's neck." If all this is what the poet is to *avoid,* certain obvious questions arise. The first is why Chaucer should have introduced, in his first ambitious addition to Boccaccio's text, an elaborate image suggesting the "horsiness" of Troilus' behavior (1.218–24); his own text implies a conjunction of Troilus with a part of a horse's anatomy other than the neck, to be sure, but connection of human and horse there certainly is. One doubts that this is mere coincidence when one sees what Pandarus himself has already done with "harping" and with mixing terms of love with terms of medicine: "What? slombrestow as in a litargie? / Or artow lik an asse to the harpe?" (1.730–31).

The word *litargie* is a technical medical term taken over from the pathologist Lady Philosophy in Boethius, and it initiates one of the more elaborate imagery patterns of the *Troilus,* that of the hero's love as sickness. It would be hard to imagine a poem that more persistently mixes "termes of physik in loves ter-mes" than does the *Troilus*. It seems to me impossible that Chaucer could have written Pandarus' speech as he did if he did not know the *Ars poetica* of Horace —as opposed to knowing a few lines of it quoted by somebody else—and if he had not given some focused and critical thought to the ideas Horace raises. We here see Chaucer both invoking Horace and, if not arguing with him, carrying on an animated conversation in which he is by no means a passive auditor.

I publish this suggestion in full knowledge of the somewhat awkward fact that a number of eminent Chaucerians are of the opinion that Chaucer mis-read rather than read Horace. I allude of course to the well-known hypothesis concerning the Horatian ancestry of Chaucer's pseudosource for the *Troilus*, "Myn auctour called Lollius." In 1873 Latham made the brilliant suggestion that Chaucer's Lollius was to be associated with Horace's pupil Maximus Lol-lius as addressed by name in the first line of the second epistle of the first book:

Troiani belli scriptorem, Maxime Lolli,
dum tu declamas Romae, Praeneste relegi . . .

(While you have been practicing declamation at Rome, Lollius Maximus, I have been reading again at Praeneste the storyteller of the war of Troy . . .)

The idea is that a careless or ignorant reading of these lines, or a reading of these lines as carelessly or ignorantly altered by a scribe, would have suggested to Chaucer that there was a Roman writer named Lollius who was a maximal writer on the Trojan War.

Latham's hypothesis was embraced, elaborated, and ameliorated by numer-ous famous scholars including, among the most distinguished, G. L. Kittredge (1917), and R. A. Pratt (1950). Though I cannot accept their conclusions, it will become obvious that, like them, I accept the connection of Chaucer's Lol-lius with the Maximus Lollius of Horace, *Epistles* 1.2.1. My small claim to originality must be my belief that Geoffrey Chaucer could read Latin.

Kittredge's essay, characterized by an awesome learning and studded with critical insights of enduring value, marshaled the full powers of a major Chau-cerian in the construction of an argument which, if accepted, would expose Chaucer himself as something of a simpleton.[34] Kittredge was convinced that

---

34. G. L. Kittredge, "Chaucer's Lollius," *HSCP* 28 (1917): 47–109.

Chaucer really did believe that there was an ancient poet of the Trojan War named Lollius. The incontrovertible truth was not in the *Troilus* but in the *House of Fame*, where Lollius was listed along with a number of bona fide poetic historians who bear up the fame of Troy. (Already I find I must part company with Kittredge, for I find no compelling prima facie reason to deny to the *House of Fame* a degree of Chaucerian playfulness clearly present in his allusions to Lollius in the *Troilus*.) Kittredge then supposed that in the interval between the writing of the *House of Fame* and the *Troilus* (according to his own unprovable chronology) Chaucer came to realize that Lollius' poem was no longer extant, so that he (Lollius) provided the poet with the perfect device to enrich the verisimilitude of his pseudoantique romance.

Chaucer could have come by the original misapprehension in one of two ways—either by misconstruing Horace's Latin himself or by being influenced by someone else who had done so. Kittredge then engaged his considerable Latinity in the search of emendations that would explain the misconception. If "Maxime" were taken not as a *nomen* but as a form of a simple adjective, and if we introduce the reading "scriptor" or "scriptorum" in place of the accusative "scriptorem," we should then have the phrase "Lollius, you great writer of the Trojan War" or "Lollius, you greatest of writers of the Trojan War."

Pratt's contribution to the hypothesis, a generation later, was to seek out and actually find medieval manuscripts in which the hypothesized corruptions did in fact exist.[35] He reported no such misreadings from actual manuscripts of Horace, but in a copy of the *Policraticus* of John of Salisbury, who cites the Horatian epistle at some length in his essay on the role of poetry in the teaching of moral philosophy, he did find the incriminated reading "scriptorum." And in a French translation of the *Policraticus* by an obscure fourteenth-century Franciscan, Jean Foullechat, he found an explicit misinformed paraphrase to the effect that Lollius was a great writer of the Trojan War.

Only one point in Kittredge's philological argument per se strikes me as shaky. His claim that the editorial recognition of "Maximus" as a *nomen* linked to Lollius is a modern one is true in the sense that the word was first capitalized in nineteenth-century editions of Horace but its connection with Lollius as a kind of nickname is clearly recognized in the Parisian scholia.[36] I think

35. Robert A. Pratt, "A Note on Chaucer's Lollius," *MLR* 65 (1950): 183–87.
36. See the *Scholia in Horatium*, ed. H. J. Botschuyver (Amsterdam: van Bottburg, 1942), 4:331: "Hic Lollius optimus placitator erat, unde a populo Maximus vocabatur."

it would be considerably harder for "maximus" to be separated from "lollius" than Kittredge suggests, though Jean Foullechat shows that it could be done.

The iron law of potential error holds its dominion over textual transmission as over other human activities: whatever can go wrong *will* go wrong. My disquiet is not with the ingenious philological argument but with the fact that, despite Kittredge's disclaimers, Chaucer would have had to be a dimwit either to have misconstrued the Horatian text or to have concluded, on the basis of someone else's misconstruction of it, that Lollius was an actual writer on the Trojan War. The least of the difficulty is the textual howler. Consider. We are invited to believe that Chaucer, who had conducted deep researches into the matter of Troy in preparation for the composition of the *Troilus*, actually believed that "a great" and perhaps "the greatest" authority on the Trojan War was a name mentioned once in all of Latin literature, and that the book or books on which his fame depended had been entirely obliterated from human memory.

By the time Chaucer wrote the *House of Fame*, whenever that was, he had had a considerable enough classical education to undertake a competition with Virgil not unworthy of that undertaken by Dante Alighieri before him.[37] It seems to me impossible that this man could have entertained the ignorant belief ascribed to him. Hence I regard as implausible the suggestion that he credulously accepted someone else's mistranslation. That he made such a mistranslation himself seems to me even less likely. Kittredge was so exercised in the pursuit of the opening two lines of Horace's poem that he seems to have abandoned altogether the issue of the broader context. There are seventy-one lines in Horace's epistle. By the time the reader gets to the fourth line and its third-person verb *dicit,* it is impossible to maintain an interpretation based on the assumption that the subject of the poem is Lollius. Furthermore, anyone who has read the *Ars poetica* knows quite well that Horace regards *Homer* as the great writer of the Trojan War, and that conclusion is likewise nearly inescapable in *Epistle* 1.2 itself.

My own hypothesis concerning Lollius is this. The name Lollius was indeed suggested to Chaucer by the opening lines of *Epistle* 1.2, but its use by Chaucer suggests an act of the poetical imagination rather than a blunder, happy or otherwise, in construing the Latin.

37. See Charles Tisdale, "The *House of Fame:* Virgilian Reason and Boethian Wisdom," *CL* 25 (1973): 247–61.

Chaucer, in common with other intelligent readers of poetry before and since, connected in his mind the concerns of Horace's *Epistola ad Pisones* and of the first epistle to Maximus Lollius. In both of them the authoritative teacher of poetry gave advice to younger men, in the first instance on the art of poetry and in the second on the moral utility of poetry. In the one Horace maintained that the poet should follow Homer both in the selection of poetic subject and in the prosecution of the poetic theme; in the other he claimed that Homer was as great a teacher of moral philosophy as the masters of the Stoa, and he sketched brief allegorical interpretations of the *Iliad* and the *Odyssey* in support of the claim.

For a variety of reasons Chaucer wanted a pseudoantique authority on which to rest the enterprise of the *Troilus*. Pseudoantique authority was in fact already a part of the tradition in which he worked. A pseudoantique original allowed him to adjust the narratorial stance of the *Filostrato* and to introduce at the end of his poem an explicit Christian judgment on pagan love. Most important, a pseudoantique "original" authorized the exercise of his historical imagination, the poetic adaptation of his considerable historical researches, in the vividly augmented "classicization" of the medieval Troy story.

In all of this he had the serious philosophical and moral intentions that were recognized by medieval readers and have been demonstrated by a number of modern scholars. Hence the question of moral as well as of historical authority was on his mind. His attempt must be to avoid moral and historical anachronism alike. In imagining the ancient poem that he might translate, he imagined the poem that Maximus Lollius, acting upon the literary and ethical precepts of his mentor Horace, might have written. In a certain sense Lollius was among the most, rather than the least, historical features of the poem. Ovid had written "heroic epistles" and attached them to names associated with the Trojan War. Chaucer toyed with the idea of ascribing a whole epic poem to a name he read in Horace. Like Troilus himself, Lollius was thus called to literary fame from the obscurity of the periphery of Roman poetry in the service of medieval classicism.

I shall not attempt to explain the presence of the name of Lollius among the Trojan historians in the *House of Fame*, but I must deny what Kittredge and Root stated as an axiom beyond the need of proof—namely, that its presence there could only be a philological mistake. It is worth repeating that we have no sure knowledge of the date of the *House of Fame*. If, as is generally accepted, it is anterior to any part of the *Troilus*, we may regard the name Lollius as a

witty "plant" or doctoring of the evidence.[38] Chaucer would hardly be the first
to have buried a false antiquity where he knew that the archaeologists were
most likely to dig.

As I read the *House of Fame* it is much less solemn than Kittredge thought
it was. In particular I find in the authorial stance to antiquity that distinctive
combination of deep respect and self-assured superiority that characterized
the Dantesque mode of medieval humanism. Kittredge found it impossible that
Chaucer should have put fictional historians of Troy among what he must have
taken to be the factual ones. I think Kittredge forgets that Chaucer is describing
images in the House of Fame—"Fame, which that false thynges egal reporteth
lik the thynges trewe."

The hypothesis briefly sketched here seems to me preferable to Kittredge's,
partly in truth because it is my own, but partly also because it finds in Lollius
an artifact of Chaucerian intelligence rather than one of Chaucerian dullness.
At the same time I am aware that neither of these reasons may entirely com-
pel its belief, and I invest no probative function in them. The more general
issue of Chaucer's response to Horace in the *Troilus*, on the other hand, is one
toward which the argument of this book cannot remain agnostic. And in this
context Horace's epistle to Maximus Lollius becomes highly relevant. I assume
that Chaucer read it (and here the subsequent argument would actually be
strengthened if he read it, as Pratt thought, in John of Salisbury's excerpts in
the *Policraticus*) and that he did not fail to understand that Horace had taken as
his subject the moral uses of poetry.[39] The testimony of the *Policraticus*, indeed,

38. However, the evidence can be (and has been) read another way. If *Troilus* ante-
dates the *House of Fame*, Chaucer is simply advertising the Trojan historian whose
ghost-writer he is. See Hugo Lange, "Chaucer's 'Myn Auctour Called Lollius' und die
Datierung des 'Hous of Fame,'" *Anglia* 42 (1918): 345–51.

39. Since I have had to abandon Kittredge's major hypothesis concerning Lollius, it
will be apparent that I cannot accept Pratt's elaboration of it. Since, however, Chaucer
certainly used the *Policraticus* at times and since it is in a (single) manuscript of that
work alone that the confusing reading "scriptorum" has thus far been found, Pratt's
idea must be briefly considered. Unless we are to imagine that Chaucer opened John's
vast book more or less at random, that his eye fell by the merest chance on the line
with the corrupt reading, and that he then immediately closed the book, the question
of *context* becomes highly relevant. The lines cited are an obvious summary of Homer's
Iliad as it was endlessly recalled in Augustan poetry and in the Latin schoolbooks of
the later Middle Ages. Thus a misreading that is theoretically credible in terms of the
first two lines of the poem in isolation becomes deeply improbable in context.

offers a telling example of the typical use of *Epistle* 1.2 by medieval humanists: Horace's poem is an argument in support of the didactic, moral, allegorical function of poetry.

Reflection may suggest that it is unnecessary and probably unhelpful to approach the question in terms of an assumed exclusive alternative: *either* Chaucer had read Horace *or* he had read other people citing Horace. Most of us who do much reading or writing must surely share the experience of discovering one author through another, one book through another, one idea through another. One of the truest claims of literary criticism in the Romantic tradition is that texts accommodate, perhaps absorb, something of the history of their previous readings; they often come to us, that is, interpreted.

The act of "interpretation" may or may not include a formal attempt to teach the "meaning" of the work; but that is not my point. My point is that it is quite likely that Chaucer read Horace both in manuscripts of Horace and in occasional citations of Horace by important medieval writers, and that "Chaucer's reading of Horace" was thus a rather complex business. It has been pointed out that when Chaucer wrote in the *Legend of Good Women* (164–66)

> But I ne clepe nat innocence folye
> Ne fals pitee, for "vertu is the mene"
> As Etik saith

he is perhaps citing Horace after John of Salisbury if not from the text of John of Salisbury. John's distinctive term for Horace is "Ethicus," "moral Horace," so to speak.[40] This is specifically a citation of *Epistle* 1.19.9 ("Virtus est medium

---

40. See J. L. Lowes, "Chaucer's 'Etik,'" *MLN* 25 (1910): 87–89. "Etik" may well in fact be Aristotle or Aristotle's *Ethics* as reported in Dante's *Convivium*, as Skeat and others thought and as Schless has reargued at length (*Chaucer and Dante: A Revaluation* [Norman, Okla.: Pilgrim Books, 1984], 150–53). Schless's criticisms of Lowes are sound, but in propounding them he may approach their opposite vice. He accepts Pratt's quite dubious theory as demonstrated probability (p. 38), and he lapses into the argument from silence. "If Chaucer knew Horace as well as Lowes implies—so well, that is, that he either had a manuscript of his works or could give a particular line from memory —it is odd indeed that he never once mentions the Latin poet by name or makes any other reference to him in his works. Chaucer, it need hardly be remarked, was not one to shun 'auctoritee'" (p. 152). Would Schless propose the same test for Chaucer's familiarity with the work of, say, Giovanni Boccaccio? So far as the *Troilus* is concerned, the absence of Horace in the poetic pentad (5.1792), as compared with the similar

vitiorum et utrimque reductum"), a line explicitly cited by John in *Policraticus* 8.13. However, even though it is possible that Chaucer is here using Horace as previously used by John, it is a non sequitur to conclude that he did not read Horace "himself."

If for the sake of argument we accept the hypothesis that Chaucer first encountered the classical Lollius from Horace's *Epistle* 1.2 *as cited by John of Salisbury*, we must then imagine that he also encountered its immediate context, including John's opinion that people who have not read Horace are "illiterates."[41] The *Policraticus* does not seem to me to be a likely text for an "illiterate" to read in the first place; but it is certainly not a book to encourage the continuing "illiteracy" of one who stumbled upon it. The two passages under discussion (*Epistles* 1.2.1–16 and 1.18.9) come from the only two poems in all of Horace that are addressed to Lollius.

The complex of ideas that unite the epistle to the Pisones (*Ars poetica*) with the two epistles to Lollius includes at least three ideas that are of thematic relevance to the *Troilus* and, in particular, to Pandarus' role as *interpres*: (1) the moral uses of literature; (2) the relationships between friendship and literary criticism; (3) the relationships between friendship and virtue. In each of the poems in question the poetic voice adopted by Horace is that of the older man who gives moral and literary advice to a younger friend—the role, that is, of Pandarus to Troilus.

Epistle 1.18 begins with Horace recognizing in his young friend Lollius an anxiety that the nature of Lollius' friendship be properly understood as that of an *amicus,* not that of a *scurra.* We have already seen, in the passage in which Troilus redefines pimping as "gentilesse, compassioun, and felawship, and trist," that he does so on the basis of a need to distinguish among things superficially alike:

---

list in Dante, where Horace is present, is easily enough explained in terms of genre alone: Chaucer gives us a list of epic poets appropriate to his own enterprise. ("Magnus Ovidius"—the Ovid of the *Metamorphoses*—qualified for the title.) Horace is not an epic poet, as he often reminds his readers; and though he proposes the matter of Troy as the poetic subject par excellence, he wrote no Trojan narrative of his own. Statius supplants him in Chaucer's list, as I suspect he would have in Dante's had not Dante chosen to save Statius, in more senses than one, for other purposes.

41. "Poetas, historicos, oratores. . . . Qui enim istorum ignari sunt, illiterati dicuntur, esti litteras noverint." John of Salisbury, *Policraticus* 7.9, ed. C. C. J. Webb (Oxford: Clarendon, 1909), 2.126.

for wyde wher is wist,
How that ther is diversite requered
Bytwixen thynges like, as I have lered.

(TC 3.403–5)

Horace recognizes a similar need:

Si bene te novi, metues, liberrime Lolli,
scurrantis speciem praebere, professus amicum.
ut matrona meretrici dispar erit atque
discolor, infido scurrae distabit amicus.

(Epistle 1.18.1–4)

(If I know you well, my Lollius, frankest of men, you will shrink from
wearing the guise of the parasite when you have professed the friend.)

The analogy here, as in Troilus' speech in the third book, though the speakers' roles are reversed, depends upon the need to distinguish within categories
of similar appearance between parameters of meretriciousness and virtue. Both
the whore and the respectable matron are women; but there the similarity
ends.[42] The text proposes that the *scurra* and the *amicus* form a similar category; but fawning is not the same thing as friendship. To see the way that the
one is different (*discolor*) from the other depends upon the act of moral perception, a discrimination between two kinds of love. Speaking of his own inability
to speak of love "feelingly," the narrator explains that "A blynd man kan nat
juggen wel in hewis" (*TC* 2.21). Troilus' colorful redefinition of pimping is, in
this context, an obvious manifestation of moral color-blindness.

The *scurra* is a type in Latin dramatic and moral literature, a kind of foppish
parasite and court jester. Here Horace uses the term to indicate a "false friend,"
a concept he turns to in a more explicitly literary context at the end of the *Ars
poetica*. The false friend, imagined as a sycophantic critic at the banquet table
of the wealthy poetaster, tells the rich man what he wants to hear about his
poems: "pulchre, bene, recte" (428). The true friend is the honest and therefore
severe critic, the man who points out literary inadequacies, infelicities, and
ambiguities that they may be corrected and improved. The true friend is the

42. This was a commonplace distinction example in classical moral literature. Augustine uses a version of it in his discussion of linguistic distinctions in the *De dialectica*.
See Fleming, *Reason and the Lover*, 111.

true interpreter; the false friend is the *false interpreter.* The Chaucerian context in which the Horatian categories are most obvious is probably the "Merchant's Tale," with Placebo and Justinus; but as we shall presently see they are fully operative in the fifth book of the *Troilus* as well.

Yet the most telling way in which the verse epistle "Trojani belli scriptorem" is relevant to Chaucer's design of the *Troilus* is in its literary theory. Horace insists, in the most unequivocal terms, that Homer's two great poems are *moral allegories.* Homer "shows us what is fair, what is foul, what is profitable, what not, more plainly and better than a Chryssipus or a Crantor," two of the most famous moralists in the Greek philosophical tradition. The *Iliad* is a powerful indictment of the disastrous social consequences of the individual passions of *amor* and *ira.* "For every folly of their princes the Greeks feel the scourge. Faction, craft, wickedness, and the lust and anger from which it springs—these are the sources of wrong-doing within the walls of Troy and without them." These claims are not incidental to Horace's poem; they are the statement of his poetic subject and his philosophical agenda. We need to remind ourselves that their author is Horace, not a twelfth-century commentator on Boethius or a fourteenth-century friar. Horace argues the centrality of Homeric allegory in the moral education of youth.

Thus it is that in the second and longer part of the epistle Horace addresses the situation of the reader rather than that of the writer. Young Lollius must take as his rule of moral life the unflinching Stoicism taught by the poet. "Sperne voluptates . . . animum rege." As I read Chaucer's poem I find a Lollius who has learned his lesson well both as poet and as moralist, if there is indeed any real distance between those two terms in the tradition in which Horace and Chaucer have alike enlisted themselves.[43]

I find in Chaucer's text certain images that may be playful echoes of his reading of this epistle. Horace exhorts Lollius to burn the midnight oils learning virtue from the reading of poetry: "so surely if you will not ask for a book and a candle (*librum cum lumine*), if you will not set your mind steadily on honorable studies and pursuits, you will lie awake on the rack of envy or passion." We may recall that part of the great "sex scene" in the third book that shows us Pandarus retiring (briefly) from the wakeful bed of Troilus and Criseyde to the chimney side, where he "took a light, and fond his contenaunce / As for to

---

43. See Colin W. Macleod, "The Poetry of Ethics: Horace, Epistles I," in Macleod's *Collected Essays* (Oxford: Oxford University Press, 1983), 280–91.

looke upon an old romaunce" (3.979–80).[44] We have in this epistle as well a conspicuous image of horse training that may enrich the complex and much discussed allusion to "proude Bayard" at 1.118.[45]

In these instances the textual allusion, if it indeed is actually there, is ironic and subversive, as is the common pattern in the poem's more obvious invocations of the *Consolatio*. But at the end of his poem Chaucer on Lollius, like Horace to Lollius, makes an explicit appeal to youth: "O yonge fresshe folkes, he or she" (5.1835). I have already expressed my belief that Chaucer wrote this line in such a way as to recognize the antieroticism of Ovid latent in the text of the *Filostrato* he translated. Yet it is precisely at the ending of his poem that Chaucer wished to, and did, part company with Boccaccio most pointedly. Bocaccio's narrator, following in the footsteps of Jean de Meun's, continues to the very end his pose of moral myopia.[46]

Chaucer did not merely invent a narrator who was a real ancient pagan rather than a pseudopagan Neopolitan trying to write his way into a woman's pants; he also, by inventing the role of the *interpres,* allowed a wholly decorous, wholly serious, and wholly decisive concluding moral interpretation of the poem. It is an interpretation that in its clarity and its ethical stability dissolves the linguistic and ethical ambiguities of the narrator's designs upon his readers as expressed at the very outset of the poem (1.15–56).

Boccaccio's narrator invites his reader to find a lesson in Troilo's love ("nell'amor di Troiolo vi specchiate," "See yourselves reflected in Troilo's love"). Chaucer's does that, but considerably more in addition. He invites the reader to a moral understanding of an entire literary tradition:

o here, of payens corsed olde rites . . .
Lo here, the forme of olde clerkes speche

---

44. Cf. Fleming, "Smoky Reyn," 10–11.
45. Cf. *Epistle* 1.18.65–66, "venaticus, ex quo / tempore cervinam pellem latravit in aula, / militat in silvis catulus."
46. Thus the narrator's "moralization" of the story is, in the best Magdunian fashion, grotesquely wide of the mark. The "moral" of the *Filostrato* (8.29–30) is that young males should try their luck with middle-aged women rather than with notoriously unstable younger ones. This is one of several echoes of the end of the *Roman de la Rose* in the ending of the *Filostrato*: specifically the amusing meditation of Jean's Lover (*RR* 21405–508) on the Ovidian maxim "Utilis, o iuvenes, aut haec, aut senior aetas" (*AA* 2.667).

In poetrie, if ye hire bokes seche.
    (5.1849, 1854–55)

His moral concern, like that of Horace, is general, comprehensive, founded in a particular perception of a whole literary tradition and addressed comprehensively to youth viewed as a condition of genuine moral option. In this regard the word *fresshe* in the line "O yonge fresshe folkes, he or she" takes on its particular importance. It corresponds to the Horatian phrase *puro pectore*: "Now while you are a boy with clean heart drink in my words, now let yourself be guided by your betters." It was indeed Horace's consistent belief in the formative experiences of youth—formative as to soundness of literary taste and to soundness of ethical precept and action alike—that is reflected in the most famous lines of his poem:

Quo semel est imbuta recens servabit odorem
testa diu. (69–70)

(The crock will long keep the fragrance with which it was once steeped in early days.)

This thought thus expressed, too, probably accounts for the fact that the first epistle to Lollius is among the Horatian poems most frequently and most approvingly cited by the Fathers of the Church—who were also the fathers, we should not forget, of medieval Christian literary culture.[47] It posits no difficulty to imagine that Geoffrey Chaucer had a familiarity with, and an intelligent attitude toward, one of the small number of classical poems best known and most warmly approved by medieval "literates."

Classical and medieval poets and lovers of poetry faced a common strategic difficulty in the powerful Platonic criticism of the lying of art. The idea that poets were liars in a morally culpable sense was endemic in certain strains of idealist thought absolutely central to medieval intellectual life; but no less

47. Some important patristic testimonia are collected by F. Klingner in his edition of Horace (Leipzig: Teubner, 1950). Two excellent essays provide illuminating discussion of "Trojani belli scriptorem" with particular relevance to my argument. Otto Luschnat, "Horaz, Epistel I 2," *Theologia Viatorum* 9 (1963): 142–55, places the poem's intellectual concerns within the context of antique theories of the role of poetry in moral pedagogy; and Rachel Skalitzky, "Good Wine in a New Vase (Horace, Epistles I.2)," *TAPA* 99 (1968): 443–52, demonstrates that the poem's unity is to be found in a pedagogic strategy.

available was the idea, likewise a resource from the ancient philosophical repertory, that the superficial lies of poetry veiled profound moral truths. This is of course the view that is forcefully advanced by Horace in the "Trojani belli scriptorem" and quite as forcefully restated by John of Salisbury, partly on Horace's authority, in the twelfth century. It is also the argument put forward by the learned "defenders" of poetry in the fourteenth century: Dante, Petrarch, and Boccaccio, among others. An influential group of modern medievalists have rewarded their efforts by, in effect, calling them liars again. Their claims on behalf of moral allegory have been taken as disingenuous, a coerced and insincere concession to a repressive culture, a smokescreen behind which they might be unobserved in the pursuit of their real interests as readers and writers, which is to say their interest in the lies of poetry.

I have no wish to enter the large debate about Chaucerian allegory which has in my opinion suffered on all sides from unacceptably broad generalizations given in answer to unacceptably narrow questions, but I shall make explicit a view of the *Troilus* that must by now be apparent in any case. Chaucer has intentionally and studiously created and placed his poem within what he takes to be the great tradition of classical poetry, the Homeric myth as translated into Latin epic and elegy; and he treats his materials—following the lead of his principal vernacular models, Jean de Meun, Dante, Petrarch, and Boccaccio —as a poet who is also a moral philosopher. Accordingly, I believe that the *Troilus* was explicitly conceived and executed as moral allegory in precisely the fashion that Horace found the *Iliad* to be moral allegory.

I further conclude that Chaucer genuinely embraced the ambition of moral pedagogy that is implied by his concluding address to "yonge fresshe folk." Two of his poetic inventions convince me that this must be the case. In the first place Troilus is presented as a young and inexperienced man with many genuinely noble instincts and qualities but without the erotic experience of the callous stud of the *Filostrato*. Until the time that his eye falls upon Criseyde he is, in amatory terms, a youth *puro pectore*. There is nothing foreordained about the disaster that overwhelms him. That disaster—and this is the second point —is brought about by his own moral inadequacies under the guidance of a fallacious *interpres,* and it is charted by a series of carefully contrived interpretive failures that establish in the clearest possible way the poet's insistent union of sound reading with sound living.

THE HERMENEUTICAL HERO

I have so far in this chapter been concerned to suggest how various strands of the theme of "interpretation" deriving from a variety of classical traditions and variously exploited by medieval classicists anterior to Chaucer are woven into the text of the *Troilus* warp and woof; for I believe that we must appreciate something of the persistence and complexity of the theme before we can aspire, even in the most general terms, to understand the literary self-consciousness of the poem before us. I would now adjust the focus of critical scrutiny to examine in some detail certain interpretive aspects of the tragedy of Troilus most insistently present in its most somber moments of the fourth and fifth books, the latter a book which, were it to be given a title of its own, might well be called, by analogy with the *Pamphilus*, "Troilus, de interpretatione."

The investigation is considerably enabled by the numerous theoreticians who have in recent years made the concepts of "semiology" or "sign theory" generally current in literary discussion. Though they are terms sometimes used in a contemporary critical vocabulary potentially misleading in its application to medieval texts, they can when used with caution denote with precise clarity the theoretical concerns of various kinds of classical and medieval interpretive enterprises centered on the understanding of "signs." The understanding of "signs" was, for example, central to the concerns of augury, oneirocriticism, and omen reading—all of which feature in Chaucer's fifth book—but it is of course most fundamentally relevant to the linguistic enterprise itself since in the Augustinian tradition continuous with important schools of antique linguistic theory, language itself is a system of "signs."

Fortunately, Eugene Vance has obviated the necessity for a certain amount of preliminary discussion by providing Chaucerians with a pioneering model of a semiological study at once informed by contemporary theory and historically responsible in its awareness of Augustinian paradigms.[48] Building on Vance's foundation even while approaching the poem from a perspective differing from that he brings to bear upon it, I propose to examine a series of cognate emblems of signification and a repertory of carefully chosen sign-bearers relevant

48. Vance, "Mervelous Signals." This essay, which has considerably influenced my thinking throughout this book, reappears in a substantially revised form in Vance's book *Mervelous Signals: Poetics and Sign Theory in the Middle Ages* (Lincoln: University of Nebraska Press, 1986), 256–310.

to the moral and intellectual analysis of Troilus' situation in the final act of his tragedy. The fifth book presents us with what I shall call the hermeneutical hero, Troilus *interpres,* a man faced with the contrived interpretive challenges of his dreams, of texts present and implied, of omens, of the signs of changing times. Yet before we turn to the series of conspicuously present interpretive challenges posed by that book, we must attend to the interpretive implications of a notorious textual *absence* of the fourth book, its aborted Boethius.

Troilus' muddled soliloquy on fatal necessity, however much discussed, still retains its remarkable versatility as a witness to Chaucer's artistic strategies. In the first place it remains, at least in my opinion, a probable example of deliberate authorial revision. I am not unaware that the very idea of authorial revision of the *Troilus* has been called into question by certain recent and challenging theories concerning "the scribal medium," but at least so far as *TC* 4.953–1078 is concerned, authorial revision remains, in my view the best explanation of a curious set of phenomena.[49]

Beyond that, I take the passage to be an important indication of Chaucer's structural design and of his thematic pursuits. From the structural point of view, it enforces the already insistent connections between his own philosophical agenda and that of Boethius. Just as near the beginning of his own book he made a prominent dramatic allusion to Boethius' first book, so now as he moves toward the end of his book he makes an equally conspicuous allusion

49. Since the question is finally irrelevant to the present argument I shall not pursue it here. Windeatt makes a careful review of the evidence, pp. 40–41, and denies that it gives convincing demonstration of revision. For the sake of argument, I limit myself to the following minimalist claims: that Chaucer wrote the passage in question and at some time intended it to be part of his poem. If this be granted and we then assume that the present manuscript evidence is a result of human intellection rather than accident, chance, or astral predestination, it means one of the following things: (1) Chaucer inserted the passage within a narrative already written down; (2) Chaucer removed the passage from a narrative already written down; or (3) someone else removed it from a narrative already written down. If one's object of inquiry—as is mine in this book—is Chaucer's poem rather than somebody else's attitude to it, (3) becomes irrelevant. We must then decide between (1) and (2). If the physical evidence of the manuscripts fails us, no definitive conclusion is possible, and we must try to decide from the criteria of common sense and literary criticism whether (1) or (2) makes the more literary sense. Disgreement on the issue is entirely reasonable; but I myself find (1) significantly more probable than (2).

to the end of Boethius'. In both instances there is a similar dramatic situation
—Troilus is surprised by Pandarus when he thinks he is alone—and in both
there is a parodic relationship between Pandarus and Lady Philosophy.

Furthermore we again see Pandarus in another aspect of his role as "textual interrupter"—a role most clearly exemplified in his first visit to Criseyde,
when he interrupts the "geste of the sege of Thebes" precisely at the point at
which Amphiaraus' plunge into the chasm of hell is announced. In the fourth
book, to be sure, Troilus is not actually *reading* a text; rather he is remaking or
performing it, as he reconstructs, point by point, what the Chaucerian translation calls the "more hard doute" of the character "Boethius" in *CP* 5.3. If I am
right, Pandarus' interruption of the Troy story served complex ends, including (1) the ironic suppression of a literary authority of considerable potential
importance to the interrupted "reader" and (2) the prominent introduction of
the theme of pagan divination. I suggest that the pattern of premature textual
foreclosure of the passage in Chaucer's fourth book repeats that of the first.

The "more hard doubt" of *CP* 5.3 is this: if God is omnipotent, He is prescient; if He is prescient, what He knows will happen in the future must happen
by necessity; if events happen by necessity, a human being lacks freedom of
the will. Lady Philosophy's solution—contained in the fourth, fifth, and six
proses of the fifth book—is both rhetorically and intellectually emphatic. It is
the "end" of the book both in a structural and a teleological sense, for it gives
philosophical justification for prayers of petition and for the voluntary pursuit
of virtue. Here, in terms of practical, tropological doctrine, is the "point" of the
book; and the "point" of Troilus' protracted soliloquy, ostentatiously stopping
short of canonical Boethian conclusion, is its pointedly pointless character.

Yet is it reasonable to expect Troilus, pagan Troilus, to get the point? The
explicit answer given to this question by several distinguished Chaucerians is
"No." It is an answer that cautions but does not convince me. Let us interrogate
the passage with the question raised in an earlier context by Minnis: are the
standards of the Christian text, the *Consolatio* of Boethius, appropriate to the
historically imagined ancient world of Chaucer's poem?

It seems to me that so far as the Boethian intervention of the fourth book is
concerned, to ask the question, surely, is to answer it. To speak of a Chaucerian
text at all is rather misleading. What we have is a Chaucerian manipulation
of a Boethian text. Furthermore, no conceivable poetic purpose is served by
the Boethian presence that does not involve a thoughtful comparison of the

Boethian text in its original and in its translated contexts. Troilus' speech is an obvious emblem of thwarted, incomplete, imperfect thought. Its very derivativeness draws attention less to its textual convergence with its source than to its flamboyant textual divergence. By what license shall we exempt Troilus from the intellectual responsibility of the Boethian text—except by first discharging him from the presumptive obligation of *rationality?*

This is much more than Pandarus, the limping Lady Philosophy of the moment, is willing to do. "Who say ever a wis man faren so?" (4.1087) he asks in disgust. Behind the English phrase "wis man" we may certainly see the Latin *sapiens.* It is one thing to fall short of the ideal of *sapientia,* another to abandon the ideal altogether. The latter is Troilus' course. Pandarus, like Lady Philosophy, though on a measurably lower level, has pragmatic aims and a tropological agenda: he wishes to instruct Troilus in a practical course of action. For him, Troilus' folly consists not in his imperfect grasp of the relationship between God's prescience and individual free will, but in his totally inexplicable belief that his parting with Criseyde is foreknown and thus foreordained.[50] Pandarus' philosophy—his advice that Troilus cross that bridge when he comes to it— is hardly profound; but it is a definite improvement on Troilus' stated plan not to cross the bridge at all but to jump off it.

If we have learned anything about the nature of Chaucer's "classical allusions" in the *Troilus,* it is surely that they have a point. He invokes not the decorative bindings of books but specific textual moments. The reader of his poem may be expected to have somewhat higher standards than Pandarus, therefore, and to make a mental invocation of the Boethian context. If we do, we find in turn that Philosophy's resolution of Boethius' doubts begins with a unique textual moment, the sole point in the *Consolatio* in which a specific philosophical text is cited. As Chaucer's translation puts it, "Than seide sche, 'This is,' quod sche, 'the olde questioun of the purveaunce of God. And Marcus

---

50. At 4.1075 Troilus silently moves from an argument based on God's prescience to one based on his own. I hope that even romantic readers of the poem will allow that there is a difference between the two. Much of the rest of the fourth book is taken up with discussions of entirely possible courses of action alternative to acquiescence in the parliamentary plan to exchange Criseyde, possibilities that in effect prove the existence of free will and that underscore the practical rather than the theoretical shortcomings of Troilus' philosophical insufficiencies.

Tullius, whan he devyded the divynaciouns [that is to seyn, in his book that he wrot of dyvynaciouns], he moevede gretly this questioun" (*Boece* 5, prose 4).

This is a certain reference to the *De divinatione*, recognized as such in the bracketted gloss that Chaucer adds to the Latin text. Whether or not he is simply copying the gloss from another commentator, we have no reason to doubt that he knew Cicero's book and that he had consulted it, as did Augustine, Holcot, Trevet, Oresme, Pierre d'Ailly, Raoul de Presles, and others who, for one reason or another, conducted original researches into the question of ancient religious practice. The passage invoked, according to most of Boethius' commentators, is Cicero's discussion of prescience in *De divinatione* 2.8–9; but I suggest that the allusion is of a more general nature, to certain fundamental preoccupations of Cicero's book.[51]

In any event I presume that in constructing Troilus' foreshortened soliloquy Chaucer was entirely aware that the intellectual problems it raised were directly addressed by Lady Philosophy's citation of Cicero—that he knew not only what was in the *Consolation of Philosophy*, but also what was in the *De divinatione* as recalled in the *Consolation of Philosophy*. If so, two points are of special interest. The first is the nature of Cicero's own inquiry; the second is Boethius' implied criticism of Cicero.

When we turn to the *De divinatione*, we find that Cicero's quarry for his history of divination is *the Trojan myth*. The opening words of his book identify the belief in divination as an "ancient belief reaching back to the heroic times" (*vetus opinio . . . jam usque ab heroicis ducta temporibus*). Cicero here alludes to the various literary memorials to ancient divination, especially in the *Iliad* and the Trojan cycle of tragedies.[52] Already the ancient, pagan Cicero brings to the Trojan myth a historically distanced attitude scornful of the ancient religious superstition. Cicero's attitude, that is, is preemptively "Horatian" if not preemptively "Robertsonian." He translates, as a particularly fantastic example, the elaborate augury of Calchas at *Iliad* 2.299–330 in which the nine birds consumed by a serpent point to the certain and proximate destruction of

---

51. The phrase *cum divinationem distribuit* is problematical. Ernst Gegenschatz, "Die Gefährdung des Möglichen durch das Vorauswissen Gottes in der Sicht des Boethius," *Wiener Studien* 79 (1966): 521–22, takes it as a general reference to Cicero's attitude toward divination in several of his books, including *De fato* and *De natura deorum*.
52. Cicero, *De divinatione*, ed. Pease, 39.

Troy. The specific passage, probably the most famous treatment of divination in classical poetry, was widely imitated in Latin texts, including some certainly known and used by Chaucer.[53] The Ciceronian context shows us Cicero the "pagan historian" of ancient divination and Chaucer's narrator the "Christian historian" of ancient divination in essential unity of attitude toward the uses of the poetic past.

But the same text that unites Cicero and the Chaucerian narrator in a certain historical sympathy implicitly divides them in terms of a more subtle examination of their philosophical position. Boethius' phrase *vehementer agitata* used of Cicero's attack on the problem of prescience seems clearly positive: Chaucer translates it as "he moevede gretly this questioun." The compliment by implication extends to the character "Boethius" himself, who has likewise strenuously but inconclusively pursued the question. "But yit ne hath it nat ben determined ne y-sped fermely and diligently of any of yow." A further and somewhat startling implication is likewise clear: Philosophia expects "Boethius" to achieve a level of philosophical understanding not achieved by the great Cicero himself. If we move back to the text of the *Troilus*, in which the character Troilus is at this moment the proxy for the character "Boethius," the implication may seem more startling still.

Can Troilus possibly be as wise as Cicero? It may prove illuminating to pursue another path of Chaucerian "imitation." Troilus is, to be sure, another textual rendition of "Boethius"; but in the *erotic* context he is another textual rendition of Amant from the *Roman de la Rose*. In chapter 3 I argued at some length that Jean de Meun's most significant innovation, from the point of view of philosophical poetry, was to subject the eroticism of Ovidian tradition to a thoroughgoing Boethian critique, thus introducing among a large number of other dialectical themes a subliminal debate between ancient (which is to say pagan) and modern (which is to say Christian) concepts of love. And in one brilliant passage (*RR* 5375–88) Jean de Meun implicitly contrasts the wisdom of Cicero and that of Raison, the Philosophia of his poem. "Am I wiser than Tully?" asks Amant in consternation. The silent answer of the text is "No—but you should be."

So far as Troilus is concerned the question is not whether he is wiser than Tully but whether he is anything like so wise. The implicit criticism of Cicero

---

53. Ibid., 454. One of the most elaborate imitations is that of Statius in the *Thebaid* (discussed in chapter 2).

in *CP* 5.3 is not that Cicero, like Troilus, is a fatalist, but that in attacking the doctrine of fatalism he was unable fully to accommodate a conception of divine prescience.

It may well be, as Klingner thought, that Boethius' "Cicero" reflects not so much his own reading of the *De divinatione* as it does his acceptance of Augustine's blunt and possibly misleading criticism of Cicero in *De civitate Dei* 5.9.[54] As with many thinkers of many philosophical schools, Cicero's commitment to human ethical dignity founded in the freedom of the will led him in the direction of theological skepticism. If Troilus could not reconcile free will with divine foreknowledge, which he takes as a given, Cicero perhaps showed insufficient interest in reconciling divine foreknowledge with free will, which *he* takes as a given.

The third meter of the fifth book of the *Consolatio* laments the "gret batayle" between the two concepts; but the problem of their reconciliation is, in fact, one that only a religious disposition and a specifically Christian theological temperament would be likely to take up. Its treatment by Boethius is certainly *the* greatest philosophical originality of the *Consolatio*, but the manner of the treatment remains curious.[55] Boethius approaches his problem as a logician. As Courcelle has taught us, he found valuable resources in the *Organon* of Aristotle, in the categorical distinctions of the possible and the necessary; but his deployment of the argument is as surprisingly original from the point of view of Christian as of pagan antiquity.

What is perhaps most unexpected in the structure of Boethius' fifth book is the understatement of the "moral" argument that dominates earlier philosophical consideration of the question by pagan and Christian writers alike, the argument at the center of the third book of Augustine's *De libero arbitrio*, for example: if a man's actions are not freely willed, he clearly bears no moral responsibility for them and merits from them neither praise nor blame. We can see from the concluding lines of the *Consolatio* that this line of argument is at the heart of Boethius' agenda; and, for a brief moment in the fifth book, it becomes explicit. Yet the major force of Boethius' argument is directed at

54. See F. Klingner, "De Boetii 'Consolatione Philosophiae,'" *Philologische Untersuchungen* 27 (1921), 102ff., as discussed by Pierre Courcelle, *La Consolation de Philosophie dans la tradition littéraire* (Paris: Etudes Augustiniennes, 1967), 210–11.

55. See the discussion by Peter Huber, *Die Vereinbarkeit von göttlicher Vorsehung und menschlicher Freiheit in der Consolatio Philosophiae des Boethius* (Zurich: Juris Verlag, 1976).

demonstrating, on categorical logical grounds, the compatible independence of divine prescience and human volitional liberty.

The argument from ethical necessity was, of course, well known to Cicero. David Amand's extraordinary book devoted to its history demonstrates both its centrality to serious philosophical discussion of the problem from the time of the academic Carneades to that of the Cappadocian Fathers and its important testimony to the continuity of "pagan" and "Christian" thought on many major moral issues.[56] In stopping short his meditation on free will at the point he does, Troilus not merely fails to achieve the incrementally Christian wisdom of Philosophia: he ostentatiously falls short of achieving the wisdom possessed by Cicero and all reputable pagan philosophers since the time of Carneades. This, I think, is Chaucer's real point. Troilus' philosophical failure—a failure that must been seen in moral as well as purely intellectual terms—is to be judged not against the exalted canons of Christian enlightenment but against those of the pagan *moyen intellectuel.*[57]

I presume that the oldest joke in the Western philosophical repertory is Gorgias' vindication of Helen of Troy, absolved of all moral culpability, indeed praised in her every action, thanks to the constraints of necessity. The tone of the *Troilus,* to be sure, is far from the deadpan absurdity of the *Encomium of Helen.* Gorgias' foolishness is ironical; Troilus' is deadly earnest in the quite literal sense that it leads Troilus to seek death. He repeatedly flirts with the idea of suicide in the last two books, and, driven by the twin passions of rage and jealousy, he dies the death of a berserker. His is a memorable fortitude,

56. At the end of his lengthy and detailed study, Amand writes thus: "Dans les pages qui précèdent l'historien de la culture antique trouvera la confirmation par les faits d'une théorie qui lui est chère: à savoir l'homogénéité de la civilization intellectuelle gréco-romaine, homogénéité maintenue même après la diffusion du christianisme dans tout le monde meditérranéen. Il se persuadera que le temps est désormais passé ou l'on étudiait à part et comme en cloisons étanches littérature 'profane' et littérature chrétienne." *Fatalisme et liberté dans l'antiquité grecque* (Louvain: Université, 1945), 590–91.

57. Thus I cannot agree with the frequently repeated view that the reader, while invited to appreciate Troilus' philosophical failure, is nonetheless to persevere in undiminished admiration for the hero's morality. I find this most recently in Derek Brewer, *An Introduction to Chaucer* (London: Longmans, 1984), 148: "Troilus, though good, is not represented as learned. . . . His speech represents the nature of his feelings as the good rationalist pagan 'who found no end, in wandering mazes lost.'" As critical as I must be of Troilus, I myself would never equate him with Belial and Beelzebub.

but a fortitude exercised at the cost of rather than in harmony with wisdom. It will not do to call it "trouthe."

The conclusion of his "soliloquy" is a prayer to Jove to grant him death or Criseyde, one or the other. The options are, from a poetic point of view, "quits." It is of course philosophically absurd to believe at once in fatal necessity and in the possible power of prayers of petition or, for that matter, in the actuality of options at all. If we hold either Chaucer or Troilus accountable for this troubling text we can hardly escape the conclusion that one of its chief functions must be to underscore that coincidence of moral inadequacy and intellectual insufficiency that is so prominent a feature of ethical analysis in the Augustinian tradition.

Those critics who have tried to "save the appearances" speak of Chaucer's *sympathy* for Troilus, or, failing that, the narrator's for Criseyde. Neither the sympathy nor its implicit poetic complications I deny; what I deny is the priority (or the equality) of the pathetic to the ethical. For I find that this same correlation of moral and intellectual inadequacy is likewise the consistent strategy of the interpretive theme in the final act of the tragedy of Troilus, Prince of Troy, the fifth book, to which we must now direct our long deferred attention.

From the outset of the fifth book, Troilus' empty nights are haunted by his dreams:

And when he fille in any slomberynges,
Anon bygynne he sholde for to grone,
And dremen of the dredfulleste thynges
That myghte ben . . .(5.246–49)

Though characterized in the poem only in terms of their vague menace, Troilus' dreams convey to him a somber presentiment, indeed a sentence of death:

"For wel I fele, by my maladie,
And by my dremes now and yore ago,
Al certeynly that I mot nedes dye."
(5.316–18)

Pandarus, his consultant on this as on all aspects of the love malady, as usual offers a good deal of commonsense advice, founded now upon a firm confidence that Criseyde "nyl hire hestes breken for no wight" (5.355), thus introducing with a wonderfully ambiguous phrase the painful truth that the statement itself would deny. Concerning the possibility of interpreting dreams correctly, he is deeply skeptical. Root, who drew attention to the fact that Chaucer has given an increased narrative importance to the brief passage in the *Filostrato*, noted also that his "conviction that dreams are not worth a bean is based on the fact that so many different explanations have been given for the cause of dreams."[58] Pandarus is also concerned with the multiplicity of *interpretations* of individual dreams: "Who woot in soth thus what thei signifie?" (5.371).

I suggest that we here encounter an instance of dramatized "creative imitation," for this latter criticism—that the wide variety of intepetations posited argues against the credibility of any particular prognostication—is very ancient, and it forms the basis of Cicero's rejection of the possibility of dream augury in the *De divinatione*.[59] Cicero's specific example is not far distant from the text of the *Troilus*. He reports that an athlete dreamed that he was transformed into an eagle, and two different augurs gave him two absolutely different interpretations of the dream, one wholly encouraging, one wholly daunting. We may wish to recall presently that Criseyde, too, dreams of an eagle.

The prominence of dreams and dream imagery in the fifth book clearly suggests that Chaucer is toying with the interpretive theme, but there is more than one pot simmering on his stove. We may note in passing that the implicit "dream debate" in the early lines of the fifth book treats in a tragic context materials to be treated in a comic context in the *Canterbury Tales*. In the "Nun's Priest's Tale" (NPT) the debate becomes explicit, with the skeptical attitude of Pandarus/Pertelote countered with authoritative arguments by Chaunticleer. There are various significant relationships between the two texts, particularly in the prominence given in both to the importance of sound *interpretation*. There is often a close filiation in tone and language between the two passages—

A straw for alle swevenes signifiaunce. (5.362)

I sette nat a straw by thy dremynges. (NPT 3090)

Their congruences once again invite us to a fairly confident reconstruction of the itinerary of Chaucer's literary imagination. In both instances we find a

58. Root, in *Troilus and Criseyde*, ed. Root, 536–37.
59. Cicero, *De divinatione* 2.70.144, ed. Pease, 574–75; see Dario Del Corno, "Ricerche sull' onirocritica greca," *Rendiconti* [Istituto Lombardo] 96 (1962): 334–66.

definite relationship to the same anterior text, the somnology of the second book of the *Policraticus* in part given its vernacular mediation in the dream discussions of the *Roman de la Rose*. The invocation of that great work, in turn, easily the most famous poem in Chaucer's vernacular repertory, should remind us that its very *incipit* is a statement of the ambiguous poetic attitude toward dreams:

Many men say that in sweveninges
Ther nys but fables and lesinges,
But men may some swevenes sene
Which hardely that false ne bene
But afterward ben apparaunt. (1–5)

The essential distinction made in these lines between "true" and "false" dreams is an ancient one, as old at least as Homer; and it has been forever enshrined in a golden page of Virgil. In classical antiquity, indeed, there was an elaborate literature devoted to the theory and practice of dream interpretation. The only treatise to survive from Greek antiquity in its integrity, the *Dream Book* of Artemidorus, can suggest the considerable ambitions of oneirocriticism or dream augury.

There is a good deal yet to be learned about the connections between antique oneirocriticism and the medieval "dream vision." The authority that Guillaume de Lorris himself cited, of course, was the Latin writer Macrobius, whose commentary on Cicero's *Dream of Scipio* preserved for the Latin Middle Ages one major school of ancient dream theory.[60] Macrobius began with the major task of oneirocritical theory, which was to provide some means of distinguishing meaningful dreams from the meaningless, and, among the former, of distinguishing between those that were literally predictive ("theorematical") and those that required figurative interpretation ("allegorical").

What emerges in the textbooks of ancient somnology is an attitude toward dreams that strictly limits the usefulness of most modern approaches toward them.[61] Significant dreams have a concrete, nearly objective character; and they are independent of the unique claims of individual personality. The focus

60. See A. H. M. Kessels, "Ancient Systems of Dream Classification," *Mnemosyne* 22 (1969): 389–424.
61. On the "alterity" of antique dreams, see A. H. M. Kessels, *Studies on the Dream in Greek Literature* (Utrecht: Rijksuniversiteit, 1972), 7–11.

of interpretive interest is not on the dreamer except to the extent that he is the subject of a prediction. The *Dream Book* of Artemidorus is essentially an iconography of dreams that assigns definite meanings to specific dream situations. It does so, admittedly, in such interpretive plurality as to invite Cicero's charge of meaninglessness.

Just as Pandarus expresses the two voices of Boethius and the two voices of Ovid, he expresses the two sides of the dream debate. It is of some interest that in the skeptical mode Pandarus links the interpretation of dreams with those superstitious ceremonies that Chaucer certainly includes among the "payens corsed olde rites," avian augury and haruspication:

> "Wel worthe of dremes ay thise olde wives,
> And treweliche ek auguryc of thise fowles . . ."
>   (5.379–80)

But his attack on the superstition of somnology trails off, and he takes up another and more positive approach, ordering Troilus from his bed and suggesting manly diversions:

> "By god, my conseil is," quod Pandarus,
> "To ride and pleye us with kyng Sarpedoun."
>   (5.430–31)

Once again there is a narrative echo in the "Nun's Priest's Tale," when Chaunticleer abandons rationality in the face of erotic provocation: "Now let us speke of myrthe, and stynte all this" (3157). And though he would much leifer sport with Amaryllis in the shade, Troilus follows this counsel out of "fyn force," and the matter of dreams is for the moment dropped. Chaucer has, however, carefully prepared the ground, and when Troilus is again menanced by a dream—a dream at once vivid in its concrete detail and dubious of import—we know that we are presented with an ambage, and with a test of Troilus' ability to move from ambiguity to truth. We have also another fine example of a competitive "classical imitation," a passage in which Chaucer at once embraces and augments a specific literary topic.

Chaucer's response to the *Filostrato* in this passage was particularly delicate, but it raises a problem too often finessed in discussions of Chaucer's "treatment" of a "source," including many of my own in this book, of course. The *Filostrato* is a brilliant if seriously flawed poem, not a lumber yard, and when Chaucer rebuilds with its materials the beauty destroyed is often quite as remarkable as the beauty created. Before assessing what Chaucer certainly gained through his reworking of Troilus' dream, we should pause for a moment to see what he lost. Troilo's dream in the *Filostrato* has a savage power and an incapacity for benign interpretation that makes it the poem's principal revelation of the perfidy of Criseida. Much of its power lies in its liberation from ambiguity, and from the conviction of Troilo's response to its clear sexual suggestion.

Troilo himself immediately recognizes the emblematic association of the dream-beast with the Caledonian Boar and hence with Diomede—an association of which Chaucer's Troilus is ignorant until he learns it from the lips of Cassandra. Boccaccio structures the dream around the image of an assault on the heart, and prepares for the content of the dream in Troilo's dramatic but unrevealed malaise which precedes it, concerning which Troilo will say only that he suffers from heartache:

> Alli quai tuti diceva ch'al core
> si sentia noie, ma quai fosser quelle,
> niun poteva tanto addomandare,
> che da lui piu ne potesse apparare.
> (Fil. 7.22)

(To all of whom he would say that he felt pain in his heart, but what it might be, none could question him so far that he could learn more of it from him.)

The centrality of the heart to Troilo's dream not merely underscores the identity of the lovers' hearts but points up the sexual truth that Troilo's pain is Criseida's pleasure:

> col grifo il cor traeva, ed al parere
> di lui, Criseida di cosi gran male
> no si surava, ma quasi piacere
> prendea di cio che facea l'animale.
> (7.24)

(With its snout it tore forth the heart. And as it seemed, little cared Cressida for so great a hurt, but almost did she take pleasure in what the beast was doing.)

Boccaccio arranged all this very successfully, as Chaucer certainly recognized, for though he changed the essence of the dream to allow the fuller play of ambiguous possibility, he did his best to preserve as much of the Boccaccian edifice as possible. Though there is no longer a *heart* in Troilus' dream, Chaucer insists on his *heartache,* doubling, in successive stanzas, an idea that appeared but once in Boccaccio:

> But whoso axed hym wherof hym smerte,
> He seyde his harm was al aboute his herte . . .
>   (*TC* 5.1224–25)

>   he nolde his cause pleyne,
> But seyde he felte a grevous maladie
> Aboute his herte, and fayn he wolde dye.
>   (*TC* 5.1230–32)

Here is a fair field for the play of word and idea: "his harm was al aboute his herte." The English pun on *herte* (heart, hurt) gives Chaucer possibilities unavailable to Boccaccio, and he is quick to exploit them, but even so it would seem that he was unwilling to have the dream-heart present in his poem only by implication. Thus in the second book of the *Troilus* Criseyde has a dream, one for which there is no source in the *Filostrato.*

> And, as she slep, anon right tho hire mette,
> How that an egle, fethered whit as bon,
> Under hire brest his longe clawes sette,
> And out hire herte rente, and that anon,
> And dide his herte into hir brest to gon;
> Of which she nought agroos, ne no thyng smerte;
> And forth he fleigh, with herte left for herte.
>   (2.925–31)

There is of course an obvious relationship between Criseyde's dream and *Fil.* 7, and the more arresting sexual implications of the latter (the bestial invasion of the female body, and its strangely pleasurable nature) are here present, further complicated by scriptural innuendo (cf. Ezek. 36.26). Careful readers of the *Troilus* can thus know what Boccaccio signaled his Italian readers by other means: that the beast's assault on the woman's heart will hurt the hero's heart for the quite literal reason that her heart *is* his heart. The idea is likewise prepared for by the imagery of Antigone's song.

Criseyde's dream tells us something else about what Boccaccio was up to, and what Chaucer knew he was up to, in its haunting half-line on the *whiteness* of the eagle. Helen Storm Corsa has surely spoken for many readers in responding to a mysterious power in the description of the bird "fethered whit as bon." "This detail remains for me completely uninterpretable. Where did Chaucer get it? Out of what corner of his imagination? Out of what text? Out of what experience?"[62] The answer to one question—out of what text?—must surely be Ovid's *Amores* 3.5:

constitit ante oculos candida vacca meos,
candidior nivibus, tunc cum credidere recentes,
in liquidas nondum quas mor vertit aquas;
candidior, quod adhuc spumis stridentibus albet
et modo siccatam, lacte, reliqui ovem. (10–14)

(There stood before my eyes a shining white heifer, more shining white than snows just freshly fallen and not yet turned by time to flowing waters; more shining white than the milk that gleams with still hissing foam or has just left the sheep drained dry.)

Criseyde's dream of the white eagle is colored by "Ovid's" dream of the white heifer because Chaucer has, probably instinctively, recognized "Ovid's" dream as the model for Troilo's. "Ovid's" dream was this: he dreamed that a heifer of preternatural whiteness lay with her bull on the soft ground. The bull slept, and a crow flew down and pecked white tufts of hair from the heifer's breast, leaving there a livid bruise. After lingering long, the heifer hurried off to greener fields to sport with other bulls. "Ovid," the ironic narrator of the *Amores*, awakes in a sweat and seeks out the dream augur (*Nocturnae imaginis augur*) who thus "reads" the dream: "The heifer was your lover—that color matches your love. You, her beloved, were the bull with the heifer for mate. The pecking of her breast by the crow's sharp beak meant a pandering old dame was meddling with your mistress' heart. The lingering long ere the heifer left her full was sign that you will be left cold in a deserted bed. The dark color and the black spots on her breast in front were signs that her heart is not without stain of unfaithfulness."

62. Helen Storm Corsa, "Dreams in *Troilus and Criseyde*," *American Imago* 27 (1970), 56n.

I have put quotation marks around "Ovid" not merely to distinguish between poet and poetic persona, but because few classicists would any longer agree that Ovid wrote the poem. The "Somnium" appears to be an ancient and unusually successful Ovidian imitation, smuggled early into the canonical editions of the *Amores*, and sufficiently convincing to gain the approbation of even highly discriminating editors.[63] It is a poem that nicely demonstrates the fashion in which the work of the *interpres*—in this instance an elegant *imitatio* —can aspire beyond its station. Furthermore, as a literary dream accompanied by its internal gloss, it gave a fixed emblematic meaning to certain details, thus offering a kind of stability in the face of criticisms such as those raised by Cicero.

Boccaccio, who doubtless thought that he was imitating Ovid, was thus probably imitating another imitator.[64] Robert Hollander has taught us to appreciate the remarkable extent to which Boccaccio artfully confused his own fictive autobiography with Ovidian biography.[65] Thus for Boccaccio, no element of "erotic biography" could have been apter than the protagonist's troubling erotic dream. Chaucer could hardly have ignored the palpably Ovidian control of Troilo's dream, with its striking parallels of content and even more striking parallels of narrative situation. He may have known more as well. The "Nun's Priest's Tale" seems to have a lateral relationship with another version of the dream, that of Talano d'Imolese in *Decameron* 9.7, and the exchange of heart for heart is perhaps related to the eating of the heart in the symbolic dreams of the *Vita Nuova*. Troilo's dream in the *Filostrato* presented a moment complex with informing intertextuality, but not, perhaps, with the associations in which Chaucer himself was at this point in his poem most interested.

The literary operation that he performed involved, in part, an exchange of text for text, Jean de Meun for pseudo-Ovid. Incidental phrases in the poetry suggest Chaucer's awareness of the rich Ovidian coherence he was losing through "interpretation." What did he gain?

He mette he say a boor with tuskes grete,
That slep ayein the bryghte sonnes heete;

63. See Franco Munari, "Sugli 'Amores' di Ovidio," *SIFC* 23 (1948), 143ff.; and E. J. Kenney, "On the Somnium Attributed to Ovid," *Agon* 3 (1969): 1–14.
64. We possess Boccaccio's autograph of the *Amores*: Florence, Laurentiana 33.3.
65. Hollander, *Boccaccio's Two Venuses*, esp. 112–16.

And by this boor, faste in hire armes folde,
Lay, kissynge ay, his lady bright, Criseyde.
(5.1238–41)

The special quality of Chaucer's dream, as opposed to Boccaccio's, is its increased ambiguity. In particular, the sexual implications of the dream have at once been made more explicit and less revealing. Boccaccio's *cinghiar* is aggressive, menacing, domineering; Chaucer's *boor* sleeps in the sun. The locus of sexual energy and initiative is ambiguous. Though the syntax seems to invite a masculine pronoun in 1240 (*his,* as printed by Skeat, Robinson, and Windeatt), Root unflinchingly followed his most trusted manuscripts with *hire.*[66] Who is the embracer and who the embraced? Several manuscripts finesse the problem by dropping the pronoun altogether—"And by this boor faste in armes folde" —but even this solution does not resolve whethter *faste* is part of the involuted phrase *fast-by* or whether it speaks of the intimacy of the recumbent embrace.

I tentatively conclude that the interpretive difficulties are intentional. Troilus' bad dream makes also a bad poem from a Horatian perspective, one in which the ambiguities have been left unresolved. It thus provides, as the dream in Boccaccio did not, genuine interpretive alternatives. One might say that like the dream of "Ovid" from which it ultimately derives it is a dream especially designed to require a dream augur, an *interpres.*

That Chaucer's intentional strategy is to make this episode serve his principal theme, the theme of *interpretation,* is here evident. The materials for Troilus' dream and its general significance in advancing the poem's tragedy Chaucer found in Boccaccio. His alteration of those materials, as we have seen, meant foreclosing certain artistic possibilities and discovering certain others. In the exploration of poetic possibilities he was guided by a text quite as important to this moment in his own poem as was the *Filostrato* itself—once again, the *Roman de la Rose* of Jean de Meun. Chaucer's revision of Boccaccio enriches the hermeneutical problem in Troilus' dream by suggesting for it alternative interpretations which become the tests not merely of interpretive skill but of moral vision. In this he certainly follows Jean's account of the ambiguous dream of King Croesus (*RR* 6459–6600).

Croesus dreamed that two gods served him at the top of a tree: Jupiter

---

66. Thus Windeatt: "his: preferred to hire, which makes awkward sense." Awkward indeed, but possibly less so than a boar with arms.

washed him, and Phoebus dried him. His daughter Phania interpreted the dream for him as follows: it meant that Croesus would be hanged from a gibbet (the tree), that the rain would fall on his dangling corpse, and that the sun would dry it. He rejected this interpretation in favor of his own literal understanding: Jupiter and Phoebus would indeed attend to his needs in a kind of divine massage parlor. But history knows he was in fact hanged. Chaucer treats this story or alludes to it several times in his poetry, most conspicuously in the "Monk's Tale," where the "tragedy" of Croesus is the last of the sad tales of the deaths of kings before the Knight's interruption.

It is instructive to observe that in terms of the ancient vocabulary of dream classification both father and daughter agree that the dream is an *oneiros,* that is, a significant dream. But whereas Phania recognizes and correctly interprets its allegorical character, Croesus takes a fallacious comfort from the mistaken belief that it is theorematical. Within Jean de Meun's scheme the dream debate is thus implicated in his discussion of literalism viewed both as an intellectual impediment and as a deficient moral state.

It seems to me not unlikely that the story as it appears in medieval moral literature still retains a certain Greek disquiet at the skeptical behavior of the historical King Croesus.[67] Chaucer's aims were somewhat different from Jean's. He probably sought out Jean de Meun's account of the dream of Croesus because it ministered to his overarching Boethian theme in the *Troilus,* the theme that examines pagan love as a species of subjection to Fortune. And at the same time it pointedly raised the necessity, as well as the hazards, of the interpretive act. Within the thematic structure of the *Roman* both Croesus' subjection to Fortune and his interpretive blunder find their moral resonances in Amant himself, a "reader" proudly ignorant of the metaphors of poets.

In the *Consolation of Philosophy,* the most important literary resource shared by Chaucer and Jean, there was already half of Croesus' story, the account of his captivity by Cyrus, his condemnation to the pyre, and his surprising escape; and it there introduces the popular medieval emblem of Fortune, the two tuns of Jupiter. Jean's proximate source for the misinterpreted dream was probably the *Speculum* of Vincent of Beauvais, where it was already a heavily

---

67. Croesus was a Lydian. He was famous for having tested, in a spirit of empirical investigation, the most renowned oracles of his day—an act that will have seemed blasphemous to many. See E. R. Dodds, "Supernormal Phenomena in Classical Antiquity," in *The Ancient Concept of Progress and Other Essays on Greek Literature and Belief* (Oxford: Oxford University Press, 1973), 166.

laden moral exemplum. It is Jean's edition of the story that Chaucer seems to depend on in the "Monk's Tale," where the story of Croesus is the last of the tragedies *de casibus*; and Jean's French text is subtly but identifiably present in Cassandra's gloss to Troilus' dream of the boar. Such is the significant context of Chaucer's "borrowing," or to put the matter more accurately, the textual arena of his classical imitation. The catalytic "subtext," here and in many other parts of the *Troilus*, is the *Roman de la Rose*.

The *Filostrato* makes no specific connection between Troilo's dream and the operation of Fortune, and in identifying the source of Troilo's knowledge of the history of the Caledonian Boar Boccaccio makes only a vague appeal to "the ancients." Cassandra connects the interpretation of the dream with Fortune's overthrow of "lordes olde" (5.1460–61), following the lead of Jean de Meun's Phania (*RR* 6490). The explicit appeal to ancient texts, repeatedly made by Cassandra, also betrays its paternity in Jean's *Roman*. The phrase "a fewe of olde stories" (5.1459) translates "d'ancienes estoires" (*RR* 6602), and his "olde bokes" (1478, 1481), Jean's "livres anciens" (6425). Thus the two royal daughters, Phania and Cassandra, truthfully interpret ambiguous dreams only to be called liars by the deluded dreamers. "'Thow seyst nat soth,' quod he, 'thow sorceresse!'" (5.1520). Croesus berates his daughter: "Servi m'avez de granz mençonges" (*RR* 6577).

Under the duress of Troilus' anxious vision, Pandarus, who has earlier expressed a Ciceronian contempt for the "science" of oneirocriticism, now becomes an *interpres* himself. His inconsistency is wholly consistent with his generally pragmatic and opportunistic behavior in the poem. His aim is to keep Troilus functional and, if possible, happy. His unscrupulous means—lies, misrepresentations, and the disingenuous manipulation of people and events—can be used against Troilus as well as against anyone else, so long as they are used to promote Pandarus' cause. Hence we do not need to ask whether he *believes* his own optimistic interpretation of Troilus' dream. That interpretation is based not on a reading of the dream but upon a reading of Troilus.

Pandarus at this point becomes a *scurra*, telling his patron what he knows his patron wants to hear, a false friend and a false critic. Troilus himself has for a moment grasped, even as Troilo had before him, the dream's quite simple truth: "O Pandarus . . . My lady bright, Criseyde, hath me bytrayed" (5.1245–47). Pandarus' interpretation *in bono* by no means resolves Troilus' doubts. It is more accurate to say that it introduces doubt, cooperating with Troilus' deep desire to avoid the truth, a desire that the narrator later describes in a

philosophical aside (5.1632–38) as a characteristic of deluded lovers, or, as he
puts it, of the man "that loveth wel."

Doubt once again alive must once again be resolved. Pandarus contrives
a safer plan to adjudicate the ambage of the dream in his favor. He can be
confident of its success because, perhaps, he intuits so clearly Criseyde's own
deep capacity for self-deception and her fully documentable craving for self-
exculpation. The test of her truth will be an invitation to her sympathetic
feelings for Troilus and her even more sympathetic feelings for herself. There
is little risk that she will decline it:

> "My red is this: syn thow kanst wel endite,
> That hastily a lettre thow hire write,
> Thorugh which thow shalt wel bryngen it aboute
> To knowe a soth, ther thow are now in doute.
> And se now whi: for this, I dar wel seyn,
> That if so is that she untrewe be,
> I kan not trowen that she wol write ayeyn."
>   (5.1292–98)

His plan is, of course, to transfer the burden of interpretation from the
dream to a text, the as yet unwritten text of Criseyde's letter. Thus Pandarus
the manipulator of texts and people alike proposes that the test of Criseyde's
truth will not be *what* she writes but *that* she writes. For she cannot be untrue,
he says, if she will so much as answer Troilus' letter.

There is a skillful poetic control in all this. In ancient literature the dream
is among the most powerful and authoritative of oracles, often involving the
direct speaking of the god. Mediated oracles are, by their very nature, more obscure and uncertain. The Virgilian ancestry of Chaucer's ambages can help us
appreciate the delicious irony of the appeal to a *written text* to resolve the uncertain interpretation of Troilus' dream. The utterances of the Cumaean Sibyl
are at best cryptic and uncertain, requiring close attention and quick wit to
interpret; but they are far less accessible in their written form when, entrusted
to leaves, they can be lost, broken, or scattered by the capricious wind. Hele-
nus has forewarned Aeneas of the danger, and for that reason Aeneas pleads
with the Sibyl that she speak rather than write her prophecy:

> Foliis tantum ne carmina manda,
> Ne turbat volent rapidis ludibria ventis;
> Ipsa canas oro. (*Aeneid* 6.74–76)

(Only trust not thy verses to leaves, lest they fly in disorder, the sport of rushing winds; chant them thyself, I pray.)

Troilus' own letter, which reveals certain similarities of vocabulary and dramatic posture with the tragic proemium to the first book, has as its theme change, mutability: *versa in luctum cithara*. The voice is that of the "Boethius" at the *beginning* of the *Consolatio*, before his philosophical curriculum has begun. Criseyde's answer—ambiguously described in terms that make it impossible for us to know whether what is being described is a single and somewhat inconsistent letter or a plurality of separate letters (5.1423–27)—is in part evasive, in part mendacious. Troilus' interpretive act is not described in detail: but he did find in her protestations of abiding love nothing but "botmeles bihestes" (5.1431).

At this point in the poem Chaucer's focus is on active rather than passive deception, on the written text designed to mislead rather than on the psychological mechanism of being misled. Chaucer, like his audience, probably would have had a sharper appreciation of the relationship between an arboreal and a bibliographical *folium* than do we, for whom the "leaf" of a book is as dead a metaphor as the "leg" of a table. It is at least conceivable that Chaucer is actually thinking of the wind-blown leaves of the Sibyl when he frames the metaphoric terms of Troilus' impasse:

But, Troilus, thow maist now, est or west,
Pipe in an ivy lef, if that the lest.
Thus goth the world; god shilde us fro meschaunce,
And every wight that meneth trouthe avaunce!
(5.1432–35)

The category of "every wight that meneth trouthe avaunce" seems to shrink with each turning leaf of Chaucer's poem. It has long since been unable to define Pandarus, who misinterprets dreams to hide the truth, nor can it now embrace Criseyde, who writes lies to prove her own truth; nor, in my opinion, can it include Troilus himself, who denies the truth that stares him in the face.

I am not unaware, of course, of the critical consensus that has identified Troilus' erotic obsession, his inability to unlove Criseyde for a quarter of a day, with his "trouthe." That is certainly how he himself would view matters. Yet though the tone of the poem invites us to respond generously and with a genuinely tragic perception alert to the tropological implications of the moment, it does so in a fashion that demands rather than obviates the reader's interpretive commitment and *moral* judgment. Troilus wants to call *lenocinium* gentility; our pimping text wants us to call irrational obsession truth. I do not deny to this textual importunity a genuinely revolutionary ambition, but I find the ambition directed in the first instance toward the appropriation of language rather than to the subversion of a moral tradition remarkably constant from Socrates to Cicero to Seneca to Augustine to Geoffrey Chaucer's moral ballad called "Truth."

We might be able, like Troilus himself, to "call it truth" were there no cultural alternative to "it" or to "truth" available; but a chief purpose of Chaucer's intertextual strategies, strategies nearly breathtaking in their comprehensiveness and complexity, is to provide definite and authoritative options from the literature of Christian humanism. Unswerving commitment to the inadequate would not be tragic in a world in which the adequate did not exist or in which its pursuit were impossible. Troilus *interpres* would construct such a world, but Chaucer *interpres* forbids it, insisting that the hero is a *tragic* hero and not a mechanically manipulated lump of soulless matter.

There is one place—the prologue to the *Legend of Good Women*—in which Geoffrey Chaucer actually talked about his motives in undertaking the task of interpreting the *Roman de la Rose* and the *Troilus*. He does so, admittedly, through the mouth of an Ovidian persona and in a highly playful context that forbids the induction of positivist conclusions. But he says there that his motive was "to forthren trouthe in love and yt cheryce." One meaning of this curiously phrased idea, certainly, is that the poet's intention is to foster amatory loyalty of the sort presumably exemplified by Troilus and violated by Criseyde. But there are ambiguities. The phrase "*in* love" may also mean "*about* love," and the poet's truth about love may not be the same thing as Cupid's truth about love.

But I suspect the more elegant ambiguity of textual allusion, to the fourth chapter of Paul's epistle to the Ephesians. Writing to antique Greeks in the context of a plea that they "no longer walk as the Gentiles also walk," Paul contrasts the oldness of the life of the flesh with the newness of the life in Christ with a possibly paradoxical analogy of infancy and maturity. The child is "tossed to and fro and carried about with every wind of doctrine, by the sleight of men, in craftiness after the wiles of error." What characterizes the mature adult is "speaking the truth in love," an untranslatable Greek phrase that the Vulgate interpreted faithfully rather than idiomatically as *veritatem facientes in charitate*. Since this is precisely what the Chaucerian voice of the prologue to the *Legend of Good Women* said he was doing, and precisely what his poem in fact does, I find no grounds to deny the textual enrichment.

Whether or not the blown leaves of Troilus and the Cumaean Sibyl have even the breeziest connection, the decisive intervention of Cassandra makes it clear that the sibylline theme was prominent in Chaucer's mind as he radically revised Boccaccio's plotting of Troilo's response to his disturbing dream. His most dramatic innovation, indeed, is to reinvest in Troilus' sister Cassandra her classical role as the unheeded prophetess of doom, a role not present in the *Filostrato*.[68] Troilus cannot drive the dream from his memory, for he fears that Jove may have shown him "the signifiaunce of [Criseyde's] untrouthe and his disaventure," and that the boar was shown him "in figure" (5.1447–49), that is, as an allegorical *sign*.

> For which he for Sibille his suster sente,
> That called was Cassandre ek al aboute . . .
>   (5.1450–51)

Still another *interpres* claims center stage. Chaucer's editors have suggested that the poet's implication that "Cassandra" and "Sibyl" are alternative personal names for the same woman is simply a medieval naïveté; once again Chaucer's classicism is rather better than that of some of his interpreters.[69] Sibyl-Cassandra has a precisely just role in the *Troilus*, but before examining it, we may observe that *all* of the women in the *Troilus* with speaking parts —all few of them—have certain definite sibylline characteristics. The distinctive difference between the Pythia and the Sibyl was this: the function of the former was the explication of vatic utterance, that of the latter the mediation of written *texts*.[70] Criseyde herself, the daughter of an augur, dresses in widow's weeds; and her fanciful self-image—a solitary ascetic, reading in her cave—is a splendid syncretism of Christian anchoritism and Apollonian manticism.[71]

Antigone, Criseyde's neice, sings a song explicitly attributed to a female author, "the goodlieste mayde of gret estat in al the town of Troye," a song in

68. See David Anderson, "Cassandra's Analogy: *Troilus* v. 1450–1521," *Hebrew University Studies in Literature and the Arts* 13 (1985): 1–17.
69. See. A. Bouché-Leclercq, *Histoire de la divination dans l'antiquité*, 4 vols. (Paris: E. Leroux, 1880), 2:148–52.
70. See R. Schottländer, "Das Sibyllenbild der Philosophen," *Acta Antiqua Academicae Scientiarum Hungaricae* 11 (1963): 43.
71. See Kambylis, *Die Dichterweihe*, 164.

praise of love in the tradition of the women lyricists in Machaut's love allegories.[72] The text is, to put it mildly, deeply ambiguous since the "love" invoked
may be as easily spiritual as romantic. Criseyde, interrupted in her audience of
the poetic history of Thebes, likewise read by a maiden, instinctively located
her options in terms of two contrasting images: young women dancing, and
the ascetic in her cave. One image suggests erotic possibility, the other erotic
denial; both suggest love. Earlier, Pandarus grounded his initial optimism in
the following anonymous wisdom:

> "Was nevere man nor womman yit bigete
> That was unapt to suffren loves hete,
> Celestial, or elles love of kynde."
>   (1.977–79)[73]

Considering her sexual resources—beauty and youth—Pandarus is confident in predicting her proclivity: "It sit hir naught to ben celestial as yit"
(1.983–84). This is a splendidly Augustinian gloss to a splendidly Augustinian
sententia. Make her chaste, o Lord, but not as yit. Criseyde's response to the
song sung by Antigone is to ask whether it is the joy of love that empowers
such fine writing. Antigone's reply is unequivocally affirmative concerning the
joy of love. Concerning love's definition, she is deeply ambiguous. She returns
to Pandarus' metaphor of the "heat of love":

> "But wene ye that every wrecche woot
> The parfit blisse of love? why nay, iwys:

72. J. I. Wimsatt, "Guillaume de Machaut and Chaucer's *Troilus and Criseyde*," *Medium
Aevum* 45 (1976): 277–93.

73. Pandarus' phrase "loves hete" (1.978) corresponds to the Latin *aestus amoris* as we
find it, for example, in the Ovidian "Somnium" (*Amores* 3.5., 36). The exegesis provided
by the *interpres* in that poem affords a stable allegorical connection between the idea
of the "heat of the day" and the metaphorical "heat" of sexual passion, as in Horace's
memorable summary of the *Iliad*: "stultorum regum et populorum aestus." There is
frequent play on the two ideas, as in Ovid's poem "Aestus erat" (*Amores* 1.5), a poem
about making love on a hot afternoon. The "heat" is literally present in Troilus' dream
(5.1239), and Pandarus tries to give it a naturalistic interpretation (5.1285). The word
aestus suggests both the heat and the turbulence of boiling water. See René Pichon, *De
sermone amatorio* (Paris: Hachette, 1902), 81–82. Cf. J. Ferguson, "Notes on Some Uses
of Ambiguity and Similar Effects in Ovid's Amores, book 1," *Liverpool Classical Monthly*
3 (1978): 124.

They wenen al be love, if oon be hoot;
Do wey, do wey, they woot no thyng of this!
Men mosten axe at seyntes if it is
Aught faire in hevene; why? for they kan telle;
And axen fendes is it foul in helle."
(2.890–96)

This is an invitation to probe ambiguity and to discriminate between things superficially, nominally alike. Criseyde changes the subject; but, like Mary, she pondered the song in her heart.

Chaucer's reinvention of Cassandra's traditional role is purposeful and enriching. It in the first place serves the design of his determined classicism. Chaucer's Cassandra, while very much his own, is Homeric, not Boccaccian. Hence the analogy to which David Anderson has recently drawn our attention —an analogy between the folly of the unheeding Troilus and the proleptic folly of unheeding Troy—dominates the poem's final movement. Cassandra reclaims our attention from the morally shallow and self-centered privatism of the lovers.

When our view moves from the periphery to the center, we see not private but public tragedy: a great city in flames, its king murdered in his household chapel, its children butchered by savage avengers. This is the vision not of Boccaccio but of Lollius. For through Cassandra Lollius reminds us of that truth he learned from Horace *interpres*: "For each folly of their princes, the Trojans feel the lash." Cassandra's interpretation of the dream is specific, coherent, historically informed, and devastating. She traces the entire mythic history of ancient wrong and bloodshed against which the immediate tragic moment of Troilus loses any claim to unique signficance beyond a ribald statement of his sexual usurpation by Diomede.

Wepe if thow wolt, or lef; for, out of doute,
This Diomede is inne, and thow are oute.
(5.1518–19)

That is one kind of surprise. There is another. I have already mentioned the fact that in the *Filostrato* Troilo himself immediately interprets his own dream correctly, basing his understanding of it on the poetic associations of Diomede with the history of the Caledonian Boar which in the *Troilus* are supplied only by Cassandra. Boccaccio, though clearly enough interested in an implied contrast of Christian truth and pagan untruth, was not in the *Filostrato* deeply engaged with the theme of ambiguity; and unlike Chaucer, he did not learn from Jean de Meun the powerful thematic association of moral failure and textual incapacity.

We have already seen that Cassandra's interpretive use of "old books" and "old stories" reflects in a specific fashion the oneirocriticism of Croesus' daughter Phania in the *Roman de la Rose*, and in a general fashion the stance of Lady Reason faced with the textually obtuse Lover. It is crucial to Chaucer's design that Troilus be a literary ignoramus. Yet what most surprises is that Cassandra's voice—a voice intimately connected with "payens corsed olde rites" —is the solitary medium of unvarnished truth in a babble of courtly cant and obfuscation.

The characteristic obscurity and deceptiveness of the pagan oracles direct the articulations of Pandarus, Troilus, and Criseyde; but the oracular "sorceresse" herself is free of it. Cassandra is of course Troilus' sister. She can therefore respond, as Cacciaguida could respond to Dante, with the "clear words and precise language" of familial love. There is in my mind a conscious connection between the two passages, but Chaucer's rehabilitation of the pagan oracle differs decisively from Dante's christianization of it. Cassandra's clear speaking shows us a pagan capable of truth—the pagan virtue almost always on the lips of the major characters of this poem, and almost always absent from their conscious intentions.

Troilus' failure to make a correct, complete, or timely interpretation of the signs placed in his path is tragic failure, the failure of his ancient analogue, Oedipus. In this instance, moreover, the failure of the protagonist may not have been irrelevant to the artistic anxieties of the poet. Chaucer's profound interest in the relationship between truth and language has many sources; but one of them surely is his perception that the art of lying and the lying of art are the double visages of a single possibility.

That is probably also what Dante Alighieri thought, and probably also feared. Without being exactly central to the enterprise of the *Troilus* Dante was nonetheless crucial for it so far as Chaucer's theme of interpretation was concerned. It was Dante who most clearly exemplified the complex attitude of the Christian poet to the ancient poetic past, an attitude at once submissive and censorious. It was Dante who had most memorably dramatized tropological moments of interpretive crisis. And it was Dante who, in the complexity of his own procedures of "creative imitation," seems to have inspired a number of Chaucer's own most subtle imitations. It is to Dante, the Christian mediator of the poetic concept of *ambages*, to whom we must finally turn for insight into Chaucer's conception of the *interpres*.

DANTE INTERPRETED, DANTE *INTERPRES*

The truth of the soothsaying Cassandra comes largely in the form of a plot summary of the *Thebaid*; but what Criseyde was not allowed to hear, Troilus is incapable of understanding. "'Thow seyst nat sooth,' quod he, 'thou sorceresse!'" As in so many passages of the Troilus, the vocabulary of truth and falsehood is oppressively ironic:

> As wel thow myghtest lyen on Alceste,
> That was of creatures, but men lye,
> That evere weren, kyndest and the beste.
> (5.1527–29)

What is referred to here is the *legend* of Alceste, that is, *written* tradition; and the suggestion of an untrue text is one that Troilus might well keep in mind when, enraged by what he takes to be Cassandra's slander, he sets off to "enquere and seche / a sooth of this with al his fulle cure" (5.1537–38).

At this point, quite abruptly, Chaucer brings into his poem the death of Hector. Hector's death is probably the most pathetic moment in the classical tragic repertory, as Chaucer twice recognizes in the *Canterbury Tales*. Here it would appear to have the understatement of a casual afterthought. Troilus' grief is said to be extreme, but it is swallowed up in Chaucer's text—and by suggestion in Troilus' mind—by the hero's erotic obsession.

The poem briefly mentions two specific initiatives taken by Troilus in his vigorous search for truth. He hopes against hope, not to mention his inner fears, that Criseyde is true (5.1569–74); and he ineffectually spins the plan of falsely passing himself off as a pilgrim and visiting Criseyde in the Greek camp—a romantic plan somewhat unromantically abandoned out of fear that he might not have a good enough excuse if the Greek police asked awkward questions (5.1576–82).[74] Truth and falsity are of course much on his mind as he writes repeatedly to Criseyde, begging

---

74. The topos of the phony "passionate pilgrim" is best known from the Tristram legend; but there is an elaborately paganized version of it in Chaucer's "Knight's Tale," 1380–1425.

syn that he was trewe,
That she wol come ayeyn and holde hire trouthe.
                    (5.1585–86)

Criseyde's response is a masterpiece of its genre—that of the Dear John letter—interlaced with savage lexical and thematic ironies. We may pause for a moment to examine two or three of them. In the first place, we here find Criseyde in an unusual role, that of Lady Philosophy reproving Troilus for his monumental impatience, his "unreste" and "haste."

"No other thyng nys in youre remembraunce,
As thynketh me, but only youre plesaunce."
                    (5.1607–8)[75]

The word *plesaunce* echoes Jean de Meun's *charnex delit* from a similar context. This statement, incidentally, comes from the same woman who recently told him that she loved him because he always subjected his desire to reason. Next, we learn that she is constrained in expressing truth in word (5.1603–4) no less than in deed (5.1610) for simple fear that the truth might be known. The invocation of the bogey man "wikked speche"—surely the Malebouche of the *Roman de la Rose*—is particularly audacious. The implication is that the hot gossip of the Greeks, whom we might presume to have other things on their minds, is all about Troilus and Criseyde; but the suspicion can be quelled by "dissimulynge"—an art at which, as she proves even as she writes, she is expert. Finally, Criseyde assures Troilus of her undying friendship:

For trewely, whil that my lif may dure,
As for a frend ye may in me assure.
                    (5.1623–24)

The lovers' language again collapses into cliché. This passage echoes the earlier interior monologue in which Criseyde, while explicitly transferring her "truth" and sexual favors from Troilus to Diomede nonetheless reserved for the former her "frendes love" (5.1080); but the idea of "frendes love" itself has by now taken on a powerfully ironic potential, since it was the deceitful pretext

75. The immediate derivation of the lines is from a speech of Jean de Meun's Reason, the Philosophia of the *Roman de la Rose:* "Mes l'amor qui te tient ou laz / charnex deliz te represente, / si que tu n'as ailleurs entente" (4570–72). We have already seen how Chaucerian *plesaunce* echoes Ovidian *concubitus*.

taken up by Pandarus in the earliest stage of his suborning of Criseyde. As so often, it is the seemingly bland, conventional phrase that jumps off the page: "trewely, whil that my lif may dure," an assurance that is by now among the most linguistically debased expressions in the poem.[76]

The Boethian concept of tragedy, an immoderate commitment to the mutable, is the tragic concept that animates the poem. Mutability is the theme of the proemium to the poem's tragic movement (4.1–28); and mutability is the de facto demonstration of Criseyde's letter. Troilus grasps this after a fashion: "Hym thoughte it lik a kalendes of chaunge" (5.1634)—another turned leaf. At the same time, Troilus' hermeneutical failure is nonetheless complete. It is not simply that desire finally blinds him to the textual truth of the letter. "Thentente is al," as Criseyde herself concludes (5.1630); and her text is by intention ambiguous and deceptive. Though his inability to resolve its ambiguities may strain the reader's credulity, it does not boggle the mind. His real failure of understanding is his failure to respond to the Delphic imperative: "Know thyself." Neither now nor at any other moment in the brief remainder of his mortal life does Troilus subject his obsessive passion to an ethical examination. Herein resides the truly tragic dimension of interpretive incapacity.

In marked contrast to his tragic hero, the poet himself demonstrates *his* interpretive capacities with flair, in the remaking of delicate textual details and in the translation of large poetic themes alike. More often than not in the final two books of his poem, it is Dante *interpres* who fires the poet's imagination. Consider, for example, Chaucer's commerce with a single ornament of traditional poetic imagery—the bestial rage of the maddened lover.

When he came to write about Troilo's fury at the caprice of Fortune that will take Criseida from him, Boccaccio had indulged himself in a bit of his habitual Dantism. Troilo thrashes about his bedroom like a bull butchered at the altar or in the abattoir:

Né altrimenti il toro va saltando
or qua or lá, da poi c'ha ricevuto
il mortal colpo, e misero mugghiando
conoscer fa qual duolo ha conceputo,
che Troilo facesse, nabissando

76. At 4.1680, Criseyde promises to belong to Troilus forever—"whil I may dure." Hardly two hundred lines later (5.153) we hear Diomede expressing the same thought with the same rhymes: undying loyalty to Criseyde, "whil that my lyf may dure."

se stesso, e percotendo dissoluto
il capo al muro, e con la man la faccia,
con pugni il petto e le dolenti braccia.
                    (*Fil.* 4.27)

(Not otherwise does the bull go leaping now here, now there, after it has
received the mortal stroke, and roaring in misery shows what pain has
come upon it, than did Troilus, flinging himself down and wildly striking
his head against the wall, and his face with his hands, his breast and
aching arms with his fists.)

Chaucer translated this stanza as follows:

Right as the wylde bole bygynneth sprynge
Now her, now ther, idarted to the herte,
And of his deth roreth in compleynynge,
Right so gan he aboute the chaumbre sterte,
Smytyng his brest ay with his fistes smerte;
His hed to the wal, his body to the grounde,
Ful ofte he swapte, hym selven to confounde.
                    (*TC* 4.239–45)

Summarizing what has been suggested about the textual relationships involved,
Windeatt writes, with full justice, "Chaucer follows Boccaccio, who is borrowing from Dante's description of the Minotaur (itself deriving from *Aeneid*,
2.222ff.) in *Inferno* 12.22–4 ('Qual è quel toro che si slaccia in quella / c'ha
ricevuto già'l colpo mortale, / che gir non sa, ma qua e là saltella')." The relevant lines in Virgil are "qualis mugitus, fugit cum saucius aram / taurus et
incertam escussit cervice securim" (His shrieks were . . . like a bull's bellow
when an ax has struck awry, and he flings it off his neck and gallops wounded
from the altar; *Aeneid* 2.222–23). Such are the textual data, and from them
I draw the premise on which the following argument depends: that we have
here a series of fully conscious literary "imitations." Dante was imitating Virgil
consciously, and Boccaccio was imitating Dante consciously. Both writers, that
is, subscribe to Russell's third law of classical literary imitation.

Virgil's image, which is an oblique way of indicating the actual moment
of the death of Laocoon, focuses upon the hideous bellowing of the dying
man. The noise is compared with that made by a bull frenzied by the terror
and pain of an atrocious blow by the sacrificer's ax. The force of the image

derives from the associations of the religious rite. The victim, though grievously stricken, escapes the altar; it is the priest, the sacrificer, who becomes the victim himself.[77]

These religious associations have no particular relevance for Dante, and he abandons them entirely. His imagination is drawn to the idea of a creature half bull, half man, a grotesque conceived, as always in Dante, in its full physical and psychological verisimiltude. The Minotaur now guards the infernal ruins as he once guarded the Labyrinth; and Dante's poetry focuses upon two suggestions—the animal's bestial wrath, and its frantic, sudden lunging movements without particular direction, the movement of one caged, trapped, or befuddled. Dante's phrase "che gir non sa, ma qua e là saltella" has no basis in Virgil. In fact, it comes from Seneca imitating Virgil.[78] Thus Dante joins Seneca in *translating* the Virgilian image precisely in the sense of moving it, physically and intellectually, from one context to another.

Dante's focus is on the Minotaur's raging brutishness. To move beyond a simple reading of texts to the imputation of attitude and motive is of course to move into a realm of speculation, but I judge Dante's relationship to Virgil here as one of respectful competitiveness. Dante's lines are an *aemulatio*. We recall that Virgil is literally at Dante's side as guide and teacher as he encounters the Minotaur; and even as Virgil instructs him, the verse shows how much he has already learned. "*You* did it that way; *I* do it this way." The process would better be described as historical evolution than poetic subversion or the "anxiety of influence." As Virgil almost casually remarks upon noting a rock newly fallen from the cliffside, the landscape of this part of hell has changed since his last visit (*Inferno* 12.33–36). Changed, too, is the spiritual landscape of the poetic universe. The agent of its change is Jesus Christ, known to Virgil only vaguely, indistinctly, imprecisely, but known to Dante through the faith of Christians. Dante's unstated assertion is that the Christ who has changed history has inevitably changed poetry and with it the function of the poet.

Before we can so much as ask the question of what if any of this is relevant to Chaucer, we must of course first consider Boccaccio. To limit myself to the immediate passage in the *Filostrato*, it does seem sufficiently plain that a moral

77. See R. G. Austin's commentary on *Aeneid* 2.222.
78. In the *Oedipus* Manto describes for the blind Tiresias the evil omens revealed in a botched sacrifice: "at taurus duos / perpessus ictus huc et huc dubius ruit" (342–43). See further Alessandro Ronconi, "Per Dante interprete dei poeti latini," *Studi Danteschi* 41 (1964): 19.

emblem of bestial wrath—such as that interpeted by Boccaccio in his commentary on Dante—is entirely appropriate to Troilo at this point in his own poem. This does not mean that Troilo is a minotaur, or that he eats people, or that he lives in a labyrinth; it means that his moral profile is justly described in the verbal iconography of the bestial fury of unreasonable and brutish passion.

Virgil was describing a man bellowing like a bull, Dante a bullish monster, Boccaccio a man poetically like a bullish monster. The image enjoys a fundamental stability, but it is not static; there is poetic change as well as poetic continuity. My hypothesis is that Boccaccio recognized the Virgil behind the Dante in this passage, but since I cannot prove that such was the case and since such proof is unnecessary to the present argument, I do not pursue the matter. What I regard as sufficiently certain is that Dante "emulated" Virgil's text, and that Boccaccio "emulated" Dante's. This brings us finally to Chaucer.

The image of the frenzied bull is not even mentioned in Schless's comprehensive review of alleged textual relationships between Chaucer and Dante. Why should it be? It is obviously a translation of Boccaccio, not of Dante. We must, however, look a little deeper. The context of the image is of course the same in the *Troilus* as in the *Filostrato*. In great dejection the hero leaves the Parliament which has just decreed the exchange of his beloved. He goes immediately to his house, retires to a bedroom, dismisses anyone who might have been there, closes the windows, and rages like a maddened bull. The "plot" is the same for the two poets, but the narration is rather different. Between *Fil.* 4.22, in which the solitary Troilo retires to his room, and 4.26, in which he begins his lament, there are three parenthetical "autobiographical" stanzas in which the narrator addresses the *donna* to whom the poem is directed, drawing a parallel between his own erotic despair and that of Troilo.[79] These three stanzas are of course omitted from Chaucer's *Troilus*, replaced by the following stanza, a stanza entirely independent of anything in the Italian text.

> And as in wynter leves ben biraft,
> Ech after other, til the tree be bare,

---

79. Boccaccio's narrator has already established in his *proemio* that the *Filostrato* is a most curious kind of personal allegory in which the situation of Troilo is the true image of the narrator's own situation and in which that of Creseida is as far from that of the *donna* as one could wish. I put quotation marks around the word "autobiographical" because I believe that the narrator of the *Filostrato* and his "lady" are no whit less fictitious than Troilo's and his.

So that ther nys but bark and braunche ilaft.
Lith Troilus, byraft of eche welfare,
Ibounden in the blake bark of care,
Disposed wood out of his wit to breyde,
So sore hym sat the chaungynge of Criseyde.

(4.225–231)

According to most of the learned annotators of this passage, the first part of the stanza, the image of the defoliated tree, is imitated from Dante (*Inferno* 3.112–14), who in turn was again imitating Virgil (*Aeneid* 6.309–12). Schless reviews the claim with a skepticism that, in my view, fairly represents an approach that in the name of methodological rigor necessarily denies much of what is most interesting in Chaucer's response to Dante. Schless's criterion of poetic relationship is the simplest form of linguistic translation, a phenomenon apparent in but a small fraction of Chaucer's poetic imitations. Thus Schless points out that there is no contextual parallel between the *Troilus* and the *Commedia*, that Chaucer has winter where Dante has autumn, that the image radically departs from Dante's beginning with its fourth line, that many poets have noted that leaves fall from trees, and that Chaucer himself probably did not have to travel to Italy to learn that fact. I leave Schless's discussion uncertain as to whether he believes that, as Chaucer wrote these lines, there was or was not in his mind any definite thought of Dante at all.[80]

What is at issue is not the question of whether a particular scholar or editor is right or wrong in affirming or denying a specific textual relationship between Dante and Chaucer. The issue is the nature of classical imitation in Chaucer's response to his poetic masters. We are to be sure in the realm of critical surmise however we decide the question, or however we fudge it; for Chaucer has left us no authorial glosses. The alternative to believing that we have here a conscious reminiscence of Dante must, however, be faced. It is this: that in expanding upon a poetic image in which Boccaccio imitated Dante imitating Virgil, Chaucer by the merest fortuity did so in language that critics have long maintained derives from another entirely discrete passage in which Dante imitates Virgil. This possibility is sufficiently unlikely, in my view, as to warrant dismissal. If we are to invoke the criterion of "context," we must

80. Schless, *Chaucer and Dante*, 130.

surely pay some attention to where Chaucer placed his image as well as to the passage in which he is alleged to have found it; and in that context—a context of poetic "emulation," "translation," and "creative transformation"—the Dantesque parentage of the defoliated tree seems obvious.

The argument that Chaucer significantly alters Dante's image—Troilus becomes encased in the tree that has lost its leaves—seems irrelevant to the question of the identification of the Dantesque "source." The poetic process with which I am concerned is one that "looses as it binds," to borrow a phrase famously used of the *terza rima* itself. There is in poetic emulation both continuity and discontinuity, original re-creation within an approved and approving tradition. Dante's own imitation of Virgil's bull has no "contextual" congruence of the kind implicitly demanded by the skeptical argument, and he departs from Virgil's image of the leafless tree no less radically than does Chaucer himself. The close translation of extended passages, though certainly a feature of the Latin "imitation" of Greek poetry, is the least common and the least interesting feature of classical creative imitation as we find it in the medieval poets. Such slavish imitation is, after all, the "vice of the *fidus interpres*." To establish its presence as the necessary and governing proof of Chaucer's use of Dante is to my mind a mistaken procedure.

What I find in these three stanzas of the *Troilus* is more evidence, if more were needed, that Chaucer played the poetic game according to the conventions established by the Augustan poets themselves and continued by such great vernacular writers of the later Middle Ages as Jean de Meun and Dante. This interpretation of the evidence does not imply that Chaucer enjoyed a memory endowed with powers of "total recall"; it does imply that he was a careful and intelligent reader of a limited number of texts by universally approved authors, that he knew how to look things up, and that he thought a good deal about how poets who had preceded him had handled the poetic issues that engaged his own attention.

Sometimes he played the poetic game very well, and at other times less well. The line "lith Troilus, byraft of eche welfare," where we must equate a plurality of welfares with a plurality of leaves, is in my opinion among the feebler of his creation. On the other hand, the inspiration of turning Troilus *into* a tree is not half bad. Windeatt adduces a number of suggestive and wholly legitimate Ovidian and Dantesque associations. It allows the pun "disposed wood" (crazy, made of wood), and it introduces the temporal parallel of pejorative seasonal change with the downturn of erotic fortunes.[81] Above all, perhaps, the suggestion of a tortured confinement ("ibounden in the blake bark of care") justly prepares the recollection of the staggering, roaring bull in all its manifestations: Laocoon locked in the serpent's grip, the Minotaur in its labyrinth prison, and the crazed lover in the artificial prison of his bedroom, with every window shut.

No unique feature of Chaucer's image of the bull justifies in the context of this book the protracted discussion it has received. My concern is to use this passage to suggest some general features of the complexities of poetic imitation as we find it in the *Troilus* and, in particular, to suggest some of the specific ways in which Chaucer enrolls his own poem in a continuous tradition linking the Augustans and Dante. For Dante, of course, Virgil occupied a special, clearly a unique position, and I find abundant evidence that Chaucer recognized and appreciated that role so far as the *Divina Commedia* was concerned.

Indeed as I search for an explanation of the curious fact that Dante's profound influence on the *Troilus* continues to be overlooked, minimized, or trivialized by some scholars, I settle on the nature rather than the obvious fact of Chaucer's use of Dante. The religious ethos of the *Commedia*, its ambitious explorations of characteristic Christian language and idea, is largely inappropriate to Chaucer's poem; what is wholly relevant, and what in my opinion clearly claims Chaucer's deep respect, not to say his aesthetic awe, is the way in which Dante responded to Latin poetry. On the other hand Chaucer himself had no unique commitment to Virgil.

He does of course turn to Virgil for a variety of ornamental epic details, and he seems to have made structural use of two Virgilian episodes—the famous love affair of the fourth book, and the betrayal of Deiphoebus. Yet I find that his "favorite" Augustan, to put the matter in somewhat flip terms, was Ovid, who perhaps necessarily had a commanding relevance for his erotic subject matter. To be sure, Chaucer often dignifies Ovid, philosophically speaking, more successfully than Ovid dignified himself; and one of the more remarkable,

81. The "chaungynge of Criseyde" primarily means her exchange for Antenor, but it foreshadows the changing of her affections from Troilus to Diomede. We recall the narrator's characterization of Troilus' reaction to her letter: "Hym thoughte it lik a kalendes of chaunge" (5.1634).

even astonishing features of the *Troilus* is Chaucer's successful consolidation of the poetic voices of exile—Ovid, Boethius, and Dante—into one harmonious body of erotic doxography. I find in this phenomenon another consequence of his readings in two great Ovidians—Jean de Meun and Boccaccio—though the intellectual uses served by the phenomenon are largely his own.

Thus it is that if we are to appreciate how Chaucer interpreted Dante interpreting Virgil, we must also pay some attention to the fashion in which he interpreted Ovid, his prestigious predecessor in the vocation of professor of desire. Once again, small details may be telling. We may consider, for example, two somewhat mysterious proper names—*Zanzis* and *Criseyde*—covertly united by a famous Ovidian text. Pandarus, trying to cure Troilus of his immoderate dependence upon Criseyde, suggests that he try a new girl; and as usual he invokes bookish authority:

> "And ek, as writ Zanzis, that was ful wys,
> 'The newe love out chaceth ofte the olde.'"
> (4.414–15)

That is the first onomastic mystery, and it is all Chaucer's own. The second he inherited from the *Filostrato*. In all versions of the story before Boccaccio the name had begun not with a *C*. but with a *B*. The forms seem to derive from two quite different Homeric women, *Chryseis* and *Briseis*, and Root, who has investigated the matter most thoroughly, concluded that the C-form was possibly based on philological error. Boccaccio, it appears, had trouble reading Latin too; and there were some lines in the *Remedia amoris* of Ovid which, "if carelessly read, might suggest that Chryseis was daughter to Calchas."[82] What Ovid had written was this—

> "Est" ait Atrides "illius proxima forma
> et, si prima sinat syllaba, nomen idem . . ."
> (475–76)

("There is one," said Atrides, "whose beauty is next to hers, and, but for the first syllable, the name is just the same.")

I suggest that the Ovidian context shows that Boccaccio understood the lines very well indeed.

---

82. Root, in *Troilus and Criseyde*, ed. Root, xxvii-viii.

A recurrent topic in the ancient critique of sexual passion was the connection between private pleasure and public calamity, especially the calamity of the Trojan War, Horace's *bellum cunni*. Patristic and medieval moralists of widely differing stripe—Ambrose of Milan and the old woman of the *Roman de la Rose*, for example—habitually make the connection between private sexual license and the disasters of war. It is only to be expected that Ovid, who developed as no other poet before or since the cognate themes of amatory and military exertion, would reflect so commonplace a moral thought, as, of course, he several times does.

The passage cited alludes to the squabble between Agamemnon and Achilles over the ownership of a sexually desirable slave girl, and it does so in a fashion that invokes the sexually brutal attitudes of the male world of warriors, attitudes by no means absent from the ethos of the *Filostrato*. Women are like the number twelve bus; another one comes by every twenty minutes.[83] Furthermore the ancient wisdom quoted by Pandarus—"The newe love out chaceth ofte the olde"—seems to derive from *Remedia amoris*, 462: "Successore novo vincitur omnis amor" (All love is vanquished by a succeeding love).

Thus whether misread or merely read, the *Remedia amoris* is relevant to the naming of Criseyde and to the mysterious Zanzian quotation, but this is not the same thing as saying that Zanzis is Ovid. To begin with, the maxim "Successore novo vincitur omnis amor," which has an obviously comic dimension within its immediate poetic context, is more than a little dubious as serious philosophy. Cicero, who was unburdened by Ovidian facetiousness, pretty clearly regarded it as bad advice that proposed a cure no less killing than the malady.[84] The dubiety of the thought is not redeemed by the dubiety of the thinker. Given Pandarus' well-demonstrated proclivites toward textual perversion, we should probably be alert to the possibility that Zanzis, like the text attributed to him, is a bit twisted.

---

83. Cf. A. A. R. Henderson's gloss on the Ovidian text (*P. Ovidi Nasonis Remedia amoris* [Edinburgh: Scottish Academic Press, 1979], 101): "forma and nomen are metonymies (possessum pro possessore) which subtly suggest that Agamemnon regards women as objects, not as persons, and as interchangeable objects at that." Pandarus is if possible even more offensive than Pandaro in this regard: "For syn it is but casuel plesaunce, / Some cas shal putte it out of remembraunce" (*TC* 4.419–20).

84. "Etiam novo quidam amore veterem amorem tamquam clavo clavum eiciendum putant. Maxime autem admonendus est quantus sit furor amoris." Cicero, *Gespräche in Tusculum*, 4.35.75, ed. O. Gigon (Munich: Heimeran, 1970).

Some years ago Donald Fry put forward the engaging suggestion that Zanzis was a form of the name of the Greek painter Zeuxis.[85] The suggestion is supported by the fact that in the "Physician's Tale" the painter is referred to by that name, probably in a form dependent upon a text of the *Roman de la Rose*. Fry also thought that the well-known story of Zeuxis, who modeled his painting of Helen of Troy after the most beautiful features of a number of different women, was thematically akin to the advice offered by Pandarus at 4.407–13. The suggestion is intriguing, but difficulties remain. The chief of them is that Zanzis is a writer (as *writ* Zanzis) and apparently a philosopher (that was ful wys). It is indeed typical of the augmented bookishness of Chaucer's character that what Pandaro ascribes to commonplace opinion Pandarus ascribes to a definite textual authority. My own suggestion—which I offer tentatively and without dogmatic conviction—is that Zanzis is Seneca, or rather a Pandaric phantasm of Seneca.

It is hardly to be expected that we have all of Chaucer's "sources" in the *Troilus*, and among the books that I would propose for closer scrutiny is the Middle French "version" of the Latin *Pamphilus*, the so-called *Pamphile et Gala-tée* of Jehan Bras-de-Fer. In this work, the go-between, a traditional crone named Houdée, is learnedly garrulous on a wide variety of topics. One of her counseling sessions with the would-be lover contains the following lines:

> Gentilz vertus est de moien;
> Zanneus, uns grans clers, mais paien,
> Moien sur toute vertu loë,
> Preus est qui si sa vie aloë.
> (469–72)

(Moderation is a noble virtue. Zanneus, a great scholar though a pagan, praises moderation above all other virtues. Upright is he who governs his life by it.)

Morawski hypothesizes that "Zanneus" is another creative error, this time the error of a scribe rather than that of the poet. What the poet had written was "Seneques" or something similar. An educated glossator had added the gentile "L.Anneus" and the gloss, misconstrued as "Zanneus" replaced the original reading. Whether or not this suggestion has merit, I think it is likely that

85. D. Fry, "Chaucer's Zanzis and a Possible Source for *Troilus and Criseyde*, IV, 407–13," *ELN* 9 (1971): 81–85.

Chaucer had read *Pamphile et Galatée* and found in it the germ of an idea he could use, what might be called the textually active go-between.[86]

The text ascribed to Zanneus—a definition of virtue as a mean—could have been derived from any number of passages in Seneca or, indeed, from any number of other pagan clerks.[87] However, the doctrine, and Senecan Stoicism generally, are highly relevant to the Chaucerian context. The advice is offered from the perspective of a double misprision. In the first place Pandarus' view of the affair as "casuel plesaunce" hardly accords with Troilus' actual perception. Hence the advice to fight fire with fire, orthodox Ovidianism though it may be, is but dubiously apt. On the other hand it does seem relevant for Criseyde who, de facto, practices it.

In the fourth book Chaucer's poem most closely conforms to the dramatic model of classical medieval erotic doxography: the hero, faced for the first time with the active persecution of Fortune, stands, like Hercules at the crossroads, before apparently starkly alternative courses of actions proposed by reason on the one hand and desire on the other.[88] In this book the role of Pandarus becomes particularly complex; and in literary terms, he reflects with some catholicity the wide range of *praeceptores amoris* of the antierotic tradition. Having been the Ovid of the *Ars*, he now becomes the Ovid of the *Remedia*. But there is also a hint of Lady Philosophy and of Lady Philosophy's daughter, Dame Reason, from the *Roman de la Rose*. Troilus refers to Pandarus' advice as medicine (*lechecraft*, 4.436) and makes it clear that he is not prepared to accept its ministrations. This idea is reinforced by the expressive terms in which Troilus chastises Pandarus for the inconstancy of his advice:

> But kanstow pleyen raket to and fro,
> Netle in, dokke out, now this, now that, Pandare?
>
> (*TC* 4.460–61)

---

86. *Pamphile et Galateé par Jehan Bras-de-Fer de Dammartin-en-Goële*, ed. Joseph de Morawski (Paris: Champion, 1917). My proposal seems to me stronger than Fry's in some ways and weaker in others. Among the problems with it is the fact that neither "Zanneus" nor any of its recorded variants is an obvious version of "Zanzis." But then Zanzis is not really an obvious form of Zeuxis either.

87. See the earlier discussion of "Ethik." Houdée repeatedly ascribes rather vague moral sententiae to specific authorities. See Morawski's note on the quotation ascribed to Solomon (cited by Pandarus as "the Wyse"), *Pamphile et Galatée*, line 2427n.

88. See Wenzel, "Chaucer's Troilus of Book IV." The conflict of Love and Reason seems to be developed by Boccaccio in terms that derive from the *Roman de la Rose*.

The sorry truth is, of course, that Pandarus is indeed the player of a game, or perhaps its referee or impressario. And from the practical point of view, his Ovidian advice—forget the old love with a new one—is not without merit, as we may see in the behavior of Criseyde: "But al shal passe: and thus take I my leve" (5.1085). But Troilus is in the grip of heroic, Apollonian, Ovidian, "courtly" love. The back-and-forth of a shuttlecock is perhaps an adequate image for instability, but the phrase "Netle in, dokke out" surely has a subversive effect in this context. It refers to the fact well known in folk medicine that the sting of the nettle is relieved by rubbing the afflicted skin with dockleaf. The patient who takes medicine is seldom described as being fickle to the pain he seeks to escape; but "love," though an illness, is not susceptible to the known pharmacopoeia. Troilus cites a vernacular charm from the folk culture of Merry England, but the guarantor of its significance is Augustan Ovid. "Ei mihi" cries Apollo, striken to the heart with Cupid's arrow,

> quod nullis amor est sanabalis herbis
> nec prosunt domino, quae prosunt omnibus artes.[89]

> (Alas, that love is curable by no herbs, and the arts which heal all others cannot heal their lord!)

If the first line defines Troilus' dilemma, the second identifies that of Pandarus. The image of shuttlecock and nettle were of course Chaucer's inventions, adornments of the idea already in Boccaccio that though Pandarus can cure others he cannot cure himself. Chaucer returns to Boccaccio at 4.484. even at the expense of a certain narrative awkwardness, to bring up the question of Pandarus' own girl friend. This lady casts a very pale shadow over the text of the *Troilus*, but she does make two emblematic appearances (of which this is the second and more explicit) to remind us of the distance between Pandaric precept and Pandaric practice.

In the "medicine of love" Boethius and Ovid join as they were joined by Jean de Meun in the *Roman de la Rose*, of which there is a textual and contextual echo in 4.428–34. Here Pandarus shares the fate of Dame Reason (4599–4613). What he shovels in, the god of Love shovels out: "Oon ere it herde, at tother out it wente" (4.434).

---

89. *Metamorphoses* 1.523–24; the *Pamphile et Galatée* (ed. Morawski, p. 60) draws explicit attention to these lines: "Tu ies celui dont li poetes / Dist—j'en voi trop bien les

Pandarus, of course, offers only metaphorical medicaments. He deals in *verba*, rather than *herbae*, and the one regimen proves no more efficacious than the other.[90] But his sententiousness, his penchant for the proverb, his thoroughgoing textuality which comes to the fore especially in the fourth book, nicely highlights one of Chaucer's inevitable concerns—the relationship between love and writing about love.

Troilus curiously rewrites what has just transpired in the terms of a feeble, failed heroic simile:

"Thow farest ek by me, thow Pandarus,
As he that, whan a wight is wo bygon,
He cometh to hym a paas, and seith right thus:
'Thynk nat on smerte, and thow shalt fele non.'
Thow moost me first transmewen in a ston,
And reve me my passiones alle,
Or thow so lightly do my wo to falle. (4.463–69)

The effect of this reformulation is to emphasize the destructive implications of Troilus' wallowing in misery rather than the misery itself. Root easily recognized the Stoic doctrine alluded to in the text, and he cited a useful parallel from Lucilius. Troilus, who regards the advice that the mind should rule matter as impossible in his situation, apparently recognized it too. This whole passage is a rhetorically extravant advertisement of the lover's constancy: unless "I were a fend," says Troilus, I could never "traysen a wight that trewe is unto me" (4.437–38). But Pandarus' advice that he find a new lover has been proffered merely in response to his inordinate suffering—and talking about his suffering —at the temporary loss of Criseyde. It is advice that could be followed only if Troilus were "first transmewen in a ston."

Let us inquire whether it in fact requires superhuman self-control to display fortitude in the face of the ten-day absence of one's beloved. As it happens, Seneca himself had written on philosophical fortitude in an essay, popular in the Middle Ages, "On the Firmness of the Philosopher" (*De constantia sapien-*

---

viettes / Quant tu maistres de toute art es—: / *Non prosunt domino que prosunt omnibus artes.*"
90. Cf. *Heroides* 5:149 and Jacob Werner, *Beiträge zur Kunden der lateinischen Literatur des Mittelalters,* 2d ed. (Aarau: Sauerländer, 1905), 47. This topos appears repeatedly in medieval literature.

tis). He listed a number of difficulties that do face the wise man: "bodily pain or infirmity, the loss of friends or children, and the ruin that befalls his country in the flames of war" (10.4). "I do not deny the wise man feels these things," he continues, "for we do not claim for him the hardness of stone or of steel." What he does claim for him is the moral courage to overcome adversity and to get on with the job. Thus once again the language of actual "moral virtue, grounded upon truth" as understood by the great pagan authors is explicitly introduced into the poem to show how far Troilus' passion—and the words of Troilus' own choosing—separates him from it.

It does not require a classical education to perceive the exaggerated irrationality of Troilus' behavior and thought patterns. The Stoic emblems are chiefly ornamental, though they also have a dramatic function. Even Pandarus is a counselor of Senecan moderation, as we see in the development of the topic we might call the topic of competitive erotic suffering—as exemplified by the competitive passion of Palamon and Arcite for Emilye in the "Knight's Tale." Nearly the first thing Pandarus says to Troilus by way of consolation is that it is he, Pandarus, who should grieve, not Troilus. After all Troilus has had the full sexual enjoyment of his girl; Pandarus cannot so much as get a smile from *his* (4.393–99).

Is it better or merely bitter to have loved and lost? Troilus is inclined to the latter view (4.484–96). His grief is the worse for the very fact of his previous joy.[91] This line of argument brings Dante back on stage; or rather, since he

---

91. Pandarus has never had the sexual enjoyment of his own phantom beloved, but we cannot be sure that he has not had Criseyde herself. The notorious stanzas (3.1553–82) describing the morning after the night before at Pandarus' house show us Chaucer Galeotto, encouraging even the sleepiest undergraduate to become a serious student of Middle English syntax. The nasty suggestion of incestuous sexual intercourse, as inescapable as it is unwelcome, is consistent with Chaucer's artistic emphasis on the Theban theme throughout the poem, with the voyeuristic element of Pandarus' supervision of the love affair, and with the Augustinian critique of antique societies which is a prominent feature of Latin writings on the Troy legend (see, e.g., J. Roger Dunkle, "Satirical Themes in Joseph of Exeter's *De Bello Troiano*," *Classica et Mediaevalia* 38 [1987]); but it is so *very* nasty and so inconvenient to the project of saving the romantic appearances that, like "Robertson's pun," it invites banishment by editorial ukase (see, e.g., Stephen Barney in *The Riverside Chaucer* [Boston: Houghton Mifflin, 1987]) or by scholarly filibuster (see Robert apRoberts, "A Contribution to the Thirteenth Labour: Purging *Troilus* of Incest," *Essays on English and American Literature* [Amsterdam: Rodopi, 1987]). I think it is wrong to make a confident judgment either way,

never left it, it brings him back into the lights. In response to Troilus' possibly hyperbolic opinion that Pandarus has harrowed hell in gaining for him the sexual favors of Criseyde,[92] Pandarus warned him,

> "For of fortunes sharp adversitee
> The worste kynde of infortune is this:
> A man to han ben in prosperitee,
> And it remembren whan it passed is . . ."
>
> (3.1625–28)

Troilus must be careful; he must not be "rakel." The philosopher of the third book is contradicted by the desperate opportunist of the fourth, but Troilus has not forgotten:

> "Why gabbestow, that seydest thus to me
> That hym is wors that is fro wele ythrowe,
> Than he hadde erst noon of that well yknowe?"
>
> (4.481–83)

Now this is a fair translation of the voice of Boethius (2.4) responding to Lady Philosophy's argument (parodied by Pandarus at 4.393ff., as reported earlier) to the effect that Boethius had enjoyed good fortune. But of course the poet and the text who most memorably applied the Boethian doctrine to tragic erotic loss was Dante in the episode of Paolo and Francesca.

I am scarcely the first to suggest that Chaucer had the episode of Paolo and Francesca on his mind in writing cardinal episodes of the *Troilus*, but so far as I know I am the first scholar to try to show its *textual* presence, a presence that seems to me certain. That is not to say that he attempted to impose Dante's dramatic situation upon the plot of the *Troilus*. His text implies a particular interest in two aspects of the fifth canto: the nature of sexual passion in an ethical context and, above all, the connections between text and desire, the idea of the book as *galeotto*. We must seek for the evidence of "influence" less

---

for Chaucer (imitating Pandarus himself) has taken great care to be ambiguous. We may, however, compare the following lines. [Pandarus of Troilus] "Syn thi desir al holly hastow had," 4.395; [Narrator of Pandarus] "And Pandarus hath hoolly his entente," 3.1582.

92. "Thow hast in hevene ybrought my soule at reste/Fro Flegiton, the fery flood of helle" (3.1599–1600).

in textual than in ideographic parallels; but there is nonetheless a textual spoor
of Dante in the English poem. Between a Senecan stanza and a Boethian stanza
in Troilus' speech comes the following:

> "My deth may wel out of my brest departe
> The lif, so longe may this sorwe myne;
> But fro my soule shal Criseydes darte
> Out nevere mo; but down with Proserpyne,
> Whan I am ded, I wol go wone in pyne;
> And ther I wol eternaly compleyne
> My wo, and how that twynned be we tweyne."
>
> (4.470–76)

This stanza, which lacks intellectual as well as linguistic coherence, offers
four eschatological propositions: (1) Troilus' love for Criseyde will survive his
death; (2) he will go to hell after death; (3) he will exist there in torment; and
(4) he will forever bewail his separation from Criseyde. The third proposition
he flatly contradicts a few lines later when he calls death the ender of all sor-
rows (501), a genuinely Stoic idea more consistently reflected by Boccaccio's
Troilo.

The allusion to Proserpina is almost certainly mediated by Dante, who calls
her—in a phrase that explains the fourth proposition—"la regina de l'eterno
pianto" (*Inferno* 9.44).[93] But the more significant Dantean association is to be
seen in the phrase "how that twynned be we tweyne."

Much of the intellectual brilliance of the system of Dante's hell lies in the
fact that many of the damned spend eternity doing what they did in their
earthly life or in achieving some version of their earthly ambitions. Paolo and
Francesca are now together *forever*. Why, then, does Troilus think he will be
forever separated from Criseyde? I suggest that we have here another example
of Troilus the misreader and failed *vates*: for when Criseyde rewrites the "sce-
nario" a few hundred lines later, it is precisely the literary error concerning
the eternal union of the departed souls that she corrects:

> "Myn herte, and ek the woful goost therinne,
> Byquethe I with youre spirit to compleyne

---

93. Schless, *Chaucer and Dante*, 131, seems to deny the textual filiation; but his skepticism has by this time lost its power to intimidate. Note the phrases "eternaly compleyne"
and "eterno pianto."

Eternaly, for they shul nevere twynne;
For though in erthe ytwynned be we tweyne,
Yit in the feld of pite, out of peyne,
That hight Elisos, shal we be yfeere,
As Orpheus with Erudice his fere.
(4.785–91)

There is certainly an allusion here to the second reunion of Orpheus and
Euridyce (*Metamorphoses* 11.61–84) in which Ovid rewrote as wistful comedy
a story already told as wistful tragedy. I accept the suggestion that we have here
textual echoes of the *Ovide moralisé*, and while I attach no special significance
to that fact, it is of interest that the phrases come from the lips of Criseyde,
by far the least "textual" of the major characters.[94] Criseyde's view of things to
come, part of her preparation for a suicide that would seem plausible enough
were not the imaginary future so starkly contradicted by the actual future,
confronts that offered by Troilus a few hundred lines earlier on one question
alone, the question of whether the lovers will or will not be separated in death:
the lovers will "eternaly compleyne," but their spirits "shul nevere twynne."

The topos, a familiar enough one in classical literature, is that of the infernal
reunion of lovers separated by mischance or disaster.[95] Dante overthrows the
idea by insisting that it is true. His lovers suffer the presence, not the absence,
of the beloved. Upon hearing the story of Paolo and Francesca—which is a
story of hearing a story—the pilgrim Dante out of pity (*di pietade*) swoons to
the floor of hell like a dead man. There is no passage of the poem that has
been more written about by critics in the Romantic tradition. But Boccaccio,
who wrote about it long before, anticipated the theological and poetic misprision on which that Romantic criticism has been posited. Boccaccio insists that
Dante's "pity" is that of a tropological reader of moral literature, a man moved
not by the "human tragedy" of unhappy love but by the terrifying realization
that the retributive justice that rewards irrational passion faces Dante as well.[96]

What might Chaucer have learned from the end of Dante's lovers that was

---

94. B. L. Witlieb, "Chaucer's Elysian Fields (*Troilus*, IV, 789f)," *N&Q* 214 (1969):
250–51.
95. See Musaeus, *Musaios: Hero und Leander*, ed. Karl Kost (Bonn: Bouvier Verlag,
1977), 546–47.
96. Boccaccio, *Esposizioni sopra la Comedia di Dante*, ed. Giorgio Padoan (Milan: A. Mondadori, 1965), 324–25.

relevant to his own project in the *Troilus*? Though the vast exegesis of the concluding stanzas of Chaucer's *Troilus* yields no consensus concerning the most provocative questions of interpretation raised by the poem, there is at least something like general agreement concerning some incidental facts of literary history and relationship. One fact is that Geoffrey Chaucer introduced into a cardinal position of his poem's ending some stanzas taken not from Boccaccio's account of the death of Troilo in the *Filostrato* but from Boccaccio's account of the death of Arcite in the *Teseida*. Another fact is that Boccaccio's treatment of the topic of the sidereal ascension of Arcite, destined to be appropriated by Chaucer, shows the undoubted textual influence of Dante's treatment of the topic of sidereal ascension in *Paradiso* 22. A third fact is that Dante's treatment of the topic quite as clearly reveals, upon subcutaneous examination, the presence of Boethius. We may wish to regard these facts as random fortuities, as the received commentary has done; but I suggest that they point out a definite pattern central to Chaucer's conception of his undertaking which is, in effect, to construct from the materials of Boccaccian pseudoantique romance a classical, Christian tragedy.

At the time that Chaucer composed his *Troilus*, Giovanni Boccaccio was arguably the most famous man of letters in Europe. He was certainly far too famous for us seriously to entertain the idea for even a moment that Chaucer did not know whose poem he was translating when he translated the *Filostrato* or that Chaucer's suppression of his name was anything but a conscious, significant artistic decision deserving of all the thought we can give it. Boccaccio's most famous vernacular work by far was of course the *Decamerone*, the work that inevitably would establish the standard for the genre that Chaucer himself would exploit in his own best-known work, *The Canterbury Tales*.

We do not know when Chaucer first came to know Boccaccio's fictions. Chaucerians have often given the impression that if he knew the *Decamerone* at all, he cannot have done so until well after the completion of the *Troilus*, but this seems to me unlikely in the extreme. On the contrary, I assume that Chaucer "knew" the work at least in the superficial sense of being familiar with its title and having some general sense, possibly secondhand, of its typical contents. He knew, that is, that Boccaccio had called it "Principe Galeotto" in an obvious allusion to the fifth canto of Dante's *Inferno*. This is the only place known to me in all of Dante where we shall find an invocation of Boethius in the service of a condemnation of sexual passion. That is the strategy of Jean de Meun in the *Roman de la Rose* and, following him, of Chaucer in the *Troilus*.

Boccaccio's "galeotto" is usually taken to be a subversive allusion, and in fact the *Decamerone* as a whole is often said to be an "anti-Dante": Boccaccio pursues a worldly, not a divine comedy. Whether such judgments will survive the increased and increasingly sophisticated scrutiny of the relationships between Dante and Boccaccio now taking place it would be premature to say. On the other hand, I feel more confident in denying the suggestion that *Chaucer* is in some sense advancing a pessimistic critique of the *Commedia*, or that in invoking a prominent emblem of misreading, he is despairing of the possibility of stably significant writing.[97]

This is not, of course, to deny the fruitful anxiety, described by E. T. Donaldson among others, arising from certain inescapable similarities between the poet and the pimp.[98] If we take Chaucer at face value in the *Retractions* at the end of the *Canterbury Tales* he was painfully aware of the culpability of texts "that sownen into synne" and, in that context, careful to include the *Troilus* among them. Yet anxiety attendant upon a realization of the necessary ambiguity of art is not the same thing as despair before the possibility of resolving ambiguity. My own view is that Chaucer's use of Dante in the concluding movements of the *Troilus*, though complex, is wholly comfortable and approbative, that he once again invokes Dante, in the company of Boethius, in silent reproof of the pseudopagan narrator of the *Filostrato*.

For the episode of Paolo and Francesca is not principally about miswriting, the carnal intention of a worldly writer; it is principally about misreading, the carnal reflex of the worldly *interpres*. The *interpres* of the fifth canto is Francesca; it is she who reports, in a false and self-exculpating fashion, the contents of a crucial scene of the Old French *Lancelot de Lake*. As Susan Noakes demonstrates, the misreading is rich and complex.[99] In the first place, Francesca misrepresents her text by transferring the locus of sexual initiative from Guinevere to Lancelot. (In the French text it is Guinevere who is the sexual aggressor, Lancelot the passive and "trembling" sexual prey.) In the second place, the suggestion that Paolo and Francesca terminated their reading of the romance with the episode of the kiss has a subtler significance than the obvi-

97. See Karla Taylor, "A Text and Its Afterlife: Dante and Chaucer," *CL* 35 (1983): 1–20.
98. E. Talbot Donaldson, "Chaucer's Three 'P's': Pandarus, Pardoner, and Poet," *Michigan Quarterly Review* 14 (1975): 282–301.
99. See Susan Noakes, "The Double Misreading of Paolo and Francesca," *PQ* 62 (1983): 221–39; the author's incidental confusion concerning the plot of the *Troilus* does not invalidate the general line of argument.

ous fact that the lovers put down the book in order to go to bed. It implies that the reading of the book was truncated before its quite transparent antierotic "moral" could have emerged. The only reader who could believe that "galeotto fu il libro e chi lo scrisse" is in a quite literal sense a partial reader, one who knows only part of its text or one whose proclivities impose upon it a meaning for which the author could in no way be held responsible.

Dante took care to make his moment a moment of textual "conversion." His great line "quel giorno piu non vi leggemmo avante" surely invokes the most famous of all textual conversions, that of Augustine in the eighth book of the *Confessions*.[100] But "conversion" in Augustine is not supine submission to an all-powerful text; it is the rational ordering of the will in symphony with a catalytic text. What we have reported by Francesca is the story of a pretextual rather than a textual encounter. What might be called her textual attitude is an attitude shared by all the major *interpretes* of *Troilus and Criseyde*, but particularly by Troilus himself and by his own arch-*interpres,* Pandarus. The fact that Francesca has misled not merely herself and her damned lover but also the classical exegetical tradition of the fifth canto is, to be sure, an eloquent testimony to the dangerous powers of the *interpres;* but it absolves no other *interpres* of fact or fiction from the sometimes onerous task of reading texts in their integrity—even their endings. To the very considerable extent that he postulated the tragedy of Troilus as tragedy of misinterpretation, Chaucer *interpres* could find no more apt an analogue than Francesca; and the subtle but certain echoes of "her" canto thoughout the *Troilus* are as harmonious as they are suggestive.

Criseyde's last letter is, however, not Troilus' last interpretive test. There is another: Diomede's armed shirt decorated with the brooch given by Troilus to Criseyde, then by Criseyde to Diomede. Chaucer underscores its semiotic importance by actually calling it a *signe:*

> And so bifel that thorughout Troye town,
> As was the gise, iborn was up and down
> A maner cote armure, as seith the storie,
> Byforn Deiphebe, in signe of his victorie;
> The which cote, as telleth Lollius,

100. See Robert Hollander, *Allegory in Dante's Commedia* (Princeton: Princeton University Press, 1969), 112–14.

Deiphebe it hadde irent fro Diomede
The same day . . . (5.1649–55)

But the "sign" of Deiphoebus' victory is the sign of Troilus' defeat. In the face of this ocular proof, Troilus is unable to persevere in his belief in Criseyde's "truth," yet his exegesis of the specific "sign" is ludicrously eccentric. In an outburst of mawkish, adolescent self-pity he cries out that Criseyde has given the brooch to Diomede with the sole intention of inflicting pain on her discarded lover:

"Was ther non other broche yow liste lete
To feffe with youre newe love," quod he,
"But thilke broche that I, with teris wete,
Yow yaf, as for a remembraunce of me?
Non other cause, allas, ne hadde ye
But for despit, and ek for that ye mente
Al outrely to shewen youre entente."
(5.1688–94)

Even once we move beyond the primary absurdity of the idea—that Criseyde's *intends* the brooch as a conscious "sign" of malice toward Troilus, as though she gave it to Diomede in order that it might be ripped from his back and carried through the streets of Troy—we see revealed a fatally shallow understanding. If Criseyde's letter with its fine phrase "Thentente is al" (5.1630) has taught Troilus anything at all, it should have taught him that the last thing in the world Criseyde is likely to do is to reveal her intentions "al outrely." We may doubt that she is any more capable of holding him in conscious "despit" than she is of being true to him in her altered circumstances. The passionate, egocentric optimism that reads his returning lover into a fare-cart on the horizon (5.1156–62) is here transformed to a passionate, egocentric pessimism that reads volitional insult to himself into an action of Criseyde's in which we may imagine that Troilus was the last concern on her mind, if indeed he was on her mind at all.

Finally, more compelling than the "sign" carried by Deiphoebus and read and misread by Troilus are the signal functions of the brothers themselves. I have elswhere tried to show how Chaucer, faithful to his artistic genius in small things no less than in large, makes brilliant use of the literary tradition of Deiphoebus *signifer*. Deiphoebus is little more than a spear-bearer in the epic of the battle of Troy. The most memorable fact concerning him in the literary tradition to which Chaucer had access had less to do with his manner of life than with his manner of death.

The sole importance of Deiphoebus in literary tradition was his grisly end, his treacherous betrayal by Helen and his brutal slaughter in his own conjugal bedchamber by Menelaus and his Greeks, a death forever memorialized in the katabasis of the sixth book of the *Aeneid*. In that famous text Deiphoebus is once again a sign-bearer, and the signs he bears—his own resonant word is *monimenta*, "souvenirs"—have been indelible symbols, in the Western literary tradition, of the perfidy of women. I have argued that Chaucer quite deliberately challenged the antifeminist tradition by making the Deiphoebus of his own poem a *signifer* of a quite different sort. Chaucer, too, shows us a Deiphoebus betrayed, but not by a woman. In the *Troilus* Deiphoebus' betrayers are men—one of them his dearest brother, the other a man whom he loves like a brother—willing to exploit his frank and fresh feelings of brotherly love in the project of deceiving a woman.

That is one clear meaning of the lengthy episode of the dinner party at Deiphoebus' house (2.1394–3.231), one of the few protracted inventions that Chaucer added to Boccaccio's plot. Thus it is that whatever else that Deiphoebus may signal to Troilus, what he must signal to a Virgilian reader of Chaucer is the deceitful abuse of brotherly love, the social manifestation of what Christians knew as the theological virtue of charity.

The death of Troilus himself is not without its own pointed semiotic purposes, purposes wholly independent of the controversies surrounding the poem's ending. The Latin literary tradition that remade the Homeric story of Troy had invested Troilus, too, with a definite sign-bearing function. A passage in the *Bacchides* of Plautus has preserved for us the antique tradition of the three signs or *fata* that were to signal the imminent death of Great Troy. The first was the loss of the Palladium, the second the death of Troilus, the third the displacement of the lintel of the Phrygian gate.[101]

The gist of these fatal auguries was preserved and very widely disseminated by Servius' commentary on the *Aeneid* in a passage meant to help explain the

---

101. "Ilio tria fuisse audivi fata quae illi forent exitio; / signum ex arce si periisset; alterum etiamst Troili mors; / tertium, cum portae Phrygiae limen superum scinderetur." Plautus, *Bacchides*, ed. Cesare Questa (Florence: Sansoni, 1965), lines 953–55.

dramatic significance of the wooden horse.[102] Virgil seems to have been the first poet to have imagined Troilus as a possibly significant dramatic role, and he called him from the obscurity of the Homeric death rolls to a brief but moving death scene. Virgil's Troilus is certainly not Chaucer's Troilus of the fifth book, but a sweet and graceful youth who, no match for the brutal Achilles, loses his life in an inglorious but wholly sensible attempt to flee from battle. It is a pathetic rather than a heroic moment.

The rhetoric of pathos is entirely absent from Chaucer's account of Troilus' death, if we can call a near afterthought an "account": "Ful pitously hym slough the fierse Achille" (5.1806). The quiet surprise in this sentence is, I suppose, the word "pitously." We want it to suggest that the reader should be moved to pity; but what the Middle English manages to suggest more easily is that Achilles has done Troilus a favor. The narrator's language insists on Troilus' nobility and the worthiness of his deeds, but it does not disguise the fact that the nobility of Troilus' last days is the nobility of a *furens,* the slaughterer of thousands, an alter-Achilles. The narrator makes clear allusion to the *Aeneid* only to say that it is not his model:

> . . . if I hadde ytaken for to write
> The armes of this ilke worthi man,
> Than wolde ich of his batailles endite . . .
> (5.1765–67)

The model, instead, is the *Iliad:*

> The wraththe, as I bigan yow for to seye,
> Of Troilus . . . (5.1800–1801)

Both Troilus and the narrator view the hero's death in terms of a private and indeed a largely secret erotic tragedy. Yet Lollius must know better than most, since Horace has spelled it out for him in such clear and dogmatic terms, that the history of the fall of Troy is one that teaches of the public and social disasters that result from private passion and private folly. As always, the reader is called upon to be a better interpreter of Troilus' signs than Troilus is himself.

We have already seen the lengths to which Chaucer has gone to construct a

---

102. For documentation and further relevant information see Austin's notes on *Aeneid* 1.474; pp. 159–60.

parallel between Criseyde and the Palladium, the idols of little Troy and Great Troy, respectively. Once Troilus realizes the implications of the permanent loss of his "sign"—and he actually refers to her as "she . . . that wont was us to gye" (5.546)—he seeks his death, and eventually finds it. Yet even in his death, a death that fulfills the second of the fatal auguries of the destruction of the city, Troilus is a "sign" of that far greater impending disaster. Now his guide will be not Criseyde but Mercury, a guide who in all of classical literature leads souls to one place and one place only, the underworld.

In his death, in a passing moment of Scipionic insight, Troilus does perceive the elemental, radical truth about the vanity of human wishes—that in comparison with the felicity of the spiritual realm the brooding tumults of the flesh are worth nothing. Such was the common doctrine of the great pagan philosophers known to the Middle Ages in unmediated study and in their oblique reflections in monuments of pagan poetry: Plato, Cicero, and Seneca. For that matter, such was the common doctrine of medieval Christianity, too, so that when Chaucer's narrator-interpreter, a fourteenth-century Christian neither more nor less religious than the general run of men of his age and class, with utter conventionality and with faultless cultural decorum makes some concluding remarks by way of interpreting his own narrative, he instinctively invokes a rather obvious Augustinian contrast of superior and inferior loves. The reader-*interpres* trained in the conventional sign-system of the poet's own choosing must find the ending of the *Troilus*, like the end of Troilus himself, wholly predictable, though not, as the hero would have it, wholly inescapable.

BIBLIOGRAPHY

Primary Sources, Ancient and Medieval; Modern Versions

Abelard, Peter. *Dialectica*, ed. L. M. De Rijk. Assen: Van Gorcum, 1966.

Anthologia Latina, ed. Alexander Riese. Leipzig: Teubner, 1894–97.

Augustine. *De civitate Dei*. See Raoul de Presles.

——. *Confessions*, trans. R. S. Pine-Coffin. Harmondsworth: Penguin, 1961.

——. *De dialectica*, ed. J. Pinborg and trans. B. Darrell Jackson. Dortrecht: North Holland, 1975.

——. *Oeuvres de Saint Augustin*, ed. F. Cayré, F. Van Steenberghen et al. Paris: Desclée, de Brouwer, 1949–.

Baudri de Borgeuil [Baldricus Burgulianus]. *Carmina*, ed. Karlheinz Hilbert. Heidelberg: Winter, 1979.

Benoît de Ste.-Maure. *Le Roman de Troie par Benoît de Sainte-Maure*, 6 vols., ed. Léopold Constans. Paris: SATF, 1904–12.

[Benôit de Ste.-Maure]. *Le Roman de Troie en prose*, ed. Françoise Vielliard. Cologny-Genève: Fondation Martin Bodmer, 1979.

Béroalde de Verville. *Le Moyen de Parvenir*, 2 vols., ed. H. Moreau and A. Tournon. Aix-en-Provence: Publications de l'Université, 1984.

Boccaccio, Giovanni. *Esposizioni sopra la Comedia di Dante*, ed. Giorgio Padoan [*Tutte le opere di Giovanni Boccaccio*, ed. Vittore Branca, vol. 6]. Milan: Arnaldo Mondadori, 1965.

——. *Filostrato*, ed. Vittore Branca [*Tutte le opere di Giovanni Boccaccio*, ed. Vittore Branca, vol. 2]. Verona: Arnaldo Mondadori, 1964.

——. *The Filostrato of Giovanni Boccacio*, trans. Nathaniel Edward Griffin and Arthur Beckwith Myrick. Philadelphia: n.p., 1929.

Boethius. *Boethii Philosophiae Consolatio*, ed. Ludwig Bieler. Turnhout: Brepols, 1957.

——. *The Consolation of Philosophy*, trans. Richard Green. Indianapolis: Bobbs-Merrill, 1962.

Bras-de Fer, Jehan. See *Pamphile et Galatée*.

Chaucer, Geoffrey. *The Book of Troilus and Criseyde*, ed. R. K. Root. Princeton: Princeton University Press, 1926.

————. *The Riverside Chaucer*, 3d ed., ed. Larry D. Benson. Boston: Houghton Mifflin, 1987.

Chaucer, Geoffrey. *Troilus & Criseyde*, ed. B. Windeatt. London: Longmans, 1984.

————. *The Works of Geoffrey Chaucer*, ed. F. N. Robinson. Boston: Houghton Mifflin, 1954.

Chrétien de Troyes. *Cligés*, ed. A. Micha. Paris: Champion, 1957.

Cicero. *Academica*, ed. James S. Reid. London: Macmillan, 1885 [Hildesheim, Georg Olms: 1966].

————. *De divinatione*, ed. Arthur Stanley Pease. In *University of Illinois Studies in Langauge and Literature* 6 (1920): 161–500 and 7 (1923): 153–474 [Darmstadt: Wissenschaftliche Buchgesellschaft, 1963].

————. *Gespräch in Tusculum*, ed. and trans. Olof Gigon. Munich: Heimeran, 1970.

————. *Tusculan Disputations*, ed. and trans. J. E. King. Cambridge: Harvard University Press, 1927.

Dante Alighieri. *The Divine Comedy*, ed. and trans. Charles Singleton. Princeton: Princeton University Press, 1970.

————. *De vulgari eloquentia*, ed. Aristide Marigo. Florence: Felice le Monnier, 1968.

Dares Phrygius. *De excidio Troiae historia*, ed. F. Meister. Leipzig: Teubner, 1873.

Deschamps, Eustache. *Oeuvres complètes*, 11 vols., ed. Queux de Sainte-Hilaire and Gaston Raynaud. Paris: SATF, 1878–1903.

Dictys Cretensis. *Ephemeridos belli Troiani libri a Lucio Septimo ex graeco in latinum sermonem translati*, ed. W. Eisenhut. Leipzig: Teubner, 1958.

Gorgias of Leontini. *Encomio di Elena*, ed. and trans. Francesco Donadi. Rome: L'Erma di Bretschneider, 1982.

Gower, John. *The Complete Works of John Gower*, 3 vols., ed. C. G. Macauley. Oxford: Clarendon, 1899–1902.

Gregorius [called Magister Gregorius]. *Narracio de mirabilibus urbis Rome*, ed. R. B. C. Huygens. Leiden: Brill, 1970.

Guido delle Colonne. *Historia destructionis Troiae*, ed. Nathaniel E. Griffin. Cambridge: Mediaeval Academy of America, 1936.

Guillaume de Lorris. See Jean de Meun.

Henry of Huntingdon. *Henrici Archidiaconi Huntendunensis Historia Anglorum*, ed. Thomas Arnold. London: HM Stationery Office, 1879 [Rolls Series, 74].

Horace. *[Ars poetica] Horace on Poetry [vol. 2]: The 'Ars Poetica,'* ed. C. O. Brink. Cambridge: Cambridge University Press, 1971.

Horace. *Horace for English Readers*, trans. E. C. Wickham. Oxford: Oxford University Press, 1903.

————. *Q. Horatius Flaccus*, 2 vols., ed. Adolf Kiessling. Berlin: Weidmannsche Buchhandlung, 1883.

Horace. See *Scholia in Horatium*.

Jean de Meun [and Guillaume de Lorris]. *Le Roman de la Rose*, 3 vols., ed. Félix Lecoy. Paris: Champion, 1965–70.

—————. *The Romance of the Rose,* trans. Charles Dahlberg. Princeton: Princeton University Press, 1971.

[Jean de Meun]. *Le Debat sur le Roman de la Rose,* ed. Eric Hicks. Paris: Champion, 1977.

John of Salisbury. *Policraticus,* 2 vols., ed. C. C. J. Webb. Oxford: Clarendon, 1909.

Juvenal. *A. Persi Flacci et D. Iuni Iuvenalis Saturae,* ed. S. G. Owen. Oxford: Clarendon, 1903.

Lefevre, Raoul. *The Recuyell of the Historyes of Troye,* trans. William Caxton, ed. O. Sommer. London: David Nutt, 1894.

Lucan. *M. Annaei Lucani Pharsalia,* ed. C. E. Haskins. London: George Bell, 1887.

Lucretius. *De rerum natura,* ed. K. Buechner. Wiesbaden: Steiner, 1966.

Marbod of Rennes. *Marbodi Liber decem capitulorum,* ed. Rosario Leotta. Rome: Herder, 1984.

Minucius Felix. *Octavius,* ed. Michele Pellegrino. Torino: Paravia, 1963.

Musaeus. *Musaios: Hero und Leander,* ed. Karlheinz Kost. Bonn: Bouvier Verlag, 1977.

Nicetas Choniates. *Nicetae Choniatae Historia,* ed. J. A. van Dieten. Berlin: de Gruyter, 1975.

Oresme, Nicole. *Livre de Divinacions.* In G. W. Coopland, *Nicole Oresme and the Astrologers: A Study of His Livre de Divinacions.* Liverpool: Liverpool University Press, 1952.

Ovid. *P. Ovidi Nasonis Amores, Medicamina faciei femineae, Ars amatoria, Remedia amoris,* ed. E. J. Kenney. Oxford: Clarendon, 1961.

—————. *The Art of Love and Other Poems,* trans. J. H. Mozley. Cambridge: Harvard University Press, 1929.

—————. *P. Ovidii Nasonis Epistulae Heroidum,* ed. H. Dörrie. Berlin: de Gruyter, 1971.

—————. *Heroides and Amores,* trans. Grant Showerman. Cambridge: Harvard University Press, 1914.

—————. *Les Métamorphoses,* 2 vols., ed. and trans. J. Chamonard. Paris: Garnier, n.d.

—————. *The Metamorphoses of Ovid,* trans. Mary Innes. Harmondsworth: Penguin, 1955.

—————. *P. Ovidi Nasonis Remedia amoris,* ed. A. A. R. Henderson. Edinburgh: Scottish Academic Press, 1979.

Ovide moralisé en prose, ed. C. de Boer. Amsterdam: North Holland, 1954.

Pamphile et Galatée par Jehan Bras-de-Fer de Dammartin-en-Goële, ed. Joseph de Morawski. Paris: Champion, 1917.

Pamphilus. *Pamphilus: Prolegomena zum Pamphilus (de amore) und kritische Textausgabe,* ed. Franz G. Becker. Düsseldorf: Ratingen, 1972.

—————. *Il Panfilo veneziano,* ed. H. Haller. Florence: Olschki, 1982.

Petronius. *Le Satiricon,* ed. A. Ernout. Paris: Belles Lettres, 1962.

Pierre d'Ailly. "De falsis prophetis." In Jean Gerson, *Opera Omnia,* 5 vols., ed. Ellies du Pin. Paris, 1706, 1:489–603.

Plautus, T. Maccius. *Bacchides,* ed. Cesare Questa. Florence: Sansoni, 1965.

Poetae latini minores, 6 vols., ed. Emil [Aemilius] Baehrens. Leipzig: Teubner, 1879.

Quintillian. *Institutionis oratoriae libri duodecim*, ed. M. Winterbottom. Oxford: Clarendon, 1970.

Raoul de Presles [trans.]. *Cité de Dieu* [of Saint Augustine]. Abbeville, 1486.

Rhetores latini minores, ed. C. Halm. Leipzig: Teubner, 1863.

Richard de Fournival [supposed translator of *De vetula*]. See Vetula.

Roman de Thèbes, 2 vols., ed. G. Raynaud de Lage. Paris: Champion, 1966–67.

Salutati, Coluccio. *De laboribus Herculis*, ed. B. L. Ulmann. Turin: Thesaurus Mundi, n.d.

Scholia in Horatium, 2 vols., ed. H. J. Botschuyver. Amsterdam: van Bottburg, 1935–42.

Seneca, L. Annaeus. *Agamemnon*, ed. R. J. Tarrant. Cambridge: Cambridge University Press, 1976.

————. *Hercules furens*. See Trevet, N.

————. *Oedipus*, ed. Bruno Häuptli. Frauenfeld: Huber, 1983.

————. *Opera Philosophica*, 5 vols., ed. M. N. Bouillet. Paris: Lemaire, 1827 [reprinted Brescia: Paideia, 1972].

————. *Seneca's Tragedies*, 2 vols., trans. F. J. Miller. Cambridge: Harvard University Press, 1917.

————. *Tragoedia*, ed. F. Leo. Berlin: Weidmann, 1878.

Servianorum in Vergilii carmina commentariorum, ed. E. K. Rand et al. Lancaster: American Philological Society, 1936.

Servii Grammatici . . . commentarii, 3 vols., ed. G. Thilo and H. Hagen. Leipzig: Teubner, 1881–1902.

Statius. [*Works*] *Opere di Publio Papinio Stazio*, ed. Antonio Traglia and Giuseppe Aricò. Turin: UTET, 1980.

————. [*Thebaid*, book 3] *P. Papinius Statius: Thebaid/A Commentary on Book III*, ed. H. Snijder. Amsterdam: Hakkert, 1968.

————. [*Thebaid*, book 2] *Publii Papinii Statii Thebaidos: Liber Secundus*, ed. H. M. Mulder. Groningen: De Waal, 1954.

Statius with an English Translation, 2 vols., trans. J. H. Mozley. Cambridge: Harvard University Press, 1928.

Trevet, Nicholas. *Commento alle Troades di Seneca*, ed. Marco Palma. Rome: Storia e Letteratura, 1977.

————. *Il Commento di Nicola Trevet al Tieste di Seneca*, ed. Ezio Franceschini. Milan: Vita e Pensiero, 1938.

————. *Hercules Furens et Nicolai Treveti expositio*, ed. V. Ussani. Rome: Athena, 1959 [vol. 2, commentary].

Vetula [pseudo-Ovidian *de Vetula*]. *Pseudo-Ovidius de Vetula*, ed. Paul Klopsch. Leiden: Brill, 1967.

Virgil. *The Aeneid*, trans. W. F. Jackson Knight. Harmondsworth: Penguin, 1956.

————. *P. Vergili Maronis Aeneidos Liber Primus*, ed. R. G. Austin. Oxford: Oxford University Press, 1971.

———. *P. Vergili Maronis Aeneidos Liber Quartus*, ed. R. G. Austin. Oxford: Oxford University Press, 1955.

———. *Publi Vergili Maronis Aeneidos Liber Quartus*, ed. A. S. Pease. Cambridge: Harvard University Press, 1935.

———. *P. Vergili Maronis Aeneidos Liber Secundus*, ed. R. G. Austin. Oxford: Oxford University Press, 1964.

———. *P. Vergili Maronis Aeneidos Liber Sextus*, ed. R. G. Austin. Oxford: Oxford University Press, 1977.

La Vieille; ou, les dernières amours d'Ovide [supposedly trans. by Richard de Fournival], ed. H. F. J. M. Cocheris. Paris: n.p., 1861.

———. *The Works of Virgil*, 3 vols., ed. John Conington and Henry Nettleship. London: Bell, 1898.

Secondary Sources

Adams, J. N. *The Latin Sexual Vocabulary*. Baltimore: Johns Hopkins University Press, 1982.

Adams, John F. "Irony in Troilus' Apostrophe to the Vacant House of Criseyde." *MLQ* 24 (1963): 61–65.

Alessio, Giovanni. *Dizionario etimologico italiano*. Florence: Barbera, 1950–57.

Amand, David. *Fatalisme et liberté dans l'antiquité grecque*. Louvain: Université, 1945.

Amandry, Pierre. *La Mantique apollinienne à Delphes*. Paris: E. de Boccard, 1975.

Anderson, David. "Cassandra's Analogy: *Troilus* v. 1450–1521." *Hebrew University Studies in Literature and the Arts* 13 (1985): 1–17.

———. "Theban History in Chaucer's Troilus." *SAC* 4 (1982): 112–28.

apRoberts, Robert. "A Contribution to the Thirteenth Labour: Purging *Troilus* of Incest." *Essays on English and American Literature and a Sheaf of Poems Presented to David Wilkinson* [*Costerus* 63]. Amsterdam: Rodopi, 1987, 11–25.

Austin, R. G. "Virgil, *Aeneid* 2.567–88." *Classical Quarterly* 11 (1961): 185–98.

Bardon, H. "Rome et l'impudeur." *Latomus* 24 (1965): 495–518.

Barwick, Karl. *Probleme der stoischen Sprachlehre und Rhetorik*. Berlin: Akademie Verlag, 1957.

Bauer, Douglas F. "The Function of Pygmalion in the *Metamorphoses* of Ovid." *TAPA* 93 (1967): 1–21.

Bayet, Jean. "La Mort de la Pythie." *Mélanges dédiés à la mémoire de Félix Grat*, I. Paris: Pecqueur-Grat, 1946, 53–76.

Benson, Larry D. "The 'Queynte' Punnings of Chaucer's Critics." In *Reconstructing Chaucer*, ed. Paul Strohm and Thomas Heffernan [*Proceedings* no. 1 (1984): 23–47]. Knoxville, Tenn.: New Chaucer Society, 1985.

Binder, Gerhard. *Aeneas und Augustus: Interpretationen zum 8. Buch der Aeneis*. Meisenheim: A. Hain, 1971.

Bishop, Ian. *Chaucer's Troilus and Criseyde: A Critical Study.* Bristol: University of Bristol Press, 1981.

Bloomfield, Morton W. "Chaucer's Sense of History." *JEGP* 51 (1952): 301–13.

——. "The Source of Boccaccio's *Filostrato* III, 74–79, and Its Bearing on the Manuscript Tradition of Lucretius' *De rerum natura.*" *Classical Philology* 47 (1952): 162–65.

——. "Troilus' Paraclausithyron and Its Setting." *NM* 73 (1972): 15–24.

Bömer, Franz. *Rom und Troia: Untersuchungen zur Fruhgeschichte.* Baden-Baden: Verlag für Kunst und Wissenschaft, 1951.

Bouché-Leclercq, A. *Histoire de la divination dans l'antiquité.* 4 vols. Paris: Ernest Leroux, 1879–82.

Boughner, Daniel C. "Elements of Epic Grandeur in the *Troilus.*" *FLH* 6 (1939): 201–10.

Broatch, James W. "The Indebtedness of Chaucer's *Troilus* to Benoît's *Roman.*" *JEGP* 2 (1898): 14–28.

Brewer, Derek. *Chaucer.* 3d ed. London: Longmans, 1973.

——. *An Introduction to Chaucer.* London: Longmans, 1984.

Brown, Carleton. "Another Contemporary Allusion in Chaucer's *Troilus.*" *MLN* 26 (1911): 208–11.

Callay, Brigitte L. "The Road to Salvation in the *Roman de la Rose.*" *Pascua Mediaevalia: Studies voor Prof. Dr. J. M. De Smet.* Louvain: Universitaire Pers Leuven, 1983, 499–509.

Chavannes, Fernand. *De Palladii raptu.* Berlin: Heinrich & Kemke, 1891.

Cohen, Henry. *Description historique des monnaies frappées sous l'Empire Romaine.* 2d ed. 7 vols. Paris: Rollin et Feuardant, 1880–92.

Cook, Robert G. "Chaucer's Pandarus and the Medieval Idea of Friendship." *JEGP* 69 (1970): 407–24.

Coopland, G. W. "Eustache Deschamps and Nicolas Oresme: A Note on the Demoustraciouns contre sortilèges." *Romania* 52 (1926): 355–61.

Copley, F. O. *Exclusus Amator.* Madison: University of Wisconsin Press, 1954.

Corsa, Helen Storm. "Dreams in *Troilus and Criseyde.*" *American Imago* 27 (1970): 52–65.

Cortes Vasquez, Luis. *El Episodio de Pigmalión del Roman de la Rose.* Salamanca: Universidad de Salamanca, 1980.

Courcelle, Pierre. *La Consolation de Philosophie dans la tradition littéraire.* Paris: Etudes Augustiniennes, 1967.

Del Corno, Dario. "Ricerche sull' onirocritica greca." *Rendiconti* [Istituto Lombardo] 96 (1962): 334–66.

Delcourt, Marie. *L'Oracle de Delphes.* Paris: Payot, 1955.

Delepierre, Marie J., "Une scene de la prise de Troie decrite par Virgile." *Monuments et Mémoirs* 56 (1969): 1–11.

Demats, Paule. *Fabula.* Geneva: Droz, 1973.

D'Evelyn, Charlotte. "Pandarus a Devil?" *PMLA* 71 (1956): 275–79.

Dick, Bernard F. "The Role of the Oracle in Lucan's de Bello Civili." *Hermes* 93 (1965): 460–66.

Dinter, Annegret. *Der Pygmalion-Stoff in der europäischen Literatur.* Heidelberg: Winter, 1979.

Dodds, E. R. "Supernormal Phenomena in Classical Antiquity." In *The Ancient Concept of Progress and Other Essays on Greek Literature and Belief.* Oxford, 1973, 156–210.

Dörrie, H. *Pygmalion: Ein Impuls Ovids und seine Wirkungen bis in die Gegenwart.* Opladen: Westdeuscher Verlag, 1974.

Donaldson, E. Talbot. "Chaucer's Three 'P's': Pandarus, Pardoner, and Poet." *Michigan Quarterly Review* 14 (1975): 282–301.

Dronke, Peter. "The Conclusion of *Troilus and Criseyde.*" *Medium Aevum* 33 (1964): 47–52.

Dunkle, J. Roger. "Satirical Themes in Joseph of Exeter's *De Bello Troiano.*" *Classica et Mediaevalia* 38 (1987): 203–13.

Ebel, Julia. "Troilus and Oedipus: The Genealogy of an Image." *ES* 55 (1974): 14–21.

Engels, J. "La Doctrine du signe chez saint Augustin." *Studia Patristica* 6 (1962): 366–73.

Ferguson, J. "Notes on Some Uses of Ambiguity and Similar Effects in Ovid's Amores, book 1." *Liverpool Classical Monthly* 3 (1978): 121–32.

Feuillet, A. "La Connaissance de Dieu par les hommes d'après Rom. 1, 18–23." *Lumière et Vie* 14 (1954): 207–24.

Fleming, John V. "The Garden of the *Roman de la Rose:* Vision of Landscape or Landscape of Vision." In *Medieval Gardens,* ed. Elisabeth Macdougall. Washington, D.C.: Dumbarton Oaks, 1986, 199–234.

———. *Reason and the Lover.* Princeton: Princeton University Press, 1984.

———. *The Roman de la Rose: A Study in Allegory and Iconography.* Princeton: Princeton University Press, 1969.

———. "Smoky Reyn: From Jean de Meun to Geoffrey Chaucer." In *Chaucer and the Craft of Fiction,* ed. Leigh Arrathoon. Rochester, Mich.: Solaris, 1986.

Fontaine, Jacques. "Demons et sibylles: La peinture des possédés dans la poesie de Prudence." *Hommages à Jean Bayet.* Brussels: Latomus, 1964, 196–213.

Frankis, John. "Paganism and Pagan Love in *Troilus and Criseyde.*" In *Essays on Troilus and Criseyde,* ed. Mary Salu. Cambridge: Boydell and Brewer, 1979, 57–72.

Frecaut, Jean Marc. *L'Esprit et l'humour chez Ovide.* Grenoble: Presses universitaires, 1972.

Frost, William. "A Chaucerian Crux." *Yale Review* 66 (1977): 551–61.

Fry, Donald. "Chaucer's Zanzis and a Possible Source for *Troilus and Criseyde,* IV, 407–13." *ELN* 9 (1971): 81–85.

Fyler, John. *Chaucer and Ovid.* New Haven: Yale University Press, 1979.

Garbáty, Thomas J. "The Pamphilus Tradition in Ruiz and Chaucer." *PQ* 45 (1967): 457–70.

Gegenschatz, Ernst. "Die Gefährdung des Möglichen durch das Vorauswissen Gottes in der Sicht des Boethius." *Wiener Studien* 79 (1966): 517–30.

Ghellinck, Joseph de. "En marge des catalogues des bibliothèques médiévales."
    Miscellanea Francesco Ehrle. 5 vols. Rome: Vatican, 1924, 5:387–402.
Giraud, Yves R. A. La Fable de Daphne. Geneva: Droz, 1969.
Goold, G. P. "Servius and the Helen Episode." HSCP 74 (1970): 101–68.
Gordon, Ida. The Double Sorrow of Troilus: A Study of Ambiguities in Troilus and
    Criseyde. Oxford: Clarendon, 1970.
Gruber, Joachim. Kommentar zu Boethius de Consolatione Philosophiae. Berlin: de
    Gruyter, 1978.
Harmening, Dieter. Superstitio: Uberlieferungs- und theoriegeschichtliche Untersuchungen
    zur kirchlich-theologischen Aberglaubenliteratur des Mittelalters. Berlin: E. Schmidt,
    1979.
Heidtmann, Peter. "Sex and Salvation in Troilus and Criseyde." ChR 2 (1968):
    246–53.
Heitmann, Klaus. Fortuna und Virtus: Eine Studie zu Petrarcas Lebensweisheit. Cologne:
    Böhlau, 1958.
Hollander, Robert. Allegory in Dante's Commedia. Princeton: Princeton University
    Press, 1969.
———. Boccaccio's Two Venuses. New York: Columbia University Press, 1980.
———. Studies in Dante. Ravenna: Longo, 1980.
———. Il Virgilio dantesco: Tragedia nella "Commedia." Florence: Olschki, 1983.
Howard, Donald. The Three Temptations. Princeton: Princeton University Press, 1966.
Huber, Peter. Die Vereinbarkeit von göttlicher Vorsehung und menschlicher Freiheit in der
    Consolatio Philosophiae des Boethius. Zurich: Juris Verlag, 1976.
Kambylis, A. Die Dichterweihe und ihre Symbolik. Heidelberg: Winter, 1965.
Kaminsky, Alice. Chaucer's "Troilus and Criseyde" and the Critics. Athens: Ohio
    University Press, 1980.
Kenny, E. J. "Nequitiae Poetae." In Ovidiana, ed. N. I. Herescu. Paris: Belles Lettres,
    1958, 201–9.
———. "On the Somnium Attributed to Ovid." Agon 3 (1969): 1–14.
Kessels, A. H. M. "Ancient Systems of Dream Classification." Mnemosyne 22 (1969):
    389–424.
———. Studies on the Dream in Greek Literature. Utrecht: Rijksuniversiteit, 1972.
Kittredge, G. L. "Chaucer's Lollius." HSCP 28 (1917): 47–109.
Koonce, Benjamin G. Chaucer and the Tradition of Fame. Princeton: Princeton
    University Press, 1966.
Kratins, Ojars. "The Pretended Witch: A Reading of Ovid's Amores, I.viii." PQ 42
    (1963): 151–58.
Kurfess, Alfons. "Die Sibylle in Augustins Gottesstaat." Theologische Quartalschrift 107
    (1936): 532–42.
Laborde, Alexandre de. Les Manuscrits à peintures de la Cité de Dieu de saint Augustin.
    Paris: E. Rahir, 1909.
Lange, Hugo. "Chaucer's 'Myn Auctour Called Lollius' und die Datierung des 'Hous of
    Fame.'" Anglia 42 (1918): 345–51.

Lausberg, Heinrich. *Handbuch der literarischen Rhetorik.* 2d ed. 2 vols. Munich: Heuber, 1960.

Lebek, W. D. "Ein lateinisches Epigramm aus Pompei (vellem essem gemma eqs.) und Ovids Gedicht vom Siegelring (Am. 2.15)." *Zeitschrift für Papyrologie und Epigraphik* 23 (1976): 21–40.

Le Bonniec, Henri. "Lucain et la religion." In *Lucain [Entretiens sur l'Antiquité Classique* 15]. Geneva: Fondation Hardt, 1970, 159–200.

Lever, Katherine. "The Christian Classicist's Dilemma." *CJ* 58 (1963): 356–61.

Levin, D. N. "Propertius, Catullus, and Three Kinds of Ambiguous Expression." *Proceedings of the American Philological Association* 100 (1969): 221–35.

Lilja, Saara. *The Roman Elegists' Attitude to Women.* Suomalaisen tiedeakatemian toimituksia, sarja B, nide 135, 1. Helsinki, 1965.

Lockhart, Adrienne. "Semantic, Moral, and Aesthetic Degeneration in *Troilus and Criseyde.*" *ChR* 8 (1973): 100–117.

Loomis, Roger S. *Arthurian Legends in Medieval Art.* New York: Columbia University Press, 1938.

———. *A Mirror of Chaucer's World.* Princeton, Princeton University Press, 1965.

Lowes, John L. "Chaucer's 'Etik.'" *MLN* 25 (1910): 87–89.

Luck, Georg. *The Latin Love Elegy.* London: Methuen, 1959.

Lungo, Isidoro del. *Dante ne' tempi di Dante.* Bologna: N. Zanichelli, 1888.

Luschnat, Otto. "Horaz, Epistel I 2." *Theologia Viatorum* 9 (1963): 142–55.

McAlpine, Monica. *The Genre of Troilus and Criseyde.* Ithaca: Cornell University Press, 1978.

Macleod, Colin W. "The Poetry of Ethics: Horace, Epistles I." In *Collected Essays.* Oxford: Oxford University Press, 1983, 280–91.

Mango, Cyril. "Constantine's Porphyry Column and the Chapel of St. Constantine." *Deltion tes christianike Archaiologike Hetairea* 10 (1980–81): 103–10.

Mantero, Teresa. *Ricerche sull'Heroikos di Filostrato.* Genoa: Istituto di filologia classica e medioevale, 1966.

Martinelli, Bortolo. *Petrarca e il Ventoso.* Bergamo: Minerva Italica, 1977.

Minnis, Alistair. *Chaucer and Pagan Antiquity.* Cambridge: Boydell and Brewer, 1982.

Müller, Richard. *Motivkatalog der römischen Elegie.* Zurich: Abhandlung, 1952.

Munari, Franco. "Sugli 'Amores' de Ovidio." *SIFC* 23 (1948): 113–52.

Nelson, Axel. "Uber der Ursprung des lateinischen Terminus *Sortes, Sor,* in der philosophischen Literatur des Mittelalters." *Eranos* 46 (1948): 161–64.

Noakes, Susan. "The Double Misreading of Paolo and Francesca." *PQ* 62 (1983): 221–39.

Norton-Smith, John. *Geoffrey Chaucer.* London: Routledge, 1974.

Ogilvie, R. M. *The Romans and Their Gods.* New York: Norton, 1970.

Olson, Paul A. *The Canterbury Tales and the Good Society.* Princeton: Princeton University Press, 1987.

Opelt, Ilona. "Griechische und lateinische Beziehungen der Nichtchristlichen: Ein terminologisches Versuch." *Vigilae Christianae* 19 (1965): 1–22.

Otis, Brooks. *Ovid as an Epic Poet.* 2d ed. Cambridge: Cambridge University Press, 1970.

Park, H. W., and D. E. W. Wormell. *The Delphic Oracle.* 2 vols. Oxford: Oxford University Press, 1956.

Pasquali, Giorgio. *Stravaganze quarte e supreme.* Venice: Pozza, 1951.

Pellegrin, Elisabeth. "Les 'Remedia Amoris' d'Ovide, texte scolaire médiévale." *BEC* 115 (1957): 172–79.

Perret, Jacques. *Les Origines de la legende troyenne de Rome (281–31).* Paris: Belles Lettres, 1942.

Pichon, René. *De sermone amatorio apud latinos elegiarum scriptores.* Paris: Hachette, 1902.

Pohlenz, Max. *Die Stoa: Geschichte einer geistigen Bewegung.* 2d ed. 2 vols. Gottingen: Vandenhoeck, 1959.

Pratt, Robert A. "A Note on Chaucer's Lollius." *MLR* 65 (1950): 183–87.

Reiff, Arno. *Intepretatio, imitatio, aemulatio: Begriff und Vorstellung literarischer Abhängigkeit bei den Römern.* Würzburg: Triltsch, 1959.

Reinhardt, Karl. *Das Parisurteil.* Frankfurt: Klostermann, 1937.

Renucci, Paul. *Dante, disciple et juge du monde gréco-latin.* Paris: Belles Lettres, 1954.

Robertson, D. W. *A Preface to Chaucer: Studies in Medieval Perspectives.* Princeton: Princeton University Press, 1962.

Ronconi, Alessandro. "Per Dante interprete dei poeti latini." *Studi Danteschi* 41 (1964): 5–44.

Roscher, W. *Ausführliches Lexikon der griechischen und romischen Mythologie.* 6 vols. in 9. Leipzig: Teubner, 1884–1937.

Ross, Thomas W. "*Troilus and Criseyde,* ii, 582–87: A Note." *ChR* 5 (1970): 137–39.

Rowe, Donald. *O Love, O Charité! Contraries Harmonized in Chaucer's Troilus.* Carbondale: Southern Illinois University Press, 1976.

Russell, D. A. "De imitatione." In *Creative Imitation and Latin Literature,* ed. David West and Tony Woodman. Cambridge: Cambridge University Press, 1979, 1–16.

Salter, Elizabeth. "Troilus and Criseyde: A Reconsideration." In *Patterns of Love and Courtesy: Essays in Memory of C. S. Lewis,* ed. John Lawlor. London: Arnold, 1966, 86–106.

Schelkle, Karl Hermann. *Paulus Lehrer der Väter: Die altkirchliche Auslegung von Römer 1–11.* Dusseldorf: Patmos, 1954.

———. *Virgil in der Deutung Augustins.* Stuttgart: W. Kohlhammer, 1939.

Schless, Howard. *Chaucer and Dante: A Revaluation.* Norman, Okla.: Pilgrim Books, 1984.

Schottländer, R. "Das Sibyllenbild der Philosophen." *Acta Antiqua Academicae Scientiarum Hungaricae* 11 (1963): 37–48.

Schrader, Richard. "The Deserted Chamber: An Unnoticed Topos in the 'Father's Lament' of Beowulf." *Journal of the Rocky Mountain Medieval and Renaissance Association* 5 (1984): 1–5.

Schwarz, W. "The Meaning of *Fidus Interpres* in Medieval Translation." *JTS* 45 (1944): 73–78.

Sherrard, Philip. *Constantinople: Iconography of a Sacred City*. London: Oxford University Press, 1965.

Skalitsky, Rachel. "Good Wine in a New Vase (Horace, Epistles I.2)." *TAPA* 99 (1968): 433–52.

Slater, W. T. "Pueri, turba minuta." *BICS* 2 (1974): 133–40.

Smith, Sharon Dunlap. "New Themes for the City of God around 1400: The Illustration of Raoul de Presles' Translation." *Scriptorium* 36 (1982): 68–82.

Soria, Claudio. "El Paraclausithyron como presupuesto cultural de la elegia latina." *Revista de Estudios Clássicos* 8 (1963): 55–94.

Stechow, Wolfgang. *Apollo und Daphne*. Leipzig: Teubner, 1932.

Strain, Michael. "Virgil Aeneid 4.188–194." *Proceedings of the Virgil Society* 14 (1974–75): 18–21.

Taylor, Ann M. "A Scriptural Echo in the Trojan Parliament of Troilus and Criseyde." *Nottingham Medieval Studies* 24 (1980): 51–56.

Taylor, Karla. "A Text and Its Afterlife: Dante and Chaucer." *CL* 35 (1983): 1–20.

Tisdale, Charles. "The *House of Fame*: Virgilian Reason and Boethian Wisdom." *CL* 25 (1973): 247–61.

Vance, Eugene. *Mervelous Signals: Poetics and Sign Theory in the Middle Ages*. Lincoln: University of Nebraska Press, 1986.

———. "Mervelous Signals: Poetics, Sign Theory, and Politics in Chaucer's *Troilus*." *NLH* 10 (1979): 293–337.

Vassano, Pico Luri di. "Modi di dire proverbiali e motti popolari italiani." *Il Propugnatore* 12:2 (1879): 203–15.

Vessey, David. *Statius and the Thebaid*. Cambridge: Cambridge University Press, 1973.

Wallace, David. "Chaucer and Boccaccio's Early Writings." In *Chaucer and the Italian Trecento*, ed. Piero Boitani. Cambridge, Cambridge University Press, 1983, 141–62.

———. "Chaucer's Ambages." *American Notes and Queries* 23 (1984): 1–3.

Waswo, Richard. "The Narrator of *Troilus and Criseyde*." *ELH* 50 (1983): 1–25.

Wenzel, Siegfried. "Chaucer's Troilus of Book IV." *PMLA* 79 (1964): 542–47.

Werner, Jakob. *Beiträge zur Kunde der lateinischen Literatur des Mittelalters*. 2d ed. Aarau: H. R. Sauerländer, 1905.

Wetherbee, Winthrop. *Chaucer and the Poets: An Essay on Troilus and Criseyde*. Ithaca: Cornell University Press, 1984.

Wimsatt, James I. "The French Lyric Element in *Troilus and Criseyde*." *YES* 15 (1985): 18–32.

———. "Guillaume de Machaut and Chaucer's *Troilus and Criseyde*." *Medium Aevum* 45 (1976): 277–93.

Wise, Boyd Ashby. *The Influence of Statius upon Chaucer*. Baltimore: J. H. Furst, 1911.

Witlieb, B. L. "Chaucer's Elysian Fields (*Troilus*, IV, 789f)." *N&Q* 214 (1969): 250–51.

Wood, Chauncey. *The Elements of Chaucer's Troilus*. Durham, N.C.: Duke University Press, 1984.

Wrenn, C. L. "Chaucer's Knowledge of Horace." *MLR* 18 (1923): 286–92.

———. Review of D. W. Robertson, *A Preface to Chaucer*. *JEGP* 62 (1963): 794–801.

INDEX

Abelard, P., 4, 5n; *Dialectica,* 5n
Achilles, 79, 111, 151, 135, 136, 149,
    181, 237, 251
Adams, J. F., 7, 7n, 8, 10, 12, 31, 31n
Adams, J. N., 130n
Adonis, 90, 105–6
Adversus Jovinianum, 18
Aeneas, 39, 57–59, 62, 64, 66–68, 77n,
    102–3, 144, 148–50, 152, 173, 177,
    220; and Dido, 172–79
Agamemnon, 111–12, 237, 237n
Alain de Lille, 142
Alceste, 227
Alessio, G., 21n
Alfred (King of Wessex), 78
Allegory, 99–107; Homer and, 197–200;
    Horace on, 197–98; *Troilus* as, 200
Alison of Bath, 13, 20, 24
Alterity, 78
Alterna regna, 49
Amand, David, 208, 208n
Amandry, P., 138n
Amant (Lover in the *Roman de la Rose*),
    29, 32, 90, 92–93, 98, 100–102,
    104–7, 117, 141, 160n, 206, 218, 226
Ambages, 1, 3, 6, 36, 43, 48, 50, 56,
    58n, 59, 61, 64, 157, 160n, 185; prin-
    cipal discussion of, 45–71; Virgilian
    uses of, 56–57
Ambag(i)o, 4, 6
Ambigua, 51–53

Ambiguitas, 4
Ambiguity, 51–53; enemy of truth, 5;
    resolution of, 6–7, 23–26; vocabulary
    of, 1, 4, 45–71
Ambrose of Milan, 237
Amis (in *Roman de la Rose*), 17, 160n
Amnon, 77n
Amours (in *Roman de la Rose*), 142,
    161n. *See also* Cupid
Amphiaraus (Amphiorax), 49, 59–61,
    85–86, 203
Amphibolia, 42, 51–53
Amphiboliques, 54, 56
Amphibologies, 1, 43, 50, 56
Amphibologies, 43
Amphion, 186–87
Amphiorax, 60n. *See also* Amphiaraus
Anchises, 64, 151–52
Anderson, D., xvi, 60n, 223n, 225
Andromache, 111
Antenor, 21n, 116, 127, 145, 176, 235n
Anthologia Latina, 136, 137n
Antigone, 213, 223–24; song of, 223–25
Antiphon, 164
Anus. See Go-between
Apollo, 52, 54n, 57, 60–61, 77, 89, 111–
    13, 118–24, 132, 134, 137, 137n,
    138n, 154, 185, 240
Apollodorus, 148n
Appius, 59
ApRoberts, R., 242n

265